David, Donne, and Thirsty Deer

Manchester University Press

The Manchester Spenser

The Manchester Spenser is a monograph and text series devoted to historical and textual approaches to Edmund Spenser – to his life, times, places, works and contemporaries.

A growing body of work in Spenser and Renaissance studies, fresh with confidence and curiosity and based on solid historical research, is being written in response to a general sense that our ability to interpret texts is becoming limited without the excavation of further knowledge. So the importance of research in nearby disciplines is quickly being recognised, and interest renewed: history, archaeology, religious or theological history, book history, translation, lexicography, commentary and glossary – these require treatment for and by students of Spenser.

The Manchester Spenser, to feed, foster and build on these refreshed attitudes, aims to publish reference tools, critical, historical, biographical and archaeological monographs on or related to Spenser, from several disciplines, and to publish editions of primary sources and classroom texts of a more wide-ranging scope.

The Manchester Spenser consists of work with stamina, high standards of scholarship and research, adroit handling of evidence, rigour of argument, exposition and documentation.

The series will encourage and assist research into, and develop the readership of, one of the richest and most complex writers of the early modern period.

General Editors Joshua Reid, Kathryn Walls and Tamsin Badcoe
Editorial Board Sukanta Chaudhuri, Helen Cooper, Thomas Herron, J. B. Lethbridge, James Nohrnberg and Brian Vickers

To buy or to find out more about the books currently available in this series, please go to: https://manchesteruniversitypress.co.uk/series/the-manchester-spenser/

Anne Lake Prescott. Photograph by Erica Zeichner Siena.

David, Donne, and Thirsty Deer

Selected Essays of Anne Lake Prescott

Edited by

William A. Oram and Roger Kuin

MANCHESTER UNIVERSITY PRESS

Copyright © Anne Lake Prescott 2024

The right of Anne Lake Prescott to be identified as the author of this work has been asserted in accordance with the Copyright, Designs and Patents Act 1988.

Published by Manchester University Press
Oxford Road, Manchester, M13 9PL

www.manchesteruniversitypress.co.uk

British Library Cataloguing-in-Publication Data
A catalogue record for this book is available from the British Library

ISBN   978 1 5261 7938 8   hardback
ISBN   978 1 5261 9543 2   paperback

First published 2024
Paperback published 2026

The publisher has no responsibility for the persistence or accuracy of URLs for any external or third-party internet websites referred to in this book, and does not guarantee that any content on such websites is, or will remain, accurate or appropriate.

EU authorised representative for GPSR:
Easy Access System Europe – Mustamäe tee 50,
10621 Tallinn, Estonia
gpsr.requests@easproject.com

Typeset
by New Best-set Typesetters Ltd

*This book is dedicated to Anne Lake Prescott,
who has taught generations that pleasure and learning can be inseparable
sisters.*

*You come to repaire
Gods booke of creatures, teaching what is faire
(John Donne to the Countess of Salisbury)*

Contents

List of illustrations	page xi
Acknowledgements	xiii

Poetic fire: an introduction   1
Ayesha Ramachandran, Susan Felch, and Susannah Monta

Part I: Spenser

1 Spenser's chivalric restoration: from Bateman's *Travayled Pylgrime* to the Redcrosse Knight   17
2 Foreign policy in Fairyland: Henry IV and Spenser's Burbon   46
3 The thirsty deer and the Lord of Life: some contexts for *Amoretti* 67–70   69

Part II: The Psalms and the psalmist

4 Evil tongues at the court of Saul: the Renaissance David as a slandered courtier   113
5 Musical strains: Marot's double role as psalmist and courtier   135
6 King David as a 'right poet': Sidney and the psalmist   160
7 The countess of Pembroke's *Ruins of Rome*   180

Part III: Imagining gender

8 Male lesbian voices: Ronsard, Tyard, and Donne play Sappho   199
9 Family grief: mourning and gender in Marguerite de Navarre's *Les Prisons*   218

Part IV: Italy, France, England

10	*Translatio lupae*: Du Bellay's Roman whore goes north	239
11	Housing chessmen and bagging bishops: space and desire in Colonna, 'Rabelais', and Middleton's *Game at Chess*	260
12	Imperfect pearls from France: Ronsard's conceits meet Donne's *Anne Lake Prescott and Roger Kuin*	280

Afterword: Anne as co-author and editor	317
The joy of partnership *Roger Kuin*	317
Anne as editor: a small florilegium *William Oram*	319

Bibliography of works by Anne Lake Prescott	322
Index	331

Illustrations

Frontispiece Anne Lake Prescott. Photograph by Erica Zeichner Siena. — page iv

1.1 Engraving, 'The armed Knight Signifieth ...' (b4r) STC 1585 copy 1 (*The trauayled pylgrime*). Used by permission of the Folger Shakespeare Library — 20

1.2 Engraving, 'Here Understanding sheweth ...' (d3r) STC 1585 copy 1 (*The trauayled pylgrime*). Used by permission of the Folger Shakespeare Library — 23

1.3 Engraving, 'The author being caried by his horse ...' (g1r) STC 1585 copy 1 (*The trauayled pylgrime*). Used by permission of the Folger Shakespeare Library — 26

1.4 Engraving, 'The Author and Memorie passeth the fielde ...' (h2r) STC 1585 copy 1 (*The trauayled pylgrime*). Used by permission of the Folger Shakespeare Library — 29

1.5 Engraving, 'The author and memorie riding forwarde ...' (I3r) STC 1585 copy 1 (*The trauayled pylgrime*). Used by permission of the Folger Shakespeare Library — 31

1.6 Engraving, 'The Author and Memorie walking on foote ...' (L3R) STC 1585 copy 1 (*The trauayled pylgrime*). Used by permission of the Folger Shakespeare Library — 33

1.7 Engraving, 'The Author beholdeth the discourse ...' (m2v) STC 1585 copy 1 (*The trauayled pylgrime*). Used by Permission of the Folger Shakespeare Library — 35

1.8 Engraving, 'By the aged or olde man ...' (G4r) STC 1585 copy 1 (*The trauayled pylgrime*). Used by permission of the Folger Shakespeare Library — 39

3.1 The thirsty deer of Psalm 42 finds God in the water's reflection. From *Les hieroglyphiques de Ian-Pierre Valerian* (Lyons, 1615), chapter III. Reprinted by permission of the Medical Historical Library, Harvey

	Cushing/John Hay Whitney Medical Library, Yale University	81
3.2	David recites Psalm 42, as a deer enacts its part in the opening simile. From Geoffrey Whitney's *A Choice of Emblems* (1586). Reprinted by permission of the Toronto University Library	82
3.3	The loving hind of Proverbs 5.19, from the title page of Thomas Churchyard's *Discourse* (1578). Reprinted by permission of the Rare Book & Manuscript Library, University of Illinois at Urbana-Champaign	94
6.1	Nathan enlightens David. From a 1533 Sarum Primer, STC 15891, fol cix. Reprinted with the kind permission of the Cambridge University Library	171
6.2	Rebuked by Nathan, David prays in repentance. From the Ash Wednesday section of the 1555 Sarum Missal, STC 16217, fol. xxxviii.r, illustrating Psalm 51 Reprinted by permission of the Harvard University Library	173
7.1	Towers falling, F2r, Engraving from Geoffrey Whitney's *A Choice of Emblemes and Other Devises*. Reprinted by permission of the Beinecke Rare Book and Manuscript Library, Yale University	181
7.2	Layout of temple and city, Ezekiel. Folding plate between leaf 3T2 verso (folio 356v) and leaf 3T3 recto (folio 357r). Used by permission of the Folger Shakespeare Library	185
7.3	Daniel in the lions' den. Bishops' Bible part 3, Daniel, leaf Y5 verso (folio clxxiij.v). Used by permission of the Folger Shakespeare Library	188
11.1	Colonna's lovers, from the *Hypernotomachia Poliphili*, 1904 reprint of the 1499 copy. Reprinted by permission of the Getty Library.	262
11.2	Recto of the engraved title page inserted from STC 17882. (Middleton's *Game at Chess*). Used by permission of the Folger Shakespeare Library.	269

Acknowledgements

We have received aid and comfort from many in the Spenserian community, but in particular from Anne Coldiron and David Lee Miller. The trinity of scholars, Ayesha Ramachandran, Susan Felch, and Susannah Monta, who put off other work, at some cost, to write the composite introduction, have our deep gratitude. Tess Grogan worked wonders in transforming unwilling formats and gaining permissions, and Henriette Rietveld compiled the bibliography. Joshua Reid, our editor, supportive, helpful, and quick, has made this book possible. Our thanks go also to Matthew Frost of the Manchester University Press, who has intervened at crucial moments.

The following libraries have given generous permission to use their illustrations: the Folger Shakespeare Library; the Rare Book & Manuscript Library, University of Illinois at Urbana-Champaign; the Beinecke Library and the Medical Historical Library, Harvey Cushing/John Hay Whitney Medical Library of Yale University; the Toronto University Library; the Cambridge University Library; the Getty Library.

Thanks to the following editors, journals, and publishers for permission to republish the essays in this book. Chapter 1, 'Spenser's chivalric restoration: from Bateman's *Travayled Pylgrime* to the Redcrosse Knight', was first published in *Studies in Philology* 86 (1989), 166–97; Chapter 2, 'Foreign policy in Fairyland: Henry IV and Spenser's Burbon', appeared in *Spenser Studies* 14 (2000), 189–214, and chapter 3, 'The thirsty deer and the Lord of Life: some contexts for *Amoretti* 67–70', in *Spenser Studies* 6 (1985), 33–76. Chapter 4, 'Evil tongues at the court of Saul: the Renaissance David as a slandered courtier', was first published in *The Journal of Medieval and Renaissance Studies* 21 (1991), 163–86, and chapter 5, 'Musical strains: Marot's double role as psalmist and courtier', in *Contending Kingdoms: Historical, Psychological and Feminist Approaches to the Literature of Sixteenth-Century England and France*, ed. Marie-Rose Logan and Peter Rudnytsky (Detroit: Wayne State University Press; 1991), pp. 42–68. Chapter 6, 'King David as a 'right poet': Sidney and the psalmist', appeared in *English*

Literary Renaissance 19 (1989), 131–51, and chapter 7, 'The countess of Pembroke's *Ruins of Rome*', in *Mary Sidney, Countess of Pembroke*, ed. Margaret P. Hannay (Surrey, England: Ashgate Publishing, 2009), pp. 223–239. Chapter 8, 'Male lesbian voices: Ronsard, Tyard, and Donne play Sappho', was published in *Reading the Renaissance: Ideas and Idioms from Shakespeare to Milton*, ed. Marc Berley (Pittsburgh, PA: Duquesne University Press; 2003), pp. 109–29, and Chapter 9, 'Family grief: mourning and gender in Marguerite de Navarre's *Les Prisons*', appeared in *Grief and Gender: 700–1700*, ed. Jennifer C. Vaught and Lynne Dickson Bruckner (New York: Palgrave Macmillan, 2003), pp. 105–19. Chapter 10, '*Translatio lupae*: Du Bellay's Roman whore goes north', first appeared in *Renaissance Quarterly* 42 (1989), 397–419, and Chapter 11, 'Housing chessmen and bagging bishops: space and desire in Colonna, 'Rabelais', and Middleton's *Game at Chess*', in *Soundings of Things Done: Essays in Early Modern Literature in Honor of S. K. Heninger Jr.*, ed Peter E. Medine and Joseph Wittreich (Newark: University of Delaware Press, 1997), pp. 215–33.

Quotations from *The Faerie Queene* use the second edition of ed. A. C. Hamilton et al. (London: Pearson Education [Longman], 2001).

Poetic fire: an introduction

Ayesha Ramachandran, Susan Felch, and Susannah Monta[1]

Donne's 'Sapho to Philaenis' begins with a question about poetic making: 'Where is that holy fire, which verse is said / To have? is that enchanting force decayed?' Art, Donne argues, ventriloquizing Sappho, cannot match Nature, because 'verse ... / ... to her work cannot draw'. The triple pun on 'draw' here, pulling close and away in the very act of representation, a splitting of self and other despite analogies of sameness (which the poem will later explore), points to the metacritical game that the verse epistle begins by announcing. It is slippery and sly, teasing and earnest all at once. Its self-reflexive tone and winking gaze have been difficult to assess, its sources contested and obscure. As recently as 2018, in his volume of essays on Sappho, Jonathan Goldberg notes the difficulty of adjudicating whether 'Donne successfully represented lesbian love' or whether 'his overwhelmingly masculinist presence precluded that possibility'.[2]

Enter Anne Lake Prescott. In a little-known essay provocatively entitled 'Male Lesbian Voices: Ronsard, Tyard, and Donne play Sappho', published in 2003, Prescott solves the mystery of Philaenis (previously considered unknown in the sources): the missing intertext is none other than the *Recueil des dames* by the French court-watcher and memoirist Pierre de Bourdeille, Sieur de Brantôme. By connecting Donne's epistle to a set of texts that emerge around queer sexual escapades at the French court, Prescott opens a new set of comparative contexts that point to a richer and more complex tradition of cross-gendered poems in the early modern period. Moreover, she explores an interpretation attuned to affect as a means of parsing the multilayered gendered tonalities of the poem. Strikingly, though, Prescott's essay is absent from the critical tradition around this poem, even though it is roughly contemporary with Valerie Traub's landmark *The Renaissance of Lesbianism in Early Modern England* and Eve Sedgwick's *Touching Feeling* (2003).[3] This is an emblematic absence.

Prescott wrote several such groundbreaking essays on a variety of subjects, essays that stand outside familiar critical historiographies and have been surprisingly left out of the theoretical conversations within which they so obviously belong. Her interest in gender-crossing poetic voices, for instance, began in the late 1980s and continues through essays written in the 2000s – a period that tracks the rise of feminist and queer readings of early modern texts. It is already evident in a 1989 essay on the genealogies of what we might call the ventriloquized prostitute poem, cleverly entitled 'Translatio lupae', which unfolds from an intertextual history of Gervase Markham's *The Famous Whore*, tracing it back to Joachim du Bellay's 'Vieille Courtisanne', and then opens into a meditation on cities and female bodies, the figure of Rome as a whore (mythic and biblical), and the ambivalent moralizing of writers from Aretino to Jonson. To take another example: in 'Housing Chessmen and Bagging Bishops' (1997), she brings together questions about space and desire, gender and power from Francesco Colonna's *Hypnerotomachia polifili*, that icon of Renaissance humanism and printing, to Middleton's *Game of Chess*, via Rabelais's *Cinquieme livre*, English translations of Colonna, a wide range of chess manuals and polemics, and cross-confessional allegory. The essay's threading together of spatial theorizations of perspective, the erotic gaze, and gendered figurations of political power ('crazy queen chess') anticipates the wave of scholarship on space, politics, and transnational cultural connections that would follow in the early 2000s.

As the profusion of texts and topics in these essays suggests, locating Prescott's work in the scholarly landscape of the last forty years is a difficult task. This difficulty is compounded by the fact that so many of the innovative essays that she wrote are hard to find. They frequently appear in edited volumes and collections to which she was asked to contribute, and to which she always generously agreed. As a scholar, teacher, and mentor who committed her career to building communities, supporting the work of others, and performing what is now recognized as the essential, invisible, frequently gendered labor of the academy, she did not focus on centering her own varied, wide-ranging research. Moreover, the confessional wars of theory and historicisms in the 1990s, particularly as they manifested themselves in early modern studies, offered no obvious critical location for Prescott's capacious, cross-cultural, multilingual, and theoretically eclectic approach to early modern texts, particularly poetry.

This volume aims to redress this critical lacuna. It collects twelve of Prescott's hard-to-find essays and places them within a critical history of early modern literary and cultural studies in the nearly four decades following the mid-1980s. It is thus both a resource for current and future scholars of early modern literature and a homage to a shaping presence in the field – one who built and led several scholarly societies (the International Spenser Society, the John Donne Society, the Society for the Study of Early Modern Women and Gender, the Sixteenth Century Society and Conference, the Renaissance

Society of America), mentored and served as a model for a generation of female-identifying scholars in the field, edited or served on the editorial boards of several publications, and helped produce a range of important pedagogical resources.

At the same time, by presenting together essays written mostly from the mid-1980s to the early 2000s, this volume offers a retrospective account of critical genealogies and models for our own moment. Anne Prescott's career spans the second half of the twentieth century – a period that saw the emergence of Renaissance studies in the postwar period, shaped by European scholars such as Paul Oskar Kristeller, Hans Baron, and J. G. A. Pocock; the rise of French theory, psychoanalysis, and feminism in the American academy; the oscillations of Old and New Historicisms; the canon wars; the 'turn to religion'; and the recent turn towards cross-cultural, multilingual literary histories. Prescott's work straddles many of these movements and the theoretical categories they engendered. She is a figure of the interstice, of critical incipience. Her work repeatedly anticipates or gestures towards theory before theory – or, more precisely, presents theoretically inflected excavations without explicitly taking polemical theoretical stands. Her easy movement within varied, even eclectic methodologies is everywhere evident.

Prescott's commitment to questions of gender and sexuality is already visible in her work from the late 1970s and early 1980s, putting her at the vanguard of this turn in Renaissance studies.[4] Her careful attention to multilingual transmission and translation, the focus of her first book, *French Poets and the English Renaissance* (1978), and eventually the spine of her scholarly corpus, looks ahead to questions of linguistic borrowing, imitation, and the politics of transnational and cross-confessional poetics almost twenty years before these were to be at the forefront of critical debate.[5] Her discussions of poetic self-making in *French Poets*, moreover, bear intriguing resemblances to Stephen Greenblatt's *Renaissance Self-fashioning*, published two years later, and even though she never explicitly intervened in debates over the New Historicism, her own scholarship borrows ecumenically from its methods, fusing it with other 'old' historicist approaches. Resisting the now-politicized dichotomies of close reading, historicism, and theory, Prescott juggles archival precision, old-school source study, and psychoanalysis within the same essay. Or in another case, she reflects calmly on the fraught tensions of history and political allegory, noting compassionately the compromises that historical actors (and critics, one suspects) must make.

Now, at a time when there are few – if any – clearly defined theoretical schools, Prescott's adroit interlacings of texts and contexts, her wide-ranging critical toolkit which sometimes seems to burst at the seams, as well as her good humor and good sense, offer *exempla* for a new generation. We have accordingly identified four distinctive areas in which Prescott's contributions – through the essays that appear here – have shaped new ways of approaching early modern texts.

Comparative study

Prescott is a practitioner of comparative literary study in an originary sense: she is always attuned to the multiple vectors of influence that may shape any given writer or text. Though she privileges French–English literary relations in the sixteenth century, she works across Latin and Italian as well, as her essays on Psalm translations and the 'Chessmen' show. Comparison is of course not only a matter of multilingual skill, but an awareness of what Prescott calls 'the cultural forcefield' of the works that gives their juxtaposition meaning. She follows the linguistic resonances of Protestant and Catholic approaches to the Word across a range of genres and a wide temporal span. Her essay on Spenser and Bateman, for instance, moves from late medieval French romances to English religious polemics.

Though she is not often explicit about the challenge of intertextual filiation, her essays return repeatedly to the question of how we might grapple with establishing sources and interpreting allusions, often providing quiet qualification of her own assertions. She is careful, for instance, in attributing 'the currently fashionable and useful terms "intertextuality" or "*imitatio*"' to Markham's translation of Du Bellay, because, she notes, the translation 'may not be self-aware enough'.[6] This throwaway comment is a condensed theoretical argument: whether intertextuality demands critical self-consciousness on the part of a writer is a thorny question, one that bleeds into assumptions about authorial intention, textual autonomy, and reader reception. In 'Chessmen', Prescott, fresh from the publication of her book on Rabelais, is very careful about asserting authorship and chains of transmission. Does the episode of the Abbaye de Thélème owe something to the *Hypnerotomachia*? Prescott is prudently suggestive and never insistent, but reminds us that strategic juxtaposition may be more useful sometimes than a rigidly philological attitude.

Philology – the groundwork of comparative literature as a discipline – is both central to and gently reshaped in Prescott's hands. It emerges in her persistent interest in making visible the networks of readers and the communities of scholars and writers who are jointly involved in an enterprise of literary co-creation. In marshalling an army of erudite sources, she embraces a richly textured literary history, one that is not fixated on a parade of canonical Great Poets but on the many mixed communities within which they lived and wrote. Markham gets equal time with Du Bellay and Bateman with Spenser. If philology is 'knowing what has been known' or '(re)-cognizing ... what has already been cognized', as Sheldon Pollock argues, citing August Boeckh, it demands a disciplinary self-understanding that is simultaneously ambitious and humble.[7] Always modest in its assertions, Prescott's scholarship helps us to reconstruct, through careful excavation, what has been known, so that we may come to recognize both our own horizons and limits. Her method, therefore, reaches back to the venerable tradition of romance philology, even as it nods towards the emerging theoretical concerns of the 1980s and 1990s.

One such concern is the centrality of translation to both literary history and contemporary comparative literary criticism, something that Prescott embraces by providing extensive citations and translations herself (as in her most recent joint essay with Roger Kuin on Ronsard and Donne, which makes available to readers in English several untranslated sonnets by the French poet), but which she also details carefully as a historical practice. She reminds us (often in footnotes) of the significance of translation as a humanistic practice in the early modern period. Under her gaze, Dallington's translation of the *Hypnerotomachia* and Marot's or Mary Sidney's translations of the psalms become significant nodes in a wider network of cultural making. Translation itself, she notes, becomes a 'politicized tradition' in the period – and a religious as well as a linguistic matter – as her cluster of essays on Psalm translation in France and England shows.

Historicism

Prescott's commitments to philology and translation point to her deeper, more complicated relationship with the struggles over historicism that have characterized early modern literary study over the last half century. Her fundamental adherence to the significance of literary history – as it was being shaped by Renaissance humanists, and as we are shaping it now in our contemporary scholarship – places her squarely between the Old and New Historicism. Already in her very early work in the 1970s she recognized the need to think more cohesively of the relationships between historical context, cultural narratives (themselves historically contingent), and the making and interpretation of literary texts. She remained insistent, however, on the distinctiveness of the literary object from other kinds of historical documents, patiently juxtaposing and probing both for mutual illumination. Thus, in her much-cited essay, 'The thirsty deer and the Lord of Life', she provides a historicist interpretation of a pivotal sonnet in Spenser's *Amoretti*, engaging the theological, cross-confessional, and literary historical contexts only to show how they are transformed by the poet in unexpected ways.

Prescott skirts the anthropological methods of the New Historicism, avoiding the historical anecdote and speculative thick description, but she is a quiet practitioner of a kind of cultural history which flourished in conversation with it. Hewing close to historical sources often derived from careful work in archives long before the present archival turn, Prescott weaves together text and context to reveal the metaphorical patterning that history itself must lean on. In the essay on the countess of Pembroke's *Ruins of Rome* she slowly shows how ruins – the very physical markers of historical passage – become emblems for religious polemic and poetic pasts, while also providing the groundwork for intellectual futures.

But Prescott's historicism shines in the essay on Spenser's Burbon, an allegory for Henri IV. The essay shows why critics' dissatisfaction with Spenser's treatment of this slippery historical figure is rooted in an inadequate understanding of the often contradictory historical sources. But though she draws on previously unpublished letters between Elizabeth I, Henri IV, and his sister Catherine (which are presented at length with translations) as well as a multitude of contemporary poems and pamphlets about the king of Navarre, Prescott never allows the seduction of the empirical document's claim to truth to override the polyvalent nuances of the poetic text. She writes,

> *The Faerie Queene* shows us Burbon the timeserver, but Henri the Gallic Hercules is there too. Erased by events and Spenser, he haunts the text as the hero he should have been … In his very historicity Burbon *is* allegorical, and one thing he allegorizes is how politics can undo allegory. That is why the Burbon episode indicates how ambiguously history and allegory can relate to each other, literary veils being twitched aside only to reveal the fog of myth on the historical mirrors.

There is a miniature theory of allegory and history contained in these lines. For Prescott, allegory does not refract history so much as it discloses the ambivalences and obfuscations of historical actors.

She is characteristically compassionate, however, in her treatment of historical and political disappointments. In writing about the promise of Henri and the inevitable disappointment of his Protestant admirers, she is also writing – albeit obliquely – of our political aspirations and how we might reckon with the compromises we must sometimes make:

> How history fractures mythology, then, can figure how circumstance pressures any plan, conviction, action: how, as the French say, 'tout commence en mystique, tout finit en politique'. Burbon's shield is broken not just by deceived or corrupted rascals but – in a book filled with dismemberings – by events in the temporal world. This does not make Spenser despair, I think, for it cannot have taken him until 1593 to notice how the world wags; even the 1590 *Faerie Queene* has few unproblematic victories. But it does suggest that Justice, even

Equity, is not enough, that a well-fashioned gentleman needs yet more virtues to help him negotiate an always lapsing world, one in which signifiers are as apt to flit as our wills are to waver and fleurs de lis are to fade.

The elegance of this extended passage belies its cheerful political hardheadedness. It also reminds us that though Prescott is never overt in her scholarship's political allegiances, they are not absent, nor is she ever apolitical. Her defense of Burbon/Henri is a defense of historical complexity, an exhortation that we examine both sides of (inevitably) flawed political heroes, not to exonerate or relieve them of complicity but to eschew a hard-edged purity which brings its own excesses. Her warm embrace of ambivalence and her refusal of righteous idealisms, in Spenser as in our critical practice, is a sharp political lesson for our own time.

It is worth noting too that Prescott's multilayered historicism is also a pedagogical reminder of the meticulous training that a deep commitment to historical scholarship demands: the unglamorous work of sitting in archives, of learning languages and paleography, of poring through historical dictionaries and volumes by early modern hack writers with unflagging attention. These are skills that are certainly in decline for structural and financial reasons; Prescott's work is an argument for our continuing defense of their value. Her essay on the annotations to the Psalter and the framing of David, the attention to image and word in 'Chessmen', and the casual deployment of the printing history of loyalist propaganda from the press of John Wolfe – all instances of the material turn and the place of book history in early modern studies – suggest the many directions in which such training can go.

Finally, Prescott's historicism is inseparable from her interest in the shaping of literary history; her work often highlights the gaps between theorizations of historical method and the less clear formations of literary historical periodization. Her essay with Roger Kuin, for instance, recuperates and interrogates historical/literary terms like Metaphysical, Mannerist, and Baroque as they are deployed across languages, in ways that suggest that we might usefully reconsider how older literary periodizations map onto various historicist arguments about the 'early modern'. As the 'global Baroque' emerges as a critical framework and scholars revisit the political and philosophical stakes of metaphysical poetry, perhaps it is time once more rethink the relation between history and literature.

Gender

The quiet refusal to oversimplify historical relations extends to Prescott's treatment of gender. Reading Donne in the context of Ronsard and Tyard, she notes that they wrote verse which 'Donne could have known, and that, even if he did not know, was part of the world in which he wrote'. Although Prescott is writing here of a canonical male author, scholars today resonate with how important it is to recontextualize less-familiar women authors within their varied, overlapping, and complex worlds – familial, social, political, religious, and the like. The 'worlds in which they wrote' were many and multifaceted, and it is the responsibility of scholars to open these worlds to new generations of readers.

Indeed, she anticipates the current interest in mapping women's social and intellectual circles, which included men as well as women. In 'Family grief', she situates *Les Prisons* within the French court and the intimate 'trinité' of Louise, Marguerite, and François. She reads François's poems and portrait alongside Marguerite's writings, showing both how the brother held political advantage and how the sister used her literary prowess to correct and corral his excesses. She then crosses the channel to connect Marguerite's family circle with that of Pembroke, noting that 'Mary [Sidney] edits and completes works by the defunct hero of Zutphen, and Marguerite makes her king her subject, if only the subject of verse', linking the two writers as exemplars of 'sisterly devotion that eventuates in the ambiguities of post-mortem control', a deliciously apt epigram.

When Prescott focuses on Pembroke in 'The countess of Pembroke's *Ruins of Rome*', it is to set the countess not only within an illustrious family circle, but also within a late sixteenth-century intellectual tradition fascinated with ruins, mutability, and Time. Spenser and other earlier poets, as well as those contemporaries who wrote with, around, and to Pembroke, employed an aesthetic of ruins, a 'verbal and conceptual cluster' that was 'self-replicating and contagious, like a lexical virus'. Pembroke herself deployed the language of ruin repeatedly in her psalms, despite not finding it in contemporary biblical translations, and thus nudged theological language toward the 'fashionable vocabulary' of ruination. Prescott's close reading illuminates at least two of Pembroke's specific lexical choices: where English Bible translations use 'waste' or 'destruction', she chooses variants of 'ruin'; to highlight the trope that writing will outlast monuments she uses terms such as 'record', suggesting script or print, to translate the more generic 'praise' or 'remember'. As Prescott notes, Pembroke makes use of this ruins aesthetic and graphocentric language for Protestant ends, conveying her concern for 'God's city and for hopes of a re-edified and renewed Jerusalem, the peaceful city lying beyond the ravages of time and sin'. Pembroke's choice of a 'fashionable' intellectual tradition and her goal of furthering a political–religious end reinforce the conclusion that her psalm translations cannot be confined to a private devotional genre; as Prescott puts it, the psalms, including those of Pembroke, 'had long provided a model for discourse at once private and public'.

Prescott is also adept at using theoretical paradigms to clarify rather than obscure what occurs in the text. In 'Family grief', she explores the ambivalence of mourning through a variety of lenses. She acknowledges the centrality of erotic desire: 'By adopting a male voice, Marguerite can relocate desire for her brother ... by in some sense *being* him, or the him he should have been, the him who eventually – in her poem – gets things right.' But she also subtly offers a corrective to theory run rampant: 'not sexual desire, I mean, but love with the erotic glow derived from power, prestige, and charm'. She adopts Julia Kristeva's work on depression to illuminate the aggressiveness in *Les Prisons* that might otherwise go unnoticed: 'It is not to dishonor her grief, only to confess our species' complexity, to observe that after years of being third in the "trinité", a queen but never a ruler, well loved but not her mother's chief pride, and bearer of only one surviving child, Marguerite effectively erases the son/brother (loved, but absent) and records maternal praise for the wise daughter/sister.' Yet to understand this text well, she adds other theoretical insights, noting the usefulness of a Lacanian movement from the Imaginary to the Symbolic to silence, traditional theology's rendering of the soul as gendered female both grammatically and conceptually, and the Jungian psychic unity of *animus* and *anima*. Prescott's characteristic turn toward a range of theoretical models opens up the text, while at the same time threading the divergent critical perspectives into complementary, rather than competitive, claims.

Religion

Prescott anticipates a number of important developments in the study of early modern literature and religion. Key to the formation of that subject area has been an insistence that the interpretive habits forged around religious texts – biblical texts but also liturgical, devotional, and hagiographic materials – were an ineluctable part of the period's literary culture, influencing sacred and supposedly secular texts in rich, varied, and subtle ways.[8] Recent important work on biblical paratexts, for instance, has underscored their importance for shaping the reception of Christianity's foundational texts.[9] Prescott's essays demonstrate how those paratexts may be used to read poetic work and as a source for poetic theory in the period. In 'David as a slandered courtier', Prescott focuses intently on exegesis in the sixteenth century, attending to those figures (Bucer, Calvin, Beza, Vatablus) whose lectures and commentaries on the psalter helped move generations of readers towards a more historical, less typological reading of the psalms. Yet Prescott does not overstate her case: careful not to exaggerate differences between medieval and Reformation approaches to the psalms, Prescott shows how historical and even political readings of the psalms also opened up possibilities for diachronic readings in light of the politics of Sidney's own day. In 'King David as a "right poet"', Prescott points to the appearance of Basil's homily on Psalm 1 in the psalter of the Bishops' Bible as a way to shape readers' engagements with the psalms; she then adduces a poetics of praise from the psalter, bringing to bear exegetes from Athanasius to Bellarmine.

With its maturation, the study of early modern religion and literature has increased its temporal range. As Prescott's essays demonstrate, religious texts from earlier periods continued to be used, studied, prayed, imitated, and ritually performed in the Reformation and post-Reformation eras.[10] Prescott converses easily with patristic thinkers who were sources for interpretive cues and habits that persist throughout the Reformation period. In 'King David as a "right poet"', for instance, she points to the reception of Athanasius's understanding of the psalter in early modern England, most importantly through material from Athanasius included in Matthew Parker's 1567 psalter. She adopts a long religious line, so to speak, not limiting her contextual reading to the immediacy of contemporary sixteenth-century religious politics, important as they were to Sidney, but instead encompassing the range of ways in which the adaptation and interpretation of patristic thinking continued to influence Sidney's poetics.

As scholarship on religion and literature has crossed temporal boundaries, so too it has learned to cross linguistic and confessional ones. Prescott's essays remain a model for how this may be done. She is clearly correct in 'The thirsty deer and the Lord of Life' when she asserts that Spenser was no Catholic. But insofar as he engages in what might be called a cultural salvage operation, scouring Catholic texts of the past for models he might use in his Protestant and Protestantizing romance epic, so too he may have turned to the Sarum liturgy – itself the basis for Thomas Cranmer's *Book of Common Prayer* – for poetic inspiration.[11] Prescott shows that even so firm a Protestant as Stephen Bateman, one who is far more skeptical about fiction's moral rectitude than is Spenser, read a Burgundian romance as inspiration for his own 'travayled pilgrim'. Her subtle work on Marguerite de Navarre – a figure not easily encompassed within the confessional boundaries that early modern governments and churches tried so hard to draw – is yet another example of the importance of approaching an author's religious thinking and writing on her own terms, not those set for her through a retrospective neatening of the period's religious changes.

In recent years, scholarship on liturgy and literature has turned from comparatively narrow studies of linguistic echoes or influence to broader understandings of liturgy as *work*, as indeed the etymology of the word suggests. Liturgical work is the work of relation: much more than a set of verbal texts, liturgy weaves together metaphorical, temporal, and communal connections. The lightness of Prescott's liturgical touch in 'The thirsty deer and the Lord of Life' and 'King David as a "right poet"' mirrors the ease with which liturgical thinking – and not simply or only liturgical language locatable in discrete confessionalized texts – shaped the literary *habitus* of Spenser and Sidney. Nor was Spenser alone in his tendency to read broadly, across confessional lines.

In Prescott's excavation of religious and literary intertexts and conversations, her learning is worn lightly. While this lightness of touch undoubtedly makes her essays a pleasure to read, it is also important as method: the ease of her broad conversations with patristic, medieval, and Reformation-era religious texts brings her closer to the analogously diaphanous interactions Spenser, Sidney, Bateman, and others had with their own broad and rapidly changing religious culture. In her essays, Prescott does not separate religious from other concerns, whether sexual, literary-historical, affective. Her weighing of emotion and experiences, affect and praxis, when thinking about religious ideas remains critical for the field: while it is perhaps easiest for the academy to imagine religion as a set of intellectual precepts to which one does or does not assent, that construction is also a terribly impoverished and fundamentally ahistorical understanding of religion. As Prescott's work on religion and literature demonstrates, religion is not mere assertion, nor are sonnets ready technologies for navigating theological inlets. Her insistence on religion as a broadly lived phenomenon remains an important guide for contemporary work in the field.

On interpretive elegance

A distinctive voice who never belonged to any critical 'school' and who happily supported colleagues and students across a very wide intellectual spectrum, Prescott's characteristic mix of critical empathy and tartly pragmatic intervention has enabled the work of many others. Far from closing down further study by insisting on a definitive reading, Prescott's criticism is one of invitation: she never assumes that her readers know (or can access) the materials she draws upon, so she often provides analytical narrations, translations, or overviews. In 'Family grief', for instance, she announces that she will offer a 'summary' of this long poem, but what follows is more anatomy than summary, a laying bare of the initial descriptions of living prisons – love, worldly ambition, books – to arrive at the deathbed scenes of mother-in-law, husband, mother, and brother. Prescott recognizes that the reader must hold in mind the poem as a whole in order to follow her finely tuned analysis of the cross-gendering dynamics at work in the French court and in Marguerite's poem, and it is only then that a holistic consideration of gender, voice, and family intimacy can unfold.

The recent essay at the end of this volume, by Prescott and Roger Kuin, might epitomize how the question of style – poetic style, but also critical style – is fundamental to her scholarship. Investigating the idea of 'conceit' through the comparison of Ronsard and Donne, the essay explores the conjunction between image and idea, suggesting that literary style – so hard to define, and too easily dismissed by some critics – is in fact at the center of debates over forms of thought and their intergenerational transformations. Describing the role of wit and irony *through* wit and irony, the essay traces the gradual move towards a Baroque poetics. As what was once a concept becomes fused with what was once an image, giving birth to a new (and transnational) form of light yet serious wit, Prescott's characteristic elegance of thought finds, once more, an ideal subject.

Throughout these essays, then, as throughout her career, Anne Lake Prescott gracefully and elegantly blends depths of learning and humanity. Her essays' dominant characteristics – careful reading of particular texts, the situation of those texts within the expansive realms in which their authors lived and wrote, the easy employment of multiple theoretical perspectives – render them both classic and exemplary. With tart humor and smiling courtesy she welcomes readers from many modernities into the world she loves: a world in no way bygone but still fascinating and sharply relevant. It is a world she invites us to regard and to approach in her own manner: with lively interest, with a thirst for knowledge, with compassion and generosity.

Notes

1. The opening of this introduction and the sections on comparative study and history were written by Ayesha Ramachandran; the section on gender by Susan Felch; and the section on religion by Susanna Monta.
2. Jonathan Goldberg, *Sappho: Fragments* (Santa Barbara, Calif.: Punctum Books, 2018), 59, 9.
3. Prescott's essay is not cited in Goldberg's 2018 essay or in Page DuBois's discussion of the literary afterlife of Sappho to which Goldberg refers: see Page DuBois, *Sappho*, (London: I. B. Tauris, 2015).
4. See the complete bibliography at the end of this volume. For comparison, Joan Kelly-Gadol's iconic 'Did Women have a Renaissance' was published in 1976.
5. Thomas Greene's *Light in Troy* (New Haven, Conn.: Yale University Press), which theorized imitation, was published only in 1982.
6. See p. 241.

7 Sheldon Pollock, Benjamin Elman, and Ku-ming Kevin Chang, eds., *World Philology* (Cambridge, Mass.: Harvard University Press, 2015), 7.
8 See for instance Jamie Ferguson, 'The Bible and Biblical Hermeneutics', *Edmund Spenser in Context*, ed. Andrew Escobedo (Cambridge: Cambridge University Press, 2016), 130–8; Carol Kaske, *Spenser and Biblical Poetics* (Ithaca, NY: Cornell University Press, 1999).
9 Debora K. Shuger, *Paratexts of the English Bible, 1525–1611* (Oxford: Oxford University Press, 2022).
10 There is no single synthetic monograph on the reception of the Church Fathers in the early modern period. For forays into the subject, see *The Reception of the Church Fathers and Early Church Historians in the Renaissance and the Reformation, c. 1470–1650*, special issue of *International Journal of the Classical Tradition* 27 (2020), eds. Andreas Ammann and Sam Kennerley; *The Reception of the Church Fathers in the West: From the Carolingians to the Maurists*, ed. Irena Backus, 2 vols. (Leiden: Brill, 1997).
11 Alison Chapman, 'National Saints and *The Faerie Queene*', in *Patrons and Patron Saints in Early Modern England* (Routledge, 2017); Susannah Brietz Monta and Lisi Oliver, 'Spenser, Wolfram, and the Reformation of Despair', *Journal of Literary Onomastics* 1 (new series; 2011), 9–30.

Part I

Spenser

1

Spenser's chivalric restoration: from Bateman's *Travayled Pylgrime* to the Redcrosse Knight

Perhaps the last thing Spenserians want is another 'source' for *The Faerie Queene*. Sources are not fashionable, liquid concepts like 'influence' have yielded to fibrous intertextuality: the water nymphs have departed and left their jobs to Bottom the Weaver. Yet one way to map Spenser's imagination is to trace how he differs from others, and difference requires similarity. So I would like to suggest a – precedent, I will call it – that provides this cartographic opportunity. The precedent is all the more valuable because in recent years it has become clear that, whatever Spenser's love of pagan fictions and tales of romance, he inscribed into his epic and deflected onto his villains certain perhaps Protestant and iconoclastic anxieties concerning his own feigning magic, his own spell weaving, the images that distract us from the straight and narrow way.[1] Spenser the creator of dreamy picture galleries has long since given way to a sterner Protestant, and at times he seems almost ready to become a sullen and disappointed Puritan. It is instructive, therefore, to see what his legend of Holiness looks like if set not against Italian or medieval romance, not against classical epic, but against another Protestant allegory of knightly quest and dynastic celebration, one also troubled by the temptations of imagined sights and the risks of repose. Luckily there is precisely such a text; it has, for all its limitations, a curious resemblance to the poem Spenser might have written had he fully shared the distrust of romance, feigning, love stories, and marvels felt by many Protestants, Counter-Reformation Catholics, and sober Humanists (including his friend Gabriel Harvey).

It is *The Travayled Pylgrime* (1569), a chivalric pilgrimage allegory by Archbishop Matthew Parker's protégé and librarian, Stephen Bateman. I am not the first to see a connection with Spenser, for Kathrine Koller, in 1942, tried to link the *Pylgrime* to the Book of Temperance; it goes better with Book I.[2] But the intertextual (or interfluvial) situation is in fact complicated. Although Bateman does not say so, his book is a reworking of the Burgundian Olivier de La Marche's nostalgic 1483 allegory, *Le Chevalier délibéré*, by way of Hernando Acuña's 1553 Spanish version published in Antwerp.³ Even the many pictures perform a translation of their own, from the Burgundian autumn that followed the death of Charles the Rash in 1477, to the Hapsburg Netherlands, to Protestant England. In his fine study of Burgundian culture and the Tudors, Gordon Kipling compares La Marche himself to Spenser, but without reference to Bateman.⁴ He is right to find similarities between the two allegorists: both follow a pattern alternating moralized wandering with emblematic structures set in a landscape devoid of specified locality or time, a world in which knights encounter abstract nouns and personages inhabiting primarily mental space.⁵ To be sure, this technique and atmosphere are also found in Deguileville, Lydgate, and, later, Hawes: that is, in a tradition owing some of its vocabulary to Prudentius' *Psychomachia* and one possible narrative structure to St. Bernard's allegorization of the Prodigal Son as an Everyyouth riding his horse Desire through a world of personifications.⁶ To this La Marche adds both his grieving loyalty in old age to a defunct line of dukes and his aching awareness of Time. This is the Book of Holiness narrated by a victim of Mutability. Bateman erases some of the nostalgia Acuña had already diminished and incorporates his own centrist Protestantism, mild anxiety about the dangers of repose and visual distractions, suspicion of history and glory, gratitude to the Tudors, and a tendency to interiorize and individualize forces that La Marche found out there in history, language, or the place abstract nouns come from.⁷

Bateman's poem is, I think, England's only significant nondramatic Protestant quest allegory before Spenser; it shows what this genre could look like after the Reformation redefined the tradition's terms but before the Christian knight dismounted to trudge as Bunyan's pedestrian.⁸ Yet Bateman faced generic complexities beyond the requirements of a new religious outlook, for his borrowed pilgrim knight is also a born-again Burgundian courtier whose dynastic homage to his defunct masters La Marche has somewhat uneasily merged into the pilgrimage tradition. True, to mingle the public and personal had ample authority in allegorizings of Vergil, but La Marche's chivalry, Bateman seems to have felt, obscures or at least fails to correspond to the general significance of the pilgrimage.⁹ It was easy to launder out the rosaries and chapels, to secularize the hermit; and, as one would expect, Bateman's fourteeners rejoice that the Gospel is recovered and the abbey-lubbers expelled. But he could not eliminate the dynastic element of his story without omitting and not merely reforming some 1553 illustrations. So he simply replaced La Marche's Burgundians and Acuña's Hapsburgs with Tudors, edging around Bloody Mary with inattentive murmurs of pity and regret. The result is that, like Spenser, he associates knightly errancy and recovery with his nation's restoration of a truth once lost to those same deceitful powers that stalk the *miles Christi*. We are on the way to Spenser, for it is precisely Bateman's combination of chivalric metaphor, pilgrimage allegory, dynastic praise, and national redemption from specifically papist darkness that makes his *Pylgrime* so interesting a precedent for *The Faerie Queene*. All Bateman lacks is love interest, better monsters (his giant is too small and talkative to be frightening), a wiser choice of meter, more awareness of the Italians, and – I admit – a greater talent for poetry.

Let me now describe this seldom-read text so as to suggest the likeness that makes difference worth noting. My method is narrative, for that is the best way to reveal how these two journeys coincide and diverge. I am not attempting to deny that Vergil, Ariosto, and Tasso are Spenser's most significant subtexts (although they do seem less central to Book I). And theoretical discussions of language and allegory in Bateman and Spenser are best postponed until the latter's place in this line of late Medieval and Renaissance personification narrative has been restudied.[10] I myself believe that Spenser read Bateman or at least looked at the pictures; he might have done so while working for Bishop Young, a friend of Bateman's employer Archbishop Parker. Skeptics, though, could consider Pilgrim and Redcrosse cognates, prodigal cousins descended from the house of Prudentius and Bernard but one of them owing more to other ancestors.

Bateman's title, *The Travayled Pylgrime*, punningly recalls how error first brought travail in field or childbed and travel far from Eden. His opening lines, indeed, evoke Adam, the namer and governor now 'exilde' from his 'accursed' land (sig. B2) – the same 'forwasted' realm from which Una's parents have been 'expeld' (II.i.5). But, says Bateman, God sent a 'newe Adam', showing us a love seen also in his rescue of the Israelites from Egypt. In other words, like St. George, whose name is more or less Greek for Adam, 'earth', Bateman's pilgrim enters on a quest immediately associated with biblical and, by extrapolation, national history. After all, St. George's name, says the Golden Legend, may also mean (among other things) 'pilgrim'. Bateman's pilgrim is armed, if not with Pauline armor then with moral virtue, and mounted on Will, a horse 'whose force few youth may stay' (B4v; Figure 1.1). Like George's 'angry steede ... disdayning to the curb to yield' (i.1), Will was sired by Bernard's Desiderium (himself a descendant of Plato's pair in *The Phaedrus*), the steed who whirls his rider up allegorical hills and down moralized dales. Pilgrim, in this also like Redcrosse, has Reason with him at least intermittently; and sometimes he has a lady: Dame Memory. Inspired by Thought, he sets forth 'couragious, some prowesse for to winne', a conventional aim: Redcrosse hopes 'To winne him worship' and 'prove his puissance' (1.3). His quest is to seek Atropos and war against Debility and Dolor, energies that La Marche reads as the entropy and chance

20 *Spenser*

The trauailed Pilgrime

¶ The armed Knight fignifieth true Obedience in all eftates, his armour, Strength : the fhielde, Hope : the fworde, Courage : the fpeare, Aduenture : deliuered to the Author, by Thought being prefent in the fielde called Time.

III

The Author putting all feare afide, armeth himfelfe, and fo rideth foorth on his horfe called Will.

Figure 1.1 Engraving, 'The armed Knight Signifieth ...' (b4r). STC 1585 copy 1 (*The trauayled pylgrime*). The Knight's identity as Obedience is not retained in the allegory.

that destroyed Burgundy but that Bateman partially interiorizes into the concupiscible and irascible faculties.

Pilgrim's adventures, like George's, are structured by the sequence Bernard had suggested: initial ignorance and folly, rashness in success, despair in adversity, and recovery and perfection in knowledge.[11] To this Bateman adds, besides the admonitions and visions he modeled on those by La Marche, his own ruminations on time and history; Spenser adds the wanderings of Una, the tale of Fradubio, some epic touches, Arthur, and a betrothal. The two authors thus differ in how they interrupt and divide the pattern, but both follow a knight from error to pride to despair to recuperative education and a final battle.

Armed and advised, Pilgrim soon comes to 'A goodly greene ... which worldly pleasure hight', a place which so 'delighted me, my selfe I cleane forgat' (B4v). Redcrosse too, 'led with delight' (i.10), wanders into serpentine greenery. What follows in Bateman and Spenser is quite similar if one looks beyond the different ways of organizing error into episodes and forgets, for the moment, that Bateman's animated nouns become, in Spenser, more imaginable figures, mobile emblems. After entering a green world that each author unsurprisingly calls a labyrinth (C2v; i.11), the knights meet figures that are at once divisive and deceitful; both are then misled into worldliness and pride. Spenser shows us a major struggle with Error, then the encounter with Archimago, then the deflection to the House of Pride; Bateman hints at error, moves at once to divisive delusion, and then, after his knight's apparently ineffective visit to the House of Reason and a temporarily sobering defeat by Age, focuses on the dynamics of wandering as a prelude to false relaxation in the World.

Spenser is structurally clearer as well as subtler, yet if one combines Bateman's two descriptions of error, anticipations of *The Faerie Queene* I.i leap out: green, delightful, tangled, the way to error is 'obscure' (Bateman, F3v) and 'shadie' (Spenser, i.7). Getting lost is easy, for this 'crooked waye' is 'not seene till some be in' and its deceit 'so steales upon a man, that scarce he can be ware', especially if, like Redcrosse relying on his own virtue, one 'puts confidence, on such as seemeth just'. Here, says Pilgrim, live illusion and 'That subtile stingbraine Error' who 'much amasde my minde' (so too Spenser's knight is 'amazde' by Error's repellent offspring). Like George, the horse Will rashly presses on 'without all dread or feare' and Pilgrim so forgets himself that 'I knew not mine owne estate nor how myselfe to name' (F4), a separation from the self that Spenser places after Archimago's machinations and that Bernard had allegorized as the 'regio dissimilitudinis', that realm of unlikeness into which prodigals pass when they have forgotten themselves and their origin. But just as Una says 'Add faith unto your force' (i.19), Pilgrim reports that 'not by force and might,

/ The shielde of faith did me defende'; it does so 'in midst of stormy showre', perhaps a reference, like Spenser's own cloudburst, to the blows of Fortune that invite us to Error's refuge.

After his initial misstep, Pilgrim meets the giant Disagreement, a figure in function not unlike Redcrosse's next enemy, Archimago.[12] Archimago promotes 'ire' (ii.5), and Disagreement rides a horse of that name, but this 'ire' is no mere wrath. Like Spenser's master magician, Bateman's giant seeks to divide and multiply, 'all fleshe to stroy and waste', to 'rent and plucke as small as sand', for he 'all would deflowre, from quiet peace and rest' (B4v).[13] He is an anti-Sabbath, and his restless destruction is a sort of mutability: as he fought, says the knight, 'Time my state did shake' (C1). In ways neither Bateman nor Spenser spell out, division is both cause and effect of temporality's breakages and slippages in the post-Edenic and sequential world. When force seems useless, furthermore, Disagreement resorts to hypocritical delusion, appealing to the knight's folly and 'fickle fantasie'. Seemingly pacified, he gives the knight a magic cap that he says restores its owner like a 'springing Well' and confounds all 'fonde device' (C2). This is an ancient fairy-tale motif, but Bateman does not believe in fairy tales or even in good marvels; not for him Prince Arthur's supernatural shield or wondrous medicine. Like Redcrosse crediting Archimago's false dreams, Pilgrim cannot read the gift's true nature, and since Bateman is not sure we can either, the margin explains that the cap signifies 'the craftie illusions of Sathan, by coloured imaginations seeking all meanes possible, to deceive if he might, even the very elect'.

Midway through his encounter with error, Pilgrim visits the House of Reason or Understanding, a place with no parallel in Spenser at this point but with a few similarities to the House of Holiness and the Hill of Contemplation, including the guest's request to stay and the host's insistence that he return to work and travel (D2v–D3; Figure 1.2). Now comes a battle with the champion Age, as famous as Corineus, conqueror of Gogmagog (F1; a marginal note tells the story, which Bateman at least affects to think historical). This defeat does not discourage Will nearly as much as younger riders might expect, nor does the knight profit from a lecture that exhorts him to avoid 'diverse Courtes', to remember that few courtiers win fame, to resist 'amorous and daintie Dames', and to content himself with 'honest mariage' (F2).

And so Pilgrim and Will come to the 'palace of disordered livers', not, unless Bateman is guilty of a brilliant pun, an anatomical allegory, but a place like Lucifera's House of Pride. Naming itself Love, it is really 'the world both fresh and gaye' (F4v), suggestive evidence that Patrick Cullen is right in identifying Spenser's version of this palace as the 'world' third of the infernal triad.[14] Self-mocking when recounted by the courtier La

Figure 1.2 Engraving, 'Here Understanding sheweth ...' (d3r) STC 1585 copy 1 (*The trauayled pylgrime*). The scene revises a 1553 illustration showing a pile of objects recalling the world's mortality.

Marche, the episode in Bateman's hands fits comfortably into a tradition of anti-court satire. There is, however, nothing like Spenser's parodic maiden queen and her deadly entourage, the negative version of Gloriana's Cleopolis. Bateman stresses the world's moral threat to a private knight (if that is not an oxymoron), but he avoids any mention of the local authorities; Spenser, thinking more politically, shows his knight dismayed by a vision of 'pollicie' and evil magnates (iv.12). Still, the two palaces are remarkably similar, even granted the expectedness of many details and the probable impact on Spenser's imagination of Cartigny's *Wandering Knight*.[15]

The disordered livers inhabit a 'faire' but 'variable' palace whose 'outward showe' (F4–F4v; compare Spenser's 'sumptuous shew', iv.7) is gorgeous with silver walls, crystal windows – altogether inviting despite a porter with 'scorning voice' (G1v, a little surprising in the Palace of Love; Spenser calls his version of this discordance 'Malvenu', although whether Lucifera's subjects know his name is another matter). 'Bedect' with gold 'like Titans gilding beames' and 'heaven Imperiall', the place challenges the skies like Lucifera's brilliance that 'shone as Titans ray, / In glistring gold' (iv.8). Pilgrim's 'eyes were dim with looking on', just as Lucifera can 'dim' her throne and 'all mens eyes amaze' (iv.8, 16). Proud beauties sit on high, spatially placed only a little lower than Lucifera, or together with their 'Champions fierce and fell' they go 'ruffeling in their brave attire' like Spenser's courtiers who 'prancke their ruffes' and 'gay attire' (iv.14); and in both places pleasure is enhanced by trumpets and 'minstrelsie'. Satan is at home in each palace: Spenser's drives the deadly sins and Bateman's triumphs over human lapse. Pluto, too, is named, for Duessa visits his realm and Bateman takes advantage of a reference to Orpheus to remark in the margin that poets feign 'Pluto' to be the Devil (G1v).[16]

Neither palace is immune to decay. Pride's 'ruinous' foundations rest on sand (iv.5) and Bateman's courtiers, aspiring on 'vaine and carnall winges', fall from the sun's melting heat as Satan blows a trump named Horror (F4v). The indirect reference to Icarus anticipates Spenser's to Phaethon (iv.9), but Bateman gives the disastrous result – plummeting worldlings – along with the ominous allusion. Spenser's periphrasis slides by Phaethon without noting his fate: the plunges and ruins in Lucifera's house happen just beyond sight and metaphor while vision is dazzled by splendor. Thus Pride's captives and corpses rot below eye level in a dungeon where only St. George's dwarf can see them, or around back in the 'privie' muck where only those fleeing the World can stumble on them. Bateman's Icarian meltdowns take place up where everyone can watch, diabolical sound effects rendering them even more impressive. The sight seems to do the disordered livers no good, though, a wryly satirical point (if deliberate) quite unlike Spenser's frightening sense that worldliness tends, as we would say now, to disappear people.

Bateman's demon ladies leave their admirers 'Bereft at length from joyfull state, until all wo and strife' (F4), even as Redcrosse will encounter an angry Sansjoy. Seeming to offer 'joyous rest' and 'ease' (Bateman, F4v), both palaces are false Sabbaths, tempting us from a weekday path on which we should be up and doing. Both knights know this in their elect hearts, for both find the inhabitants 'no fit companions' (Bateman, G1) and 'unfit' (Spenser, who, however, also stresses George's 'knightly vew', iv.37, 15).[17] Each, though, needs his memory jogged. Looking in a mirror, Pilgrim sees his own sins and the face of Age; Lucifera also has a mirror, but hers is the normally Venereal glass wrenched to the use of unmarried pride, not the 'crystal glass of reformation' on which Bateman wrote a book published this same year. In Bateman's picture (Figure 1.3) the mirror's holder looks like Reason, but the text identifies the reminder as Memory. Redcrosse, too, is taught by reason and memory, for his dwarf gives him a lesson in history resembling the one which Reason had fruitlessly given Pilgrim several episodes before the latter's deviation into folly. Needless to say, the prudent dwarf prefers effective and sober nonfiction, so, unlike Lucifera's 'chroniclers' who – like Spenser – record 'Old loves, and warres for Ladies' (v.3), George's teacher shows him the more humanist 'ensample' and 'sight' of political disaster (v.45–52). Pilgrim's rescuers, however, bypass both doubtful amorous records and vivid moral example in order to present unmediated self-knowledge. Within the fiction, that is, they do not use history as a mirror but show the mirror itself, directly. It is true that Memory has *energia*, speaking with 'words of lively force' (G2), so perhaps she uses 'ensamples' like those her friend Reason had relied on earlier (D3v–E1). Still, here Bateman separates the image of the image-making mirror from the report of unspecified words on sin. For him the 'sight' is of the self, even if behind that allegory may be another in which Memory's possibly more general lecture in some sense 'is' the mirror. Spenser's fiction at this point contains an image of effective history-telling; Bateman's fiction contains an image not of history or fable but of the hero looking at himself and seeing the results of time on his own face. In any case, both knights make their furtive escape, Redcrosse fleeing by Pride's filthy 'privie Posterne' (a witty anatomical allegory), though 'Scarce could he footing find in that foule way' (v.53), and Pilgrim, who 'scarce could finde [his] way' in the Palace (F4), instructing Memory to tell any sin who asks after him that she does not know his whereabouts. A clever move, if unheroic.

After pride comes despair. Spenser's arrangements are again more structurally interesting, his language generates more implications, some of them grimly funny, and he infolds more tradition, but the cousinship of the two narratives remains striking. Spenser has two episodes. The first, the defeat by Orgoglio, continues Redcrosse's struggle with Pride while anticipating

Figure 1.3 Engraving, 'The author being caried by his horse …' (g1r) STC 1585 copy 1 (*The trauayled pylgrime*). The mirror-holder looks like the Reason or Understanding of Figures 1.1 and 1.2.

and in part causing the ensuing temptation by Despair.[18] And now Spenser indicates specifically the sexuality that Bateman had put into his combined houses of Pride and Eros. The sequences are the same; the timing and persistence of individual elements vary.

Despite Reason and Memory, then, Pilgrim staggers into a place where the air dims, the earth shakes, and infections fly (G2v); Spenser's trembling earth (earthy George's as yet unsanctified old Adam) generates a giant whose behavior, physiology, and function indicate his earthquake nature, for giants sometimes signified earthquakes and earthquakes were read as admonitions to the sinful.[19] That Orgoglio seems also to be a phallus, the infected will grown devilishly erect and proud, dimly parallels the allegorized frailty of Pilgrim's body.[20] Spenser's trembling terrain ('all the earth for terrour seemd to shake', vii.7) is thus both George's weak flesh – cause and result of his sexual encounter – and the giant to which it gives birth in the next stanza. True, Redcrosse's forces 'faile' and he gets chills and fevers because 'carelesse of his health' he has been up to no good with Duessa (and therefore with Rome), not because he has aged further. Since we age and sicken because long ago we sinned, the two allegories are not entirely distinct, and in any event Bateman has moralized a landscape whose shaking began as La Marche's rueful representation of decrepitude. Yet the physical and moral significance of Spenser's episode has polemical implications missing at this point in Bateman, who, separating private from public discourse, preferred to have his Protestant arguments march boldly unveiled on their confident flat feet.

Released by Arthur from Orgoglio's prison, Redcrosse nearly despairs. And just as Orgoglio's victim is 'Disarmed, disgrast, and inwardly dismayde' (vii.11), a soon to be 'dismaide' Pilgrim finds this land ruled by 'Dispaire, Dispraise, Disdaine and Ire' (H2v, G3). Like Orgoglio's castle the place seems a 'dungeon', but like Despair's home it is a 'tenebrous' and thorny wasteland (G2v). There is a well, not enervating like the one Redcrosse drank from before meeting his giant double, but bitter and named Violation. Recognizing himself in this 'vacant', malodorous, and trap-filled land, Pilgrim thinks some of the thoughts that Spenser puts in the mouth of Despair, no mere noun now but a powerful rhetorician. As so often, what is scenery and names in Bateman, in Spenser becomes a vocal emblematic personage. Despair is in many ways chthonic, sitting on the ground that generated Orgoglio and out of which God shaped Adam and George, although his cave is 'a greedie grave' (ix.33), not a womb. But in another sense, too, he is landscape's child, symbol and creation of the desert in which he lives: crouching amid trees that like Bateman's have 'nor fruit, nor leafe', he wears the thorns that grow in Bateman's scenery and his body is as withered and dishevelled as Pilgrim's surroundings.

What Pilgrim tells himself, Despair tells Redcrosse: he has sinned and should die. La Marche's stress had been on aged regret, but Bateman has imagined a scene closer to Bernard's sequence and so emphasizes that what his knight sees is the world without God. Divine wrath hangs over it, and Pilgrim quakes to recall that 'the count is great, that I to Jove must make' (G3). Like Bateman's careless world that forgets Heaven and Hell, Despair's rhetoric slithers past what follows the sleep of death to which he invites his visitor; but he remembers a just God's payment for accumulated sins:

> Is not the measure of thy sinfull hire
> High heaped up with huge iniquitie,
> Against the day of wrath, to burden thee? (ix.46)

Bateman thinks of 'grace' (G3v) and Una recalls mercy, adding logic – as the elect pile up sins they must increase God's mercy – and – denigrating mere rhetoric – 'Ne let vaine words bewitch thy manly heart' (ix.53).

But Pilgrim still hates himself. Tired, lonely, and 'despairing of my selfe', he rides 'halfe dead' into a 'hollow cave'. Even Will starts to 'reele' (H2v–H3). Like Redcrosse, Pilgrim would gladly die; and he too feels filthy. Despair had rightly accused his victim of dirtying himself with Duessa 'in all abuse' and Pilgrim must remember that the porter of the Palace of Love was named Abusion. Now he wishes that a 'hollow grave, with bloudie bones, of me should be defilde' and longs 'not in such a Laberinth, of endlesse woes to wende'. Among his griefs, however, is one Spenser spares Redcrosse. Pilgrim has begun to question glory itself in a world where 'ech man himselfe doth love' and sudden death makes hope of fame problematic: 'For while he strives to get renowme, the thred of life is cut' (G3; cf. Milton's 'Lycidas'). Here and elsewhere Bateman sets limits on the chivalric pursuit of even good glory, limits Spenser doubtless considered but Despair does not mention. That Book I's 'glory' may indicate divine glory does not alter the fact that within the fiction Redcrosse desires 'worship', something the hermit Contemplation does not discourage despite his doubts about bloodshed and ladies' love. For Bateman, finally, the New Jerusalem and knightly fame cannot be reconciled, whatever the continued usefulness of chivalric discourse as metaphor.

Bateman's knight raises his grieving eyes and sees Dame Memory. When cheering Redcrosse, Una had also been Memory, in a way, recalling him to himself and his task. Bateman's Memory offers Pilgrim something rather different this time, not a mirror of reformation but the assurance that he 'should not go alone' on his quest to find Atropos (Figure 1.4). Her history is less for moral education than for companionship, and it is perhaps because of this that Pilgrim calls Memory's conversation 'mery tales and stories true' (H3v). Her nonfiction fashions a good death, not a many-virtued gentleman enabled by twelve or twenty-four books of dark conceit to serve the crown.

Spenser's chivalric restoration 29

The trauailed Pilgrime

The Author and Memorie paſſeth the fielde of worldly pleaſure, and after talketh of the dreadfull combats not yet ſeene.

With his Horſe as yet nothing tired, for all his long trauaile in the fielde of worldly pleaſure.

Figure 1.4 Engraving, 'The Author and Memorie passeth the fielde ...' (h2r) STC 1585 copy 1 (*The trauayled pylgrime*). Memory guiding the Knight.

Una now takes Redcrosse to the House of Holiness, a correctional institution closer to similar structures by Bernard and Cartigny than to anything in *The Travayled Pylgrime*. Dame Memory, too, will bring her knight to a house, one where Reason (no hermit or palmer but a theologically informed layman) prepares him for his last duel. But first she gives him a tour of what Spenser was to call the Ruins of Time. It is now that Bateman introduces, through explicit and visionary nonfiction (Memory at her best, he must have thought), with a personification or metaphor here and there, the national history that in Book I Spenser both veils and figures forth in an allegory never calling the Tudors by their names. Bateman does so, however, while showing that Truth's champions also unwillingly teach us about death. The Tudors, like their Burgundian counterparts, enter the lists heroically to fight and lose – good is the life ending faithfully. But their chivalry is personal. As warriors against Dolor and Debility they enact their courage in terms familiar from court pageantry and knightly combat, but as Protestant reformers they act like statesmen with no time for courtly fiction. As individuals they play knights and as kings they play kings, for the monarch's two bodies yield two discourses: the metaphoric and the historical. True, Memory finds biblical names and analogies, together with images that anticipate Spenser's extended fictions: Edward defeats the Pope Goliath (a real giant, however, not a pagan fable) and Henry battles the Catholic Church with a bright shield of faith. On the whole, though, allegory ceases when Bateman describes the Reformation. Spenser's anti-papist triumphs are more consistently and elaborately feigned.

Memory starts with a 'Pageant' of Henry VIII, splendid on his way to battle Debility in the field called Time (Figure 1.5). This is the king

> Which made all forrein powers to quake, through magnanimitie ...
> Which brake the neck of Papistrie, and gave a deadly wound,
>   Unto the Masse that romishe Hell, that did our soules confound ...
> And did by Target bright of faith, the Popes high curse receave,
>   And washing of the same gan first, on Christes truth to cleave,
> Which staide the Popes revenues here, and puld the Abbeys downe,
>   And spoylde the Romishe lubbers all, which lurckte in every towne.
> The same is he which did commaunde, Gods pastors for to preache,
>   And gave them leave in Popes despite, Gods holye worde to teache. (I1)

In words the wind makes nearly inaudible, Thanatos tells a reluctant Henry that all creation 'must chaunged be by mortall law' but that 'Mori non turpe est, sed turpiter mori' (I2), consolation for the mere *shame* of dying that Bateman explores more subtly than the crudity of his thumping fourteeners might suggest.

Next Pilgrim sees Edward VI on progress to death while Memory tells how he expelled the priests of Baal and felled the Pope Goliath. He

> set up Tables by and by, as Christ himselfe did use.
> The bookes of God he made be read, I meane Christes Testament,
>   Quoth she which Antichrist the Pope had hid long time and rent:
> And made them playne in mother tongue, translated for to be,
>   And made the people serve the Lorde, in truth and veritie. (I4)

Spenser, too, introduces unveiled dynastic history into his allegory, but not in Book I, and when he does so later the stress is genealogical, moral,

Figure 1.5 Engraving, 'The author and memorie riding forwarde ...' (I3r) STC 1585 copy 1 (*The trauayled pylgrime*). Henry VIII on his way to Death.

political; Reformation polemics in *The Faerie Queene* are seldom as naked as the Truth Spenser believed he had seen rescued from the dark.

Avoiding all but the barest mention of Mary, Dame Memory guides Pilgrim toward her field of monuments, showing him that he will 'not alone, / Treade on the path of mortall steppes' (K3). The geography of the place, though, suggests her indecision about its status. The field lies near a hill that Memory compares to 'Pernassus as they faine', a reminder that the mountain of 'the worthy Muses mine' is a fiction (how complicated for the mother, an abstract noun, to have given birth to pagan fables who inhabit a poetic fancy). The path on *this* slope, she says, 'hath turnings none' (L3v): flowers beautify her hill but her road never winds, as though her rhetorical tropes worked with no indirection – a neat trick.

While they travel, Pilgrim stares with fascination, but Memory soon becomes oddly scornful about what he sees, as if remembering deeper truths. That is, she perceives behind history, and thus in a sense beyond herself, a sort of abyss against which our records and recollections seem not so very different from fiction after all. Spenser may have shared some of her doubts, but Memory's reminders have a directness he himself avoids. Her lesson in skepticism comes when she notes that her pupil is inattentive and replies only 'hum and ha' when she speaks to him. He has in fact been so enchanted by *seeing* that he forgets to *listen*. Distracted by 'toyes, and fancies that I sawe' and 'fancies newe and straunge' (L4), his mind has forsaken words for images, just as many Protestant reformers said Christians had been drawn from God's Word by Catholic glitter and idolatry. 'Me thou doest not heere', scolds Memory. 'I am ravisht with the sight', explains Pilgrim. Spenser knew this danger, calling one of his chief villains '*Archimago*', but if only for self protection as an arch-imagemaker himself he usually separates those who abuse sight – deceivers like the creator of Redcrosse's false dreams or the manufacturer of the snowy Florimel – from the granters of true insight like Contemplation or Colin atop Mt. Acidale. Memory, though, bears her own risks with her. She may be irritated with her knight, but it is her landscape they ride through, visual correlative of her 'mery tales'. At least she can set him straight and point his eyes forward. This looks lovely to you, she tells him, because you read it from your own perspective (L4v):

> This Fielde is time that nowe appeeres of such a lively hew,
>   To thee and certayne other mo, which perill never knew,
> Which have ynough as helth and wealth, and ease withouten paine,
>   To whome eche hap of wordes and deedes, still fall out perfite gayne.

To the sad, the poor, the scared, Memory's sights are less attractive:

> To such this pleasaunt fielde of Time, which thou doest thinke so gay,
>   A joylesse plat they holde it sure, devoyde of comfort thay.

For example, she says, Catholics find this scenery ugly, for in it they lost 'all their comfort'. Without pitying them, she knows that Tudor history is not the only one visible.

Eventually the two arrive at Memory's cemetery to inspect 'the auncient showe and Funerals of mightie Conquerours past' (Figure 1.6). These

Figure 1.6 Engraving, 'The Author and Memorie walking on foote ...' (L3R) STC 1585 copy 1 (*The trauayled pylgrime*). Memory's Cemetery, showing what Spenser was to call the ruins of Time.

'Pyramides, and Monuments right hie' (M1) memorialize the fame that the Renaissance liked to imagine for the virtuous, yet Memory understands that to live in the mouths of men is not a reward or consolation, only a neutral fact: we know of the good, the bad, and the ugly because they have caught history's sometimes amoral attention. Memory had claimed for a moment to have forgotten the unworthy 'bitter floure' Mary Tudor, but now she remembers Goliath, Herod, Nero, and (Bateman was a Euhemerist) Bacchus, pointing out the markers that 'stande to their shame' (M1v). Pilgrim is impressed, but Memory rebukes him for his spiritually ignorant gawking at celebrity:

> The sights not seene with Jove above, doth breede more joy and ease:
> For these are things though faire, yet vaine, a time to please the eye,
> The life to come doth far surpasse ...

Doubtless Spenser would agree, as would Milton, but when Arthur reads the Britons Moniments in Book II he is given no such advice; like chivalry, history survives Spenser's doubts better than it does those of Archbishop Parker's librarian. Bateman's ambivalence remains curious; knowledge of a history more significant than chronicle and more trustworthy than national fantasies had acquired increased importance for many humanists and theologians, whether as political and moral instruction or as an aid to better informed if less imaginative scriptural exegesis. More than Spenser, much more than his Burgundian model, Bateman seems to have regarded even history as potential deviation from the path to God, at least when visualized. History, apparently, is not only more fictional, more constructed by the projecting sight, than the straightness of Memory's path had at first implied – it offers us, in addition to consolation and company, the danger of premature rest as we glut the inner eye. We must, says Memory to her charge, push on to those better sights above: 'that journey let us hye'.

The only way to those sights, in Bateman's mind, is death; his poem is less visionary than Spenser's in this regard too, for the work's chief religious spectacle comes early, when Reason shows Pilgrim a chamber full of virtues – very pretty, but not the New Jerusalem (see Figure 1.2). Before his last liberating battle, it is true, Memory provides one more glorious image: Elizabeth (Figure 1.7). Yet even her splendor is shadowed, for the enthroned figure in the picture is Thanatos, ruler of dynasties.

Memory reacts more like a subject than an abstract noun, unless she is here Pilgrim's personal recollection: the queen is 'our supreme head' whose benefits 'No tongue ne pen may well expresse' (M3). We need fear no enemy 'if we eche other love' and obey one whose 'splendent face and Christan eyen, hir comly corps and gate, / Is able sure a hart of stone, to cause relent and quake'. Guiding 'hir publike wealth' with 'sage sobrietie', Elizabeth

Spenser's chivalric restoration

Figure 1.7 Engraving, 'The Author beholdeth the discourse …' (m2v) STC 1585 copy 1 (*The trauayled pylgrime*). Elizabeth on progress to death, accompanied by her Council and by Fame.

has no equal Memory can recall. And yet Memory also draws Pilgrim's attention to the 'bony figure' who 'endes the life of every degree'. To say that queens die is not normally *scandalum magnatum*. Still, the mention of Elizabeth's human frailty gently moves the historical woman away from her mythology. The queen on this particular progress rides from her immortal rule as an image to the mortal event of her individual death.[21]

As Pilgrim watches, however, a structural strain in the allegory reveals itself, together with further commentary on historical development and personal story. The genre Bateman is reworking was first designed to express the forgiven prodigality of an individual life, and indeed to figure forth the redemption of mankind travelling from Eden to Heaven. To wander off the path – the literal path within the fiction, the straight and narrow way of a good life, and the path of the chief narrative line – makes sense if life is imagined as a road from which *deviation* is dangerous if interesting (after all, unless the initial Word multiplies into potentially errant words there can be no poetry). But La Marche had taken this structure and applied it to himself as an aging person suffering dolor and debility on 'la marche' (La Marche often puns on his name); his 'marche' is life's path, the frontiers of getting old, the periphery – now – of Empire, and perhaps his own identity seen *seriatim*. On *this* long march, toward age and beyond, there is alas no rest or digression; La Marche's narrative thus combines with some strain two linear movements, one twisting through moral error and return, the other leading straight through time to the grave. To this La Marche adds the dynastic material that never quite merges with the individual pilgrimage allegory because the Burgundians, although sharing La Marche's mortality, appear literally circumscribed by the lists in which their combats take place while the 'aucteur' presses on the 'marche' of his quest. The line of his path touches the circles of their fighting spaces and he pauses for a while to watch, but finally the dynastic and personal stories do not connect in any serious way.

Bateman, I have suggested, links the dynastic and the personal by having Bernard's plot of prodigality and recovery parallel a national history of loss and recuperation. He remains, however, largely limited by the text before him, if only because of the illustrations, and so a straight line running from youth to death shows behind the tracery of error, just as it does in his model.[22] And he too, although after more of a struggle, finally separates his pilgrimage from his politics. For La Marche, this may have been an essentially structural necessity; for Bateman, there is a hint of dissatisfaction with history and politics themselves, the same sense he had shown a few pages earlier that the images we hold of the world, the glorious show, are mere mirages compared to the Word in a dying world.

No doubt Elizabeth is a great and pious queen, sailing 'on seas of troublous time' with 'Gods gospell' as captain and keeping such a sharp eye on her coastline that 'Pope and Jewe' stand 'in feare, of hir most splendant face' (M3v). To include the Jews, hardly a geopolitical threat to England, may imply that her care is as much religious as military: the supreme head bewares both popish superstition and 'Judaic' legalism as found, perhaps, in Geneva. But Bateman intrudes touches that qualify the splendor beyond the shadow already cast by Thanatos. The queen and her cabinet ride 'Through worldly pleasures trapped way', and although she seeks 'the life to come' and although her progress 'goes forward on, not minding once to stay', her constant if virtuous activity ('so that she feares scarce time to have, such is hir godly zeale') leaves little space for Memory and Pilgrim. Those two remain observers, and neither seems to think that the knight owes further service or is indeed attached in any way beyond admiration to this mobile court. Even Memory's praise, under these narrative circumstances, remains internalized in Pilgrim (Bateman himself, of course, has gone public). The vision moves out of sight and beyond relevance as dynastic celebration and personal allegory part company: 'Forth on we needes must take our way, for we two will alone / Debate of matters past and gon' (M4).

At Memory's words, Pilgrim's color changes and 'grayer head did then appeere'. The two pass through an increasingly barren countryside while Memory argues with remarkably good cheer that 'nothing bides in one estate' (N1). The knight broods over this thought in language close to that Spenser uses when reflecting on Nature's crisp rejection of Mutabilitie's similar claim: 'When I considered hir words, and weyde them well in minde', he begins (cf. VII.viii.1), although his mind then moves not to the pillars of eternity but to Memory's kindness in showing 'the daungers great, which passed were and gone'. Eventually the two come to the shining House of Hoped Time, where True Zeal puts Pilgrim to bed in a room called Pain. It is here that the knight at last finds, more briefly described, the enlightenment his equivalents are allowed earlier in their careers by La Marche, Cartigny, and Spenser. Reason sends Diligence, Patience, and the three theological virtues. He even suggests that Pilgrim can win fame, although after what Memory has said about history the knight should perhaps greet this with some skepticism. Comforted by these bedside nouns, rested and instructed, Pilgrim summons his strength, mounts Will, and rides forth to his inevitable defeat in this world. And yet the poem does not quite close. Spenser's refusal to conclude is more elaborate and allegorically necessary: Redcrosse cannot rest with Una while there is work to be done for God and Gloriana, and so long as there are lies and divisions in a world of time mankind cannot join Truth in marital bliss. Bateman's humbler nonconclusion is merely the admission that his is not a very good poem and that he hopes someone will write a better. Someone did.

I hope I have shown that there are enough similarities between Spenser's masterpiece and Bateman's thinner but by no means stupid allegory to give the differences between the texts some interest. That Spenser is not like any number of minor early Elizabethan poets is more a blessing than a surprise. What gives this particular unlikeness some positive significance, however, is Bateman's status as the only other published *Protestant* allegorist who described the journey of a knight from error to salvation while praising the Tudors and denouncing Rome. Personification allegories by Lydgate, Hawes, Googe, and especially Cartigny (who includes some of the 'history' lying behind Book V's Egyptian matter) must also have given Spenser food for thought when he was not thinking about Vergil, Ariosto, and Tasso. But none of them except Googe was a Protestant, and although Hawes may well have had a political subtext none attached Reformation dynastic history to pilgrimage allegory.[23]

What can one conclude? Like romance itself and even like Bateman's allegory, criticism such as this resists conclusions not only because of the number of interpretative variables and the subjectivity involved but because each little moment of difference opens out to infinite space: after all, the set of what is *not* congruent between texts is almost by definition (so to speak) limitless. Still, a few incongruities seem particularly relevant in calculating – negatively – the parameters of Spenser's larger imagination.

Spenser is more seriously engaged by the chivalric metaphor that Bateman also adopts, more moved by knightly loyalty, service, and sacrifice. Not surprisingly, then, Redcrosse has more context than Pilgrim: he has a foster father, one true love, an evil mistress, future in-laws, a friend, a dwarf, 'merie England' to patronize one day, and a queen to serve. Pilgrim's company is found chiefly in the ranks of the dead; despite his early identification in one of the early illustrations as 'Obedience' (see Figure 1.1), his only true liege is God; and when as an aged knight he sees Elizabeth he does not even offer to be her beadsman. Even more than our literature's most famous pilgrim, fleeing his city and family to find eternal life, Pilgrim makes a lonely journey; Bunyan's Christian at least has fellow travellers. Redcrosse's task is to restore a lost kingdom; Pilgrim's last effort is to die well, not to rescue others. La Marche's knight, to be sure, was similarly isolated, but he was made so by the death of his duke. It seems appropriate, then, that one of the few pictures Bateman or his printer added to those derived from the Spanish translation shows an elderly man walking through a desert wood, on foot (Figure 1.8). In his heart, I think, Bateman did not believe the chivalric mythology that he adopts, whatever its still very audible Christian resonance. Pilgrim looks like a knight and wears, finally, all the right metaphoric armor, but

The trauailed Pilgrime

By the aged or olde man traueling in the wood, is signified the desert of Age, that is, when youth is consumed, and the vitall powers decreased, mans time is nothing else but paine of body possessed with Dolor and Debilitie, still looking for the last combat, which is Death.

In the desert of Age there is no going out, decrepite or consumation of the body may not escape the prefixed time appointed. Also the Author goeth further, being not yet come to Decrepitie, and sheweth of certaine combats done by diuers valiant Champions, as followeth.

Figure 1.8 Engraving, 'By the aged or olde man ...' (G4r) STC 1585 copy 1 (*The trauayled pylgrime*). The illustration has no parallel in the 1553 Antwerp translation by Acuña.

somewhere within himself he is this determined but lonely pedestrian, not so much a *miles Christi* as one of the Lord's civilians.

Redcrosse is in love. With a little ingenuity, Bateman could have added something of the sort, although the pictures would have made it a challenge. Protestants valued marriage, and indeed Bateman's employer had annoyed Elizabeth by marrying, but beyond a hint in Age's lecture to the knight that the latter is married, chivalry in this poem is, here too, a solo affair with little room for an accompanying, distracting, or inspiring 'other' – Pilgrim has Memory, true, but she is not his beloved, only his teacher.[24] It is tempting to recall the stereotypical middle-class Protestant whose family is doubtless dear to him but who wrestles alone in his chamber without wifely or even priestly counsel. La Marche's knight had no wife but did have the clergy and the sacraments. Bateman disallows these, and while he may simply have thought it undignified for decent clergymen to appear veiled in fiction (in the wrong vestments, so to speak), it can also be said that his imagination is quite unsacramental. La Marche's 'aucteur' goes to mass, but Bateman's pilgrim receives moral instruction and does not even go to church. Although detesting the Whore of Babylon as much as the next Protestant, Spenser is happier with certain Catholic remnants and seems even to have worked into Redcrosse's betrothal scene elements of the Sarum Missal's baptismal rite.[25] As a knight, then, Redcrosse has intermediary and preliminary loyalties, and as a Christian he has a faith likewise mediated through, for instance, a hermit, the sight of Heaven, and open references to baptism.

Spenser admits the marvellous; Bateman minimizes it, and behind this rejection of something he may have considered papist and medieval lies an even deeper worry about fiction itself. Recent criticism has, as I have said, identified Spenser's own inner quarrels with the spectacular and imagined, but although Bateman liked pictures, it is also evident that much more than Spenser he feared what might slink out of the gates of ivory. Yet the gates of horn seem not quite to have pleased him either, for the 'sights' of history are almost as dangerous to Pilgrim as the feigned magic of Disagreement and the disguised demons of Love's Palace. In Book I, anyway, Spenser is less in a hurry for a final 'sight', perhaps precisely because he can see it in the distance while standing here – or can at least imagine that his hero sees it. Bateman has *heard* good news and wants to press on. He seems more radical than Spenser, impatient to see face to face, to get going; even the pleasures of learning about history appear to him like dallying on the grassy ground when one should be putting on the new man as fast as possible. And the history Bateman enjoys most is that of the Tudor Reformation and not, despite a somewhat credulous reference to the defeat of Gogmagog, the ancient sources of Britain. Translation of empire interests him little; nor does he say that he himself is translating, if also subverting, a late Medieval and Catholic work as adapted for the Hapsburgs.

In sum, while Spenser was more up to date than Bateman in looking at Italian romance and dynastic epic he was also more hospitable to older tones and affections, both more humanist and more medieval. He is chivalric beyond mere metaphoric trappings, for his hero serves, rescues, and loves others in a knightly fashion and for knightly motives of duty and glory. He is more impressed by what we can envisage and invent, more willing to linger a while in fictions thicker and more multivalent (and multi-veiled) than the nouns that delay or push Bateman's knight on his way to disappear. Much of this difference derives from the nature of Bateman's tradition, but some comes from his deeper distrust of the eye, of digression, of the feigned – an ancient distrust almost certainly accentuated by the Reformation. That Bateman wrote allegory at all is a testament to the part of his mind that could not resist gods, illustrations, and encyclopedic learning. Whatever his own Sabbath longings and whatever his own fear of Archimago, Spenser was surer than this earlier Protestant allegorist that the artist may by indirections find directions out; and, in finding them, he was more willing to take his time.

Notes

1 Our lying 'devil' derives from double-speaking 'diabolus', but as Isabel MacCaffrey says, 'A forked tongue is the poet's stock in trade': *Spenser's Allegory: The Anatomy of Imagination* (Princeton, N.J.: Princeton University Press, 1976), 55. For more on this increasingly noted ambivalence see, e.g., Kenneth Gross, *Spenserian Poetics: Idolatry, Iconoclasm, and Magic* (Ithaca, N.Y.: Cornell University Press, 1985). Ernest B. Gilman's *Iconoclasm and Poetry in the English Reformation: Down Went Dagon* (Chicago, Ill. University of Chicago Press, 1986) has a fine chapter on 'Spenser's "Painted Forgery"'. 'Puritan' iconophobia did not, however, preclude imagery and stageplays; for a salutary reminder, see John King, *English Reformation Literature: The Tudor Origins of the Protestant Tradition* (Princeton, N.J.: Princeton University Press, 1982). And for Spenser's positive uses of magic, especially as an allegory or analogue of poetry, see Patrick Cheney, '"Secret Powre Unseene": Good Magic in Spenser's Legend of Britomart', *Studies in Philology* 85 (1988): 1–28.

2 '*The Travayled Pylgrime* by Stephen Batman and Book Two of *The Faerie Queene*', *Modern Language Quarterly* 3 (1942); her comments on faculty psychology bring out an element I downplay here, and she may be right to find a touch of Debilitie (who sports a skull and crossbones) in Spenser's Maleger. Patrick Cullen, *Infernal Triad: The Flesh, the World, and the Devil in Spenser and Milton* (Princeton, N.J.: Princeton University Press, 1974), finds Koller's evidence 'slight'.

3 The revised STC identifies Bateman's poem as a translation of La Marche, although with no mention of Acuña. I have used the unillustrated Paris 1842 edition, consulting *'Le Chevalier délibéré', the Illustrations of the edition of Schiedam*, with a preface by F. Lippman (London: Chiswick Press, 1898). So far as I know there is no modem edition of Acuña. There can be no question that Bateman knew who wrote the allegory, and Acuña even retains the puns on 'la marche'. La Marche and Acuña call the pilgrim 'Author' (and 'Acteur', as it was spelled, also means 'actor'); except for a few references to the 'author', Bateman never names his own hero, so I call him Pilgrim.

4 *The Triumph of Honour: Burgundian Origins of the Elizabethan Renaissance* (Leiden: Leiden University Press, for the Sir Thomas Browne Institute, 1977), 154. Kipling cites, e.g. 14, the role of La Marche in keeping the court of Edward IV informed about proper chivalry; Edward was brother-in-law to Charles the Rash, and Henry VII's mother's people, the Woodvilles, had Burgundian connections.

5 'Mental space' is Coleridge, quoted by Michael Murrin in *The Allegorical Epic: Essays in Its Rise and Decline* (Chicago, Ill. University of Chicago Press, 1980), 131. Murrin says, 'Images and personifications appear and disappear in a largely deserted landscape. This dreamy sense contrasts markedly with the Italian romance epic' (144). Bateman adds one scene that stands out precisely because the landscape is so crowded: Pilgrim finds a valley filled with foolish women like Dame Flingbraine and Mrs. Nice (sigs. G4v–H1), who seem to have wandered in from Vanity Fair.

6 For the importance of Bernard's *Parabola I, De pugna spirituali* see Dorothy Atkins Evans' introduction to her edition of an allegory by the Flemish Carmelite, Jean Cartigny: *Le Voyage du Chevalier Errant*, 1557, translated by William Goodyear as *The Wandering Knight*, 1581 (Seattle: University of Washington Press, 1951); Bernard's sermon is quoted 126–130. In '*The Wandering Knight*, the Red Cross Knight and "Miles Dei"', *Huntington Library Quarterly* 7 (1943/4): 101–34, Evans shows how Cartigny often anticipates Spenser; Cullen (16) agrees. The issue is muddied by Cartigny's evident debt to La Marche and by the possibility that Bateman read Cartigny. See also Sigfried Wenzel's important article, 'The Pilgrimage of Life as a Late Medieval Genre', *Mediaeval Studies* 35 (1973): 370–88; he mentions La Marche and Bateman but does not appear to notice their connection. Edgar Schell, *Strangers and Pilgrims: from 'The Castle of Perseverance' to 'King Lear'* (Chicago, Ill.: University of Chicago Press, 1983) argues well for Bernard's impact on the drama. Personification allegory is not much admired in modern times; Rosamond Tuve curtly dismisses La Marche in her *Allegorical Imagery: Some Mediaeval Books and Their Posterity* (Princeton, N.J.: Princeton University Press, 1966), 17. What depth the mode can offer, however, receives thoughtful sounding in Carolynn Van Dyke, *The Fiction of Truth: Structures of Meaning in Narrative and Dramatic Allegory* (Ithaca, N.Y.: Cornell University Press, 1985), ch. 1.

7 The companion piece to this article, by Susie Speakman Sutch and Anne Lake Prescott, 'Translation as Transformation: Olivier de la Marche's *Le Chevalier délibéré* and Its Hapsburg and Elizabethan Permutations', *Comparative Literature Studies* 25 (1988): 281–317, treats the transformations by Acuña, Bateman, and

Lewis Lewkenor, who in 1594 published an unillustrated prose translation quite faithful to Acuña except for the added Tudors.

8   See, however, Hendrick Niclas' familist *Terra Pacis* (STC 18564, c. 1575), a prose pilgrimage allegory (the splendid frontispiece shows the Lamb of God crushing the world, flesh, and devil). There are a few parallels with Spenser, who might have found its defense of 'Similitudes, Figures, and Parables' intriguing despite the notorious author's risky and perhaps not very Protestant theology, but its chief kinship is with Bunyan, for Niclas is indifferent to the chivalric metaphor and ignores the Tudors.

9   Since *The Aeneid* had long been allegorized it could seem to offer just what La Marche (and Spenser) offered: dynastic celebration like that by Ariosto joined to a pilgrimage like those by Dante or Deguileville. On such readings of Vergil see Andrew Fichter, *Poets Historical: Dynastic Epic in the Renaissance* (New Haven, Conn.: Yale University Press, 1982), chs. 1–2.

10 Spenser's relation, especially in Book I, to older French, Burgundian, and native allegory needs a new look. In *Unfolded Tales: Essays on Renaissance Romance*, ed. G. M. Logan and Gordon Teskey (Ithaca, N.Y.: Cornell University Press, 1989), Carol Kaske studies what he might owe Hawes' *Example of Vertue* (1504?). It is also entertaining to compare his methods to those of Barnaby Googe's *Shippe of safegarde* (1569), a seagoing pilgrimage that sails past sins such as sky-piercing Presumption and dark Desperation (sig. E3). Like Bateman's, Googe's doubts about images go beyond Spenser's even as he, too, relishes them: when his sailors reach Heresy they find among other abominations a picture of Saint George killing a dragon (sig. D5v). M. S. and G. H. Blayney, 'The Faerie Queene and an English Version of Chartier's *Traite de L'Esperance*', *Studies in Philology* 55 (1958): 154–63, find some parallels between I.ix–x and an early fifteenth-century allegory, a copy of which was in Leicester's library.

11 Evans implies on occasion that Bernard's suggested structure is tripartite, but he is clear that there are four stages: 'Primo enim est egens et insipiens; postea, praeceps et temerarius in prosperis: deinde, trepidus et pusillanimis in adversis; prostremo, providus, et eruditus et perfectus in regno charitatis' (Evans, 130).

12 To my inexpert eye there seems little of allegorical interest in the minutiae of combat or dress in Bateman's battles (beyond the obvious and explicit), although it may be that La Marche himself gave such details chivalric or moral significance (and see his deliciously elegant arming of a lady in allegorical finery, the *Parement et triumphe des dames*). Here again Spenser is restorative; see Michael Leslie, *Spenser's 'Fierce Warres and Faithfull Loves': Martial and Chivalric Symbolism in 'The Faerie Queene'* (Cambridge: D. S. Brewer, 1983).

13 Compare Orgoglio, by whom Red Crosse is nearly 'pouldred all, as thin as flowre' (vii.12). Error, too, is divisive, of course; Gordon Teskey remarks of Red Crosse's encounter with her that 'Spenser generates his narrative by driving good and evil apart so that a variety of adventures will unfold in the space opened between them' ('From Allegory to Dialectic: Imagining Error in Spenser and Milton', *PMLA* 101 [1986]: 13). Bateman's pun on post-Edenic travel and travail suggests the same dynamic. The pulverizing giant is curiously like Arthur and his shield: 'Men into stones therewith he could transmew, / And stones to

dust, and dust to nought at all' (vii.35). Gilman (66) notes the blank shield's iconoclastic power; Disagreement's force, on the other hand, is backed by an ability to manipulate fraudulent mental imagery.

14 Cullen, 40–43.
15 Spenser seems to me closer in content, wording, and tone to Bateman; it is typical, for example, that Cartigny's palace has tennis courts, very specified landscape, and a closely described indoors. Compare, too, Googe's description of the rock of worldly pride (sigs. B2v–B5, including the competition to be chic) and his palace of lust (C5v ff.), where the eyes dazzle and a scornful queen tortures her prisoners by tearing their hearts in a sort of Petrarchan parody, like Spenser's Busirane. There was, in fact a fashion for describing the beautiful but dangerous building, the 'pseudo-amoenus' topos, we could call it. Reaching towers, gold, crystal, and dazzled eyes are *de rigueur*. Thus Gavin Douglas describes the 'Palice of Honour' as 'like the hevin imperiall' with silver, jewels, and gold that daze the sight even though the visitor eventually learns that 'eirdlie gloir is nocht bot vanitie'; he too has a mirror, in his case a magic glass in which one sees not the face, as in Bateman and Spenser, but 'The deidis and fatis of everie eirdlie wicht' (*Poetical Works*, ed. John Small, Edinburgh, 1874, I, 57–74).
16 Such vocabulary is found elsewhere, of course, particularly in love poetry (cf. Desportes, passim) and polemic; William Fulbecke, *An historicall collection of the continuall factions, tumults, and massacres of the Romans and Italians* (1601) refers to 'aspiring Icarian Romaines' and 'Popish Phaetons' (sig. *3) and remarks that after the defeat of Carthage the 'Romanes were now in the ruffe of their pride' (sig. D2).
17 Knights, particularly free lances, need not admire courts; indeed, the chivalric romance is particularly adroit in exploring tensions between public and private life. Nonetheless, Red Crosse judges according to a standard that is feudal and aristocratic as well as moral, even if the 'knightly vew' itself signifies some spiritual awareness.
18 See MacCaffrey, 175, and notes.
19 S. K. Heninger, 'The Orgoglio Episode in *The Faerie Queene*', *English Literary History* 26 (1959): 171–87. Like La Marche and Bateman, Cartigny also at this point subjects his protagonist to an earthquake and then to a bog of despair. His knight, however, quits the worldly palace more or less inadvertently, not thanks to a warning.
20 John Shroeder, 'Spenser's Erotic Drama: The Orgoglio Episode', *English Literary History* 29 (1962): 140–59.
21 That there may be something a little uncomfortable about the image of Elizabeth and Thanatos is amusingly indicated by the printer who recycled the picture for Anthony Munday's *Fountaine of Fame* (1582), literally erasing Death from the celebratory scene and leaving an awkward blank; true, several other pictures Munday or his printer borrowed from Bateman are similarly de-shadowed by simply excising Death. I thank Ruth Luborsky for alerting me to Munday's use of these illustrations.

22 If such a line appears at all in Spenser it is that straight sequence of centuries from the Fall to the Millennium against which both human deviation and Providential time may be seen.
23 In 'Stephen Hawes and the Political Allegory of *The comfort of Lovers*', *English Literary Renaissance* 17 (1987): 3–21, Alastair Fox makes a good case that Hawes associates Henry VII with St. George and thus 'shows himself to have been one of the first exponents of the Tudor myth'. Hawes, however, was a Catholic.
24 Pilgrim has Memory, but although a necessary guide she would make a dangerous wife; so he must go it alone, directed toward Heaven but not to a divine marriage or self-completion through unity with the feminine. On such matters see the fascinating study by Benjamin G. Lockerd, Jr., *The Sacred Marriage: Psychic Integration in 'The Faerie Queene'* (Lewisburg, Pa.: Bucknell University Press, 1987).
25 Links between the Holy Saturday baptismal ceremony in the Sarum Missal and the betrothal scene at the end of Book I are noted by Harold Weatherby, 'What Spenser Meant by Holinesse: Baptism in Book I of *The Faerie Queene*', *Studies in Philology* 84 (1987): 286–307. Recently he has also argued for a connection between St. George, so scorned by humanists and so doubted by the Church of England, and the Eastern Orthodox liturgy; see 'The True Saint George', *English Literary Renaissance* 17 (1987): 119–41. For more on Spenser and Sarum, see my 'The Thirsty Deer and the Lord of Life: Some Contexts for Amoretti 67–70', *Spenser Studies* 6 (1985): 33–76.

2

Foreign policy in Fairyland: Henry IV and Spenser's Burbon

This essay examines a moment in Book V of *The Faerie Queene* – Artegall's dispiriting encounter with Sir Burbon – when the veil of allegory becomes particularly fact-torn. Readers may understandably suspect that they can now too easily glimpse the historical events behind the poetry, that the final episodes of Book V have too few moving images from wit's zodiac and too many by now mouse-eaten records from an often repellent foreign policy. The very names that Spenser invents, if 'invents' is the right word, gesture too obviously at actual European geopolitics in the late 1580s and early 1590s: Belge, Irena (Ireland, Peace), and Burbon – Henri de Bourbon, king of Navarre, whom French Huguenots and Catholic loyalists called Henri IV after the murder in 1589 of Henri III, last of the Valois dynasty and brother of Elizabeth's deceased and unlamented might-have-been husband, Alençon.

In Book V, it will be recalled, the beleaguered Burbon, to whom the Redcrosse knight had given a now broken shield, abandons that shield so as to win a fickle-hearted and indifferent lady, Flourdelis (France). The deed evokes Henri's conversion to Catholicism in July 1593, a deed that would for a time end France's religious civil wars.[1] Since the shield signifies Faith, giving it up cannot be defended by Burbon's claim to be, as Shakespeare's Biron puts, 'forsworn on mere necessity'.[2] Asked for support in the name of 'courtesie' – the virtue explored in Book VI – the knight of Justice continues to help him, but with little enthusiasm and only after hesitations and distaste not unlike those of Elizabeth's government: 'Fie on such forgerie (said Artegall) / Under one hood to shadow faces twaine. / Knights ought be true, and truth is one in all: / Of all things to dissemble fouly may befall' (V.xi.57). Although Burbon hopes to resume his shield 'when time doth serve', the narrator condemns him in terms that Protestants usually reserved for Henri's enemies: the Guise family and other leaders of the ultra-papist and Spanish-supported Holy League:

> O sacred hunger of ambitious mindes,
> And impotent desire of men to raine,
> Whom neither dread of God, that devils bindes,

> Nor lawes of men, that common weales containe,
> Nor bands of nature, that wilde beastes restraine,
> Can keepe from outrage, and from doing wrong,
> Where they may hope a kingdome to obtaine.
> No faith so firme, no trust can be so strong,
> No love so lasting then, that may enduren long. (V.xii.1)

In this essay I hope to complicate the admittedly no longer universal view of Book V as so fat with 'facts' that the allegory starves (fascination with Spenser's relation to Ireland and belief in the ties between poetics and politics having energized the study of its closing cantos and made their seeming transparency less subject to critical condemnation). The poem's treatment of Henri/Burbon suggests, I think, that Spenser had come to believe, and perhaps always had believed, that history, as it appears to its participants and recorders, is itself a veil, one nearly as well embroidered with allegory and myth as *The Faerie Queene*. A number of historians would be quick to concede this, of course, but many of us still prefer to distinguish between *poesis* and actuality. Spenser probably did too, but he knew that their interconnections are a tangle.

The real Sir Burbon, so to speak, had been familiar in England as a heroic figure; although all kings are mythified, Henri IV was more mythified than most. Spenser would have known his legend from a flood of loyalist propaganda, much of it printed by Gabriel Harvey's friend John Wolfe.[3] Behind Book V's flimsy veil of allegory, that is, falls a scrim of history, but a scrim on which is painted yet another allegorical portrait. (Behind this scrim in turn stands, to be sure, a worldly politician with an enigmatic heart visible only to God.) *The Faerie Queene* shows us Burbon the timeserver, but Henri the Gallic Hercules is there too. Erased by events and Spenser, he haunts the text as the hero he should have been. Taken together, the two selves – the ideal absent mythic hero and the all-too-historical and present Politique – perform a sort of meta-allegory of what happens to heroes, myths, magnates, even stars and suns, that sidle through a fallen chronometrical cosmos not yet stayed upon the pillars of Eternity.[4] In his very historicity Burbon *is* allegorical, and one thing he allegorizes is how politics can undo allegory.[5] That is why the Burbon episode indicates how ambiguously history and allegory can relate to each other, literary veils being twitched aside only to reveal the fog of myth on the historical mirrors.

Burbon renders this service especially well because as Henri IV he had been a national myth. Indeed, despite the narrator's assertion that 'Amongst all Knights he blotted was with blame, / And counted but a recreant Knight, with endles shame', he was long to remain quasi-mythic, even in England.[6] What was there about him or his reputation that made him easy to allegorize? A major component of his 'image' was virility. Elizabeth might boast of having the heart and stomach of a king, but Henri had more than a man's heart and stomach. He had a jaunty beard, for example, not to mention other parts he would later put to better ends, dynastically speaking, than those relished by the sexually ambiguous Henri III. Whatever the exasperation of his advisers, the erotic energy of 'le vert galant' could seem engaging. (In 1606 John Chamberlain wrote Dudley Carleton with amusement that Henri had told his jealous queen she was his *panis quotidianus* but he needed 'a collation'.[7]) Although destined to intensify the French monarchy's evolution into political absolutism, in England Henri could appear as a more feudal and surrogate king: manly, smart, and at ease with his martial nobles. Once, they say, he offered to fight the duc de Guise in single combat; even the prince of Parma (Alessandro Farnese) faltered before him; and the duc de Mayenne (the English writers' 'de Maine' or 'Dumaine') must be carried from battle in a litter.[8] No wonder Michel Hurault's 1592 *Excellent discourse upon the now present estate of France*, a text that inspired Gabriel Harvey to add multiple comments and squiggles in the margins of his copy, asks why anyone would want to forsake a 'quicke' and active man, a 'mightie king of War' who can establish justice and keep the realm from dismemberment, a 'brave and flourishing Prince, replenished with vertue, justice and experience', so as to follow 'an old stranger [Philip II]: Impotent, trembling with diseases and age' (sigs. H1v–H3v).

Henri's armor itself drew attention. *An Answere to the Supplication exhibited unto the King* (1591, STC 664) says that unlike those friars and monks 'that fight rather for their wallet then for their faith, and the great ones to make way to their ambition, … Our king buildeth not his hope upon eyther the Nobility or the commonalty, but upon God only: he is his buckler, his fortresse, and his upholder' (sigs. A2v–A3). And L. T. A.'s 1592 *Masque of the League and the Spanyard discovered*, when objecting that Henri's enemies betray their religion by resorting to force, recalls that 'The Armes given by GOD to a Christian, are justice, in sted of a Corselet, the Helmet of Health, the inexpugnable Target of Equitie, the Shield of Fayth, the Sworde of the Spirit, which is the worde of GOD' (sig. F2v). It is perhaps Christian armor that graces the beplumed knight who illustrates a 1590 broadside (STC 385) celebrating Henri's victory at Ivry on March 14 of that year. Ascribing the victory to God, the poem records Henri's exhortation to 'Be valiaunt now and fight like men' and says that

> On either side they curredge cride,
> The king was not dismaied.
> But like a Souldiour and a king,
> A standard he did take:
> And slew the man that bare the same,
> Which made his enemies quake.

The figures carry standards left blank by the printer, perhaps to indicate a Bourbon white, and inscribed above is the legend, 'God save the King' – words then seldom heard in English but doubtless attractive to many.

No mere strongman like the younger Artegall or his iron deputy Talus, Henri is chivalric, someone to whom St. George might well give a shield; by 1593 he had, after all, been elected a Knight of the Garter, and cuts of St. George appear in several texts praising him.[9] He is more honorable than Duke Alva, Philip's governor of the Low Countries, of whom one pamphlet sneers that this member of the order of the Golden Fleece had indeed fleeced the Netherlands.[10] True, charity alone – one aspect of Spenser's Mercilla – would justify intervening in the French wars. Pierre Erondelle's anti-Guisard *Declaration and Catholick exhortation to all Christian Princes to succour the Church of God and Realme of France* (1586) makes a case that rescuing 'so florishing a realme' as France from usurping tyrants would 'accomplish the workes of charity, and fulfill the Commaundement of GOD, which is, love thy neighbour as thy selfe' (sig. B1).

Others were more specifically chivalric in their rhetoric. To help Henri is knightly, says G. B.'s *Newes out of France for the Gentlemen of England*, a report on the campaigns of summer, 1591:

> Imitate the virtues of your Ancestours, that all the world may ring of your noble acts, of your Ancestours said I, nay of our Cavaliers yet living, who as they be equall in valour to the test of any time; so are they before al other to be folowed of your persons at this time. Remember the fortitude of Norris never quailed, consider the magnanimitie of Williams never daunted, and worthie Yorkes forwardnes never impeached ... [T]he whole commonwealth intreates you, that as whilom your politique Predecessours, and now these your martiall Progenitours by their exploytes have attayned the heighth of renowne in the world; so yee like renowned Children of so renowned Parents, would by your couragious enterprises brandish your names and fames throughout the world. (sigs. A3–A3v)

Henri himself is 'the flower of Chivalrie, and mirrour of Curtesie', while Sir Roger Williams is Henri's 'approved champion', a 'redoubted Chevalier' who in the French wars has 'found a danger equall to his heart' (sig. B2).

Exactly. And here may be another reason for Artegall's ire. It has been much remarked that the Renaissance revived a chivalric tonality through such enterprises as tourneys, masques, and *The Faerie Queene*, presenting court notables as knights of old. But such lords were of course not knights of old, subjected as they were to economic and political imperatives Lancelot and Amadis could ignore. There is a connection, thematically and discursively, between Artegall's dismayed realization that, whatever his sins against chivalry, the troth-breaker Burbon would have to be helped and Mammon's ugly but largely accurate reminder to Sir Guyon in Book II that nowadays somebody must pay cold cash for a knight's equipment and service. That Artegall responds to Burbon's plea in the name of the very courtesy that the latter has violated, although important as a hint of the Legend to follow, is as much an obfuscation as Guyon's self-satisfied insistence that money has nothing to do with *him*.[11] So, perhaps, is Spenser's demotion of a public and political figure – a king with a court and armies – into a sole knight, a 'Sir' in need of brotherly help from another 'Sir'. Spenser insists on Burbon's chivalric status, thus stressing his failures as a Garter knight and weakening excuses that might be plausible in a king. (Poets were not alone in this maneuver; François I liked to swear 'foi de gentilhomme', as though he were not a mere monarch whom *raison d'état* might make lie.) The chivalric 'courtesy' that Artegall extends to Burbon, albeit grudgingly, is in truth a victory of expediency over moral absolutism; but the gentlemanly gesture is also a mystification of the move toward a political absolutism that Henri's policies accelerated.

Henri's virility reinforced his image as *pater patriae* and France's husband. In the 1594 *Order of Ceremonies observed in the annointing and Coronation of the most Christian King of France and Navarre, Henri the IIII* readers would note, besides an English presence at the subsequent festivities, how the new king, decked out with 'flowers de luce', a scepter, and a 'hand of justice', 'marrieth the Realme', putting a ring on his finger as a token.[12] And, in an allegorical picture reprinted in *The Spenser Encyclopedia* under 'Burbon', an armed and about-to-be-garlanded Henri IV holds a lady France by the hand. He steps firmly on a friar, doubtless in the pay of Spain, whose slithery lower parts coil around a royal leg. Although no giant, the friar is *tortus*, twisted. Make him bigger, grander, and he would be a Grantorto. That giant, enemy of Irena and oppressor of Flourdelis, is 'Great Wrong', in legal terms a supertort. But he is also 'Great Twist', tortuous and torturer, as serpentine in his way as were the ancient snake-footed Giants. Similarly, the anonymous *The Flower de Luce* (1593) envisions France as a dying mother urging her children, descended from those Gauls who feared only that the sky might fall, to 'gather strength, yea albeit all weapons should fayle you, even with your handes to stifle these serpents who having once wrethed you within their traines will sucke forth the very marrow out of your bones'.[13]

Flourdelis is so sulky a lady that only allegory explains why Burbon wants her. Spenser has imagined her not as another Florimel, say, but as having a trace of that villainess dear to those writing on France: the League. Like France, Flourdelis is not sure what she wants and who she is: is she already Henri's spouse, merely his intended, or does she belong to someone else? If to someone else, anti-League writers had two words for her: whore and witch. The League, parodic twin of Henri's true wife, figures over and over in the pamphlets as a promiscuous sorceress, a Duessa (and the 'real' Duessa, Mary Stuart, was a Guise on her mother's side).

I. L.'s *Birth purpose and mortall wound of the Romish holie league* (1589), for example, tells how Satan visits Rome to chat up the Pope and talk tactics against Elizabeth and Henri de Navarre. This 'spirite of malignitie' begets the League, who at Satan's request is disguised as a 'Holie League'; rather like Duessa, she holds a 'superstitious cup of Romish abhominations'. Together with Spain, the Pope and Satan think to swallow England like a crocodile; they are merely lunar, however, and God outshines them (sigs. A2–A3v). The next year saw *A letter written by a Catholic Gentleman, to the Lady Jane Clement, the haulting Princesse of the League* (1590), one of Wolfe's pamphlets. A 'sweethart' of Henri III's assassin, Jacques Clément, Jane has played on the credulity of the 'common sort of the French men' with 'glosed speeches' and witchcraft; set up 'Idols' in the 'Temples of God'; summoned foreigners; and seduced Clément into regicide by 'crafts, disguisings, allurements, drifts, and stratagems', by 'lascivious lookes, gestes of countenance and body, inticing wordes', by 'dishonest gropings' and 'pretended chastity'. Nor is she sincerely religious, for the League's motive in rousing 'rakelles and maisterlesse rogues, the scomme and lyes of the worlde', is ambition, covetousness, and 'unbrideled appetite to command'. And if Jane really cannot bear to be ruled by a Huguenot, we read, she can always go to Canada (sigs. A2v–B3v).

More subtly, Michel Hurault's *Discourse* warns France that she resembles women 'at strife with their husbandes' who draw the hopeful attention of would-be cuckolders. These gentlemen first offer commiseration, then 'honest offers and presents', and at last 'themselves come divers waies to visit you'. So too, foreigners have come to Brittany, Languedoc, and Picardy to see

> whether wrath might not intice you to harken to new love. Well, thankes be to God at the first ye escaped well inough: ye returned them without anything of yours; without any gaine at your handes, except some small favour in Brittaine, and some kisse in Picardie. They were content, the fornicators, to see that at the first ye did not utterly denie them: that ye refused them not to speake, but gave them the hearing: But feare not: that old courtisan of Castile is too crafty to be so easily said nay.

If you take up with him, though, he 'will prove more suspitius than your good husbandes' and 'keepe you under locke and key after the Spanish and Italian maner'.[14]

Like Artegall, Henri IV was also a Hercules, specifically the Gallic Hercules: son of Osiris, ancestor of the kings of Navarre and France, eloquent enchainer of men's ears, and the hero who rid the West of monsters while Dionysius was attending to the East. Such political flattery was common all over

Europe, if at times misapplied: Elizabeth's François-Hercule, duc d'Alençon, was Herculoid in name only.[15] Wreathed about the temples of the victor of Coutras and Ivry, the rhetoric was convincing but still banal. That, however, is my point: not the mere fact of making Henri IV – or Artegall – Herculean but the intensity, frequency, and appropriateness of the image. When Artegall scolds Burbon he may recognize some strayed and desperate self, a fallen fellow Hercules.

Aside from a Busiris or Anteus here and a Hellhound or Harpy there, the monsters Henri most often quells are Geryon (father of Spenser's Geryoneo) and the Hydra. A three-headed giant aptly figures a Spain that had eaten much of Belge and most of Navarre, while the Hydra well represents the multiple evils besetting France and the many-headed populace encouraged by Philip II and the Guise family. Thus *A Comparison of the English and Spanish Nation* tells how

> Geryon king of Spain (if we give credite to Poeticall fables) had three bodies: and although it be a Poeticall fiction, yet will it not be found so strange of him that will thoroughly consider the nature and disposition of the Spaniarde, in whom may be seene togither incorporated, a craftie Foxe, a ravenous Wolfe, and a raging Tygre. And let that be spoken in respect of the least insupportable of that Nation. For he which shall neerely looke into those of greatest account amongst them, ... shall find in everyone of them the Cube: yea oftentimes the verie Sursolide of this ternarie monster.[16]

The *Masque of the League* compulsively repeats such comparisons. Spain has 'engendred Monsters, more horrible and hiddious, then those that (of old) are sayd to be subdued by the valour of Alcmenaes Sonne', turning France into 'an Anarchie of many headed government'. Her enemies are furious to see 'The vertue, the Lawrell, the fortune and victories of our Hercules of Gaule, the queller of so many Monsters'. But despite the League's walls and fortifications it cannot withstand 'our valiant Hercules', our 'Alcides', even though 'thou makest the earth tremble where thou pacest'. So go ahead and 'Ayde thyselfe' with Cerberus and the 'horrible route of hell'. Was not 'Geryon of Spayne' enough to succor you? No – even allied with these monsters of 'in-justice and ambition' you will be defeated by 'our Hercules' because it is 'GOD onely that established him'. Why persist? 'Hydra, dooth more heads stil bud forth, having alreadie lost so many?'[17] Hurault's *Discourse* is less given to such mythologizing, but even it calls Mayenne a 'chimere', and the League a many-headed 'mightie serpent engendered of the corruption of the earth' (sigs. E3v, F2).

The *Masque* also calls Henri's enemies Python, (Gran)tortious foe of Apollo (sig. E1v). Indeed, as a hero of justice, Henri is solar – a *sol justitiae* – even if his career's elliptical path took him slantwise against the sun from

Navarre to Paris. In this he outshone his predecessor. Just before the assassination of Henri III, for example, Hurault's first, 1588, *Discourse on the present state of France* calls that sad king his realm's 'declining sunne, and so weake in his declination, that even in his presence he seeth them dispute, both by writings and weapons of him that shall rise after him'.[18] And *Flower de Luce*, its title punning on words for Wyand light, expects France, whose 'glory and majestie' now 'wholly glister in her eldest sonne', to see all 'stormes driven away by the beautifull beames of the sonne which shall restore unto us the lightsome day of contentation and perfect liberty'. To be sure, some depressingly dim monarchs have been told how much they luminesce, but Henri's more credible radiance suits the astronomical and Herculean pattern likewise exploited by Book V from the Proem on. Like the Burbon-that-had-been, Artegall is solar. And like Hercules, like the malingering and sloping sun, like Henri, he can be deflected from his right and original path.

Henri appears amusingly as *roi soleil* in the satirical *Divels legend* (1595, hence post-conversion). The author puns on the name of the League's chief in Brittany, the duc de Mercueur. The Leaguers, we read, view the heavens more like dogs than doctors, for while refusing to follow 'the other Planets which acknowledge the Sunne as their common Prince, or principall substance of their borrowed splendor, yet will they that Mercury of Britaine, and Venus his wife, and all such wandering starres like themselves, shall bend their borrowed bonfiers against the true sonne of Fraunce, [who] ... of his owne benevolence, hath given them the little glimmering brightnesse which they have'. And, after losing 'the true naturall heate of that glorious sunne, they search the coldenesse of the Satournian Spaniard, both frostie in goodnesse, dried up with covetousnesse, and as mellancholly as ambition can make him' (sig. B3). Such astronomical wordplay must have been irresistible, but to Spenser it would also seem, if he read it, usefully problematic: neither a mercurial nor a saturnine temperament suits Justice, yet the sun, too, in a fallen world, cannot run its course perfectly but lags and slopes.[19]

Henri's solar and hence implicitly temporal aspect suggests other issues that fascinated Spenser: lineage and succession. One reason for Flourdelis' moodiness is that the Guise family – figured in Book V as Guizor and his kin – had asserted not only that Henri was a heretic but that their own line stretched further back, attaching itself to Charlemagne, to the Merovingians, to Pharamond (legendary first king of France), even to the eponymous Trojan, Francus.[20] Laughing at such claims is *A necessary Discourse concerning the right which the house of Guyze pretendeth to the Crowne of France* (1586), translated by Edgar Aggas from a text perhaps by Duplessis-Mornay. The Guises, it says, call themselves 'undertwigges' of Charlemagne and peddle 'fables' about how their rights were stolen by rulers from Merovee to Hugh Capet. If you doubt one ancestor, they pull 'others readie crowned out of the bellie of the Troyan horse' (the author forgets that the Trojan horse held Greeks).[21] But history has dynastic bracchiations, when what would later be called alpha maleness swings from one branch of a family tree to another. If the Carolingians could replace the Merovingians, the author wonders, why cannot Bourbons replace the defunct Valois? That Spenser was drawn to such matters is clear from Mutabilitie's accusation in Book VII that Jove is a usurper, from his taste for genealogies, from the dispute early in Book V over land displaced by time and tide, from the Equality Giant's desire to rewind Time. Time has shifted the French dynastic sands, unbalanced the scales by sending the childless Valois brothers one by one up to Heaven and lowering their crown upon Henri. Even in astrological houses, as Book V's Proem says wittily, constellations have jostled each other out of place. What they do in their starry circle, Valois and Bourbons do in more linear style down here.

The author of the *Necessary Discourse* knows this, arguing that even if Guisard 'fables' were true, once 'an Estate is established in a famelie by lawfull calling and approbation of the Commonwealth and people, and that for so many hundred yeeres, it is a manifest token that God ... hath transferred such a Realme or Estate into that familie' (sig. B4). *The Masque of the League* spells out this notion at some length. God's justice, it says, will never allow St. Louis's line to be confounded after maintaining it for so long. Some 'cunning Rebell' may reply that 'all thinges are subject to alteration and change, and there is nothing that perpetually continueth in one selfe same estate, for heaven it selfe is not exempt from change and ending'. Well, yes. There is indeed 'a course of ages and dispositions of things in the world'. Just as in our bodies, 'flourishing estates, are no lesse exposed to remoovings, varieties, and changes'. But the Guise family's motive is mere 'greedy desire to reigne' disguised as piety, and in any case 'alteration in all things, but chiefelie in these publique affaires, is most dangerous' (sigs. R3–S1v). *Masque* sounds like a combination of Artegall rebuking the Equality giant and Spenser's narrator conceding that Mutabilitie has a point.

Related to questions of time and succession are hints that the civil wars, like the events in Book V, point to the day of Doom when Astraea the harvest queen has done her job and the sheaves are gathered in, perhaps to be threshed by the flail of Talus. Thus G. B.'s *Newes Out of France* credits Henri's success in 1591 to how 'God now in these latter times vouchsafeth to bring things to speedie end, thereby to hasten the comming of his Sonne to judgement', when 'butcherlie' Rome, 'founded in bloud, ... shall ende in bloud'. That is why we now see Mayenne fleeing like Cain 'from citie to Citie, from Coast to Coast, from Countrey to Countrey'. Now 'the kingdome of Antichrist is falling' as 'a mayne [a pun on 'de

Maine'?] proppe of his pavilion begins to shrink, his golden Metropolis (Spaine I meane) who ... is wearie of hir burden'.[22] The natural world itself foreshadows Henri's victory, for according to *The miserable estate of the Cittie of Paris at this present, with a true report of sundrie straunge visions*, 'At the comming of the Prince of Parma into the French countries, it is reported there was visibly seene in the Aire to all his army, three raine bowes, and betweene every one of them the forme of a toade, and presently the rivers therabout seemed nothing but bloud.' This presaged the ruin of the 'unwholy Leaguers, upholden by the Pope and the king of Spaine, and contrariwise the good successe of the French King, whose ancient armes is the three toades'; only fear of summary execution kept Parma's men at their posts (sigs. A3v–A4).[23]

One other cluster of images relates to Book V's concern with broken bodies. Dismemberment is a danger to any body politic, not least in a civil war worsened by the volatility of the many-headed populace. A hydra, after all, is always halfway to flying apart, made one single thing only by its tail. Henri's real task, as he came to understand it, and in this he was like Elizabeth, was not to kill a hydra but to meld it into one governable entity and be its sole head. Over and over, the French wars were read as illness and dismemberment: religious division and geographic particularism.[24] The doctor specializing in mutilation and dispersal is of course Apollo's son Aesculapius, who at Diana's request restored the torn Hippolytus to life. An alarmed Jove struck Aesculapius with a thunderbolt, but he survived as patron of health to whom one offered a cock, a *gallus* – later to be a punning symbol of Gaul. The Gallic Henri is a 'wise Chirurgian' who can piece his nation back together, cure her fevers, and ply the sword because to 'rip up old sores' is better than to let them 'fester inwardly'.[25] Who, the *Masque* asks League-occupied Paris, in 'thys mortall malladie ... shall be thy Aesculapius'? (sig. B4)

The wittiest compliment to Dr. Henri, one which assumes – as does Spenser's Mercilla – that monarchs must sometimes cure the state by letting blood, comes in a set of Latin verses on French politics (one calls the queen's deceased suitor, Alençon, 'turpis'):

> For a long time, Gaul, you were sick from Medications [a pun on the queen mother, Catherine de Medici] and finally you stabbed your doctor [Henri III]. You remain moribund, pierced by raging illness. What doctor could cure you? There remains one, whom you will have as your Paracelsus or, if you prefer him, behold: you have Galen. The latter is wont to achieve ['Navare'] a sound cure without fraud and promises sure succor no matter how lost you are. He will gently apply health-giving plants [that is, the old Galenic herbal medicine] – and, if you refuse herbs, he has metal [Paracelsian chemicals – or cannon and swords].[26]

In truth, whatever his resort to metal, to Talus, Henri did prefer Galenic remedies. From temperament and policy he and his friends stressed his reluctance to force consciences, one reason why so many pamphlets claim to be by moderate Catholics and why, perhaps, Harvey could write in the margin of his *Excellent Discourse*: 'French pragmaticians: the chiefest emploied men of the court, and state'.[27]

In sum: Henri is virile and knightly, armed in the arms of God, a Herculean queller of Spanish giants and of that Hydra who well represents the rascal mob and centrifugal urban or provincial rebellion. Nobly descended, he is solar, medicinal, worthy to bear the 'hand of justice', solidly Protestant yet no bigot and longing to rule by equity and loving prudence. A mini-epic by Du Bartas on Henri's stunning victory at Ivry on March 14, 1590, portrays just this figure, in effect sketching a portrait of Burbon before he threw away his shield: the Burbon who, had he kept faith, could have been another Artegall (and whose ambiguous relation to that hero Spenser underlines by having the latter likewise drop his shield).[28] Joshua Sylvester's translation, *A canticle of the victorie obteined by the French king, Henrie the fourth. At Yvry*, was published by Wolfe in 1590 and reprinted in 1592 with Du Bartas's *Triumph of Faith*. Harvey had a copy of the 1592 volume, scribbling in its margins such cries of ecstasy as 'here Dubartas rowsed his inspired hedd, to excell [Homer and Virgil] bothe'. The notes are undated, but Harvey certainly admires Henri, citing 'His Prudence, & Temperance, like his Valour, & Justice', calling him a 'wise, & most curteous King: gratious & magnificent', and noting his acumen, for 'It interesseth a Prince, to be as Cautelous, as Valorous'.[29] In some moods, Artegall and even Arthur would agree.

Few now would call *Yvry* a fine poem, not with lines like 'Ah! now begins my rapted Brain to boyle, / With brave Invention', but Spenser, who admired Du Bartas, probably shared Harvey's warm opinion. Du Bartas's Henri radiates: 'O! What a Sun-shine gilds us round-about!' He is also Jove, hurling 'Sulphury Thunder-stowers' of justice at the League and at 'fatall Philip', who 'right Foxy-wise' waits for France to fall apart so that he can snatch the pieces. Too magnanimous for a Talus and too metallic and grizzled for a court fop, Henri 'doth not nicely prank / In clinquant Pomp' but goes

> ... arm'd in Steel; that bright abilliment
> Is his rich Valour's sole rich Ornament.
> Steel was his Cradle, under steel he dight
> His chin with Doun, in steel begins it white:
> And yet by steel he conquers, bravely-bold
> Towns, Cities, States, Crowns, Scepters, kings and gold.

Not that he is grim, for his famous *panache* has a gaiety recalling Arthur's: 'a plume dread-dancing light' that moves 'like a Willow' in the wind. Preferring chivalry to modern inventions, he brushes aside a pistol: 'Hence, guileful Arms; the glittering Sword for Me'. Then, 'nimbly tossing light / The flashing Horror of his Fauchin bright / (Like an Autumnal ruddy streaming Star / Presaging Famine, Pestilence, and War)', Henri sends his foe to Hades, where he can boast of being slain by 'th'Hercules of France'. Other images link the king to the skies: Ivry is fought 'under the weeping Kid' (Capella's rainy child who rises in March), while the king is a Numidian lion (not unlike the Nemean one who prances the summer sky as Leo) and his sword an autumnal star. As a doctor he can cure France's fever and – evoking another constellation – he can kill the Hydra besetting her.[30] The Guise-incited mob has 'many heads', while France, almost as though she were the Church addressing Christ, calls Henri her 'Dear Son', 'Second-founding Father', and 'deare Spouse', who as victor 'worthy Spouse, shall beare [her], for Bride, away'.

Most important, Henri has a capacious but firm faith. After 1593 Spenser would have read with some bitterness that

> ... never did the all-discerning Sun ...
> Behold a Prince religiously more loth
> To shake, for ought, his honour-binding Oath....
> Yea, make him Monarch of the World, by wile;
> Hee'll spurn all Scepters yer his faith hee file.[31]

Yet Henri is no persecutor:

> Hee firm beleeves, that God's reformed Awe,
> Hee from his Cradle, with his milk did draw:
> Yet is not partiall, nor prejudicate.
> And if the church, now neerly ruinate, ...
> May ever look for ... happy Peace, to dure;
> It shall be, doubtlesse, under such a Prince,
> So free from Pasion's blinded Vehemence.

If Artegall would call this policy timeserving, England's Gloriana came to find it consoling.

After the events of July 1593, Elizabeth needed consoling.[32] Angrily, without real surprise, she wrote the convert in terms anticipating Artegall's reproof. Whatever her genuine upset, however, the queen's letter is also a necessary political move. It or another missive was made public, for Dutch Protestants said they were pleased by her rebuke.[33]

> Ah what Doulours! oh what greifes! oh what sorrows have I felt in my soule....
> Oh my God is it possible that any worldly respect should make us forgett the

terror that the feare of Gods vengeance doth threaten unto us? ... I hope that in tyme you shall be possessed with a more holy inspiracion. In the mean season I shall not cease to place you in the cheifest ranke of my Prayers, to the end that the handes of Esau may not put away the Blessings of Jacob. And whereas you doe promise me notwithstanding, your best amytyes and Freindshippe, I confesse that I have dearly merited the same, and I shall not repent me therof, soe long as you change not your Father: for otherwise I can be unto you but as a Bastard Sister, at least on the Fathers side: For I shall in my love allwayes preferr the naturall before the adopted, as God best knowes, whom I beseech always to guard and direct you in the path of his most chosen and righteous wayes. Your most assured Sister, if it be after the Ancyent manner, but with Noveltyes I take noe pleasure. E. R.[34]

In late August, though, Elizabeth and Henri agreed on a bond of 'Amity', and on October 7, even while hoping that God and Time will open his 'sealed eyes' ('celés yeulx') so he can recognize his 'seductive betrayers' ('seduisants traïstres'), she asks resignedly that God in his grace amend all and assures the king that he will never find a 'franker and freer friendship' ('une plus franche et libre Amitié').[35] By December of 1594 a now crowned Henri is her 'beloved brother' whose lucky escape from a Catholic assassin drives her to her knees in gratitude.[36] Queens do what queens have to do, and in fact may even feel what they have to feel. After his conversion she and Henri could show affection despite their disagreements: a gallant Henri admires her portrait and envies the painter who saw the lovely original; a smiling Elizabeth refers gaily to a 'dance of love'.[37] The queen could scold her 'brother' bitterly (although untactful candor was nothing new for her, as witness her ungracious distaste for the African elephant he sent her), but the courtesy with which she sometimes writes shows an urbanity most unlike Artegall's surliness.[38]

Elizabeth also wrote Henri's unconverted sister, Catherine, her letters mixing pained exhortation, smiles, and wily advice; they read as though composed jointly by Redcrosse, Calidore, and Machiavelli. Since they have not been published, so far as I know, I quote them in full. The first, dated August 25, 1593, says:

Madame, If my paper had the color of my heart, I would not dare to show it to you, the color black suiting too ill with the young. It is, I thank God, in no way for myself that I feel regret but for him for whom I wish the greatest good, [and] upon whom I see so many misfortunes fall that I feel them too much to [want to] be part of them. And in response to your desire to be able to serve me in place of [or perhaps 'close to'] the king your brother, nothing you could do for me would so please me as to purchase for him so much honor and security that whatever harm he has wished to do to himself may not crush him through his forgetting the care of those of the true religion who for so many years have consumed their means [and] poured out their blood to safeguard his cause. Not only does he owe this in good conscience, policy of state invites him to it, which is so uncertainly grounded on marshlands that he needs to grasp some very strong poles to get himself out. Remind him, Madam my good sister, in God's honor, that he must keep so much reputation even among his enemies that at no price he abandon those devoted to him just to please wickedness. Rest assured that if you do this you will oblige me to remain

Your most affectionate and devoted sister. ER.

The other, dated November, 1593 says:

Madam, as I am sending this gentleman to the King, I have been unable to restrain my pen from revealing to you one of the urgent reasons for sending him at once: he must serve as tablets to remind him [i.e., Henri] of the important reasons why he must have consideration for those of the Religion, not only for the danger to their lives, bodies, and goods when he was not too near his [current] dignity to reward them for it, but for his own salvation and the firm maintenance of his state. For if his enemies see him even slightly leaning on them, they make sport of him ['en joueront leur parsonage', an obscure phrase that seems to suggest mockery or manipulation], knowing he has lost all other hope. See here, Madame, my boldness in minding somebody else's business: if this is a sin, I merit pardon for acknowledging it. Nevertheless, I beg you to add your urging [to mine]. And rest assured always to have in me Your most faithful sister. ER.[39]

If Elizabeth writes to Catherine of both prudence and honor, her advisers were similarly torn between Protestant solidarity and political need. One memorandum notes that denying support might drive Henri 'into some desperate corse' such as allying with the League or marrying the Infanta; that a Spanish or League-held Brittany would be 'noysome unto Englande'; that Henri might seek revenge; that the French crown might fall to the 'house of Guise'; that Huguenots, 'disconforted to see the queen of England w[ith]drawe her succors', would be forced to flee 'or leave their throates to the sworde'.[40] Both Cecil and Robert Sidney feel the tug between wanting a world fully liberated from great wrong, from Grantorto, and awareness that only by compromise could they untwist a few of evil's coils. Henri should not be punished by denying him funds and men, for English national security requires his success. Foreseeing the king's conversion, Cecil writes that the situation is 'more to be lamented than remedied'. First he lists the differences between an English Church obeying Christ and a Catholic one whose 'corrupt doctryne' makes kings yield to the pope. 'And yet though her Ma[jesty] shall do well ... to censure the Fr[ench] kyng, yet it is to be considered what shall be mete in pollecy for her Majesty to doo to help the

Fr[ench] kyng ageynst the K[ing] of spayne the Guises and such as will not submit their selves upon his conversion.'[41]

Sidney's dispatches from France speculate that Huguenots have all the assurances they can expect from a king under great pressure from his new co-religionists and that Henri will remain friendly to his old supporters. Sidney hopes the queen will appear honorable and be realistic, writing Essex from Flushing in November, 1595 that whatever the risk of 'some Toutch of Reputation' she must go on helping Henri. '[Q]uestionless, the good of the State of England, and generally of all them that profess Religion, is by all Meanes to keepe the King of France in Affection and in Abilitie a Ballance against the Greatnes of Spaine.' But the queen should 'seeme to do it with her most Honor; and that must bee beinge againe intreated and perswaded; which I think there bee Ways to bring about, if the Queene be not to hasty'.[42] In other words, let her help Henri but arrange to be begged to do so. And that is exactly the pattern that Spenser follows, whether with approbation, irony, or both: Burbon breaks faith, is rebuked, pleads for help anyway, gets it, and together with Gloriana's knight and iron Talus, saves Flourdelis.

Many must have understood, as the pain wore off, that Henri had done what he had to do to outflank the League, prevent more bloodshed and economic ruin, and neutralize Spain. Sir Burbon is right – necessity compelled his action. This does not make Henri a hypocrite. There is no evidence that he ever called Paris worth a mass (even if he did later tell a fellow convert, 'Oh, I see – you have some crown to win').[43] Rather, he had every psychological and political reason to feel and show sincerity. It was skeptical Leaguers and wistful Huguenots who doubted his good faith, although one would love to know what he told his Protestant chaplain when the two met privately for a tearful farewell, the king's new advisers en route to escort him to mass and the Huguenot minister ready to leave tactfully by the back door.[44] In making Burbon a timeserver, Spenser either agreed with Henri's papist enemies that the king was a liar or retained a frail hope that he was biding his time.

Spenser does have his facts more or less right, whatever his exaggeration of England's role and his suppression of any campaign's unchivalric concern with massed armies, money, disease, and policy disputes. Unlike Artegall, though, Elizabeth's government was soon back on friendly terms with Henri (when not furious with him for ignoring his debts, disagreeing over where to focus military efforts, refusing England an urban military base, putting out feelers to Spain, or just being French).

Yet Henri's conversion lacerated many hearts. Perhaps it was after July, 1593 that Harvey wrote in his copy of *Yvry*: 'What if heroic virtue cools? Whatever is not of faith is a sin, lest the sun hide or even suffer eclipse.'[45] Was Spenser disappointed as a poet as well as a Protestant to find Henri's sun in eclipse? Perhaps not entirely, for he puts the eclipse to good use. In some brilliant pages on the episode Lowell Gallagher argues that Artegall's rebuke, although not exactly 'wrong', is smugly self-assured, whereas Burbon's excuses move the relevant terms into an ambiguous world of subjectively understood motivation, from allegory to something like the novel.[46] I would go further. If history often comes to us draped in myth and allegory, myth and allegory are never unpressured by history and it is unwise ever to assume their separation.

The Burbon episode figures this pressure as Book V first incorporates the heroic allegories with which Leicester was greeted during the Dutch Revolt, then evokes a civil war in which a French king chooses to stop being a champion so as to dwindle into his nation's husband, and finally demonstrates how in Ireland knightly heroics are precluded by England's own politics. It is not simply that in the Burbon episode Spenser too thinly allegorizes real events – the campaigns of Norris and Essex, the negotiations over strategy, money, and troops. He also meta-allegorizes the move from myth to actuality. Henri IV, that failed Hercules, and Artegall, that slandered hero who fails to reform Irena's country, are solar figures who, like the sun, are swayed by the pull of primal sin and passing time. Hercules himself, after all, did not make a good end and notoriously had problems with self-control. Not even he could be entirely heroic in a world of time, of a disordered zodiac and a lax sun, of compromises necessary lest worse injustice ensue. Kenneth Boris, who comments that the Burbon episode 'emphatically marks a transition from the Arthurian plane of ideal resolutions to the compromises of human history', has well shown the degree to which Book V is apocalyptic, but with the apocalypse itself postponed as historical time marches on.[47]

Judith Anderson has argued that by the end of his legend Artegall is more human and less absolute, questions of geopolitical justice allowing no pure answers.[48] Yes. And it is no accident that after helping Burbon he has his first real failure. His aborted effort to pacify Irena's lands is presented in terms relevant to Burbon's career: the project is at odds with an ideal but impossible time and timing, not least because he is halted by slander, the besmirching that he and Burbon, for different reasons, had feared.

How history fractures mythology, then, can figure how circumstance pressures any plan, conviction, action: how, as the French say, 'tout commence en mystique, tout finit en politique'. Burbon's shield is broken not just by deceived or corrupted rascals but – in a book filled with dismemberings – by events in the temporal world. This does not make Spenser despair, I think, for it cannot have taken him until 1593 to notice how the world wags; even the 1590 *Faerie Queene* has few unproblematic victories. But it does suggest that Justice, even Equity, is not enough, that a well-fashioned gentlemen needs yet more virtues to help him negotiate an always lapsing world, one in which signifiers are as apt to flit as our wills are to waver and fleurs de lis are to fade. One virtue Artegall might try is courtesy, the empathetic if devious grace that he offers Burbon so grudgingly and that he himself is denied by Envy and Detraction. Spenserians, too, should cut Sir Burbon some slack: even if Grantorto did not die in late sixteenth-century France, he did slink off, taking his Jesuits with him when Henri expelled them in 1595. By the age's own standards, if not by ours, the new husband did prove more Irenic than many had feared, as witness the Edict of Nantes in 1598. And Flourdelis did learn to love him; reborn as the Republic's Marianne, she still does.

Notes

1 V.xi.43–xii.2. For a subtle reading of Henri's dilemmas and motivations, see Mack Holt, *The French Wars of Religion, 1562–1629* (Cambridge: Cambridge University Press, 1995). The fullest study of the conversion is Michael Wolfe's *The Conversion of Henri IV: Politics, Power, and Religious Belief in Early Modern France* (Cambridge, Mass.: Harvard University Press, 1993). My thanks to the committee for Spenser at Kalamazoo for inviting me to give this paper as the 1996 Kathleen Williams Lecture. In quoting early modern texts I have normalized i/j and u/v.

2 *Love's Labors Lost* I.i.152. This play, with an oath-breaking King of Navarre who loves a French princess and has companions with the names of French magnates (including 'Dumaine' – de Mayenne, known in England as the duc de Maine, leader of the Guise faction), makes no explicit comment on Henri's conversion but certainly takes a sardonic view of great men's vows.

3 See Clifford C. Huffman, *Elizabethan Impressions: John Wolfe and His Press* (New York: AMS Press, 1988) and Lisa Ferraro Parmelee, *Good Newes from Fraunce: French Anti-League Propaganda in Late Elizabethan England* (Rochester, NY: University of Rochester Press, 1996). Parmalee, focusing on the material's intellectual rather than mythical content, thinks that much of the propaganda encourages royal absolutism. Wolfe, *Conversion*, finds similar implications in French disputes over Henry's religion. Parmalee has a useful bibliography of pamphlets, and Paul Voss's *Elizabethan News Pamphlets: Shakespeare, Spenser, Marlowe and the Birth of Journalism* (Pittsburgh, Pa.: Duquesne University Press, 2001) examines their social and material context. I thank Professor Voss, whose work in certain areas overlaps my own, for his communications and advice.

4 As A. C. Hamilton puts it in *The Structure of Allegory in The Faerie Queene* (Oxford: Clarendon Press, 1961), 173, 'Throughout Book V the reader is aware of fact pressing down upon the fiction.' That pressure increases in the final cantos. Hamilton himself says that focusing only on fact would further 'tilt' the poetry's balance (177). In this essay I do focus on fact, but 'fact' that had been gilded by metaphor before Spenser began writing.

5 By 'allegory' I mean such 'other-talk' as sustained allusions to ancient myth, repeated personifications, and extended metaphors. Historically, Henri led his men to victory at Coutras in 1586; allegorically he slew a giant. The many references to his role as a solar Hercules add up to allegory if, like good Spenserians, we define 'allegory' loosely.

6 For the iconography of Henri's myth, see Marie-France Wagner, 'Représentation allégorique d'Henri IV *rex imperator*', *Renaissance and Reformation* 17.4 (1993): 25–40. After a pause, English praise of Henri resumed. In 1599, for example, Joshua Sylvester translated Jean de Nesme's sonnet sequence on Henri tricked out in the usual mythological finery. Henri's assassination in 1610 provoked a flood of grieving admiration; in 1625 the future Charles I married Henri's daughter.

7 The *Letters of John Chamberlain*, ed. and intro. Norman Egbert McClure, two vols. (1939; Westport, CT: Greenwood Press, 1979) I, 231. Henri's virility makes an intriguing contrast with the feminization of the French that Andrew M. Kirk finds in his *The 'Mirror of Confusion': The Representation of French History in English Renaissance Drama* (New York: Garland, 1996).

8 See the *Declaration of the King of Navarre touching the slanders published against him*, trans. Claude Hollyband (1585). In *A journall, or Briefe report of the late service in Britaigne, by the Prince de Dombes [and] Sir John Norris* (1591) the Spaniards will not stand and fight the English whom the queen sent to aid Henri. On Mayenne, see *The Continual Following of the French king upon the Duke of Parma, the Duke of Guise, the Duke of Maine, and their Armies* (1592; STC 13130, one of Wolfe's quartos, on a battle in late April of that year). A woodcut of St. George appears both at the start and end of the quarto; it applies well to Henri, a Knight of the Garter. Wolfe also used it in J. B.'s *A Mirrour to all that love to follow the warres* (1589), verses on the chivalric doings of Peregrine Bertie, Lord Willoughby, in the Dutch campaign; on this pamphlet and the woodcut's relevance to Spenser's Redcrosse and Sir Burbon see Paul Voss, 'The *Faerie Queene*, 1590–1596: The Case of St. George', *The Ben Jonson Journal* 3 (1997): 59–73.

9 At least two writers, though, explicitly dissociate Henri from the diagonal Burgundian red cross (St. Andrew was patron of Burgundy), I assume because the duchy was now Hapsburg. See *Masque* sig. D2v and *An advertisement from a French Gentleman, touching the intention and meaning which those of the house of Guise have in their late levying of forces and Armes in the Realme of France* (June, 1585). The latter answers a proclamation by the aged Cardinal de Bourbon, Guisard claimant to the throne; it defends Henri III against the charge of (homosexual) favoritism, scoffs at the cardinal's claim to descend from Pharamond, and says 'let us shew our selves rather reunited under the white Crosse, being the ancient banner of our Kings, against the redde Crosse of Burgundie in Spaine' (sig. E2). That Spenser's Redcrosse gives Burbon his shield may hint that the pre-Hapsburg Burgundy, object in the 1580s of political nostalgia, is one with Burbon in a common struggle against Spain. A red cross, whether perpendicular or diagonal, has a Burgundian overtone and suggests

that deeds by men like Sidney in the 1580s have now moved westward from Belge to France.

10 *A Comparison of the English and Spanish Nation*, sig. D3v.
11 II.vii.8–18. Spenser satirizes the corruption of chivalry by the newly rich who buy themselves arms and ancestors. But Mammon's scorn also recalls the unhappy truth that armor and horses do not come from nowhere, that knighthood is sustained by an economic system run as much by cash as by fealty and gift-giving.
12 The 'hand' of justice translates 'virga' (sig. C3, 'wand'), a wand terminating in a hand performing a blessing; William Segar's 1602 *Honor Military and Civil*, ed. Diane Bornstein (Delmar, NY: Scholars' Facsimiles and Reprints, 1975) has a picture of Henry III holding one.
13 Sig. A2V. Like some other works on French affairs, *Flower* exploits stories of Spain's greedy cruelty in the Americas; sig. C1v adds that recent deaths among French royalty were largely poisonings arranged by Philip II.
14 Sig. F2. For less cleverly worked out scoffs see L. T. A.'s *Masque*: the League is Pandora (sig. B1v), a false Venus whose skirts bear cabalistic signs (sig. D2), a Circe (sig. D4), 'deceitfull Courtezane' (sig. N1), and 'subtill Thais' with 'a thousand baytes and sleights' (sig. T3v).
15 On the habit of comparing royalty to the Greek hero, see Marc-René Jung, *Hercule dans la littérature française du XVIe siécle* (Geneva: Droz, 1966).
16 Sigs. D3–D3v. Philip II is also Pharaoh. *An Answere to the last tempest and villanie of the League* (STC 662 [53]) compares the League to Herod, Busiris, and Indian dragons who get drunk on elephant blood and die.
17 In order, sigs. B1v–B4, D3v, E4v–F1, and M4; for similar Herculean allusions, see sigs. E3v–E4, F1v, G1–G1v, N1, and N2v.
18 Sigs. A2v–A3; Hurault adds that he blushed to hear how the faint-hearted Henri III 'stoode but as an O in Ciphre, which of it selfe can do nothing, but being added to anie other number, encreaseth the value thereof'. As for Philip II, he looks impressive only because he is rich and has been opposed by women rulers in France and England and an idiot in Turkey. Now that he faces Dutch rebels and Henri of Navarre, we will see what his current preparations against England can accomplish (sig. E3 ff.).
19 The calendrical symbolism of *Epithalamion*, which Spenser probably wrote at the same time or shortly after writing the Burbon episode, shows that the sun's imperfections and all they imply were on his mind in the mid-1590s.
20 One genealogy is given in Jung, *Hercule*; I thank Barbara C. Bowen for a list of Renaissance texts tracing the Valois back to Pharamond and thence to Francus and Hector. Despite his royal blood, Henri was a little vulnerable to such scoffs, for Navarre was, from a French perspective, minor and marginal; the *Masque of the League* reports, sig. B2, that Henri's enemies called him a 'Bearn-ish man' – merely from Béarn.
21 Sigs. A2v, B1v. Similar taunts appear in *The Flower de Luce*, sig. A4v, and Hurault's 1592 *Excellent Discourse*, sig. A4v.
22 Sigs. B3v–B4. A sarcastic version of this appears in *A Comparison of the English and Spanish Nation* (1589), sig. D3v: if the sun in the sky had been eclipsed

as often as the wisdom in the supposedly great duke of Alva's head 'wee might well thinke that we were on that daies eve, which shal bring an end to all things of this world'.

23 Sigs. A3v–A4; toads did indeed figure on the ancient French royal coat. Ronsard's *Franciade*, Book IV, tells how when Clovis became Christian the toads became fleurs-de-lis.

24 Hurault, 1592 *Discourse*, fears that as other cities ('Orleans ... Also Roan, Lions, Burges, Tholouze, Troye, Dion, and many more') and the provincial parliaments follow Paris into rebellion France will see 'Provinces against Provinces' and 'Governours against Governours' (sig. F1).

25 *A Comparison of the English and Spanish Nation*, trans. Robert Ashley (1589; one of Wolfe's pamphlets), sigs. A2, B2. *The Masque of the League*, sig. B4, prescribes hellebore for France's madness and thinks that Henri, 'no vulgare Phisition', can cure 'the disease of this estate' (sig. N3–N3v; also, O4, P4). Cf. Hurault's 1592 *Discourse*, sigs. K1v–K2. Henry's conversion did not end English admiration of his medical prowess: Robert Dallington's *View of France* (1604) calls him 'the Hercules that now reignes, [who] conquered this monstrous Hidra, and like a skilfull Esculapius, recovered her of this pestilent fever' (sig. G3).

26 'Ad Galliam de Rege Navarreno', *De caede et interitu Gallorum regis, Henrici tertii, epigrammata* (Oxford, 1589, sig. A3): Aegra diu fueras Mediceis, Gallia, philtris, / Et tandem Medicum transfodis agra tuum. / Nunc moribunda taces furiali percita morbo. / Immeritam medicus quis tibi praestet opem? / Unicus en superest, quem vel [Theophrastus, i.e., Paracelsus] habebis, / Vel (si illud mavis) ecce [Galen] habes. / Ille operam Navare solet sine fraude fidelem, / Et certam (quamquam es perdita) spondet opem. / Ille salutiferas tibi molliter admovet herbas, / Et, si herbas nolis ferre, metalla parat.

27 Sig. I3v; see sig. L1 for an argument that all Christians are in some sense of one body, that Henri would never persecute Catholics, and that he will not convert. *The Masque* is full of such assurances (see sigs. G1, L3, S3–S3v, and T3).

28 I thank Carol Kaske for sending me some wonderful pages on shields in *The Faerie Queene*, although I myself would go further in allowing for Spenser's ambivalence toward Burbon.

29 For these and other comments, see Eleanor Relle, 'Some New Marginalia and Poems of Gabriel Harvey', *Review of English Studies* 23 (1972): 401–16. Harvey also admired the poet's own political savvy: 'Dubartas sawe the errour of the Duke of Guises popularitie, in a Monarchie. Himself wiser, to be a liege Subject in a Kingdom.' I quote Sylvester's works, ed. A. B. Grosart (1880; Hildesheim: Olms, 1969, 2 vols.), II: 245–51. Sylvester shared with Spenser a hopeful attitude toward Essex: Grosart's introduction to vol. 1 prints two 1597 letters from the earl trying to get him some secretarial work.

30 Once but 'rich in hope', Henri is also now Caesar ('Thou cam'st, saw'st, overcam'st'), 'Earth's Ornament', and the 'honour of our Times'.

31 Cf. *The oration and declaration of the French king, Henrie the fourth of that name, and by the grace of God King of Navarre* (1590, for Richard Field; STC 13114a): 'Let than this companie of evill speakers cease, and let them truely

beleeve that neyther this Crowne, nor the Empire of all the whole earth sere able to make me change the Religion wherein I have bene brought uppe and instructed from my mothers pappes, and the which I uphold to be true' (sig. A3). The title page has the anchor of hope that Field used for his edition of Spenser's *Amoretti*.

32 On English reaction during these weeks, see Wallace T. MacCaffrey, *Elizabeth I: War and Politics 1588–1603* (Princeton, N.J.: Princeton University Press, 1992), 178–83. John Bennett Black, *Elizabeth and Henry IV, Being a Short Study in Anglo-French Relations, 1589–1603* (Oxford: Blackwell, 1914) remains useful as well.

33 On the Dutch reaction see the brief account by Richard Bruce Wernham in his invaluable, *List and Analysis of State Papers, Foreign Series, Elizabeth I* (London: Her Majesty's Stationery Office, 1964–93) V, 212. These papers have not been calendared but Wernham's analysis almost makes up for this lack. I have worked from a microfilm of the documents lent to me by Joseph Black when he was director of Victoria University's Centre for Reformation and Renaissance Studies and in reading the relevant ones have been guided by the paleographical prowess of Roger Kuin. Fulke Greville's account of the affair shows the continuing ambivalence of some English observers. Greville paraphrases with seeming approval Elizabeth's suggestion that Henry had sold God to purchase the Earth but later calls Henri 'that brave king' and praises Elizabeth's 'timely and princely help'. See his life of Sidney in his *Works*, ed. A. B. Grosart (1870; repr. New York: AMS Press, 1966) IV: 178–81, 213–14.

34 From a translation dated November 12, 1593; BL Harley MS 787, fol. 15v. I have used a transcription graciously provided by Janel Mueller, who is editing a selection of Elizabeth's letters.

35 On the bond of amity, see Wernham, *List and Analysis* V, 364. Elizabeth's letter to Henri is State Papers France 78.32, fol. 205.

36 *The Letters of Queen Elizabeth I*, ed. G. B. Harrison (New York: Funk and Wagnalls, 1968), 232–33.

37 For Henri's letter, see J. Nouaillac, ed., *Henri IV raconté par lui-même* (Paris: Picard, 1913), 242–43; Nouaillac dates the letter 'vers 1594', although I would be more confident if Henri were not explaining that he has kept for himself a portrait that Elizabeth had sent his sister, Catherine, which could be the same one referred to in the queen's letter to Catherine on July 21, 1592 (State Papers France 78.28, fol. 40, analyzed in Wernham, *List and Analysis* IV, 313). Elizabeth's 'dance of love' letter is in Harrison, *Letters*, 246.

38 On the voracious elephant, see Wernham, *List and Analysis* IV (May 1592–June 1593), no. 512.

39 Catherine was herself an experienced politician, having at times served her brother as regent in his ancestral domains. I have added a few accents for the sense.

SPF 78.XXXI, fol. 74 (Aug. 25):

Madame: Si mon papier eust le taint resemblant ... mon coeur, Je ne le vous oseroi presenter, le couleur noir sayant trop mal aux jeunes gents. Ce nest point que grace ... dieu de moy je sents regret, mais de tel a qui le plus de bien je desire, sur qui j'appercoive tomber tant de malencontres que me senble trop avoir senty pour en estre participante. Et pour entendre l'envie que vous tient de me pouvoir servir en l'endroict du Roy vostre frere, Je useray de de ceste franchise en vostre endroict, que rien de vous me peult tant complaire qu' ... luy pourchasser tant d'honneur et seurete que quelque mal qu'il s'est voulu faire qu'il ne l'accable en outliant le soing des vrais religieux qui tant d'années ont consumés leur moyens, espandus leur sang pour garder son partie. Car oultre qu'en conscience il le doibt, la police mesme de son estat le convie, qui n'est point si bien fondé sur de maretz qu'il n'ayt bien le besoing de conserver bien fort bastons pour s'en despestrer. Souvenez le pourtant madame ma bonne seour en l'honneur de Dieu quil se conserve tant de reputation voire entre les enemys mesme, que ... nul pris il abandone ses tresacquises pour complaire le mal assurez Quy faisant vous m'obligerez ... vous demeurer

Vostre tresaffectionee soeur et vray devote.

E. R.

(SPF 78.XXXI, fol. 74 [November, 1593]):

Madame, Envoyant ce Gentilhome au Roy, je n'ay sceu refreyner ma plume, qu'elle ne vous [ne cancelled] represente une des instantes causes, qui m'a convie ... le mander presentement, qu'est pour luy servir des tablettes pour luy faire souvenir des grandes raisons, qui pour ceulx de la religion il doibt tenir, non tant seulement pour leur dangiers de vie de corps et des biens, quant il ne fut trop pres de telle dignité pour leur en guerdonner, ains pour son propre salut, et solide conservation de son estat. Lequel si ses ennemis verront s'appuyer du tout sur les espaules d'eux, ilz en joüeront leur parsonnage, scachant qu'il aura perdu toute autre esperance. Voila Madame, mon outrecuidance de me mesler des affaires d'aultruy, laquelle estant picché Je en merite pardon, pour le recognoistre. Ce pendant je vous supplie adjouster vostre instance. Et de moy asseures vous d'avoir tousjours V[ost]re tresfidele soeur.

ER

40 'The Dangers that may insewe to her M[ajesti]e & the realme by abbandoning the present action of the French K[ing]', State Papers France 78.32, fol. 287 (October 1593, unsigned).
41 State Papers France 78.31, fol. 222, dated c. July 10, 1593; Wernham V: 57 gives some context and see also MacCaffrey, *Elizabeth I*, on Cecil's concerns. Cecil's use of 'yet' and 'and yet' sounds a little like Artegall's.
42 *A Collection of State Papers Relating to Affairs in the Reign of Queen Elizabeth, From the Year 1571 to 1596*, ed. William Murdin (London: William Bowyer, 1759), 698.
43 See, e.g., François Bayrou, *Henri IV: Le Roi Libre* (Paris: Flammarion, 1994), 261; Henri's teasing comment, quoted from the memoirs of Pierre de l'Estoile, says 'Ah! j'entends bien ce que c'est: vous avez volontiers quelque couronne à gagner.' As Bayrou says, the jest proves nothing, for 'Henri savait rire des choses les plus graves'.
44 Wolfe, *Conversion*, 147.

45 Relle, 'New Marginalia', 413–14 ('An unquam fides heroica frigeat? Quicquid non est fide, est peccatum. Nisi quatenus Sol interdum latet; aut etiam patitur Eclypsin').
46 *Medusa's Gaze: Casuistry and Conscience in the Renaissance* (Stanford, Calif.: Stanford University Press, 1991), 190–97. For Gallagher, Burbon's shield has 'polysemy', not Artegall's 'hegemony of a programmatic allegoresis'; but it is too simple to call Artegall's the 'official' view, which was less univocal and, after a brief time, much less censorious.
47 K. Boris, *Spenser's Poetics of Prophecy in 'The Faerie Queene' V* (Victoria: University of Victoria English Literary Studies 52, 1990), 62. The stanzas are further evidence that, as Borris says (35), 'Spenserian allegory is not a disguised repetition of outmoded orthodoxies ... but rather an exploratory mode of apprehension.' On apocalyptic delays, see especially Richard Mallette, *Spenser and the Discourses of Reformation England* (Lincoln: University of Nebraska Press, 1997), 168, who also notes that 'the apocalyptic view of the world comprehends human failure as deeply as tragedy does'; and contrasts the limits of homiletic exhortation in the Burbon episode with Arthur's more forceful methods in rescuing Belge (162).
48 '"Nor Man it Is": the Knight of Justice in Book V of Spenser's *Faerie Queene*', *PMLA* 85 (1970): 65–77. Sean Kane, *Spenser's Moral Allegory* (Toronto: University of Toronto Press, 1989), likewise finds Artegall 'self-righteous', thinking that Spenser does not criticize 'contemporary politics from the point of view of moral vision' or 'the moral ideal from the point of view of political exigency' but, rather, feels the 'ambiguity and irony' arising from 'the disparity of the ideal and the real' (171, 169). I am puzzled by Kane's statement that Henri's conversion 'did buy him time' much as the appeasement of Hitler at Munich bought time. Time was on Henri's mind, for he feared the growth of a *tiers parti* of impatient Catholic moderates and war-weary Leaguers, but he stayed Catholic and there is no evidence that his conversion was consciously insincere. Richard A. McCabe, *The Pillars of Eternity: Time and Providence in The Faerie Queene* (Dublin: Irish Academic Press, 1989) is subtle but less sympathetic to Burbon than I am.

3

The thirsty deer and the Lord of Life: some contexts for *Amoretti* 67–70

As the huntsman of *Amoretti* 67 sits resting in the shade, he may think he is alone with his hounds and the approaching hind. Readers of the poem, however, know that he is accompanied by the ghosts of many deer and hunters past. Two of the most famous hunters, of course, are Petrarch and Wyatt. Less often noted but probably around somewhere is Tasso's 'fera gentil', and recently a little attention has gone to the panting hart of Psalm 42. I would like to examine the relevance of these and other deer, particularly some biblical ones, to the significance of *Amoretti* 67 (*Am.* 67), and also to suggest a hitherto unremarked source or analogue for the lover's unusual situation in this sonnet and for several sonnets that follow it. Finally, I will try to tie these sonnets even more closely than they have been linked so far to the liturgy, both to that of the relatively deer-poor Book of Common Prayer and to the older Sarum rite.

As the notes to the Variorum edition of Spenser demonstrate, it is hard to read *Am.* 67 without recalling Petrarch, so much so that one may well suspect an almost mischievous invitation to compare the successful courtship of Elizabeth Boyle to the disasters and losses in the *Rime*. Petrarch is left weltering in a weatherbeaten galley charged with forgetfulness (*Rime* 189), but Spenser's lover can with some confidence 'descry the happy shore' after 'long stormes and tempests sad assay' (*Am.* 63). Petrarch's 'candida cerva' eludes him (*Rime* 190), but Spenser's deer is 'goodly wonne'. After this capture, we may assume that the 'sweet warriour' of *Am.* 57 will now give him the 'peace' he wants but that Petrarch, like Wyatt after him, cannot find (*Rime* 134). Sounding through the echoes of Petrarch, especially in *Am.* 63 and 67, then, is a certain boastfulness; Petrarch may be among Spenser's poetic progenitors, but the later poet is the more successful lover. Yet despite this possibly playful intertextuality, there remain limitations on the relevance of Petrarch to *Am.* 67. Not only is the hunter a failure, he has every reason to be. As the commentaries of, for example, Gesualdo and Vellutello make clear, the white hind is not merely reluctant but chaste, liberated from enamoured lovers by God and the laws of marriage.¹ The two hinds may be similar in goodness, but the huntsmen differ in their situations.

On several occasions Tasso's 'Questa fera gentil' has been cited as Spenser's source.² Such a debt would not be surprising, for like the birds in the Bower of Bliss, although presumably with less purely lascivious intentions, the lover in *Amoretti* seems to know Tasso well. There are certainly some parallels between the two poems. Tasso's kindly/noble beast has recently fled among the thorns, brush, and rocks of steep and uncertain paths. But now, its will changed, it wanders modestly and descends to a softer and lower path and, abandoning hardness, makes itself glad and graceful. Henceforth it will smile, says Tasso, and its eyes will shine on its lover. If the lover is so happy now, how will it be when love kisses him with burning pity? Some phrasing anticipates Spenser: *fera gentil* and 'gentle deare', *fuggia* and 'fly', and *onesta posa* and 'mylder looke', if indeed the new mildness in *Am.* 67 is the deer's and not the lover's.³ Above all, *cangiato voler* is not unlike the 'owne goodwill' and 'owne will beguyld' of Spenser's hind. Again, however, there are significant differences between Spenser and this 'source'. Tasso congratulates another man on the animal's change of heart; Spenser speaks in the first person. Tasso has no dogs, no brook, no shade, no binding, and his creature descends whereas Spenser's 'returnd the selfe-same way'. Most important, there is no indication that the lucky recipient of the beast's favors had despaired or even rested before the animal's desertion of the high thorny path.⁴

Behind Petrarch and Tasso themselves, of course, there is an immense body of literature comparing a relationship to that of hunter and hunted.⁵ No one, I imagine, has seen it all, but Renaissance readers would remember the most famous deer. One appears in Horace's lovely reassurance to Chloe, a poem on occasion cited as a source for *Am.* 78 but with a fawn more closely resembling the beguiled and trembling hind of *Am.* 67 observed at a somewhat earlier stage in the process of persuasion. 'You avoid me', the lover tells the girl, 'like a fawn that in the trackless mountains seeks its anxious mother, afraid without cause, of breezes & woods. If the coming of spring makes loose leaves quiver, or greening lizards move a fruit bush this way and that, a deer's pulse speeds up and her legs start to tremble. But I am not chasing you like a Gaetulian lion, or a violent tiger, to tear you to pieces. Stop this habit you have of following mother – it's time [*tempestiva*] that you followed a man.'⁶ Several words would have struck Spenser's ear: the fawn is filled with *metus* that her pursuer finds *vana*, just what Spenser's lover tells his own quarry elsewhere in the sequence, and because of this fearfulness, like Spenser's deer, it trembles (*tremit*); furthermore, the maturing fawn is *tempestiva*, anticipating one of Spenser's favorite words: timely (and perhaps recalling to him the whole complex of *tempus, tempestas, temperantia* and 'goodly temperature' so basic to Book II of *The Faerie Queene* [*FQ*]).

Buried in Horace's seductive mildness, however, and in Tasso's man-to-man congratulation as well, is an unspoken implication. Horace says he has no desire to mangle the fawn, but just what *does* one normally do with a captured deer if one does not want to provide it with a diamond collar? The hunting imagery hints at an almost inevitable anxiety about captivity and dismemberment; deer are not wrong to tremble, even if, like Amoret after her rescue from Busyrane, they later discover that they are, if no longer intact, then not so severely hurt that their wound will not close (*FQ* 111.12.38). In other words, the ancient metaphor touches on one of *Amoretti*'s major themes, a feminine fear of imprisonment and wounding that must be put by when it is timely to do so. Indeed, the hunt in *Am.* 67 may itself be 'timely', because the capture, death, or even sighting of a deer has often meant a new beginning, a necessary or desirable change in relationships.[7] Such references to deer at moments of transition can be unhappy. When Vergil compares Dido to a pierced hind wandering in anguish through the city (*Aeneid* 166–73), he indicates something about the cost of refounding a dynasty. For Aeneas, and in this tragic division he differs from many other heroes, the stricken deer and the Italic shores are altogether different quarries. The doe herself finds just what many hunted animals fear – death – and in Italy the hero will again have trouble with deer when the killing of a pet fawn starts a war between the natives and the Trojans, a savagery once more associating empire with blood and sorrow.[8]

Many deer legends, it has been pointed out, have a deep and archaic connection with the foundation of cities, churches, empires, and dynasties, although the deer seldom suffer as much as Dido or Silvia's fawn.[9] Stories of Caesar's long-lived and collared deer, the cruciferous deer of saints like Eustace, the deer-chase leading to sovereignty in Celtic legend, the deer associated with the beginnings of cities, even the deer who guide Charlemagne or Roland to places of crossing or safety – all tie the establishment or attaining of something new (religious or political) to a creature whose pursuit nonetheless normally involves pain and exhaustion. Within the endearing sweetness of *Am.* 67's pastoral repose, in other words, hide disturbing recognitions of potential violence and the at least symbolic death involved in any transition from an old to a new life. Acteon, after all, learned from his own transformation what hounds do to deer, although in at least one esoteric reading of the story his distribution into a multiplicity of canine stomachs may be seen as the bliss of mystical dissolution into the divine.[10] When Scudamor leads Amoret out of the Temple of Cupid in *FQ* IV.10.55, her hand trembles in his like a 'warie Hynd' gone to soil (i.e. hiding from the dogs in shallow water; the lover himself is the deer seeking soil in *FQ* III.12.44 [1590], but he does not tremble). Scudamor's behaviour as a lover and husband is not beyond reproach, and Amoret may have more to worry about than the beloved in *Am.* 67, but even the latter still shivers some at the prospect of what comes next. At least she is in her weary hunter's charge, not torn by his irrational dogs, an important consideration for any female meditating surrender. So too, in a possibly relevant poem by the Petrarchist sonneteer Sasso, Acteon offers to submit to Diana, preferring to die directly at the hands of the goddess.[11]

By the time Spenser wrote *Am.* 67, then, there was not only a vast herd of classical and medieval deer for a later poet to chase but considerable ambivalence available as well, ironies and energies generated by the situation of hunter and hunted, man and beast, love as pursuit and love as captivity or destruction. These complexities, furthermore, work as well in religious poetry as in amatory. So, needless to say, Renaissance poetry is also crowded with deer, sometimes indicating the poet and sometimes the object of his desire. Puns on serf/cerf encouraged such poetry in France, and puns on deer/dear or hart/heart proliferated so in England that sometimes it is difficult to know if the author intends his metaphor as anatomical imagery, hunting allegory, or both. Thus Thomas Lodge cries out, 'Triumphant eies, why beare you Armes, / Against a hart that thinks no harmes. / A hart alreadie quite appalde, / A hart that yeelds, and is enthrald.'[12] If a hunting poem of sorts, there is a certain kinship with *Am.* 67, although yielding deer are not impossible to find elsewhere. Tasso's 'fera gentil' condescends to love and one medieval hunting poem ends by begging the deer to grow tame. Closer to home, George Gascoigne, a self-confessed failure at shooting all sorts of game from legal studies to courtly place, manages to hit a doe standing quietly in front of him, an allegorical doe sent by Jehova for his moral and satirical instruction.[13]

Among these hundreds of hunting poems there may be several in which the hunter chases the deer with dogs, gives up, sits down by water to rest, and then finds the deer comes to him to be bound. It would be rash to think that no one during all the centuries from Horace's *tempestiva* trembling fawn to the pleading poetical stag in Gascoigne's *Noble arte of venerie* (1575; sigs. 4v–5) thought of such a variation on the more usual images of escaped deer and captured deer. So far, however, I have found only one poem besides Spenser's that contains all these elements. There are major differences: this poem is explicitly religious, eleven stanzas long, and not so much the story of successful capture as the anticipation of one now that the hunter is initiated into evangelical wisdom. Nevertheless, the lyric is remarkably relevant to Spenser in a number of important ways. Either Spenser knew this lyric, which is intriguing, or two Renaissance poets independently arrived at a similar conceit with similar religious implications embedded in a similar series of poems with seasonal and liturgical significance – and that is intriguing too.

The poem is the sixth lyric in the *Chansons spirituelles* (1547) of Marguerite de Navarre. Although it is long and available in a good modern edition, I give it here for the convenience of Spenserians:

> 1. Un jeune Veneur demandoit
> A une femme heureuse et sage,
> Si la chasse qu'il prétendoit
> Pourroit trouver, n'en quel Bocage;
> Et qu'il avoit bien bon courage
> De gaigner ceste venaison
> Par douleur, mérite et Raison.
> Elle luy a dit: Monseigneur,
> De la prendre il est bien saison:
> Mais vous estes mauvais chasseur.
>
> 2. Elle ne se prend par courir,
> Ne pas vouloir d'homme du monde,
> Ne pour tourment, ne pour mourir,
> Et si ne fault point que l'on fonde
> Son salut, fors qu'au Createur:
> Vertu peu vault s'il n'y abonde
> Par son Esprit, force et valeur.
> Las, vous en seriez possesseur
> Si de David aviez la fonde:
> Mais vous estes mauvais chasseur.
>
> 3. Ce que cherchez est dens le bois,
> Où ne va personne infidèle:
> C'est l'aspre buysson de la Croix,
> Qui est chose au meschant cruelle.
> Les bons Veneurs la treuvent belle,
> Son tourment leur est vray plaisir;
> Or si vous aviez le désir
> D'oublier tout pour cest honneur,
> Autre bien ne voudriez choisir:
> Mais vous estes mauvais chasseur.
>
> 4. Lors quand le Veneur l'entendit,
> Il mua toute contenance,
> Et comme courroucé luy dit:
> Vous parlez par grand ignorance;
> Il fault que je destourne et lance
> Le cerf, et que je coure après;
> Et vous me dites par exprès

Qu'il ne s'acquiert par mon labeur.
– Seigneur, le cerf et de vous près,
Mais vous estes mauvais chasseur.

5. S'il vous plaisoit seoir et poser
Dessus le bort d'une fontaine,
Et corps et esprit reposer,
Puisant de l'eau très-vive et saine,
Certes sans y prendre autre peine,
Le cerf viendroit à vous tout droit;
Et pour l'arrester, ne faudroit
Que le retz de vostre humble coeur
Où par Charité se prendroit;
Mais vous estes mauvais chasseur.

6. – Or, ma Dame, je ne croy pas
Que l'on acquière ou bien ou gloire
Sans travailler ne faire un pas,
Seulement par aymer et croire.
De l'eau vive ne veux point boire;
Pour travailler, le vin vault mieux.
La Dame a dit: de Terre et Cieux
Serez Seigneur et possesseur,
Si la Foy vous ouvre les yeux:
Mais vous estes mauvais chasseur.

7. Le cerf est sy humain et doux,
Que si vostre coeur voulez tendre,
Par amour il viendra à vous;
En vous prenant, se lairra prendre:
Et alors vous pourra apprendre
De manger sa chair et son sang
A ceste curée par reng;
Pour estre remplis de douceur
Vous désirs courront à ce blanc;
Mais vous estes mauvais chasseur.

8. En ceste délicate chair
La vostre sera transmuée;
O bien heureux qui peult toucher
A ceste grand teste muée,
A la chair courue et huée,
Mise à mort, rostie pour nous,
Sur la croix pendue à trois cloux!
Hélas, elle est vostre, ô pecheur,
Si vous croyez ces saintz propous:
Mais vous estes mauvais chasseur.

> 9. Le Veneur entendit la game,
> Et descouvrit la Poësie,
> Et soudain luy a dit: Ma Dame,
> J'abandonne ma fantaisie;
> De la Foy mon âme est saisie,
> Qui trompe et cor me fait casser,
> Colliers, couples et laisses laisser;
> Croyant la voix de mon Sauveur,
> Autre cerf je ne veux chasser
> Pour n'estre plus mauvais chasseur.
>
> 10. Empereurs, Roys, Princes, Seigneurs,
> A vous ma parole j'adresse;
> Vous tous Piqueurs, Chasseurs, Veneurs,
> Renoncez travail et destresse,
> Dont en lieu de plaisir, tristesse
> Vous rapportez le plus souvent.
> Las, vostre plaisir n'est que vent;
> Laissez comme moy ce malheur:
> Autre je suis qu'auparavant
> Pour n'estre plus mauvais chasseur.
>
> 11. Venez, Veneurs, venez, venez
> A la salutaire curée;
> A laisser le monde apprenez,
> Qui est de si courte durée;
> Car charité immesurée
> De son Tout vous fait le présent,
> Par lequel Rien est fait plaisant,
> Remply de divine liqueur:
> De moy, je m'y rens à present
> Pour n'estre plus mauvais chasseur.[14]

Spenser might have noted several matters here, not least the shift from a positive to a negative wording in the refrain, the same device used in his *Epithalamion*. But would he have looked at so obscure a collection? It would not be surprising. Marguerite was an important and famous woman, sister of François I, author of the popular *Heptaméron* (which Gabriel Harvey read), patron of Marot and Rabelais, celebrated by Du Bellay and Ronsard, and grandmother of the recently triumphant Henri IV – the Sir Burbon of *FQ* V.xi–xii. Marguerite had encouraged the belief, not wholly unfounded, that she, the king's mistress Mme. d'Estampes, and the Cardinal Du Bellay (cousin and employer of Joachim) formed an English party at the French court, and her evangelical tendencies, although stopping short of Protestantism, were so close to what the Sorbonne considered Lutheranism that one of her early works was briefly banned. The work in question, the

Miroir de l'âme pécheresse, was translated in 1544 by Gloriana herself when she was merely the Lady Elizabeth and published several times thereafter.[15] George Puttenham says of her, 'Queenes also have bene knowen studious, and to write large volumes, as Lady Margaret of Fraunce, Queene of Navarre, in our time.'[16]

The *Chansons* as a whole had much to intrigue a poet like Spenser. There are thirty-three poems, a good Christological number, yet some of these pious verses wittily rework popular lyrics. Chanson 6, for example, parodies an ingeniously obscene song about a bad hunter who does not know how to chase the 'conin' in a pretty lady's personal forest, hit it right in its moist middle, and 'bien brasser la venoison'.[17] Marguerite's Erasmian piety was intense, but she was no prude. Nor was she reluctant to describe her longing for God in the sensual terms made available to her (as to Spenser) in the Song of Songs. May God take her as his wife, she prays; Christ is her 'vray amant', and while she passes the weary hours waiting for her bridegroom she begs him, 'Baisez moy, acolez moy, / Mon Tout en tous.' Once joined to him, she will 'se perd et pasme / En son Tout joyeusement'.[18] The pain of languishing anticipation is less cleverly worked into the collection's structure than into Spenser's, however, and whereas Spenser ends his sequence with anacreontics about little Cupid, Marguerite ends hers with a noël (it is interesting that each series of poems concludes with images of infancy, the new life). The chief threat during this separation is not, as in Spenser, venomous tongues, but what Marguerite calls 'cuyder', a belief in one's own virtue, merit, and self-sufficiency, a false goodness who appears like a hypocrite with 'dévot maintien' and speech of silk, a danger and even an image found elsewhere in Spenser, of course. 'Cuyder' seeks to persuade us that good works can earn us the Bridegroom's embrace; but to believe this is to join Orgueil's chain of prisoners and to forget the true 'repos' – one of Marguerite's favorite words – for which the soul aches.[19]

Marguerite's vocabulary is fairly narrow, her symbolic language resonant but repetitive, her allusions chiefly scriptural and liturgical. If he read the sequence, however, Spenser would have found pleasant metrical variety and some clever conceits. Certain metaphors parallel his own, such as the siege imagery of chanson 22 (cf. *Am*.14), and he might have been especially taken by chanson 30, which compares the speaker to a thirsty deer, a ship straining towards harbor, and a captive seeking freedom, all images found in the Roman liturgy for Good Friday or Easter Saturday and all relevant to *Amoretti*, particularly as the deer and ship appear just as the sequence is approaching Easter. Three poems leap to the eye of any reader of Spenser, not only because of their similarity to certain Amoretti but because taken together they acquire a liturgical significance that parallels that of *Am*. 67, 68, and, possibly, 69 and 70.

The first is chanson 6, the deer hunt. The next, chanson 7, is a ninety-four-line Easter poem. Like *Am.* 68 it refers to Christ's harrowing of Hell and his conquest of death and sin, and it too ends with an impassioned hope for lover's union: 'Je seray vostre Espoux, vous tous un, mon Espouse: / Venez au vray repos où sera endormie / Entre mes bras toujours mon Espouse et amye.' The lover who speaks is a pelican, the bird long associated with redemption and cleansing. According to the printer William Ponsonby, Spenser wrote a now lost poem called 'The dying Pellican', a topic appropriate to the Easter season.[20] Is it mere coincidence that two poets who described a resting hunter whose deer returns willingly also wrote of dying pelicans? The third, chanson 8, celebrates the new season: 'Voicy nouvelle joye', for the dry tree flowers and the soul 'devient amoureux'.

If Spenser did know this series of poems that moves, like *Am.* 67–70, from a deer's surrender, to Easter victory, to dawn, spring, and love, he must have recognized in it not just a sequence of attractive conceits but a web of scriptural and liturgical allusions, among which the obliging deer is only the most striking. Marguerite's references are fairly obvious because of her explicitly religious matter, but Spenser's sonnets, too, even when primarily secular, have muted biblical echoes particularly audible to readers who take into account recently discovered connections between the sonnet sequence and the church calendar.[21] About *Am.* 68, of course, there can be no doubt. Like Marguerite's pelican poem, it is a brief anthology of scriptural quotations suited to the Easter season. The Harrowing of Hell is never mentioned in the Bible and alluded to only in texts requiring exegetical nudging (e.g. Ps. 107: 'He broght them out of darknes, and out of the shadowe of death, and brake their bands a sunder'), but many other phrases can be traced to scripture or to its Genevan editors.[22] 'Most glorious Lord of lyfe' is from Acts 3:15 ('and killed the Lord of life'), which Spenser had used earlier in *FQ* II.7.62, and 3:13 (God 'hathe glorified his Sonne') or John 13:31–32. Leading Captivity captive is from Ephesians 4:8 and hence also from Psalm 68, which Paul is quoting. It has not been remarked, I think, that the Geneva gloss on this verse inspired Spenser's second line, 'Did'st make thy triumph over death and sin': Christ went 'to *triumph* over Satan, *death* and *sinne*, and led them as prisoners and sclaves' (my emphasis). Just before this passage Paul exhorts us to support each other with love, although the end of Spenser's poem also recalls John 13:34–35, 15.12, Ephesians 5:2, and 1 John 4:19. The washing in blood is from Revelation 1:5 and 'all lyke deare didst buy', says the Variorum, from the Bishops' Bible: 'For ye are dearely bought' (1 Corinthians 6:20). Two psalms with Easter significance also contribute. Psalm 47:5 says 'God is gone up with triumph', words the Geneva editors apply to the Resurrection and that may have suggested Spenser's 'This joyous day, deare Lord, with joy begin' if he was thinking of the verse as used in the Sarum rite for Ascension Day: *Ascendit deus in jubiliatione,* or in the Edward VI prayer-book: 'God is gone up with a mery noyse.'

Psalm 16, which also refers to 'joye', offers the Messianic assurance that 'thou wilt not leave my soule in the grave: nether wilt thou suffer thine holie one to se corruption'. The next verse, 11, says that with God 'are pleasures for evermore', and Spenser's eye may have been caught by the marginal comment: 'Where God favoreth, there is perfite felicitie.' Verse ('for evermore'), gloss ('felicitie'), and context (Easter), I think, lie behind *Am.* 68's 'may live for ever in felicity'.

The Word quoted with such density of allusion in Spenser's Easter sonnet does not, I think, fall quite silent at the end of the sequence bounded by Ash Wednesday (*Am.* 22) and Easter (*Am.* 68). If Spenser is still remembering his Easter texts in *Am.* 69, furthermore, this reminiscence would help resolve a critical puzzle. The sonnet's vocabulary is close to that which Spenser first used in *The Ruines of Rome*; 'anticke', 'Trophees', 'eternity', 'immortall monument', 'posterity', and 'spoile' in close proximity, although used by a few Renaissance poets about women (and in Shakespeare's verse about a young man), form a cluster Spenser knew best as ambivalent evocations of Roman or sometimes British glory.[23] There may be ambivalence here, too. Has not the lover, so recently humble and gentle, relapsed into pushiness?[24] Is this the 'cuyder' Marguerite feared? And has he not noticed that the lady freely gave herself to him, beguiled by her *own* will and not won, so far as we can see, by labor and toil?

There is no reason Spenser need be consistent, one might reply, for the pleasure of a sonnet sequence is its ingathering of multiple moods and perspectives. The contradiction between the lady's submission and the lover's boastfulness, however, may point to a religious complexity analogous to the psychosexual one. Marguerite's deer poem states explicitly what Spenser's implies: grace and love are unearned (Christ buys us, we cannot buy him), which is why to speak of the successful lover in *Am.* 67 as having become 'worthy' is a little off the mark.[25] Yet even if, according to Protestants, we can do no acceptable works without prior faith, God can still congratulate the one to whom he has presumably given that faith, saying 'It is wel done good servant and faithful' (Matt. 25:21).

Spenser's two versions of his beloved's capture are not much more contradictory than Christian feeling and experience, whatever the fierce clarities of reformed theology. The lover's juxtaposition of gratitude and pride is, in fact, similar to that in some of the scriptural passages to which Spenser and Marguerite allude in their Easter poems – Psalm 47, Psalm 68, Ephesians 4:8 – and in some other related texts. As Marguerite's Pelican puts it, man may be nothing, but when he realizes this then Christ can 'En moy le réunis, l'embrasse et l'incorpore' and hence make him partaker in victory. Thus the verses that celebrate Christ's triumph pass that triumph on to us. Ephesians 4:8 says that when God 'ascended up on hie' and 'led captivitie captive' he 'gave giftes unto men'. The margin explains that Christ gave his 'victorie' over death and sin 'as a most precious gifte to his Church'. So, too, in 1 Corinthians 15:57, Paul cries, 'But thankes be unto God which hathe given us victorie through our Lord Jesus Christ.' The top of the page says boldly, 'Our victorie'. Even Spenser's 'happy purchase of my glorious spoile' recalls the 'deare didst buy' of *Am.* 68 and perhaps Acts 20:28, in which God has 'purchased' the Church. That 'purchase' is now ours: in Ephesians 1:14 God has 'purchased' our 'inheritance' – 'unto the praise of his glorie'. So in some sense the lover's claim that this is *his* conquest is not wholly wrong, even if in his pleasure he forgets to mention that his victory is also a gift.

Do these religious echoes reverberate as far as *Am.* 70? Perhaps so. Marguerite's happy chanson 8 welcomes Spring: 'voicy le jour' when 'L'hyver plein de froid et de pleurs / Est passé' and the new year flowers; the nightingale sings; and the faithful soul, who had trembled hidden in the Law, now sees clearly and falls in love, freed from damnation and drunk with joy at its election; the deadly cross is now a comfort and the soul need no longer lurk at home, for what was dry is now 'Florissant'. Spenser's sonnet, too, celebrates Spring and flowers; the speaker urges the lady to leave her 'winters bowre' and since she is 'not well awake', he is also asking her to greet new light. For both poets, then, images of sacrifice yield to those of triumph and passionate love and then to new day, new season, flowers, 'nouvelle joye' / 'joyous time', and love that had been fearful (if not in *Am.* 70 then in earlier sonnets) and will now 'les gens hanter' or join Love's 'lovely crew'. Marguerite has clear scriptural references: to passages like Galatians 3:23 describing the old law as a prison, to speaking in the light (Luke 12:3) or walking in the light (Revelation 21:24, 22:5), and to the Song of Songs ('For beholde, winter is past: the raine is changed, and is gone away. The flowers appeare in the earth: the time of the singing of birdes is come' [2:11–12]; the margin reminds us that this means 'sinne and error is driven backe by the comming of Christ which is here described by the spring time, when all things florish'). Both poems also recall Psalm 104:30: 'if thou send forthe thy spirit, thei are created, and thou renuest the face of the earth', or several passages in Isaiah foretelling the day when 'the budde of the Lord' (either the Church or Christ, say the Geneva editors) will be 'beautiful and glorious, and the frute of the earth shalbe excellent and pleasant' (4:2), when Israel 'shal florish and growe' (27:6), and when 'the desert and the wildernes shal rejoyce: and the waste grounde shal be glad and florish as the rose' (35:1; the headnote calls this 'the great joye of them that beleve in Christ' and the 'frutes that followe thereof'; see also Ezekiel 17:24).

Read in isolation, *Am.* 69–70 would probably not elicit such memories, and each sonnet has a secular lineage of its own. Yet following so hard upon an Easter poem, they may vibrate sympathetically, so to speak, with what has gone before, even if they are less insistently scriptural than Marguerite's melange of Psalm 104, the Song of Songs, and Isaiah. Like the central temple scene in *Epithalamion*, *Am.* 68's energies radiate outwards, alerting us to the analogies and relationships between human and divine love expressed more metaphorically on either side of the explicit statement. The Resurrection rends the veil of fable, and the fictive imagery – deer and moniment/spring – are illuminated by that more direct light.

If this is so, then the thirsty hind of Spenser and the dog-torn hart of Marguerite should also have biblical relatives, and so they do. It has been suggested that Spenser's closest scriptural reference is Psalm 42:1, 'As the hart braieth for the rivers of water, so panteth my soule after thee, O God'[26] (Figure 3.1). I agree that this deer is important to *Am.* 67, but there is more to be said about it and about related scriptural *cervidae*. Indeed, certain other texts to which Marguerite alludes in her deer poem seem relevant here too, even though they mention no animals. Spenser has no wise lady (a 'Personnification de la Sagesse' as in Proverbs 14 and Ecclesiasticus 14–15, says Marguerite's modern editor), but the juxtaposition of defeated searcher and approaching quarry is not unlike Acts 17:27: we 'grope' after God, 'though douteles he be not farre from everie one of us'. The brook recalls several springs such as that of Proverbs 5:18 or 'the fountaine of living waters' in Jeremiah 2:13, which the margin calls God's word and contrasts to mere human 'invencions, and vaine confidence' (Marguerite's 'cuyder').

Several critics have found the deer in *Am.* 67 Christlike, and Marguerite's poem is further indication that they are right – and also support for a reading of the poem that stresses the utterly free nature of the lady's surrender, not the merit, improvement, or psychological development of the lover/speaker.[27] Biblical deer, to be sure, have shifty and multiple identities. Harts in one translation are hinds in another, and it can sometimes be difficult to divide the deer from the goats. Nevertheless, it seems safe to say that incorporated into the deer of *Am.* 67 are the most famous Old Testament harts and hinds, all thought by one or another authority to represent Christ, the Christian, or the Church, and by some to signify more than one of these. Together they form a small family of symbolic creatures who on occasion are pressed *en masse* (and out of context) into exegetical passages of considerable metaphoric intensity. That is to say, the sighting of one deer in a single biblical verse often summons up remembrance of its cousins in other texts. Some of them I have already mentioned: the light-footed deer

Figure 3.1 The thirsty deer of Psalm 42 finds God in the water's reflection. Note the double implication: first, that like a good Christian the deer sees Christ in the living waters of Scripture and, second, that the scriptural deer reveals his allegorical significance to us (even as he 'reads' or contemplates) through the artist's indication of his two-fold nature. As in patristic commentary and after, the deer sees Christ or is Christ or both. From *Les hieroglyphiques de Ian-Pierre Valerian* (Lyons, 1615).

(hinds in Geneva, harts in Augustine) in Psalm 18 and Psalm 104 and the thirsting deer of Psalm 42 (Figure 3.2). Others who invite study inhabit Proverbs, the Song of Songs, and (more doubtfully) Psalm 22.

Wherever they live, deer have certain well-established habits that explain their usefulness to exegesis, art, and poetry. Even in the Reformation, when biblical commentary had for some time been sobering up after what now

Figure 3.2 David recites Psalm 42 as a deer enacts its part in the opening simile. From Geoffrey Whitney's *Choice of Emblemes* (1586)

seemed its allegorical excesses and was turning more and more to history and philology, the behavior of deer remained well understood.[28] Deer, as almost any reader of classical science, the Church Fathers, and bestiaries knew well, are thirsty by nature. Their thirst increases after contact with their mortal enemies, serpents, whom they force from their holes with saliva or warm breath and then snuffle up in their nostrils and swallow (either from hatred or as rejuvenating medicine) or trample under foot. Snake-killing can be dangerous and thirsty work; so, filled with venom, deer race to a spring or brook whose waters will refresh and renew them. Deer move quickly, leaping on the hills and rocky places. Although timid, they may be lured by music. Extremely long lived, they know that to eat dittany will make an arrow fall out. They cross a wide river by swimming in single file, each deer's head resting on the rump of the preceding one; when the leader is exhausted he retires to the rear of the line and the next one takes over. It was not Christian theologians who discovered that deer do these things, but they took advantage of the allegorical possibilities afforded by this particularly compelling chapter in the Book of Nature, and even some Reformation commentary perpetuated the old readings. Luther, for example, agreed that the beloved in the Song of Songs is like a deer because the Word of God leaps from city to city.[29]

Spenser would have come across this deer lore in any number of places, from Pliny to Valerianus, from Hugh of St. Victor to Conrad Gesner. For practical information on how to catch deer, one might consult Gascoigne's *Noble art of venerie*, which also suggests uses for left-over bits of animal; dried deer pizzle, for instance, when powdered and mixed with plantin water, is good for a bloody flux.[30] Furthermore, *The noble art* tells the proper time to hunt each sort of deer; as a hind, the lady of *Am.* 67 is indeed in season, at least if she is 'fatte or in good plight'. Harts are in season from Midsummer to Holy Cross (September 14), and hinds at all other times if they appear healthy (sig. P7v).

Of all biblical deer the one with the most obvious relevance to Spenser is that in Proverbs 5:18–19, although I have not seen the text cited in discussions of the poem: 'Let thy fountaine be blessed, and rejoyce with the wife of thy youth. Let her be as the loving hinde and pleasant roe: let her breasts satisfie thee at all times, and delite in her love continually.'[31] The Geneva editors say merely that this shows that 'God blesseth mariage and curseth whordome', but the loving hind has a richer heritage than this moralizing suggests, for the 'cervus amicitiae' of patristic commentary (the creature is a hind in the Vulgate, a hart in Augustine and other fathers) was above all a symbol of Christ or of Christian love and celestial contemplation. God tells us to carry each other's burdens (Galatians 6:2), says Augustine, and deer do just this when crossing a river, so perhaps Solomon was thinking of their habits when he wrote Proverbs 5:19 (*Patrologia Latina* [*PL*] 40.80–81). Ambrose calls the deer our lover, Christ (*PL* 14.849–850). The fountain, says Origen, is knowledge and the *cervus/wife* is good doctrine, for the deer signifies contemplation and a love of God that makes us not his servants but his friends. Yet, he says elsewhere, the 'cervus amicitiae' is also he who destroyed the serpent who seduced Eve, Christ (*Patrologia Graeca* [*PG*] 17.74, 13.171–77). Procopius calls the *cervus/wife* Wisdom, the ancient Word (*PG* 87¹.1266). After such symbolic wealth, it is disappointing to read in works like Thomas Wilcox's *A short yet sound commentarie; on the proverbes of Salomon* (1589) that 'these allegories, or metaphors' mean only that we should be loving to wives. Harts, he adds, are known for fondness towards their mates (Wilcox maneuvers the text to stress masculine sentiment, not the wife/hind's own friendliness). The older reading was by no means forgotten, though, and Valerianus cites Eucherius on the hart of friendship as Christ, master of all love and charity.³²

Still relevant to *Am.* 67 despite their gender are the loving roes and harts of the Song of Songs, symbols of the Bridegroom (e.g. 2:9: 'My welbeloved is like a roe, or a yong heart'). To marry a deer, as Marguerite's hunter will also do (after he has finished eating it), is to participate in the divine marriage that sanctifies human unions. Needless to say, this hart received much attention in the commentaries. Particularly interesting, because of its implications for *Amoretti*'s sonnets of waiting and separation, is the Geneva gloss to the last verse: 'flee away, and be like unto the roe, or to the yong heart upon the mountaines of spices'. The editors say the Church asks of Christ that if he leaves he will still be ready 'to help them in their troubles'.³³ The great answer to this prayer, of course, is Pentecost.

More of a puzzle, but clearly figuring in Marguerite's poem and, I think, in Spenser's, is Psalm 22, the psalm Christ quoted from the cross and which was assumed (with a little help from mistranslation) to foretell the crucifixion. It is said by David speaking for Christ, for as the Geneva headnote puts it, he was 'past all hope' but now 'recovereth him self from the bottomles pit of tentations and groweth in hope', just as Christ 'shulde marvelously, and strangely be dejected and abased, before his Father shulde raise and exalte him againe'. David says, 'dogges have compassed me' and laments that the wicked have pierced his hands and feet; the note adds, 'this was accomplished in Christ'.³⁴ The psalm, assigned in the Sarum Missal for Palm Sunday and in the Edward VI prayer-book for Good Friday, is certainly about a victim, but is it also about a deer? Little cervidological commentary mentions Psalm 22, but St. Jerome says clearly (*PL* 26.931) that this animal is the hart, slayer of serpents, destroyer of poison, and that 'nullum alium nisi Christum intelligimus'. Richard Sampson's *In priores quinquaginta Psalmos* (1539) says the same, adding that the dogs are bad clergymen. (As a one time close associate of Wolsey, Sampson probably knew what he was talking about, although his own shifts and turns during those difficult years show that he himself was more of a dog than a friendly deer.)

Sampson is led to identify the victim as a deer because he takes the title of the psalm as referring to a 'hind of the morning'. Some preferred 'De susceptione matutina', and Geneva likes 'To him that excelleth', although the margin adds, 'Or, the hinde of the morning'. Jerome says 'Pro cervo matutino', as does Bede; *PL* 26.931, 93.590.) Calvin is unhappy with the title and calls it 'darksome'; some have rejected any reference to a literal hind, he says, and because 'Chrystes Dignitye could not be avaunced royally inough, onlesse by an allegoricall sense, they transposed the name of hynde unto a sacryfise' (*Commentaries*, trans. A. Golding, 1571). The hind of the morning must be the name of the tune, he says, and twentieth-century scholars are inclined to agree. The fact remains that Spenser knew of an Eastertide psalm thought to concern the hunted Christ and often calling itself a poem about a hind. And, as Bishop Sampson says, 'Non absurde, cervo seu cervae, comparatur Christus', for as deer snuffle up serpents and kill them, so likewise Christ killed the serpent when he harrowed Hell and liberated our race 'ab illis carceribus', and all this by his own will (sigs. T2v–T7).

Commentators on deer, however, more often cite Ps. 42 and the thirsty hart. True, this creature, too, is probably a hind. Henry Ainsworth argues the point cogently in his *Annotations* (1617, 2nd. ed.) and gives his own less than elegant translation: 'As the hind, desirously-brayeth for the streams of waters: so my soule desirously-brayeth unto thee O God.' Hinds, he adds, are more passionate than harts. Earlier translators like Robert Crowley (1549) and Matthew Parker (1567) also knew the animal's likely gender, so Spenser may well have imagined a panting hind. In any case, this deer too was associated with Christ, although it more often represented apostles, saints, the faithful, and penitents.[35] To some commentators the deer is both ourselves and Christ, for Christ as man speaks and acts for us and as his followers we can become him. Like most early exegetes I have read, Augustine is content to equate the deer with the faithful and especially with penitents who have killed the serpents of vice and now run to the waters of baptism and the fountains of life. Let us love each other like deer, he urges, who bear one another's burdens (*PL* 36.464–67). John Chrysostom, whose writing may have influenced *The Faerie Queene*, goes further.[36] In an impassioned meditation of the sort that earned him his name, Chrysostom reverts over and over to this verse. The implied serpents are vices and we too should eat the 'intelligible serpent' so as to acquire a holy thirst. After all, we are contracted to God, promising to cherish him more than others and to burn with love. So when in the forum you see silver or golden clothes or other wealth, say to yourself, 'Just a little while ago I sang, "As the hart thirsts ..."' (*PG* 55.155 ff.). In other words, the verse is a mnemonic to recall a contract, an engagement; as in the Song of Songs and Proverbs 5:19 the deer is our partner in a love affair.

In his own fashion Luther continues this metaphoric pattern. Like Augustine and Jerome, he finds an etymological and mysterious connection between Psalm 42 and the Passion, for the title refers to the 'sons of Korah' and, since 'Korah' can be read as 'baldhead' it anticipates Christ's execution on Calvary, cognate with Latin *calvus*. The whole psalm, he says, is a 'sigh of human nature seeking to enter the church of God', but so long as we are outside the Church we cannot speak the word: 'Therefore this psalm is ascribed to Christ speaking for mankind', and refers to the exodus from Egypt to the Jordan, from Synagogue to Church, from sin to grace.[37] Calvin's reading leaves behind the ancient fascination with deer symbolism, but he too emphasizes David's longing for the temple. The argument has an odd relevance to *Am.* 67, for Calvin insists that this pastoral scene actually means we should hasten to church, where, indeed, Spenser's lover and lady are soon to be found, certainly in the next sonnet with its liturgical rhythms and eventually in the center of *Epithalamion*. *Am.* 67 is refreshingly rural in imagery, but its implications are not. The point, says Calvin, is to remind us that we are not to live in spiritual isolation, ignoring ceremonies and the congregation: 'For he biddeth us not clymb streight up into heaven, but favouring our weaknes, he commeth down neerer untoo us' (*Commentaries*, on what is here verse 2). To Calvin, the deer is David, not the saviour himself, but this argument, too, moves the discouraged human lover towards union with a beloved who comes voluntarily and whose love is not private and separate but sociable, joining the soul, in the words of *Am.* 70, to Love's 'lovely crew'.[38]

One commentary on the psalmist's panting hart seems particularly germane to Spenser: Victorinus Strigelius's often delightful *A proceeding in the harmonie of King Davids harpe*, which appeared in sections from 1582 to 1598 in the translation of R. Robinson. The discussion of Psalm 42 (1593) paraphrases the opening verse in words that strikingly anticipate Spenser's own: 'As the Hart in *chase* fleeth, and in *long pursute* made *wearie*, doth most greedily covet and *thirst* after the lively running springs', so I thirst not for puddles but for 'springs of livelie Water' (my italics). Standing water is mere philosophical consolation, the arguments of necessity and virtue; flowing water is curative evangelical comfort. This consolation is the forgiveness of sin through Christ, for 'The acknowledgement of Gods presence in calamaties, and the hope of the very last deliveraunce and of eternall salvation, doo call back languishing soules, as it were from the jawes of hel, and effectually heale the woundes of the hart'. Sometimes, he adds in commenting on the next verse, we suppose ourselves abandoned, but God 'Sheweth us a gentle and joyful countenance' through his doctrines and ceremonies, and 'by his Embassadors speaketh familiarly with us, calling and inviting us unto everlasting salvation'. Let us wait for him.

Strigelius gives his remarks a significant direction, from thirst for salvation and comfort, to deliverance from Hell, to the anxiety of desertion relieved by the loving 'embassy' of messengers. In other words, he applies the opening verses of Psalm 42 not only to the Passion but to Pentecost; and rightly so, for the psalm had long been sung on both Easter Saturday and Whitsun eve, and was so sung in England until Cranmer's reformation of the prayer-book confined its special use to the burial service. For the rest of this essay I will argue, although with some hesitation, that Spenser, too, relates his deer, and indeed this cluster of sonnets, to the liturgy, if for the most part less overtly than Marguerite had done when she created her own filiations between her chansons and the Roman rite.

This suggestion is not wholly new, but a link between *Am.* 67 and the church calendar has been only tentatively proposed and no one, so far as I know, has claimed a liturgical connection for *Am.* 69 or 70. Furthermore, Spenser's calendrical implications and hints have perhaps been investigated too exclusively in terms of the Elizabethan Book of Common Prayer. Spenser must have known the prayer-book more or less by heart. Yet even though it seems clear that *Amoretti* is associated somehow with the liturgy, the scriptural allusions that it shares with the Anglican prayer-book are fewer than one might expect. So it is not unreasonable to look as well at the Sarum Missal (readily available to Spenser) and to the first prayer-book of Edward VI. Spenser was no Catholic, and doubtless he agreed with his church's views on ceremonies and on the elements of rigidity, excess, and superstition in the older rite. Yet to a poet, to anyone sensitive to the resonance and energy released by texts structured into a soaring pattern of mutual references and buttressed with reiteration and typological gravity, Sarum's liturgical architecture might seem a good place to visit, even to a Protestant preferring to live in reformed simplicity.[39]

Certain sonnets in the sequence seem at least faintly to recall Sarum. *Am.* 61, correlated by some with Palm Sunday, celebrates the beloved as angel, saint, light, and flowers. As William Johnson says, after making what to my ear are some rather strained comparisons with the prayer-book's readings for that day, Palm Sunday was also called 'Flowering Sunday'.[40] Whatever actual church practice, the prayer-book has shed the old floral rites, but Spenser's 'bud of joy' and 'blossome of the morne' recall Sarum's blessing of the flowers and branches, when we are asked to remember the olive leaves of Noah's dove that first announced a world recovered and a journey over (this is suitable, for the forty-day rain and the ship's safe passage fit Sarum's Lenten/Paschal number symbolism and its interrelated recollections of journeys, wanderings, and escapes; not surprisingly, Spenser's own ship reaches safety and 'eternall blisse' two sonnets later). Like the Book of Common Prayer's epistle (Isaiah 7) and Gospel (Luke 1) for Lady Day, *Am.* 62 welcomes new life and new light, but the connections are tenuous. Sarum's fragments from Isaiah 45.8 offer a little more: 'aperiatur terra et germinet salvatorem'.

As these examples make all too obvious, however, attempts at such linkages oversimplify the liturgical context. The Sarum Missal, and even the Book of Common Prayer, is so rich in intratextuality that at the end of each day in the church calendar the reverberating complex of scriptural references merely rotates forward a notch in its emphasis. Anticipation and reiteration are central to the liturgy and to Spenser's sonnets as well. For this reason alone the hunt for direct correspondences may be hopeless. The storm-tossed ship of *Am.* 63 is found in Sarum's Maundy Thursday blessing of the oil as well as in Palm Sunday's celebration. The shiny lady of *Am.* 66 responds to the Passion Sunday prayer, 'Emitte lucem tuam' almost two weeks late, and on that same Sunday the dogs of Psalm 22 are already out, if briefly, looking for an animal like the deer of *Am.* 67. This is not to say that certain sonnets have no liturgical referents, only that the connections are more likely to be between two seasons or movements than between one sonnet and one day. From *Am.* 22 and Ash Wednesday, Spenser's sonnets and the prayer-book move through longing and hope, to a series of celebrations involving the beloved's amazing grace and gift of self, a victory, vernal renewal and concord, to a period of waiting. Yet these partial circles, these arcs of the fuller annual rotation which the prayer-book describes and to which *Amoretti* refers, are so complicated by little epicycles of imagery (light, binding, flowers, water, and the like), regressions, and foreshadowings, that while the larger similarities are easy to see, plausible specifics are hard to find, as much because of an excess of echoes as because of any dearth.

Sometimes the ground seems a little firmer, to be sure. Spenser's Lenten poem, *Am.* 22, recalls both the Book of Common Prayer and the older rite, as is fitting in a sonnet that naughtily mentions relics, an image, and saint worship. Like Sarum, the Book of Common Prayer's appointed readings have a less idolatrous version of Spenser's sacrificed heart and burnt offering (from Psalm 51), priests around an altar (from Joel 2:17), and averted wrath, although the hope to 'apease her ire' may be closer to the Sarum prayers' stress on propitiation and the assuaging of 'iracundae tuae'. Only in Sarum, however, is there a worshipper 'qui meditabitur ... die ac nocte' (from Psalm 1), whose thoughts attend 'day and night' like those of Spenser's lover.[41]

The liturgical connections tighten up somewhat for *Am.* 67, too, although ambiguities remain. William Johnson, who has thought hard about *Amoretti* and the prayer-book, says that 'There are no parallels between any of the propers for the day and what is contained in the poem. The closest scriptural reference appears in the familiar "Sicut cervus"', but he adds that the sonnet 'by a remarkable incorporation of liturgies ... represents the penitents who, during Lent, prepared themselves for acceptance into the body of the Church and who, on Easter eve, were finally baptised'. He cites Augustine on the early church custom according to which the catechumens went to the font singing Psalm 42.[42] This is helpful indeed (even when one remembers that a deer *hunt* goes better with Palm Sunday or Good Friday), but Easter eve's use of Psalm 42 was less remote from Spenser's day than Johnson suggests, for, as I have mentioned, the psalm figures prominently in the Sarum Missal for that day and for Pentecost eve. Nor, I think, is it quite right to say, 'As the Church accepts the readied Christians, so at this point the lady also quietly and tenderly accepts the now-prepared lover.' The panting deer in the liturgy is the accepted one, not the one who accepts, and, as I have said, in much still current deer symbolism the serpent-killing font-seeking hart of Psalm 42 is also Christ, sacrificed for us this season by his own will. The deer can be the accepted penitent or the yielding savior thirsty from slaying vices, or both, but I do not see how it can also be the welcoming Church under these liturgical and metaphoric circumstances. And Spenser here imagines, as does Marguerite in her own Easter-season deer poem, grace and victory coming to us *despite* our lack of deserving, our unpreparedness. For that reason, too, I doubt the lover is the catechumen thirsting for the font. He is just sitting there, tired from fruitless labor.

Spenser might have known one other ancient reason for associating Psalm 42 with Easter eve: according to the Catholic count, this is Psalm 41.[43] The number is wonderfully appropriate because as this ceremony is taking place the forty-day fast of Lent is ending, and the prayers and readings also recollect Noah's forty days of rain and the Israelites' forty years in the wilderness; hence the Good Friday prayer that God 'famem depellat peregrinantibus reditum, infirmantibus sanitatem, navigantibus portum salucis indulgeat'. And Spenser, the forty-year-old lover who has been living under a fantasized planet with (he says in *Am.* 60) a forty-year orbit, is through with his waiting as well, at least for a time, and he too can move on to Easter and the promised land.

The Easter poem, as I have shown, crowds in even more biblical fragments than have been hitherto identified. The relation of *Am.* 68 to the liturgy is, however, more complex than it first appears. The sonnet's rhythms have been rightly compared to those of the Anglican collects, but the 'on this day' formula is in fact very rare in the Elizabethan prayer-book, although found in the collect for Whitsun.[44] In this regard, Sarum's chief Easter prayer, ancestor of the Book of Common Prayer's Easter collect, is much closer to the syntactic pattern and content of *Am.* 68, as though Spenser had its shape and rhythm in the back of his mind: 'Deus qui hodierna die per unigenitum tuum aeternitatis nobis aditum devicta morte reserasti: vota nostra quae praeveniendo aspiras, etiam adjuvando prosequere.' Several prayers later we hear, 'Concede nobis famulis tuis ut in resurrectionis eius gaudiis semper vivamus.' Combining and condensing these two Easter prayers in effect gives us a structure and even a thought quite like Spenser's: 'Lord who on this day didst open for us the gate of eternity, having conquered death (an English equivalent to the Latin ablative absolute) ... grant that we (concede nobis) may live forever in the felicity of his Resurrection.' No prayer I can find in the Book of Common Prayer is as close to Spenser as this, further evidence that whatever his theology, he remained moved by the patterns and language of an older time.

Thus *Am.* 68's movement, much of its sentiment, and some of its wording recall the liturgy, especially Sarum. Curiously, however, not one of its scriptural phrases is from readings set for Easter Day in the Book of Common Prayer, although Psalm 16:10–11, which may have generated 'live forever in felicity', is appointed for Easter in the first Edward VI prayer-book (words from the same psalm, 'Caro mea requiescet in spe', end the Good Friday service in Sarum, an image of mortality resting in hope that adds resonance to *Epithalamion's* 'So let us rest, sweet love, in hope of this'). The biblical phrases Spenser incorporates certainly refer to Easter, but *liturgically* these are texts associated with the weeks that follow the Resurrection and culminate in Ascension Day. Acts 3:15 in all three prayer-books is set for some time during the week after Easter; 1 Corinthians 15:55 with God's (and our) victory is likewise post Easter. Most significantly, Psalm 68 ('captivitie captive') is appointed for Ascension; both Sarum and the first Edward VI prayer-book give Psalm 47 (God's joyful arising) and the central Ephesians 4:8 to Ascension. What is going on? Is Spenser directing our attention forward, anticipating the great feast day that completes Christ's earthly life? *Am.* 68 is obviously about the Resurrection, but like Marguerite's pelican poem, which in some ways it resembles in content and direction, it foreshadows through allusion the next great feast day in the calendar, day of victory and triumph.

In this regard, furthermore, Spenser's sequence of sonnets follows the movement of the church calendar, for in its secular fashion *Am.* 69 expresses this victorious mood. The vocabulary is drawn largely from Du Bellay and Desportes, but also relevant is Psalm 21, set for Ascension Day in the Book of Common Prayer: 'Thou hast given him his hearts desire, and hast not denied him the request of his lippes ... His glorie is great in thy salvation: dignitie and honour hast thou layed upon him.' (To be sure, Psalm 47, appointed in Sarum and Edward VI, also says that 'the shields of the worlde belong to God', a warning not to let victory lead to pride.) And the echoes of the church calendar may linger a while longer, since after the triumph of *Am.* 69 come the flowers and light of *Am.* 70, just as in the church year the next major feast is Whitsun, the day of hope and revival that through the coming of the Holy Spirit confirms and in some sense concludes the earthly events surrounding the redemption. Again, Spenser would have found a precedent in Marguerite's verse; as I have said, the stanzas with which she follows her Easter (and Ascension) poem have recollections of Isaiah, the Song of Songs, and other texts that welcome fertility, joy, and fellowship. The readings in the Protestant prayer-books have less on renewal and fertility than Sarum, which appoints Isaiah 4 ('the frute of the earth shalbe excellent and pleasant' and the chosen shall 'spring up like a bud'), but all three prayer-books require Psalm 104: 'thou renewest the face of the earth'. Sarum's processional, a version of 'Salva festa dies' echoed several times by Marguerite, exults in flowers, sun, clear sky, spring growth, and painted fields; compare Spenser's Spring, in whose coat 'are displayed / All sorts of flowers the which on earth do spring / In goodly colours gloriously arrayd' with Sarum's 'vernales opes': 'Mollia purpureum pingunt violaria campum / Prata virent herbis et micat herba comis.'[45]

Like the season that finds chief expression in Ascension Day and Whitsun, then, *Am.* 69 and 70 recollect, recapitulate, and complete the triumphs and renewals of Easter, but like the earlier sonnets that prepare for Christ's 'lesson' of love through erotic imagery, they disguise these aftershocks of the Resurrection in metaphor and internalize them in the lover's amatory experience. To point this out is not to suggest modifications of the symmetrical pattern most readers now find in the Amoretti or to claim that these two sonnets take place on Ascension and Whitsun the way *Am.* 22, for instance, 'happens' on Ash Wednesday; the two sonnets that follow *Am.* 67 and 68 do, however, enjoy both seasonal *and liturgical* relevance to their position in a sequence that makes clear if infrequent reference to the Christian year.

There is, moreover, one additional and important piece of evidence that ties *Amoretti* to the liturgy in a general way. So far as I am aware, no one has pointed out that the number of sonnets in Spenser's sequence is exactly the same as the number of Sundays and holy days for which communion collects and readings were assigned in the reformed prayer-book.[46] The Sundays and holy days from Advent through Trinity do not correlate by number with sonnets in Spenser's sequence for at least one obvious reason: some of the forty-seven sonnets from *Am.* 22 to *Am.* 68 must also 'count' as ordinary days to give us the central Lenten pattern. Nor does the sequence's implied narrative, such as it is, correspond with the church calendar, for the courtship takes more than one year and ends in a June wedding, although not in the sequence itself. The period of waiting at the end is not wholly unlike the end of the church calendar, however, and Spenser refers to the cold and dark; even his references to slander, common enough in love poetry, have a parallel in the readings for All Saints. Calendars as gifts to ladies, furthermore, were not unprecedented. Du Bellay's *Olive* has a Nativity poem near its start and a Good Friday poem near the end, associating the lady not only with Christ but specifically with his life in the liturgy.[47] And in 1593 Giles Fletcher had published fifty-two sonnets to 'Licia' that parallel the fifty-two 'weeks'; the sequence contains what one could call three hundred and sixty-six 'days' (1592 was a leap year and one sonnet has some extra lines to make the numbers work) together with a pattern of images that suggest increasingly warm and then once more cold weather and thus express not only the lover's frustration but the lady's solar radiance.[48] Perhaps it amused Spenser to do something similar for Elizabeth Boyle, although his own poetry has more religious and psychological significance than Fletcher's and more calendrical specificity than Du Bellay's. He had already made a calendar of months and was about to give her a calendar of a secular year in the long lines of *Epithalamion*. Why not press into her lily hands some happy leaves that form yet one more imitation of the yearly circle, a sort of engagement ring?

The prayer-book's eighty-nine sets of prayers and readings, however, take account of fifty-three Sundays, as is required by that minority of years with an extra Lord's Day. In most years, of course, there are fifty-two Sundays and thirty-six special communion days to remember, making eighty-eight; some of these will coincide, like Epiphany in 1594 and its first Sunday, or Lady Day and the Monday of Holy Week that year. Fifty-two Sundays would also be insufficient because Easter's mobility creates, so to speak, slightly different narratives during its nineteen-year cycle, if not in terms of plot then in terms of pacing; 1593/4 has a fairly early Easter, for example, so it skimps on Sundays after Epiphany and adds one at the end of Trinity to make fifty-two. Furthermore, the prayer-book's opening list of lessons for morning and evening prayer services comprises fifty-five possible Sundays and thirty-three holy days (Ash Wednesday and Holy Week's Monday and Tuesday are omitted) to give us, again, eighty-eight. The Elizabethan prayer-book, in other words, contains an opening list of eighty-eight days with lessons for Matins and Evensong and a long collection of eighty-nine days with assigned communion readings and collects. Neither sequence, especially the first, is entirely 'real'; for in order to provide for the calendar's annually varying stretches and shrinkages, each has too many Sundays for most years (including the liturgical year 1593/4). Of these two sets of readings, however, the communion collects and propers form the more important collection, not only because of the sacrament but also because they bulk so large in the prayer-book, taking up more than half of its pages.

The wavering between eighty-eight and eighty-nine communion services (eighty-nine for possible use, eighty-eight for actual if sometimes coinciding use in an average year) offers one additional explanation for Spenser's repetition of *Am.* 35 as *Am.* 83. The repetition, whatever its other purposes or its role in other numerical structures, converts a total whose number is associated with a 'real' liturgical year (1593/4) of fifty-two Sundays and sometimes coinciding holy days into one like that of the usually impossible but necessary calendar of days as given in the prayer-book. *Am.* 83 thus calls attention to the prayer-book's calendrical ambiguity, for both sequences appear at least to hover between two numbers, two totals, and if *Am.* 83

is not in fact quite the same poem as *Am.* 35 because a new context creates a new text, the same might be said of communion readings omitted during the Epiphany season and used at the end of the church year. *Am.* 83 thus signals the issue of number and order; specifically, and in conjunction with Spenser's explicit references to Ash Wednesday and Easter, it recalls through such signaling that there are eighty-eight actual communion services for Sundays and holy days that year (because in one sense there are only eighty-eight *Amoretti*) and simultaneously reminds us of the disparity between this pattern and one accommodated to the exigencies of mortal time (because there are also, after all, eighty-nine printed sonnets, just as there are eighty-nine sets of readings in the prayer-book). But what is Spenser's point? Together with any other functions it may have, the repetition parallels a liturgical wavering between numerical totals that is necessitated in part by a solar cycle containing one too many days for a stable number of Sundays from year to year and in part by Easter's link to a lunar cycle whose mutability is the human race's own ancient fault – the fault being, of course, the reason we have Easter. The reappearance of *Am.* 35, in at least this regard, is not unlike Spenser's numerical manipulations in *Epithalamion*: it reenacts the imperfections in our fallen world of time, imperfections for which sexual love and generation offer some healing consolation and from which divine love redeems us.[49]

Spenser's *Amoretti* are witty and urbane, often bantering, playful, and affectionate, never solemn minded. Yet there is no reason to deny Spenser religious depth and sexual insight as well as sophisticated charm, and recent critics are surely right to grant him all these. If I am correct in some of what I have written here, Spenser composed a sequence that at least on occasion alludes not only to the reformed prayer-book with its eighty-nine communion days but to the typologically richer Sarum Missal as well. These scriptural and liturgical allusions, overt in *Am.* 22 and hinted at elsewhere, intensify around *Am.* 68, whose explicitly religious exhortation is flanked by more veiled associations of sexual love with the acts and love of Christ. The deer in whose surrender some readers have recognized Christ's submission to death comes to *Amoretti* from the older liturgy, as well as from classical and Renaissance poetry, either as the animal given to dogs in Psalm 22, recited on Palm Sunday or later on Good Friday in memory of Jesus' returning to Jerusalem to be killed, or as the thirsty hart of Psalm 42, recited on Easter eve to symbolize a burning wish for regeneration – or as both, because the panting hart had long been taken for the savior as well as the saved and equated with other deer who, thanks to their allegorical situation in scripture or their well-known behavior in the wild, were also called Christ. Interestingly, some of these deer had recently become better known as females,

Figure 3.3 The loving hind of Proverbs 5.19, from the title page of Thomas Churchyard's *Discourse* (1578)

but nearly all, whatever their gender, served as symbols of a love at once spiritual and erotic and one, in Proverbs 5:19, is recommended by Solomon himself as a wife (Figure 3.3).

Finally, Spenser was not alone in writing of a deer who comes when not chased, and he may well have seen Marguerite de Navarre's similar pattern of paradoxical hunting, Easter victory, invitation to love or marriage, and post-paschal celebration of spring and conviviality. Perhaps Spenser 'borrowed' from Marguerite, as mathematical probability and the Pelican speaker would invite one to believe, but to call this 'intertextuality' would claim too much. Marguerite was still famous, but her verses were not well enough known to allow the dynamic relationship Spenser could establish with Petrarch, say, or with the Bible and the liturgy. Yet Marguerite's chansons make it even easier to hear the religious overtones of *Am.* 67–70 and to consider

Spenser's unusual treatment of the old belief, so often forgotten in all Christian centuries, including our own, but never quite dead, that sexual love can participate in and body forth divine love, that the love that moves the sun and the other stars can move us into each other's arms.

But why a captured deer and not some other pre-Easter symbol? To provide a pastoral moment, maybe, or to show up Petrarch, Tasso, and others. To sound again the theme, apparently of great emotional significance to Spenser, of binding and loosing, of constraint that is liberating because freely chosen.[50] Also, I think, to make a deeper acknowledgement than some readings of *Amoretti* allow: the understanding that human sexual love is like divine love also in its experience of pain and loss. Spenser's sonnet nowhere mentions the dismemberment Marguerite's deer must experience but the implications may be there, and feminine anxieties (whether widespread in real life is probably beside the point) about what follows even loving capture certainly receive ample and sympathetic exploration elsewhere in his poetry. By accepting the risk of suffering, either as physical intrusion and later parturition or, also scary, as the penetration of an emotional and psychological perimeter, and by taking on the inevitable and natural sense of some loss, the half-trembling deer assures for herself and for others – her lover, her family – a future triumph over doubt, bondage, and fear. It is hard to imagine what deeper or wiser compliment a poet could give a young woman.

Appendix

Amoretti

LXVII

Lyke as a huntsman, after weary chace,
   Seeing the game from him escapt away,
   Sits downe to rest him in some shady place,
   With panting hounds beguiled of their pray:
So, after long pursuit and vaine assay,
   When I all weary had the chace forsooke,
   The gentle deare returnd the selfe-same way,
   Thinking to quench her thirst at the next brooke.
There she, beholding me with mylder looke,
   Sought not to fly, but fearlesse still did bide:
   Till I in hand her yet halfe trembling tooke,
   And with her owne goodwill hir fyrmely tyde.
Strange thing, me seemd, to see a beast so wyld,
   So goodly wonne, with her owne will beguyld.

LXVIII

Most glorious Lord of lyfe, that on this day
   Didst make thy triumph over death and sin,
   And having harrowd hell, didst bring away
   Captivity thence captive, us to win:
This joyous day, deare Lord, with joy begin,
   And grant that we, for whom thou diddest dye,
   Being with thy deare blood clene washt from sin,
   May live for ever in felicity:
And that thy love we weighing worthily,
   May likewise love thee for the same againe;
   And for thy sake, that all lyke deare didst buy,
   With love may one another entertayne.
So let us love, deare love, lyke as we ought:
   Love is the lesson which the Lord us taught.

LXIX

The famous warriors of the anticke world
   Used trophees to erect in stately wize,
   In which they would the records have enrold
   Of theyr great deeds and valarous emprize.
What trophee then shall I most fit devize,
   In which I may record the memory
   Of my loves conquest, peerelesse beauties prise,
   Adorn'd with honour, love, and chastity?
Even this verse, vowd to eternity,
   Shall be thereof immortall moniment,
   And tell her prayse to all posterity,
   That may admire such worlds rare wonderment;
The happy purchase of my glorious spoile,
   Gotten at last with labour and long toyle.

LXX

Fresh Spring, the herald of loves mighty king,
   In whose cote-armour richly are displayd
   All sorts of flowers the which on earth do spring,
   In goodly colours gloriously arrayd,
Goe to my love, where she is carelesse layd,
   Yet in her winters bowre, not well awake;
   Tell her the joyous time wil not be staid,
   Unlesse she doe him by the forelock take:
Bid her therefore her selfe soone ready make,
   To wayt on Love amongst his lovely crew,
   Where every one that misseth then her make
   Shall be by him amearst with penance dew.

Make hast therefore, sweet love, whilcst it is prime;
For none can call againe the passed time.

Marguerite de Navarre

Chanson 7

Sur l'arbre de la Croix, d'une voix cíere et belle,
J'ay bien ouy chanter une chanson nouvelle.
L'oyscau qui la chantoit esmouvoit le courage
De tout vray Pèlerin, disant en doux langage:
5   Je suis le Pélican qui sante donne et vie
Pour faire vivre ceux que sauver j' ay envie.
La Mort qui eux et moy pcnsoit ses subjets rendre,
J'ay prise et mise à mort, me laissant d'elle prendre:
Mais estant en ses laz, n'a pas esté sy forte
10 Que n'en soye eschappé en rendant la Mort morte.
Par quoy sur mes enfans n'ha plus nulle puissance,
Qui par mort de vie ont parfaite jouyssance.
Où est ton aiguillon, ô Mort tant redoutée?
Ta puissance par moy de ta force est ostée.
15 Je suis la Vérité et la Vie et la Voye,
Mort n'a plus de povoir en quelque part que soye:
Les pécheurs seulement la trouveront cruelle,
Mais les miens l'aymeront, et la trouveront belle.
Par moy l'horrible Mort est belle devenue,
20 Et les portes d'Enfer n'ont contre moy tenue;
Car au mylieu d'Enfer me trouve le Fidèle,
Qui suys son Paradis et sa joye éternelle.
Mes enfans sont en moy sy très-unys par grâce,
Qu'Enfer, Péché, ny Mort, n'ha plus en eux de place.
25 Adam plein de péchés j'ay mis en croix austère,
Je l'ay crucifié en jouant son mystère;
J'ay prins ce vieil Adam et sa concupiscence,
Lequel j'ay mis a rien par Foy et congnoissance;
J'ay gousté le morceau de Mort en patience:
30 Nul ne le goustera qui ayt en moy fiance.
J'ay entré en Enfer, sentant ses douleurs fortes:
Pour en tirer les miens j'en ay rompu les portes;
Nully ne demourra plus en ces trois limites
Si bien se fie en moy, recevant mes mérites:
35 Mais s'il se veult fier en son labcur et peine,
Estimant mon tourment et ma passion vaine,
Il congnoistra qu'Enfer, Mort et Péché, et Vice
Vaincre ne pourra pas par sa propre justice:
De péchés se verra charge a sy grand somme

	Qu'à la fin pourra voir ce que peult sans moy l'Homme.
40	

Qu'à la fin pourra voir ce que peult sans moy l'Homme.
Mais l'Homme au cœur contrit, petit, humble et infime,
Qui ne sent rien de soy, et nul bien n'en estime,
Qui tout en ma bonté se confie et s'arreste,
A luy tousjours ma main de secourir est preste;
Je le mets en Enfer, lui monstrant son ordure,
Et qu'il a mérité par Péché mort très dure;
Je le metz tout à rien, luy monstrant que son Estre
Et sa Vie je suis, son seigneur et son maistre.
Mais quand le Très-petit du tout Rien se confesse,
Je le retire à moy, luy monstrant ma promesse
De ma chair, de mon sang, luy fais présent encore,
En moy le réunis, l'embrasse et l'incorpore:
Luy transformé en moy hors son péché immunde,
Rien que grâce ne voit, qui en son lieu abonde.
En moy il voit la Mort sy très-bien acoustrée
Qu'il la désire voir comme de Vie entrée,
Par moy de son Enfer voit les portes brisées,
Là congnoit Paradis et les Joyes prisées;
Povreté, Faim et soif, travail, peine et tristesse,
Trouve, vivant en moy, tout repos et liesse.
Or venez donc, Pécheurs, escouter ma doctrine:
Apprenez ma chanson pleine de discipline.
Je suis monté en hault afin que chascun m'oye,
Et qu'escoutant mon chant soyez remplis de joye.
Par Charité j'ay soif du salut de toute âme,
Pour la faire brusler de l'amoureuse flamme.
Las, donnez moy de l'eau de vraye amour à boire
Au vaisseau de voz cœurs par fermement me croire.
De n'avoir fait nul bien, ne craignez ce langage,
Car tout est consommé; j'ay gaigné l'héritage;
J'ay accomply la Loy, j'ay gaigné la partie:
Tout est pour vous, Pécheurs, pour lesquelz Eli crie;
A vous tous ignorans pardonner vostre offence;
J'ay pour vous délaissé ma vie à mort amère,
Et en très-grand douleur ma très aymée Mère,
Pour vous monstrer que chair, tant soit elle estimée.
Puys j'ay recommandé entre les mains du Père
Mon esprit, pour monstrer qu'en luy fault qu'on espère.
Or ay-je le salut de chacun fait sy ample,
Et pour y parvenir me suis mis pour exemple.
Venez, venez, trestous chargez outre mesure
De labeurs et travaux; voyez ma peine dure,
Voyez ma croix, mes clous, mes douleurs non petites,
Mon cœur d'amour ouvert et trestous mes mérites.

85   Tous ces biens sont à vous; par grâce je les donne
       A qui par ferme Foy tout à moy s'abandonne.
       Venez, embrassez moy, mon troupeau, mon Eglise,
       Mes Esluz humbles et doux, desquelz fais à ma guise,
       Car vous, uniz en moy, estes la mesme chouse;
90   Je seray vostre Espoux, vous tous un, mon Espouse:
       Venez au vray repos où sera endormie
       Entre mes bras toujours mon Espouse et amye.

Chanson 8

Voicy nouvelle joye.
La nuict pleine d'obseurité
Est passée; et voicy le jour
Auquel marchons en seureté,
Chassans toute peur par amour,
   Sans que nul se desvoye:
   Voicy nouvelle joye.

  L'hyver plein de froid et de pleurs
  Est passé, tremblant et glacé;
L'esté plein de verdure et fleurs
Nous vient plus beau que l'an passé;
   Or chacun le voye:
   Voicy nouvelle joye.

L'arbre sec et facheux à voir,
Raboteux et dur à toucher,
Que nul ne désiroit avoir,
Maintenant povons le toucher:
   Il fleurit et verdoye;
   Voicy nouvelle joye.

Le rossignol qui s'est fâché
Pour la rigueur de l'hyver froid,
Maintenant il n'est plus caché,
Mais sur la branche se tient droit;
   Il gergonne et verboye:
   Voicy nouvelle joye.

Le Fidèle dedens la Loy
Tout caché, tremblant et peureux,
Par la lumière de la Foy
Voit cler, et devient amoureux
   De Dieu, qui le convoye:
   Voicy nouvelle joye.

> Il se congnoit tout délivré
> De péché et damnacion;
> Il se sent de Joye enyvré
> Par la divine Election
>   Qui tout bien luy ottroye:
>   Voicy nouvelle joye.
>
> L'arbre de Croix, de peine et mort,
> Que tant avoit eu en horreur,
> Maintenant c'est le reconfort
> Où il a attaché son cœur
>   Afin qu'il ne desvoye:
>   Voicy nouvelle joye.
>
> Luy qui craingnoit les gens hanter
> Et cachoit par crainte sa voix,
> Maintenant ne fait que chanter
> Dessus l'espine de la Croix;
>   Il fault que l'on le croye:
>   Voicy nouvelle joye.
>
> Il est dehors d'yver et nuict,
> Il n'est plus sec, mais florissant;
> Mort et Péché plus ne luy nuist;
> Il est content dans le Puissant,
>   Vérité, Vie, et Voye:
>   Voicy nouvelle joye.

Acknowledgement

I would like to thank A. Kent Hieatt for reminding me of several deer I had forgotten, Edmée de M. Schless for advice on French hunting terminology, Edward W. Tayler for thoughts on the significance of *'tempestiva'*, and my research assistant Anne Himmelfarb for more help with German than I enjoy admitting.

Notes

1 Petrarch, ed. Alessandro Vellutello (Venice, 1568), sig. P7, and G. A. Gesualdo (Venice, 1581). sig. Dd2, which has more deer lore. On the significance of this commentary to Wyatt and the problematic relationship between 'Una candida cerva' and 'Who so list to hunt', see Alastair Fowler, *Conceitful Thought* (Edinburgh: Edinburgh University Press, 1975), 2–6. See also Jon A. Quitslund, 'Spenser's *Amoretti* VIII and Platonic Commentaries on Petrarch', *Journal of the Warburg and Courtauld Institutes* 36 (1973): 256–76.

2 Torquato Tasso, *Opere*, ed. Bruno Maier (Milan: Rizzoli Editore, 1963), I.453. On *Amoretti*'s sources, see the Variorum edition of Spenser's *Works*, ed. Edwin Greenlaw et al., VIII, *The Minor Poems*, Part II, ed. C. G. Osgood and H. G. Lotspeich (Baltimore, Md.: Johns Hopkins University Press, 1947); Janet C. Scott, 'Sources of Spenser's *Amoretti*', *Modern Language Review* 22 (1927): 189–195; Veselin Kostic, *Spenser's Sources in Italian Poetry: A Study in Comparative literature*, Filoloski Fakultet Beogradskog Univerziteta Monografije: XXX (Belgrade: Novi, 1969), especially 54–56. R. W. Dasenbrock, 'The Petrarchan Context of Spenser's *Amoretti*', *PMLA* 100 (1985): 38–50, says Tasso 'describes the capture' of the deer, but the poem makes no explicit reference to capture, only to descent and new friendliness.

3 Edwin Casady, 'The Neo-Platonic Ladder in Spenser's *Amoretti*', *Philological Quarterly* 20 (1941): 284–95, insists that the 'mylder looke' is the lover's, which makes sense too. Each syntactic possibility supports an equally plausible understanding of what is going on: the lover is less aggressive and the deer more willing. Perhaps the ambiguity is intentional.

4 The wild animal is now tame, and this in some circumstances could imply loss of sexual integrity. Furthermore, a mountain-going animal on the high trails has specific biblical parallels. Thorny paths on rocky hills are fit for deer and for the 'hinds feet' God gives David. See Ps. 18 and 104 and Hab. 3:19: 'he wil make my fete like hindes fete, and he wil make me to walke upon mine hie places' (Geneva translation). To many authorities the high-stepping hinds meant, as Augustine said in his commentaries on the psalms, that God perfected his love so he might rise above the dark and thorny snares of the world (*Patrologia Latina* 36.152). Peter Lombard, and he was not alone, compares such deer to Christ: like them, Christ steps atop the thorns and entanglements (*foveas*) of sin. See Jean Bayet, 'Le symbolisme du cerf et du centaure', *Revue archeologique* 44 (1954): 21–68, a mine of information about deer in patristic tradition. Whatever Tasso's intended implications, it was possible for Spenser to see a noble animal's abandonment of the thorny hills as a descent in more ways than one.

5 On deer and hunting poems, see especially D. C. Allen, *Image and Meaning* (Baltimore, Md.: Johns Hopkins University Press, 1968), 165–86; M. J. B. Allen, 'The Chase: the Development of a Renaissance Theme', *Comparative Literature* 20 (1968): 301–12; Claus Uhlig, '"The Sobbing Deer"', *Renaissance Drama* n.s. 3 (1970): 109; Marcelle Thiébaux, *The Stag of Love: The Chase in Medieval Literature* (Ithaca, N.Y.: Cornell University Press, 1974). Less central but useful are Edward S. Le Comte, 'Marvell's "The Nymph Complaining ..."', *Modern Philology* 50 (1952): 97–101; Nicholas Guild, 'Marvell's "The Nymph Complaining ..."', *Modern Language Quarterly* 29 (1968): 385–94; Earl Miner, *The Metaphysical Mode from Donne to Cowley* (Princeton, N.J.: Princeton University Press, 1969), 258–66 (Miner says [259], 'nowhere that I know of in seventeenth-century writing will one find Christ represented by a female type'; I am not sure what 'type' means here, but I have found earlier female *deer* representing Christ).

6 *Odes* I.23. Translation by Lydia Kirsopp Lake, Still Waters Arts & Services.

7 Thiébaux's *The Stag of Love*, opening chapter is particularly helpful on deer and transition. One might add that legends of ghostly riders condemned to perpetual hunt demonstrate a negative version of this topos; neither capturing the deer nor letting it escape, the hunter is caught in an infernal and compulsive repetition.
8 Guild and Miner both mention the dead deers' implications for empire and change.
9 See Thiébaux, *The Stag of Love*; Michael Bath, 'The Legend of Caesar's Deer', *Medievalia et Humanistica* n.s. 9 (1979): 53–66; and Rachel Bromwich, 'Celtic Dynastic Themes and the Breton Lays', *Etudes celtiques* 9 (1961): 439–74.
10 Giordano Bruno's theory, outlined by C. C. Gannon, 'Lyly's *Endimion*: From Myth to Allegory', *English Literary Renaissance* 6 (1976): 220–43.
11 Lars-Håken Svensson discusses Acteon in Renaissance poetry in *Silent Art: Rhetorical and Thematic Patterns in Samuel Daniel's 'Delia'*, Lund Studies in English, 57 (Lund: CWK Gleerup, 1980). Like Scudamor, Sir Arthur Gorges is a deer: 'Yow are the brooke, and I the Deare Imboste [i.e. foaming at the mouth with exhaustion]', in *Poems*, ed. Helen E. Sandison (Oxford, 1953), 66.
12 *The Phoenix Nest* (1593), ed. Hyder E. Rollins (Cambridge, Mass.: Harvard University Press, 1931), 67. For wordplay in *Amoretti* see William C. Johnson, 'Spenser and the Fine Craft of Punning', *Neuphilologische Mitteilungen* 77 (1976): 376–86.
13 Thiébaux, *The Stag of Love*, 230; 'Gascoignes Woodmanship', in *Works*, ed. J. W. Cunliffe, 2 vols. (Cambridge: Cambridge University Press, 1907), I, 348–52. Gascoigne is also the probable author of *The noble art of venerie* (1575), once assigned to George Turberville.
14 *Chansons spirituelles*, ed. Georges Dottin (Geneva: Droz, 1971), 17–20; the *Chansons* were first published in 1547 as a subsection of the punningly titled *Marguerites de la Marguerite des princesses*. Dottin's notes identify many of Marguerite's biblical and liturgical references. The translation is mine.

> A young hunter asked a happy and wise woman if the chase he was looking for could be found in that forest, and he said he had plenty of heart to win this venison by grief [or, we might say, by taking pains], merit, and reason. She said to him, 'My lord, it is indeed the season to take it, but you are a bad hunter.
>
> 'It is not to be taken by the chase [by 'coursing'], nor by the will of a worldly man, nor through its pain nor through its dying; and so one must base salvation only on the Creator: virtue is worth little if there is no power or strength abounding in the spirit. Alas, you would possess this if you had David's sling – but you are a bad hunter.
>
> 'What you seek is in the woods, where no faithless person goes: this is the bitter wood [literally, 'bush'] of the Cross, cruel to the wicked. Good hunters find it lovely, and its pains are their pleasure. Now if you wished to forget everything for this honor you would not want to choose any other good – but you are a bad hunter.'

When the hunter heard her he screwed up his face as if angry and said, 'You speak with great ignorance: I must turn and rouse the deer [make it dash from its hiding place so the dogs will run after it] and must chase it; yet you expressly tell me it cannot be caught by my effort'. 'My lord, the deer is close to you – but you are a bad hunter.

'If you would please to sit and place yourself on the edge of a spring, and rest your body and spirit, drinking the health-giving and living waters, indeed without your taking other pains the deer would come straight to you, and to take it would require only the net of your humble heart, in which it is caught by Love – but you are a bad hunter.'

'My lady, I do not believe one wins either goods or glory or gets anywhere without work or with only loving and believing. I don't want to drink the living waters – for working, wine is better.' The lady said, 'You will be lord and owner of Earth and Heaven if Faith opens your eyes – but you are a bad hunter.

'The deer is so human/humane and gentle that if you wish to tender your heart [a possible pun: in French one can 'tendre' a rope or snare] it will come to you through love. In taking you it will let itself be taken; and then it will be able to teach you to eat its flesh and blood by rank at this curry [i.e. at the ceremony in which the entrails of the deer are given to the dogs on the deerskin; in the allegory we are the dogs]. To be filled with sweetness your wishes will aim at this goal – but you are a bad hunter.

'Into this delicate flesh your own will be transformed: Oh happy he who can handle this great unhorned head, this sought-after and harried flesh, done to death, roasted for us, hung on the cross by three nails! Alas, it is yours, oh sinner, if you believe the holy words – but you are a bad hunter.'

The hunter understood the scale [the musical notes] and discovered the idea [the 'posie'] and suddenly said to her 'My lady, I give up my fantasy; my soul is seized by Faith, which makes me break trumpet and horn, abandon collars [i.e. dog collars, but also the chains and necklaces of rank and chivalric honour], couples [braces or ties connecting a pair of dogs together], and leashes. Believing the voice of my Savior, I will chase no other deer, so as no longer to be a bad hunter.

'Emperors, kings, princes, lords, I address my speech to you all; you whips, huntsmen, masters – renounce the labor and anxiety which instead of pleasure most often bring you sorrow. Alas, your pleasure is but wind; leave off, like me, this wretchedness. I am not now what I was, so that I might be no longer a bad hunter.

'Come hunters – come, come [a play on 'venir' and 'venerie'] to the holy deer-feast; learn to leave this world, which is so ephemeral; for the measureless Charity of his All gives you the gift whereby (your) Nothingness is made pleasing, filled with divine liquor. I now give myself over, so as to be no longer a bad hunter.'

15 Harvey mentions the *Heptamtéron* on fol. 47 of L. Domenichi's *Facetie*, now in the Folger Library. On Marguerite and England, see my 'Pearl of the Valois', in *Silent but for the Word*, ed. Margaret P. Hannay (Kent, Ohio: Kent State University Press, 1985).

16 In *The Arte of English Poesie* (1589), *Elizabethan Critical Essays*, ed. G. Gregory, Smith, 2 vols. (Oxford: Clarendon Press, 1904), II, 23.

17 Dottin gives some of Marguerite's originals; as he says (ix–xvii), there was then a fashion for pious parodies. For another laundered hunting poem, one which makes Christ the hunter, see John Wedderburn's *Gude and Godlie Balates*, quoted in J. M. Gibbon, *Melody and the Lyric from Chaucer to the Cavaliers* (1930; rpt. New York: Haskell, 1964), 38: 'With hunt is up, / With hunt is up, / It is now perfect day. / Jesus our King, / Is gone hunting – / Who likes to speed, they may.' This is a born-again version of Gray of Reading's popular ballad about a friend of Marguerite: 'The hunt is up, the hunt is up, / And it is well nigh day; / And Harry our King is gone hunting, / To bring his deer to bay.' Dottin prints thirty-two poems as Marguerite's grouping of spiritual songs, relegating one on the death of François I to an appendix because of its typographical surroundings. I have looked at the Lyons 1547 edition and despite the bar and 'fin' I would still include it; the matter is ambiguous.

18 Marguerite, chansons 3, 24, 17, and 21.

19 *Ibid.*, ch.16, 23 (a fairly dramatic dialogue with the soul tempted by the diabolical Orgueil and 'gens de là bas').

20 Spenser, VIII. 33. Marot wrote a less erotic and more anti-Jewish Easter pelican poem, Ballade XIII (1532). On the pelican, see L. Charbonneau-Lassay, *Le bestiaire du Christ* (Paris: Desclée de Brouwer, 1940), 558–68.

21 On Spenser and the calendar (the theory at its most basic is that *Am.* 22 falls on Ash Wednesday, Febrruary 13, 1594, and *Am.* 68 on Easter, March 31, the right number of fast days and Sundays later; *Am.* 62 falls, correctly, on the old new year, March 25), see Alexander Dunlop, 'The Unity of Spenser's *Amoretti*', in *Silent Poetry*, ed. Alastair Fowler (London: Routledge & Kegan Paul, 1970), 153–69. O. B. Hardison, Jr., '*Amoretti* and the Dolce Stil Novo', *English Literary Renaissance* 2 (1972): 208–16, wittily calls the resulting pattern a 'triptych'. More specifically on the liturgy is William C. Johnson, 'Spenser's *Amoretti* and the Art of the Liturgy', *Studies in English Literature, 1500–1900* 14 (1974): 47–61 and his '"Sacred Rites" and Prayer-Book Echoes in Spenser's "Epithalamion"', *Renaissance and Reformation* 12 (1976): 49–54. For some objections, see G. K. Hunter, 'Unity and Numbers in Spenser's *Amoretti*', *Yearbook of English Studies* 5 (1975): 39–45. Carol Kaske's vigorous 'Spenser's *Amoretti and Epithalamion* of 1595: Structure, Genre, and Numerology', *English Literary Renaissance* 8 (1978): 271–95, has not dissuaded me from seeing a calendar in *Amoretti*. Her skepticism is sobering, but when she says *Am.* 22 refers to a season and not a day she ignores 1.3 and I am puzzled by the fuss over *Am.* 60's reference to a year spent loving; no law requires the duration of love to correspond to the real or fictional time it took to write the love poems or to that of a calendrical sequence to which the poems might refer. For a calendrical

reading that groups Lenten Sundays together, see A. K. Hieatt, 'A Numerical Key for Spenser's *Amoretti* and Guyon in the House of Mammon', *Yearbook of English Studies* 3 (1973): 14–27. James Neil Brown, 'Lyke Phoebe: Lunar, Numerical, and Calendrical Patterns in Spenser's *Amoretti*', *Gypsy Scholar* 1 (1973): 5–15, finds a lunar calendar and references to Elizabeth; the theory is clever but relies too much, I think, on considerations of tone and seems to me overingenious. I will give my own calendrical suggestions later in this essay. Charlotte Thompson's dense and suggestive article, 'Love in an Orderly Universe: A Unification of Spenser's *Amoretti*, "Ancreontics", and *Epithalamion*', *Viator* 16 (1985): 277–335, appeared too recently for me to use. Her conclusions complement my own.

22 The Variorum Spenser and Scott mention many but not all of the biblical phrases I cite. I quote the Geneva translation of 1560 (and at Carol Kaske's suggestion I have checked the marginalia against a later revised edition) unless I am citing the biblical passages in an English-language prayer-book.

23 Spenser, however, would also have known Du Bellay's *Olive* 34 (closer to *Am.* 69 than is Desportes's *Cléonice* 11) and Gorges' translation in *Works*, 67–68.

24 Alexander Dunlop, 'The Drama of *Amoretti*', *Spenser Studies* 1 (1980): 107–20, sees *Am.* 69 as evidence that the lover's 'education is clearly not yet complete'.

25 This insistence that the lover earns the lady, *learning* something, is widespread (Spenserians are usually also teachers), even among scholars who recognize that for Protestants there is no justification by works. Thus Don Ricks, 'Persona and Process in Spenser's "Amoretti"', *Ariel* 3 (1972): 5–15, says that the lady waits for her suitor 'to become worthy' and that he 'finally becomes acceptable'. Dunlop, 'Drama', rightly says *Am.* 67 and 68 show that 'True love is ... ultimately a gift of grace', but in the next sentence he says the 'bond of love' depends on 'the proven worth of the lover'. A. Leigh DeNeef, in a fascinating chapter on *Amoretti* in *Spenser and the Motives of Metaphor* (Durham, N.C.: Duke University Press, 1982), sees that *Am.* 67's deer 'reenacts Christ's sacrificial act', but he too finds the lover 'reformed' (71). Robert S. Miola, in his 'Spenser's Anacreontic', *Studies in Philology* 77 (1980): 50–66, recognizes the poetry's religious significance yet refers to the lover's 'well-deserved bliss'. In some sense all this is true, for like Marguerite's hunter, the lover, by giving up his struggle, makes room for the grace that gives him imputed merit. But he is 'reformed' and 'worthy' only in a negative and possibly unknowing way. Spenser's whole point, it seems to me, is that mercy is above the scept'red sway of education and earning power. For a recent study of Spenser's views on faith and works, see Anthea Hume, *Edmund Spenser: Protestant Poet* (Cambridge: Cambridge University Press, 1984). Arthur F. Marotti's '"Love is not Love": Elizabethan Sonnet Sequences and the Social Order', *English Literary History* 49 (1982): 396–428, says love offered Spenser a realm in which merit, not birth, is rewarded, a provocative argument that also raises this troubling issue.

26 Johnson, 'Liturgy', 57.

27 On the deer's association with Christ see DeNeef, 67; Robert Kellogg, 'Thought's Astonishment and the Dark Conceits of Spenser's *Amoretti*', in *The Prince of*

Poets: Essays on Edmund Spenser, ed. J. R. Elliott (New York: New York University Press, 1968), 139–51 ('the ancient religious and erotic conceit of the beloved as a tame deer' [in fact, such deer are seldom tame]); and especially John D. Bernard's excellent 'Spenserian Pastoral and the *Amoretti*', *English Literary History* 47 (1980): 419–32. No one, I think, discusses both the deer's Christlike surrender *and* the scriptural/liturgical deer. Robert G. Benson, 'Elizabeth as Beatrice: A Reading of Spenser's "Amoretti"', *South Central Bulletin* 32 (1972): 184–88 discusses the Easter paradox of surrender and triumph, a related topic. Elizabeth Bieman, in '"Sometimes I ... mask in myrth lyke to a Comedy": Spenser's *Amoretti*', *Spenser Studies* 4 (1984): 131–41, mentions Ps. 42 and the habits of deer as snake-eaters. I heartily agree that Spenser is witty and that the deer in *Am.* 67 is 'earthly' as well as spiritual (that, after all, is the point of the Incarnation as well as of Spenserian love poetry); that *Am.* 67 has a 'Good Friday location in the sequence' (139) is less certain if we count by sonnets from Lady Day to Easter (or by Sundays, like A. K. Hieatt).

28 On deer see Thiébaux, *The Stag of Love*, Bayet, 'Le symbolisme du cerf', Charbonneau-Lassay, *Le bestiaire du Christ*, and Henri-Charles Puech, 'Le cerf et le serpent', *Cahiers archeologiques* 4 (1949): 17–60, which quotes many authorities. For some more eucharistic deer, see Louis Poinssot and Raymond Lantier, 'Trois objets chrétiens du Musée de Bardo', *Revue archéologique* 5th ser. 28 (1928): 66–89. Herbert Kolb, 'Der Hirsch, der Schlangen frisst', in *Medievalia Litteraria, a festschrift for Helmut de Boor* (Munich: C. H. Beck, 1971), 583–610, shows how the application of allegorized natural history diminished in the late Middle Ages, sometimes further eroded by scientific doubts about deer lore. As Kolb says, however, the symbolic reading of the deer by no means disappeared. I mention here the most famous deer, but there are others, e.g., Ps. 29, Prov. 6:5, Isaiah 13:14, 35:6, Job 39:4 and Lam. 1:6.

29 Martin Luther, *Works*, ed. Hilton C. Oswald (St. Louis, Mo.: Concordia Publishing House, 1974), XV, 217–18, commenting on S. of S. 2:9.

30 Sigs. C4 ff. Edward Topsell's *History of Four-footed Beasts* (1652), an adaptation of Gesner (1551), cites Pliny saying that 'the teeth of a Dragon tyed to the sinews of a Hart in a Roes skin, and wore [sic] about ones neck, maketh a man to be gracious to his Superiors' (92).

31 Breasts may satisfy biblical husbands in Prov. 5:19 and inspire lovers (see *Am.* 76–77), but they can worry readers. To Peter M. Cummings, in 'Spenser's *Amoretti* as an Allegory of Love', *Texas Studies in Literature and Language* 12 (1970): 163–79, Spenser's delight in them 'threatens to warp the poet's view of the lady in favor of fleshly rather than spiritual qualities', and Marotti, '"Love is not Love",' calls such feelings 'an oral longing that has become a predatory greed' (415). Spenser's thoughts may press beyond what he himself quite approves, but passages like Prov. 5:19 would give him some excuse – if any were needed.

32 Valerianus (G. P. V. Dolzani), *Hieroglyphica* VII, 16. I have used the French translation of Jean de Montylard in the Garland series, *The Renaissance and the Gods*, ed. Stephen Orgel. For Eucherius see *PL* 50.795. Wilcox, *Commentarie*, says 'thy youth' can also refer to a young wife.

33 DeNeef, *Spenser and the Motives of Metaphor*, 74, compares the separation in *Amoretti* to that in Song. Kaske, *Spenser and Biblical Poetics*, 273–80, points out the resemblance to several betrothals in *FQ*, and Dunlop, 'Drama', 114, associates it with the period after Ascension. I would say after Pentecost, for complaints that one cannot physically see the beloved, the 'comfort' (*Am.* 89), are accompanied by awareness of her image within (*Am.* 88). Carol T. Neely, 'The Structure of English Renaissance Sonnet Sequences', *English Literary History* 45 (1978): 359–89, discusses inconclusive endings. Geoffrey Hartman's '"The Nymph Complaining for the Death of Her Fawn": A Brief Allegory', *Essays in Criticism* 18 (1968): 113–35, connects the hunting theme to the role of the Comforter during Christ's absence: 'The end may be near, yet there remains a space of time not redeemed by the divine presence. One can hardly blame the expectant soul for showing impatience' (V, 122).

34 Commentators had long equated the dogs with persecuting Jews, but services ordered by the Elizabethan government in times of trouble sometimes use this psalm with the clear implication that its dogs and lions are foreigners, Turks, and Catholics. William K. Clay prints these services in *Liturgies and Occasional Forms of Prayer set forth in the Reign of Queen Elizabeth* (Cambridge, 1847: Parker Society 27).

35 One reason any given deer could symbolize both parties in a relationship was the tendency of commentators, as I have mentioned, to cite other deer as well and merge their identities. For example, deer huddle together in Origen, *PG* 13. 171–77, Ambrose, *PL* 14. 849–54 (who mentions new year games with deer), and Raban Maur, *PL* 111. 204–05.

36 Harold Weatherby, '"Pourd out in Loosnesse"', *Spenser Studies* 3 (1982): 73–85 argues for Chrysostom's influence on *FQ* I.

37 Luther, *Works* X, 194, 197.

38 In this regard, Calvin might applaud William Johnson's observation in 'Amor and Spenser's *Amoretti*', *English Studies* 54 (1973): 217–26 that Spenser's sequence is Christian and not Neoplatonic, although Johnson, I think, Platonizes medieval mysticism too much. I do not mean to deny the pastoral element here, only to add a complexity to those discussed by John Bernard.

39 For the Sarum Missal I have used J. W. Legg's edition (Oxford, 1916, rpt. 1969), based on medieval MSS, and the less convenient *Missale ad usum ... Sarum* ed. F. H. Dickinson (Oxford: Clarendon Press, 1861–63), based on later texts. Sarum was not the only use, of course, but it was by far the best known. 'Sarum' is Salisbury, whose cathedral was rumored to have a numerological architecture surprisingly relevant to Spenser; see my 'Licia's Temple: Giles Fletcher the Elder and Number Symbolism', *Renaissance and Reformation* 2 (1978): 170–81. For the first prayer-book of Edward VI, I have used the Everyman edition (London, 1910) and for the Elizabethan prayer-book Clay, *Liturgies and Occasional Forms of Prayer* and *The Book of Common Prayer*, ed. John E. Booty (Folger Library, University Press of Virginia, Charlottesville, 1976). Harold Weatherby, in a paper read at Kalamazoo in 1984, has suggested a link between Sarum's baptism rite (found in the materials for Easter eve) and *FQ* I. I agree that *Amoretti* has a

liturgical aspect, but like most others I doubt Spenser relates each sonnet to a specific day. A little experiment will show that too often the same sonnet seems to work well with different sets of readings, thus making any one correlation less convincing. By counting backward from Ash Wednesday, Johnson puts *Am.* 1 on January 23, citing readings for that day that mention food, eyes, hands, handling, and leaves (see his '"Sacred Rites"'). True enough, although at some expense to context, but suppose *Am.* 1 represented St. Andrew's day, at the start of the liturgical year: *its* readings have eyes, food, leaves, and the laying on of hands, not to mention angels, stars, 'might', captivity, and singing to one's beloved. Johnson also says that *Am.* 3 echoes the readings for St. Paul's day, and indeed it does, but if one wanted Spenser to have begun the sequence at Christmas so as to end when both his lover and the faithful are waiting, *Am.* 3 would then seem to recall the St. John's day collect ('Cast thy bright beams of light') and the readings: 'God is light', and we grope blinded in darkness; like Spenser, the speaker in Rev. 1 is 'ravished', at least in the Geneva translation. Furthermore, Johnson bases some of his argument on psalms he says are set specifically for the Sundays he examines; but in addition to the monthly progress through the psalter, the Elizabethan prayer-book has proper psalms only for Christmas, Easter, Ascension, and Whitsun. The psalms he cites are, however, in the first Edward VI prayer-book as propers for those days. Professor Johnson, who read this essay with generosity and attention, told me he is working to resolve some of these difficulties in a book on *Amoretti*.

40 Johnson, 'Liturgy', 55.
41 Ps. 51 in the Elizabethan prayer-book is found in the 'Commination against sinners' traditionally used, as the opening words say, on Ash Wednesday. These unusually specific echoes of the Ash Wednesday service are not noted by Dunlop or Johnson, although of course both critics relate the sonnet to the day generally. In the magnificent Sarum Missal published in Paris in 1555 (with, as Harold Weatherby noted in his 1984 Kalamazoo paper, St. George and the dragon on the title-page), there is a woodcut accompanying the Ash Wednesday service showing David, harp laid near by him, kneeling before an altar on which blazes a heart.
42 Johnson, 'Liturgy', 57.
43 Puech, 'Le cerf et le serpent', 39–43, discusses Ps. 42 (i.e. Vulgate 41), Easter eve, and number symbolism.
44 The similarity to the collects was first noted by James Noble in 1880; see *Variorum* VIII, 443. There may be one more possible link between Spenser and the 1555 Sarum. In the Book of Common Prayer, as in preceding uses, the collects and readings for Lady Day (March 25) are placed, like those for other saints' days, after the sequence of readings for Sundays, Christmas, Easter, and so forth. In the 1555 Sarum Missal this is also true, but appearing just before Easter, on Easter eve, there is a mass for Mary. Professor Richard Pfaff tells me that such an anomaly was probably intended to stress the connection between the Annunciation and the Passion, often said in the Middle

Ages to have taken place on the same day of the year. The readings are from the Song of Songs on the beloved's beauty and perfumed body, readings not found in other services for the Virgin, passionate though those are in their own manner. Spenser would perhaps have detested the Easter Eve mass for Mary simply as a mass, a papist perversion, but he pays his own lady similar compliments in *Am.* 64. This sonnet corresponds with neither Lady Day nor Easter Eve, but its language seems appropriate to an annual and liturgical season that here, just as in the 1555 Sarum, inspires vocabulary linking human and divine love.

45 *Epithalamion*, too, may echo Sarum as well as the Book of Common Prayer. In Sarum's marriage rite, the priest blesses the bed, a ceremony later played down by the Catholic Church, and asks that it be free 'ab omnibus fantasmaticis demonum illusionibus'. Spenser likewise expels 'deluding dreams' and hobgoblins who 'Fray us with things that be not'. Here and in st. 23, which like the marriage service in Sarum and the Protestant prayer-book includes prayers for a large posterity and the inheritance of 'heavenly tabernacles' (the prayer-book's 'inherit ... everlasting kingdom') the poignancy lies partly in the husband's assumption of roles traditionally played by others. Just as he needs no Catullus to sing his wedding, he can bless his own bed (the displacement of these prayers to the end of the poem also brings the movement into line with the structure of the classical epithalamion). There is more on the bed-blessing tradition in *The Rathen Manual*, ed. and trans. Duncan MacGregor, Transactions of the Aberdeen Ecclesiological Society (Aberdeen, 1905). Johnson, '"Sacred Rites"', notes some parallels with the Elizabethan prayer-book but not the 'inherit' of st. 23. Hard-core Protestants would not call these associations 'sacramental' (53), for Spenser's church did not acknowledge marriage as a sacrament, and the prayer-book does not refer to a sign of the cross (52), only to a blessing.

46 By these I mean days in the calendar, both moveable and immoveable, not, e.g., the wedding or burial service. All days had lessons found in the opening almanac plus the collects, epistles, and gospels of the preceding Sunday, but these are not the special days, Sundays and holy, to which so much of the prayer-book is devoted.

47 V.-L. Saulnier, *Du Bellay* (Paris: Hatier, 1968), 63. Du Bellay's scheme involves some symmetry, for each poem is four sonnets from its end of the sequence, but despite a few seasonal references and a total number of sonnets that corresponds roughly to the number of days from Christmas to Good Friday in the years 1549–50, *L'Olive* has no indication I can find of a particular year; Spenser's calendar is both more complex and more specific than Du Bellay's.

48 Prescott, 'Licia'. On Spenser's amatory sun symbolism see Richard Neuse, 'The Triumph over Hasty Accidents: A note on the Symbolic mode of the "Epithalamion"', *Modern Language Review* 61 (1966): 163–74.

49 I can find no liturgical reason to repeat *Am.* 35 instead of an earlier one. In the church year, of course, no Sunday is repeated, only postponed, not an option available to Spenser (how could we recognize a previously omitted sonnet?). On

83 and 35 see also Dunlop, 'Drama', who speculates on Spenser's reasons and summarizes earlier theories of Fowler and Hieatt. On Spenser, numbers, and mutability, see A. Kent Hieatt, *Short Time's Endless Monument: The Symbolism of the Numbers in Edmund Spenser's 'Epithalamion'* (New York: Columbia University Press, 1960).
50 On binding see J. C. Gray, 'Bondage and Deliverance in the "Faerie Queene": Varieties of a Moral Imperative', *Modern Language Review* 70 (1975): 1–12.

Part II

The Psalms and the psalmist

4

Evil tongues at the court of Saul: the Renaissance David as a slandered courtier

To Renaissance Christians, as to their ancestors, King David was both a great if flawed man and a sacred 'psalmograph', the 'sweet singer of Israel' whose words, said George Wither, could burn the heart inside the body like lightning melting gold hidden in a purse.[1] It would be perverse to deny the religious impulse that led such Renaissance poets as Wyatt, Sidney, and Milton to imitate such psalmography, yet few scholars today share the once widespread assumption that the urge to rewrite the psalms derived solely from devout hopes for a 'divine' poetry to rival profanity and for a 'Christian muse' who might silence or subsume her sisters.[2] Some who imitated or discussed David were also responding, for example, to the culture's evolving attitudes to words, voice, self, and interiority.[3] This essay will explore yet another reason why English poets were drawn to David, a reason that spoke to the private self but placed that self in a larger public world. I suggest that, to a greater degree than is often thought, post-Reformation concern with the psalms looked outward to history and politics as well as inward to the soul and its utterances. It did so because, compared to their patristic and medieval predecessors, commentators such as Bucer, Calvin, and Beza now read the psalter even more specifically in terms of David's life as they found it recounted in the Bible's historical books. Particularly fascinating to such commentators was what they took to be the prevalence of bad-mouthing and slander in the political world they thought David described in his poetry. Meantime, for the process was synergistic, they read the historical books of the Bible with a keener ear for the role of wicked tongues in David's sufferings first as Saul's servant and then as a beleaguered ruler.

In this more politicized tradition of Renaissance translation and commentary the facts as found in 1 and 2 Samuel and 1 Chronicles had not changed. David, the youngest son of a humble family, a shepherd and harpist, slays an ogre, marries the king's daughter, escapes his jealous father-in-law thanks to the king's son, heads a band of outlaws in a resistance movement while sparing the life of his anointed persecutor, and as foretold becomes ruler himself, uniting several territories into a kingdom riven for a time by family tragedy and wicked counsel. The love interests include incest, rape, and gazing on naked beauty that inspires cleverly planned violence. The story has nearly everything: politics, sex, blood, treachery, male friendship, family divisions, God, adventures, armies, madness, upward mobility, even a giant. Rulers could sympathize with David's anguish as he replaced a tyrant only to be beset by rebellion from below, poets could admire the power of David's harp or Nathan's eloquence, and fathers could identify with the king's grief over his son Absalom. Spatially, the adventures move from fields to city to wilderness or foreign courts and back; and in one of the best cave scenes in literature Saul encounters his enemy David and calls him 'son'. There is, furthermore, a final tragedy: although forgiven for stealing Bathsheba and murdering her husband, David remains 'a man of blood' and cannot build the Temple. What the original story lacks, however, is precisely that emphasis on slander that appeared in the Renaissance and that emerged as an effect of reading many of David's lyrics as meditations on events in his life.

To be sure, seeing the psalmist as a public man had always been permitted by the belief that the hero of the Book of Samuel wrote many or all of the psalms. This belief was supported by long tradition, a few Hebrew titles, Paul's reference to David in Romans 4:6, and David's recitation of Psalm 18 in 2 Samuel 22, even though no one thought the psalms were in chronological order and even though there was not always consensus on which episode any given psalm refers to. Renaissance scholarship on the psalter was not, therefore, quite as innovative as some then claimed. Twelfth-century readings by Andrew of St. Victor would interest the Protestant radical Servetus, and medieval exegetes who wanted to fashion such historical readings had often had fairly ready access to Hebrew scholarship and scholars.[4] Yet the sixteenth century had soberer philology, better textual criticism, and a greater sense of anachronism than did the earlier writers. No wonder there was new interest (interest in both senses of the word) in the author of the psalms as a political and historical figure.

Not everyone, of course, regarded David as something like a Renaissance anti-court poet. To some he was still, for instance, a feudal worthy, the 'conquerous David' who maintained 'princely chivalry and knighthood'.[5] Nor did the calumnies that beset the younger David ever appeal as much to writers of plays and fictions as did his fight with Goliath, his love for Bathsheba, or his war with Absalom.[6] Nevertheless, in many Renaissance eyes the psalmist seemed to be entangled in the scornful gossip and manoeuvring that his sympathetic observers thought typical of royal courts. He is a braver brother of Skelton's Drede, beset by hypocrites scrambling for the 'bowge of court', an early victim of the Blatant Beast who prowls through

Spenser's *Faerie Queene* VI. This interpretation appeared, moreover, at a time when at least in England the courts' slander caseload was increasing and the common law's view of bad-mouthing was developing further.[7] The Reformation only exacerbated such anxieties: many controversies were about language – about signs and things signified – and polemics were astonishingly scurrilous. Commentators' obsession with slander was not devoid, I suspect, of uneasy if unconscious dismay at the taste of their own tongues. David's denunciation of sycophantish calumny, furthermore, was deeply gratifying to anyone with cause to view European courts with suspicion – if also with the desire that even people who know better feel for centres of power.

Few called David himself a courtier, perhaps because of the word's overtone of butterfly frivolity or ingratiating ambition, but he lived at or near court (when not in exile or on the run), attended his king, and provoked envy in Saul's other servants.[8] To translate or write about his songs was therefore to engage, if only incidentally, an ancient political and military drama involving abuses of language that many claimed were typical of courts. David had long been famous as a humble penitent and chosen king.[9] He now appeared, more than before, as a king's victim – albeit one with sources of authority and inspiration unavailable to his rivals or to the sullen tyrant whose own prophecies failed. Listening hard to literary psalm paraphrases would probably reveal his presence, or at least the pressure of interpretations made explicitly in scholarly and homiletic comments on David's verse. That, however, is not my enterprise here.[10] I will, rather, describe the attention David the slandered courtier received in annotated psalters, particularly that in the Geneva Bible of 1560, and in a few commentaries and poems. I hope their relevance to Renaissance psalmody and to other responses to David will be clear.

In describing how emphasis on the psalmist's tribulations at court increased and how the tongues of which he complained became located more exactly in courtly mouths, I will use works I know were available in England. It should be borne in mind, though, that Renaissance readings of David – even brief marginalia – depend on and borrow from each other in such complex ways that tracing their affiliations would be a lifetime's labour. Moreover, what seem particular thoughts by individual exegetes, translators, or editors may well be not personal invention but personal selection among the available possibilities. We need a word for units of biblical commentary on the analogy of narreme or phoneme: interpreme? exegeme? Some 'exegemes' passed like small change from hand to hand, rendering very difficult the task of sorting out the larger exegetical economy. The following discussion therefore assumes no single family tree, only a tangle of branches whose trunks I cannot specify. Nor does it claim a development after a certain point, for the slandered courtier so vividly present in the Geneva Bible's running meditation on courts and the abuse of language is virtually missing from several important but more 'establishment' texts.

Medieval psalters offer little on David's biography. As Dom Pierre Salmon puts it, few Christians read the psalms 'en cherchant à les comprendre dans la perspective du temps où ils avaient été écrits'.[11] Medieval *tituli* speak often of Christ, seldom of David. There are exceptions: the title of Psalm 120 in what Salmon calls series 2 of the *tituli* refers to David's 'tribulation' under Saul and his 'peregrination' among foreigners. Psalm 3 is 'Prophetatio David de quibus passus est' (series 4), even if others said it shows that Christ 'pro nobis in mortis somno obdormiat et resurgat' (series 5). There is a little on tongues (e.g. Psalm 109, 'quod ipse maledictioni subjacuit ut nos a legis maledictione erueret', series 5), but the stress remains Christological: if Psalm 7 refers to the war with Absalom, David himself applies this to the mystery of Christ (series 6). And there is virtually nothing on courtiers. The 1535 Vulgate Bible printed in London does better by David in translating the Hebrew titles that on occasion position him historically; readers are reminded of his escape 'de manu Saul[is]', his hiding in a cave, Nathan's rebuke, and Doeg's cruelty, while some marginal notes expand a little on his adventures and on their typological significance. But there is not much here compared to elaborations to come, and the apparatus ignores courts and the sins found there.

Times were changing, though. Five years earlier the slandered courtier had occupied some headnotes in an English translation, published at Antwerp in 1530, of Martin Bucer's 1529 Latin psalter. We should not, warns the preface, judge according to 'the comen texte', for this work is 'fetched more nyghe the Ebrue verite'.[12] Bucer's David is afflicted by 'krafty deceitfull flaterers' who 'occupy all places' (Psalm 12; 'places' means positions as much as locales). He sings Psalm 58 as 'an Invective ageinste the flaterers of Saule', prays 'ageinste sclaunderers and false accusers' (Psalm 64), and offers 'cruel bannynges or wisshinges ageinst Doeg and wother flaterers of Shaule which withe their lyes stered hym up ageinste David' (Psalm 109). When David looks for vengeance against Saul and 'his flaterers' (Psalm 35), we are told that he did so not for his own sake but for God's glory. In fact, one attraction of the psalms as invective against those powerful and foul-spoken *others* must have been that even in only marginally typological readings the onus of the speaker's – and hence the reader's – anger could be put onto Christ, who is in this regard, too, the bearer of the world's sins: in him, accommodated to our understanding, the language of condemnation, wrath, and cursing is lawful. Spiritually, this is dangerous if seductive ground, and commentators knew it, advising against applying the psalms' irascible or punitive language to the private self and its enemies.

Bucer's psalm headings provided wording for those of Clement Marot and Theodore Beza, whose French metrical psalms eventually became the great Huguenot psalter of 1562 that the Sidneys, among many others, knew well. Neither poet needed encouragement to think about Saul's court. Marot had a 'place' with Francis I and served him as best he could when not driven to flight by slander, the king's fear of 'Lutherans', and his own imprudence; whatever his ambitions and pleasures, he cannot have regarded kings and courts with utter serenity. Beza was no courtier, and he denigrated Marot for having been one, but as civil war swept his native France he came to find in the Valois court the sins David had lamented in Saul's.[13]

Psalm 12 readily elicits thoughts on words and courts (although in his commentaries Beza was to deal with it perfunctorily). It describes those who flatter and lie with lips they vainly insist are subject to no one else: 'Nous serons grans par noz langues sur tous; / A nous de droict noz levres appartiennent; / Flattons, mentons; qui est maistre sur nous?'[14] These mouth-proud men separate themselves from two communities: from the court where words should serve king and commonweal, and (typologically) from Christ's body. To assert power over one's own lips is also to claim originality, to locate discourse's authority within the self and not, say, in ancient letters, law, or tradition – or in a patron. Such poets as Marot (or Sidney) must have found this thought both exciting and disturbing. Yet David's enemies are also a 'we', a faction, not isolated individuals finding their own vices. In any case, Marot's headnote goes beyond Bucer's: 'Il parle contre les flatteurs de la court de Saul qui par flatteries, dissimulations & arrogances estoient moleste à chascun, & prie Dieu y donner ordre. psaulme pour tout peuple vexé de gouverneurs de princes.'[15] Other editions even more pointedly refer to Saul's 'mignons'. And other headings, too, if less dramatically, indicate the atmosphere around the tyrant: Psalm 5, read as a complaint against Saul's henchmen, is 'propre contre les calumniateurs', reminding us that God 'favorise' the good (we may fall from our king's good graces, but there is a higher 'court' with better favour). Psalm 11 offers, we hear, consolation for those 'mis hor de grace de leurs seigneurs' (like Marot); some editions add 'les banniz à tort'. And Psalm 143, written when David hid from Saul (some others said from Absalom), is for 'prisonniers pour la foy'. For some reason, and whatever his later comparison of David's situation to that of the Huguenots, such headnotes in Beza's much larger portion of the 1562 psalter are fewer and more subdued. Still, his David grieves for false friends (Psalms 41 and 69), denounces 'les vanitez et bestises des riches et puissans' (Psalm 49), laments his 'injures et faux blasmes' (Psalm 56) and the 'reproches et moqueries' of the 'malins' (Psalm 71), and recalls how he was 'banni par le faux rapport' of the 'envieux' (Psalm 120).[16]

The arguments do associate these griefs with Saul, even if they are reticent on courts.

Christians lacking Hebrew were increasingly able to learn about the psalmist from scholars in touch with Jewish tradition, a job that became easier as editions and translations proliferated. So the fastest way to inform oneself concerning the psalms' diction and historical context was to read notes like those of the Hebrew professor Francis Vatablus or commentaries like those of Calvin or Beza. It seems likely that Sidney, for one, had studied something like Robert Estienne's 1546 Paris psalter, which has the Vulgate text, a fresh Latin translation by Leon Jud (schoolmate of Bucer and himself part Jewish), and copious marginalia derived from Vatablus's lectures.[17] Vatablus presents a tyrannical king's loyal servant, one beset by the arrow-tongues of those the margins often label 'sectatores', 'adulatores', and 'assentatores': followers, flatterers, and yes-men. David suffers from 'calumniam ... apud Saulem' (Psalm 7), from cruel witnesses' insinuated slander ('insimulando'). Hypocrites treat him with empty mockery ('sannis ... futilibus et vanis'), useless and light talk signifying nothing ('inutilem sermonem, levem et nihili', Psalm 35:16). (Vatablus is here explaining the difficult phrase 'cum hypocritis illusionum placentae', meaning more or less 'with the hypocrites at their cake [Hebrew *mahnog*] of vain play/deceit/jeers', which elicited a variety of comments and translations.) The teeth that wound the psalmist in Psalm 57 belong to sycophants and delators: 'falsas et noxias delationes assentatorum Saulis'. So too, in Psalm 64, which a marginal note calls a prayer 'contra delatores', David undergoes 'linguarum virulentiam'.

On occasion Vatablus creates or at least hints at little scenes in the implied drama of a persecuted royal servant. Skelton and Wyatt would have been impressed. Psalm 12, as I have said, is especially significant for those who think about words and authority. Vatablus identifies the proud speakers as 'aulicis Saulis', Saul's courtiers, for in the court of Saul everyone 'assentationi student', strove after flattery. True, the arrogant 'adulatores Saulis' also sound like uppity masters of the trivium when they boast that 'periti sumus artis dicendi' (we are skilled in the art of speech). This is technical academic language, and if Professor Vatablus used it with students he must have expected a laugh. It might be thought paradoxical that court yes-men would brag of being answerable to no one, but while such grovelling arrogance is psychologically plausible, the writer of the notes ignores the irony. The danger of such skilled mouths is strikingly realized in the notes to Psalm 52, here assumed as usual to refer to how Doeg, Saul's chief servant, first slandered and then murdered a number of priests ('sanctes'; see 1 Samuel 22). Some say, we hear, that David calls Doeg's tongue a 'razor' to indicate that traps lie beneath it, but the marginalist pans to a more lurid close-up: the tongue/razor 'meant for the beard, going astray, seeks/desires/assaults the jugular' ('ut novacula adhibita barbae aberrans, jugulum petit'). The words are brilliantly chosen, for 'adhibita', with the primary sense 'be turned to', suits an edge properly aimed at a hairy cheek or chin, but it was often applied (says Lewis and Short's dictionary) to summoning counselors, dinner guests, and even quotable authorities. Doeg's tongue, furthermore, does indeed perform an 'aberration', the participle itself suggesting slipperiness, as it goes sliding in cheek-flattering smoothness to sudden murder under the jaw. The owner of the tongue takes no responsibility for the slip – it is the wandering razor, not the guiding hand or mind, that seeks the throat, as though Doeg, unlike the detractors of Psalm 12, were putting distance between himself and his mouth.

Doeg's imagined tongue-stroke is only a brief moment in a long parade of notes, but even when working on this small a scale Vatablus indicates the terror at Saul's court, a world of hidden threat and nearly disembodied speech for which the victim cannot always find a source. Renaissance poets and playwrights (to say nothing of Renaissance courtiers) would find the air familiar. Some would also recognize the bad-mouths of Psalm 58, identified by Vatablus as 'adulatores', 'assentatores', and 'aulici'. If Doeg is an insidious murderer, these magnates are irresponsible in a different way. They claim to consult 'de rebuspublicis' at their get-togethers, says the note, but do these 'courtiers' in fact care for equity? No. All their talk is to please Saul and win favour. (In fact the psalm says nothing explicit on courts and flatterers.) As I have said, David's persecution by Saul never produced the wealth of visual and literary treatment given to his adventures with Goliath, sex, and family, but annotations like these suggest a political drama staged just outside the text. It comprises scenes of court whispers, treachery, and violence that were in good part projected onto the Bible's less institutionally particularized anger at injustice, mockery, snares, and lies.

Aside from its brief run in Bucer's headnotes, this drama did not play well in the early Tudor psalters I have seen. A 1534 version of Campensis translates the Hebrew titles; Coverdale's Latin and English psalter (1540) has a charming picture of David's servant tipping his hat to a naked Bathsheba smiling in her tub, but there are no annotations. The 1548 Coverdale psalter is likewise unannotated, and despite mention of the great Jewish scholar Kimhi the psalm section of the Bible printed by Day and Seres (1550) has little of the Vatablus tradition beyond a remark in the headnote for Psalm 12 that 'gylefull flatterers rule all' and a reading of Psalm 58 as 'An invectyve agaynst the flatterers and adherentes of Saule'.[18] It would not be surprising, perhaps, if in Henry VIII's later years a stress on royal tyranny and courtly slander seemed risky, but in fact throughout the Renaissance such a focus is found more readily in less official texts. Hence its presence in the Geneva Bible and absence from the Great Bible and the Bishops' Bible, its intensity in Beza's Latin psalter and its very muted appearance in the psalters of Archbishop Matthew Parker and Sternhold-Hopkins.[19]

One partial exception is the *Godly meditacion upon .xv ... psalms* (1547) 'compiled and set forth' by Sir Anthony Cope. Although he did not share the attitude of Vatablus when it came to courts (he had just been knighted by Edward), Cope had no doubt concerning the psalter's political significance. He begins by asking Queen Catherine Parr, whose chamberlain he was, to read about David singing the evil spirit out of Saul. So too, he says, *we* may have power through the psalms, probably a hint that modern psalmody might help clean up residual papistry at her stepson's court. More than precedent demanded, then, Cope could hear the psalms implying truths known to Catherine and those who supported further reform. Psalm 12 foresees 'the corrupt maner of lyving of the greatest sort of people' – but also the darkening of scripture 'through mens tradicions'. Nowadays people try with 'fayr painted' words to 'deceyve and prevayle', for like David's enemies 'They say their tongues are their own as though there were no lord over them', thinking 'eloquence to be a gyft of nature and not of god'. Cope thus nudges the psalm closer to good Protestantism, glancing sourly at traditions, self-reliance, and verbal deception in high places.

By the time the translators of the Geneva Bible set to work in the 1550s and continued the efforts of Bucer, Vatablus, and other historicist commentators, they could also use Calvin's vigorous and learned commentaries (I quote Arthur Golding's 1571 translation[20]). Calvin devotes most of his space to philology, moral implication, and remnants of typology, but on occasion he stops for thoughts on courts. Probably referring to life with Saul, says Calvin, David laments in Psalm 12 that 'there is no more courtesye or truthe remayning among men', for 'every man entrappeth his neybour with fayre speeche'. The 'first cause' of this is 'that they speake with a dubble hart. And this dubblehartednesse (as I may terme it,) maketh men dubbletunged and woordwresters ... And surely, falsehod and slaunder are more deadly, than all swoordes and weapons.' Some 'flatter after a slavish and vyle sort', but David notes 'another maner of fellowes, namely, which in their flattery doo notwithstanding set a stowt countenance upon the matter, and meddle their undermyning with boldness. Therfore he speaketh not of the stinking and rascall kynd of flateries: but he crossebytheth the courtly Clawebackes, which not only wynd themselves in by pleasant devyses, but also overwhelme silie [i.e. innocent] sowles with their greate jolytie of lowd lying.'

Psalm 35, the one with the puzzling cake (Golding's Calvin has 'bred baked under the embers'), prompts analogous remarks: 'As long as Saul was displeased with David, the noblemen and such as at that time bare any authority (according as flatterie reigneth always in the Courts of Kings) had spitefully conspired the destruction of the innocent soule', drawing 'almost all the comonalitie into the felowship of their hatred and crueltie'. Therefore, says the note to verse 16, 'in expresse woords hee blameth the joly Courtiers ... that they gnash their teeth upon him like woode bestes'. (In fact David uses no such express words, merely calling the teeth-gnashers 'falsharted scoffers'.) Like Vatablus, in explaining the mysterious cake/bread Calvin warms to the scene: 'For some taking (Magnog [sic]) for a Tarte or a Custard, are of opinion that in this place bee touched the liktrenchers that hunted after fyne and deynty fare; such as alwayes swarme much about in princes Courts.' 'Othersome' (those who know about patronage?) see a reference to 'slavish and rascall felowes' who 'set theyr tunges too rayling for little or naught, like as in all ages they have bin to bee fownd that woold (as men say) set theyr tungs to sale for a bit of bred'. To Calvin, though, these are the 'tablejesters which gave their verdit of [David's] death among the cups'. The 'venemousnes' of 'false reportes and slaunders' (Psalm 64:3–4) accompanies crafty 'policy'. When David fears 'covert' malice, 'he meeneth that they exceed in manifold policie, and that they be ... wittie and politik'. Saul flatters David only 'to allure him into his trappes, and no doubt but his Courtyers folowed the same suttletye of his' (Psalm 55:22). Such indirection generates division, doubleness, what Spenser was to call Duessa. Christians seek Una, the One, unity: 'the Holy Ghost, condemning all overthwart wyles, and cheefly deceytfull flatteries, exhorteth them too folowe singlenesse'.

The Geneva translators would in any case have found a preoccupation with sins of the tongue in other parts of the Bible, particularly the Wisdom books, and with what tongues can do to social cohesion and personal 'name'. Whatever the later role of scripture in encouraging guilt and interiority, the impression given by the text and notes of the Geneva Bible is of anxiety about shame, something the Renaissance understood thoroughly. Hence the comfort of God's stable single Word in a world of labile multiple words – words that one translator of Beza called 'bibble-babble' or words that slide like Vatablus's razor down the visible face to go for the dimness below.[21] When the Bible does not mention slander as such, the translators can supply it: although Ecclesiastes 10:11 compares a biting serpent to a 'babler', the headnote calls him 'a sclanderer'. But outside the psalms, it is the Apocrypha's Ecclesiasticus 28:13–21 that expresses with most passion what Proverbs and Ecclesiastes say more briefly: 'Abhorre the sclanderer and double tongued: for suche have destroyed many that were at peace. The double tongue hathe disquieted manie, and driven them from nacion to nacion: strong cities hathe it broken downe, and overthrowen the houses of great men ... The stroke of the rodde maketh markes in the flesh, but the stroke of the tongue breaketh the bones. There be manie that have perished by the edge of the sworde, but not so manie as have fallen by the tongue.'

Mockery is as bad as slander to a shame-fearing culture. When God makes his covenant with Noah (Genesis 6:18) the Geneva translators add, 'To the intent that in this great enterprise and mockings of the whole worlde thou maist be confirmed.' The commonweal is at risk, if Solomon is wise to say that 'Scornful men bring a citie into a snare' (Proverbs 29:8), and even clergymen are threatened: next to Ezekiel's thoughts on derision (Ezekiel 33:31) we are told to hear God's word with 'zeale and affection' lest we 'make of his ministers as thogh they were jestes to serve mens foolish fantasies'. This concern with language is repeated in the New Testament, although not often by Jesus himself – who does warn, however, that 'everie idle worde that men shal speake, they shal give acounte thereof at the day of judgement' (Matthew 12:36). Paul forbids foolish joking (Ephesians 5:4; the margin says this does not mean 'pleasant talke', just harmful jesting – what Bishop George Webbe, citing this verse and Psalm 1:1, calls 'an Arrow framed in the shop of the Scornefull' with feathers of 'Morologie and Eutrapelie').[22] In the last days there will be mockers (2 Peter 3:3), and notes to Revelation 12:4 and 16:13 call the devil a flatterer and compare the frogs coming out of the satanic dragon's mouth to deceits from the pope's 'ambassadours'. The Bible begins and ends with mouths. In between is the world of sneers and slander in which David (usually) followed God's 'singlenesse'.

Because 1 and 2 Samuel have little to say on sins of the tongue, the Geneva translators did not have much to work with on that topic (preachers, moralists, and poets had a freer hand), but they occasionally read David's history in terms familiar to Renaissance politics. In the notes to 1 Samuel, Saul is a tyrant but also a Machiavel. When he hides after being offered the kingship, a note says wisely: 'as thogh he were unworthy and unwilling'. When he is kind to young David the margin makes sure we are not fooled, saying, 'for under pretence of favour he soght his destruction' (1 Samuel 18:21), and when, thanks to Jonathan's pleas, he readmits David to his presence the translators are unimpressed: 'Whatsoever he pretended outwardly, yet his heart was full of malice' (1 Samuel 19:6). Second Samuel, says the headnote, shows the 'insurrections, uprores, and treasons' wrought by 'fained friends and flatterers', for 'by slander, flatterie, and faire promises the wicked seke preferrement' (2 Samuel 15:4, on Absalom).

It is in the notes to the psalms that David the slandered courtier emerges most vividly as the events of 1 Samuel find fruitful conjunction with David's laments over evil speech. Those to Psalm 4 establish the *mythos* by reading the phrase 'sonnes of men' as 'Ye that thinke your selves noble in this worlde' and God's chosen 'godlie man' as 'A King that walketh in his vocation'. The margin of Psalm 12 says of those who 'speake with a double heart' that David 'meaneth the flaterers of the courte, whiche hurt him more with their tongues then with their weapons'. A bit surprisingly in so Calvinist a text, the courtiers recall the confident rhetoricians of Vatablus more than Cope's self-reliant Pelagians: they 'thinke them selves able to persuade whatsoever they take in hand'. No wonder David feels encircled by those the margin says seek his death (Psalm 17). He calls them proud men, 'inclosed in their owne fatt', which the margin takes to mean 'Thei are puft up with pride, as the stomake that is choked with fat.' Over and over, then, the Geneva translators hear David's psalms as exclamations concerning Saul's court; if not the first to do so, they were among the most willing. The psalms indeed show a passionate regard for speech, but the translators aim it more pointedly at Saul and his court, their paraphrases surrounding and transforming the psalmist's less specific language.

Beza was to express astonishment that David could remain good in these surroundings, for courts usually corrupt manners and loosen faith.[23] This court is, notably, a place of seemingly unmotivated enmity where Saul's men 'raged without anie cause given on [David's] parte' (Psalm 17), for example falsely charging David with 'gredie desire to reigne' (Psalm 131, note). To worldly and experienced ears, a politician's denial – 'Lord, mine heart is not hawtie, nether are mine eies loftie' – can seem confirmation, as witness the margin's sceptical reading of Saul's reluctance to be king. But the translators take it as exemplary, saying, 'He setteth forthe his great humilitie, as an example to all rulers and governers.'[24] Most rulers can well use such instruction, although David also offers as proof of innocence that he has 'kept silence'. It is his enemies who are hypocrites (Psalm 7), these 'adherents' of Saul who 'diffamed' David (Psalm 55, note) with 'false reportes' (Psalm 57, identifying verbal 'speares and arrowes'). Saul's 'counselers' both 'secretly and openly soght his destruction' and 'under pretence of consulting for the commune welth conspire [his] death' (Psalm 58, note on 'Speake ye justly? o sonnes of men, judge ye uprightly?'). They give David himself 'wicked counsel', telling him to despair (Psalm 11). He 'praieth against the furie and false reportes of his enemies', their 'sclanders' (Psalm 64, note on 'bitter wordes'), and asks God to hide him from those who search out thoughts with 'secret and subtil' ways. 'Vexed by the false reportes of Sauls flatterers', he 'sheweth that there is nothing so sharpe to perce, nor so hate to set on fyre as a sclanderous tongue' (Psalm 120; the psalm itself does not quite specify slander). But why so many calumniators? No early reader of Estienne's psalter, Calvin, or the Geneva Bible would ask. Virtue and faith always incur envy, and frustrated envy breeds slander. Strong kings kill; weak ones and courtiers bad-mouth. So when David suffers 'falsehode and injuries', the venom and snares of backbiters, he tells 'what weapons the wicked use, when power and force faile them' (Psalm 140, notes).

Sometimes the translators frown more generally on political elites. The great are often atheists, they say, explaining Psalm 29 as David's exhortation to 'the princes and rulers of the worlde, (which for the moste parte thinke there is no God)'. So too, the behaviour of those David calls 'the proude' and 'the assemblies of violent men' shows 'that there can be no moderation nor equitie, where proude tyrants reigne' (Psalm 86). Witness the 'arrogant tyrannie' (Psalm 52) of Doeg, whose 'credit with the tyrant Saul' gave him 'power to murther the Saints of God', a credit – the margin implies – that works through 'craftie flateries and lies'. And Psalm 35, as one would anticipate, provokes testy social criticism. Says the headnote, echoing Calvin, 'So long as Saul was enemie to David, all that had anie autoritie under him to flatter their King (as is the course of the worlde) did also moste cruelly persecute David.' Courtiers 'sclander him', not allowing him to 'purge [him] self'; this annotates the vaguer complaint that 'Cruel witnesses did rise up: thei asked of me things that I knewe not.' Without guiding annotations the psalm would still evoke a world of defamation, ambush, and scorn, but strictly speaking there is nothing in it on courts and kings. Enemies 'have hid the pit and their net for me'; they 'imagine deceitful wordes' and 'gaped on me with their mouthes, saying, Aha, aha, our eye hath sene'. (*What* they have seen is disturbingly unclear.) The translators omit the *mahnog/placenta/* cake/bread enjoyed by 'false scoffers at bankets', but the margin explains that 'The worde signifieth cakes: meaning that the proud courtesans at their deinty feasts skoff, raile, and conspire his death.'

Even when translators do not mention Saul, they can further politicize the texts. Psalm 26 describes one who has kept himself apart from 'bloodie men' with hands 'fol of bribes', from 'vaine persones' and 'dissemblers'. The title, 'A Psalme of David', allows the translators to picture this as life at court, but there is nothing in the text that requires them to say that David had been 'banished by Saul'. When David has God condemn the 'workers of iniquitie' who 'eat up my people as they eat bread', the margin refers not, say, to the rich, but to 'governers, who having charge to defende and preserve Gods people, do moste cruelly devour them' (Psalm 53). David's lovely celebration of brotherhood (Psalm 133), which without its marginal note might seem, in the Bishops' Bible or the King James Version, to apply to any group from shepherds to merchants to professors to courtiers, is here applied primarily to the last: 'Because the greatest parte were against David, thogh some favoured him, yet when he was established King, at length thei joyned all together like brethren' (one wonders if the translators hoped the dead Queen Mary's supporters would ponder this). So too, a note to Psalm 109, identified as a prayer made after the psalmist was 'falsely accused by flatterers unto Saul', says of the phrase 'those that wolde condemne his soule' that 'he sheweth that he had not to do with them, that were of litle power, but with the judges and princes of the worlde'.

Most good satires and complaints establish a norm against which deviations may be seen and known, even if that norm is ironically modified. In *Mother Hubberds Tale*, for example, Spenser's imagined ideal courtier makes the corruptions we witness look even worse. In the Book of Psalms, and with no irony or complexities audible to generations of readers, Psalm 101 is that norm. David anticipates a household governed by 'mercie and judgement', one free of slander and infidelity in which only the good will 'serve' him. The Geneva Bible's margin is excited by the political implications and assumes that he refers to his future palace. Patiently awaiting his 'kinglie dignitie', says the margin, and living as 'a private man', he expects the time when 'he that telleth lies, shal not remaine in my sight' and when 'workers of iniquitie' shall be 'cut of ... from the Citie of the Lord'. The notes pronounce on the government of kingdoms and churches: 'He sheweth that magistrates do not their dueties, except thei be enemies to all vice.' For 'in promising to punish these vices [slander and pride], which are moste pernicious in them that are about kings, he declareth that he wil punish all.' And if 'heathen Magistrates' must repress wickedness, 'how muche more thei that have the charge of the Church of God?'

'At the time appointed', the man 'rejected of Saul and of the people' (Psalm 118, argument) comes into his kingdom and sings, 'This was the Lords doing, and it is marvelous in our eyes.' The margin calls David's joy gratitude for God's mercy in 'appointing [him] King, and delivering his Church', an event with much resonance for English Protestants after 17 November 1558. Yet David himself was occasionally to sin. As verse 9 warns, it is unwise 'to have confidence in princes'. So too Psalm 146:3: 'Put not your trust in princes.' The only king one can rely on is God, and sometimes the translators, more than they need to, see God's behaviour in courtly terms. They do not radically misread, but given a choice they choose like exiled subjects of Mary and vastly relieved subjects of Elizabeth. An example: when the psalmist prays, 'Send thy light and thy trueth', the note says, 'To wit, thy favour' (Psalm 43). A Florentine neoplatonist, for instance, might read that light differently. Beyond the reach of Saul, of Doeg, of sycophants and slanderers, beyond Achitophel and beyond even the penitent murderer of Uriah, is another court where because 'God favoreth' there is 'perfite felicitie' (Psalm 16, note). Most of this is in the text, of course, but not quite all of it, and the translators' fascination with the notion of favour, especially, makes even clearer the Bible's awareness of two kingdoms, earthly and heavenly.

Whatever officialdom's taste in Bibles, the Geneva translation was loved by the people, including Shakespeare and Spenser, and the slandered courtier David was not to be ignored. He appears in other biblical texts known or published in England, such as Beza's huge Latin psalter with comments that

Gilby translated in 1580. The heavily annotated *Biblia sacra* of Tremellius and Junius,[25] which Sidney cites in his *Apology*, at least mentions David's problems with 'aulicorum calumnus' (Psalm 12). And Henry Ainsworth's *Book of Psalmes* (Amsterdam, 1612) recalls the calumnies of Saul's 'nobles' and the 'scoffing parasites' who feast on 'juncates' (Psalm 35): not much, but doubtless enough to remind Massachusetts pilgrims, who admired Ainsworth, what decadence they had left behind. To characterize David's mistreatment by his enemies still allowed some room for individual preferences, though. A striking instance of how scenes of his persecution could be reimagined is the commentary on Psalms 12 and 35 in Alexander Top's *Book of Prayses, Called the Psalmes*.[26] Top's own posture is itself courtierlike. His epistle tells Charles I that the king is 'a prince of peace' shining with the 'glory of the law', fit for 'the Throne of David'. In what follows, there is much on slander, little on courts. So far is Top from Calvin's tone that he says Psalm 12 (the one with the haughty mouth-owners) shows what happens when 'base people [are] in authority', when braggarts act with 'churlishness' and 'riot'. He denigrates 'worldlings', to be sure, but his worldlings are upstarts only. In his translation of Psalm 35 (with the *mahnog* of mockery), David's enemies wink and sneer, 'Oh, Oh, ah Sirr ho, we saw it', but these are not the sycophants of Estienne's psalter, the Geneva Bible, and Beza; they are 'slaves'. Top might argue that the word 'slaves' works well for flatterers or parasites, that Calvin had called the cake-eaters 'slavish' (but he also called them 'courtiers'), and that in the previous verse are people variously translated but termed 'slaves' by Sternhold and Hopkins and 'abjectes' by the Great Bible and by Sidney. Top had choices, however, in creating the scene's atmosphere. Here he suggests social disorder, an inverted hierarchy, by stressing the lowly origins of those who scorned a future king.

In many other works, though, the David I have described flourished. John Boys's *Exposition of the Proper Psalms* speaks eloquently of David's faith: not for him Achitophel's 'politicke counsell', Goliath's strength, or the worldliness of those who 'trust in Princes, and make the Kings Minion their mediator'.[27] His eclectic reading of Psalm 57 combines typology, a search for modern relevance, and concern for context. David's anguish in the cave, he says, foreshadows Christ's burial in the tomb – this is from Augustine – and also anticipates the sufferings caused by Catholic 'Machiavelismes'. As for the lions who threaten David, these are 'backbiting Slanderers and Sycophants in the Court of Saul' (sigs. H2v–H8). The margin cites Robert Estienne and Bucer. Sometimes thoughts on David's calumniators lead, as in some annotations, to fragments of an imagined narrative, to lively miniscenes. In *A Mirrour of Mercy*, Nehemiah Rogers traces Doeg and his fellows 'windingly and crookedly' developing their slanders.[28] 'The

Detractor', he says, 'beginneth with a Question aloofe off; proceeds with a kind of praise, and then comes with a (*But*) at which he shooteth all his envenomed arrowes [a pun on but/butt]; But this and this I heare: I could wish it were amended, etc. His Commendation is like a Law-writ, always with a Clause and exception which he makes to smooth the way for scandall' (sig. R4v).

More examples would serve no purpose, although a study could be made of the uses to which David's life as a courtier was put. Such a study would examine how his persecutions served to instruct modern monarchs, how Saul's flatterers were summoned in trying sins of the tongue, how the psalmist's career provided a language for expressing the ambiguities of rebellion, authority, and social mobility.[29] I will end, rather, with the suggestion that when we read Renaissance psalms or 'divine poetry' we remember how often Christians had come to hear the psalter as referring to courts, plots, 'policy', and political tyranny. Its fragmentary but dramatic story seemed exciting, and Francis Quarles was quite right to credit the psalmist with several muses, not just divine Urania, when he asked in a splendidly inept couplet, 'Who ever sung so high, so rapt an lo / As David prompted by heroick Clio?'[30] Why David needed a muse at all is a puzzle, but one sees Quarles's point: as ancient tradition claimed, the psalms are history as much as lyric.

Awareness of this story accompanied a broader range of considerations in psalm translation than is sometimes allowed. I do not mean only that some Renaissance psalmists searched for arcane musical numbers, that some wanted to demonstrate the competitively aesthetic value of the psalter, that rewording his psalmody could express a possibly new sense of personhood, and that David could be drafted to serve political ends. All this is true. But the political strife often heard in the psalms also made the situation of David's imitators more piquant. There were several possible responses. Marot and Wyatt, consciously or not, chose a resonant ambiguity.[31] Others, putting their trust in princes after all, could write as though the great would of course welcome godly song. That is to say, a 'divine' poet could inscribe a courtly system without the tensions that Marot and Wyatt absorbed from David's story – and from their own. A good example is a work that helped create England's vogue for 'divine poetry', Guillaume Du Bartas's 'Urania'. The poem has conflicts, indeed, but they are not so much within the speaker as between the verse's ostensible goal – to promote scriptural poetry – and the worldliness of its hopes.

Du Bartas is often said to express an anti-secular poetics, but not only has his Urania been reading Plato, Horace, and Ovid, she is herself a pagan fiction; that she tells her poet to give up pagan fictions is generous but paradoxical. More to my point, she has rewards to give: widespread admiration, 'eternall Bayes', and 'fair Renown' for 'time-proof Poems'.[32] Curiously, though, she depoliticizes the poet whom Du Bartas's fellow Protestants found so relevant. Thanks to her, she says, the shepherd boy David sang as he did (Urania forgets that scholars dated many or most of his psalms from his days as a great man), and she remarks fondly that 'my David on the trembling strings / Of his divine Harp onely sounds his God', even though many thought that David also sounded his political and military tribulations. Yet this poem is not uninterested in courts. Not only will Urania's devotees win places as 'Secretaries' (officials with security clearance) in the 'Heav'nly Court', here on earth 'Majestie would make you wait upon her, / To manage Causes of the most import.' Du Bartas's English readers knew his friendship with Henry IV, and was not the first translator of this poem James I? A quite secular glamour glows around Urania's 'divine' poet. But not around David; he is with his sheep, eyes fixed on the heavens.

George Wither is not a glamorous figure among psalmists (or poets), but his quite different attitude is the clearer for lacking dazzle. Some of his views would have pleased Urania: 'For, knowe', he says in a poetic 'Soliloquy' written to ready himself for translating the psalms, 'the Deitie that guides my quill, / Haunts not Parnassus, but faire Sion hill'. He does not need Urania's bribes, though, because holy song is its own reward: 'let ... vaine Esteeme goe by: / My soule and I will to our Poesie.'[33] Wither, then, is neither a courtly psalmist with signs of stress like Wyatt nor yet a 'divine poet' like the nobleman Du Bartas basking in anticipated admiration from unthreatening kings. So his long 'exercise' on Psalm I simply transfers his courtly terms to the skies – not changing the game but raising the stakes.[34] The reward for psalmody is to go where Saul and Doeg cannot come. 'Let Kings of Earth; affect an earthly Crowne', he says grandly, 'Let Courtiers at the Court attend their Fates' and fools wonder at 'bubbles of renowne'. Heaven offers better company: 'You, shall be deere unto the Saints above, / And into fellowship with Angels grow.' There love is without 'distrust, or Jelousie', and no one rises only to fall, since 'death, or time, of nought deprive you shall'.

The court to which the psalms transport Wither is not unlike that which David and his commentators imagine in Psalm 101. Filled with 'bliss', God's courtiers live in God's eyes without 'distinction' of person, judged by one not swayed by 'purest beauties', impressed by costume, bribed with 'Indian Ore; / Nor moved, by the flattring tongue'. In his court are no subtle manoeuvres and 'No bribed Favorites', for this happiness 'is neither made by strength / Nor humane policie' (compare, e.g., Beza's notes on Psalm 26). Encouraged by metaphors in the Bible itself, then, Wither has no objection to the system, only to its usual earthly management. So if you 'slight those favors, which each worldling craves; / You shall be Favorites, to that great Prince, / To whom, Earths greatest Monarks are but slaves'. Your 'honours' will be such as 'Kings can neither give; nor take away', and you will be 'full as great as they'. Wither was no Leveller, and this vision of liberty, equality, and fraternity in God's kingdom was not new, but his terms indicate some of the same resentment and vision that animate the Geneva Bible. His David, too, is an anti-court poet, and his heavenly court precisely opposes the one where the psalmist was so infamously treated.

Sterner men than Wither were to sing the songs of David while marching to battle their king, and laxer Christians doubtless wrote psalms without thinking about courts one way or another. Yet so long as the texts I have quoted – to say nothing of the many I have ignored – were read in England and early America, the David I have described could not be forgotten even when unmentioned. It would be instructive to know more exactly which psalmists allowed him to affect their translations and which did not. In the meantime it remains thought provoking that when Sidney wrote, for example, 'With scoffers false, I was theyr feasts delight' (Psalm 35:16), he must at several points in his preparatory reading have visualized the well-fed mockery at court 'bankets'. When he came to Psalm 26 ('Lord, judge me and my case'), he would have known that Beza, for one, had recently identified it as the cry of a misdeemed poet in a social world designed to break 'synceram religionem et vitae integritatem'. As his sister worked on Psalm 58 ('And call yee this to utter what is just'), did she remember how Vatablus pictured courtiers ostensibly gathering to discuss the commonweal but in fact seeking to fawn and flatter?[35] Genevan exiles and Cromwell's troops were not alone in feeling kinship with the psalmist. Aristocratic poets like the Sidneys (and George Herbert) had their own understanding of what David suffered. To meditate on his words had always consoled both rulers and ruled, but the Renaissance view of his lyric poetry encouraged, more than ever, a sceptical scrutiny of the historical world of power and ambition where the discourse of faith could be honestly pronounced only amidst slanders, derision, and lies.

Acknowledgement

This essay expands a paper read at the 1989 convention of the Modern Language Association. I thank John Wall for inviting me to participate, John Shawcross and Carol Kaske for their helpful comments, and Betty Travitsky for advice on Hebrew.

Notes

1. *A Preparation to the Psalter* (London: Nicholas Okes, 1619; reprint in Publications of the Spenser Society no. 37, 1884), sig. H2. 'Psalmograph' is from Thomas Becon, *The sicke mans salve* (London: Richard Day, 1587), sig. A3. A fine study is Rivkah Zim's *English Metrical Psalms: Poetry as Praise and Prayer, 1535–1601* (Cambridge: Cambridge University Press, 1987); on the next century see Philipp von Rohr-Sauer, *English Metrical Psalms from 1600–1660* (Freiburg: Poppen & Ortmann, 1938). Also useful are Hallett Smith, 'English Metrical Psalms in the Sixteenth Century', *Huntington Library Quarterly* 9 (1945/6): 249–71, Coburn Freer, *Music for a King: George Herbert's Style and the Metrical Psalms* (Baltimore, Md.: Johns Hopkins University Press, 1972), and Johannes A. Gaertner, 'Latin Verse Translations of the Psalms, 1500–1600', *Harvard Theological Review* 49 (1956): 271–305.
2. On 'divine' – scripturally based – poetry, see L. B. Campbell, *Divine Poetry and Drama in Sixteenth-Century England* (Cambridge: Cambridge University Press, 1959) and idem, 'The Christian Muse', *Harvard Library Bulletin* 8 (1935): 29–70. Michel Jeanneret, *Poésie et tradition biblique au XVIe siecle* (Paris: J. Corti, 1969), shows the range of motives behind much translation.
3. The fullest study is Barbara Lewalski, *Protestant Poetics and the Seventeenth-Century Religious Lyric* (Princeton, N.J.: Princeton University Press, 1979). See also Ira Clark, *Christ Revealed: The History of the Neotypological Lyric in the English Renaissance* (Gainesville: University Presses of Florida, 1982), who calls the poetics in question post-Reformation, and Annabel Patterson, '*Bermudas* and *The Coronet*: Marvell's Protestant Poetics', *English Literary History* 44 (1977): 478–99.
4. Beryl Smalley, *The Study of the Bible in the Middle Ages*, 2nd ed. (Notre Dame, Ind.: Notre Dame University Press, 1964), ch. 4; the literal events of Scripture so appealed to some that in one religious order the Bible's historical books were not to be read before bedtime for fear of overexcitement (24). I do not wish to oversimplify exegetical history; the evangelical Lefèvre, for example, retained a primarily typological David. See Guy Bedouelle, 'La lecture christologique du psautier dans le *Quincuplex Psalterium* de Lefèvre d'Etaples', in Olivier Fatio and Pierre Fraenkel, eds., *L'histoire de l'exégèse au XVIe siecle* (Geneva: Droz, 1978), 133–43, and Jerome Friedman, 'Servetus and the Psalms: The Exegesis of Heresy', in ibid., 164–78.
5. Richard Robinson, tr., letter to T. Smith in the anonymous *Auncient order... of Prince Arthure* (London: John Wolf, 1583), sig. ***2.
6. On the giant-fight, see Anthony Allingham, 'David as Epic Hero: Drayton's *David and Goliath*', in R.-J. Frontain and Jan Wojick, eds., *The David Myth in Western Literature* (West Lafayette, Ind.: Purdue University Press, 1980), 86–94. Inga-Stina Ewbank's 'The House of David in Renaissance Drama', *Renaissance Drama* 8 (1965): 3–40, describes dramatizations of David's lust and family conflicts. No competition for Dryden's *Absalom and Achitophel*, but deliciously disillusioned in its view of power politics, is *Davids Troubles*

Remembred, thought to have been written by Robert Aylett (London: Richard Hodgkinson, 1638). One author did present a rightful heir who, like David, feigned madness to defeat the plots of his royal 'father' and politic slanderers destined (like David's enemies) to fall into their own traps; see Gene Edward Veith, Jr., '"Wait upon the Lord": David, *Hamlet*, and the Problem of Revenge', in Frontain and Wojick, eds., *The David Myth*, 70–83. Cf. David Evett, 'Types of King David in Shakespeare's Lancastrian Tetralogy', *Shakespeare Studies* 17 (1981): 139–61, who shows the relevance of 2 Samuel to Shakespeare's *Henry IV* and *Henry V*.

7   Frank Carr, *The Law of Defamation* (London: n.p., 1902); Theodore Plucknett, *A Concise History of the Common Law*, 5th ed. (Boston, Mass.: Little, Brown, 1956), ch. 5.

8   An exception is George Chapman's *Petrarchs Seven Penitentiall Psalms* (London: Matthew Selman, 1612), which has David admit that in his sinful days 'No Courtier could so grosly flatter' (Psalm 143). I define 'courtier' as one who serves a monarch in an important capacity, is or wishes to be near him much of the time, and depends on his favour for much of his own position and identity. As a designated king and type of Christ, to be sure, David has no exact parallel with later courtiers.

9   Charles A. Huttar, 'Frail Grass and Firm Tree: David as a Model of Repentance in the Middle Ages and Early Renaissance', in Frontain and Wojick, eds., *The David Myth*, 38–54.

10 That translating the psalms could have political implications has been noted by several scholars. Stephen Greenblatt, in *Renaissance Self-Fashioning: From More to Shakespeare* (Chicago, Ill.: University of Chicago Press, 1980), ch. 3, excavates the commentary on power – God's and King Henry's – buried in Wyatt's adaptation of Aretino's *Sette Salmi*, and Margaret Hannay, in '"Princes you as men must dy": Genevan Advice to Monarchs in the *Psalmes* of Mary Sidney', *English Literary Renaissance* 19 (1989): 22–41, finds subtle admonitions to Elizabeth. Hannay's *Philip's Phoenix* (Oxford: Oxford University Press, 1990), 103–4, notes the importance of the psalms' concern with slander. More generally, see Hardin Craig, Jr., 'The Geneva Bible as a Political Document', *Pacific Historical Review* 7 (1938): 40–49. Huguenots thought that David's troubles anticipated their own: after the 1572 St. Bartholomew massacre, Doeg's slaughter of holy men (1 Samuel 22; Psalm 52) took on fresh horror; see Edward A. Gosselin, 'David in Tempore Belli: Beza's David in the Service of the Huguenots', *The Sixteenth Century Journal* 7 (1976): 31–54, and idem, *The King's Progress to Jerusalem: Some Interpretations of David During the Reformation Period and Their Patristic and Medieval Background* (Malibu, Calif.: Undena, 1976), which notes Beza's references to courtly evils. To be sure, using psalms as political commentary was not new: the *Psalter* of the fourteenth-century hermit Richard Rolle (Oxford: Clarendon, 1884) frowns at 'ill pryncys' (Psalm [89]), 'oure pryncys now, that ledis thaire life in filth of syn' (Psalm [105]), and 'ill leders of cristen men' (Psalm [107]), which the editor, H. R. Bramley, says means Edward II and his nobles. The David on whom I focus, however, is specifically the victim

of evil-tongued magnates, one whose story inscribed a drama opposing God's poet to a king's court.

11 *Les 'Tituli Psalmorum' des manuscrits Latins* (Rome: Abbaye Saint-Jerome, 1959); the introduction describes an exception, Theodore of Mopsuestia. Salmon's observation seems generally true despite the Hebrew-Latin versions Smalley notes and occasional consultations of Jewish tradition.

12 Bucer was highly regarded in England and actually lived there from 1549 until his death in 1551; the translation uses his pseudonym, 'Felinus'. The psalter was republished in London in 1544(?) but without credit. Its 'Hebrew verity' was less irenic than competitive, according to R. Gerald Hobbs, 'Martin Bucer on Psalm 22: A Study in the Application of Rabbinic Exegesis by a Christian Hebraist', in Fatio and Fraenkel, eds, *L'histoire de l'exégèse*, 144–63. The translator, George Joye, fled to Strasbourg after being denounced for 'heresy'; there is a section on him in Lewis Lupton's engaging multi-volume *History of the Geneva Bible*, vol. 4 (London: Olive Tree Press, 1972), 79–84.

13 In his *Icones* (Geneva: I. Laonius, 1580), sig. Y4, Beza makes Marot an anti-David unable to resist the court's indecency.

14 Marot, *Traductions*, ed. C. A. Mayer (Geneva: Slatkine, 1980). Marot began his translations in the 1530s; by his death in 1544 he had finished forty-nine. Mayer doubts Marot's authorship of the arguments, as well as the debt to Bucer that others have seen, but Marot accepted them, and the similarities to Bucer are in fact often close. Huguenots did not always retain the full headings; the psalter printed with Olivetan's French Bible as revised by the Genevan leadership (I have seen the 1567 edition) softens them.

15 Ibid.

16 *Psaumes mis en vers français (1551–1562)*, ed. Pierre Pidoux (Geneva: Droz, 1984).

17 I shall refer to Vatablus as the author of these marginalia, though they may have come to Estienne through the mediation of one of Vatablus's students. My copy of this text, which was reused in one of Estienne's Bibles, has verses by Sternhold and Hopkins squeezed into the margins in a Renaissance hand. Studying the notes has convinced me that Sidney probably knew Estienne's psalter and that it should be added to the commentaries and translations listed by Seth Weiner in 'The Quantitative Poems and the Psalm Translations: The Place of Sidney's Experimental Verse in the Legend', in Jan van Dorsten, Dominic Baker-Smith, and Arthur F. Kinney, eds., *Sir Philip Sidney: 1586 and the Creation of a Legend* (Leiden: Brill, 1986), 193–220. Professor Weiner kindly showed me a related paper, 'Sidney and the Rabbis: A Note on the Psalms of David and Renaissance Hebraica'.

18 Bishop Richard Sampson, *In priores quinquaginta psalmos* (London: Thomas Berthelet, 1539), sees the eloquence in Psalm 12 as 'pestifera' trickiness promoting bad religion. He cites as an example the courtier who called Luther 'Luder' (i.e. fool) not once but *passim*, a slap at Thomas More's *Responsio ad Lutherum*. Sidney makes the same rhetoricians boast of having 'tales to tell', an intriguing choice of words by the author of *Arcadia*, implying both slander and fiction.

19 King James himself cordially disliked the Geneva Bible's interest in political dynamics, and it is to his unhappiness with its annotations that we owe the translation bearing his name. See Maurice S. Betteridge, 'The Bitter Notes: The Geneva Bible and its Annotations', *The Sixteenth Century Journal* 14 (1983): 41–62. True, kings could themselves be called Davids; two remarkable instances of such identification are a carving of Francis I as David in the cathedral at Auch and a psalter made for Henry VIII with illustrations showing His Majesty as the psalmist. Henry's marginal notes are described by John King, *Tudor Royal Iconography: Literature and Art in an Age of Religious Crisis* (Princeton, N.J.: Princeton University Press, 1989), 76–80; Henry did not annotate the (unillustrated) Psalm 51 in which David repents his adultery.
20 London: Thomas East and Henry Middleton.
21 Theodore Beza, *Christian Meditations upon Eight Psalmes*, trans. I. S. S. (London: Christopher Barker, [1583?]), Psalm 102, sig. H4. I quote *The Geneva Bible: A Facsimile of the 1560 Edition*, ed. Lloyd E. Berry (Madison: University of Wisconsin Press, 1969).
22 *The Araignement of an Unruly Tongue* (London: G. P[urslow], 1619), sig. D7. The arrow will fall back on the archer (sig. D4v). Also at risk are blasphemers, if Webbe is right that in Mansfield one was snatched by the devil in mid-blasphemy.
23 *Psalmorum Davidis et aliorum prophetarum libri quinque* (London: Thomas Vautrollier, 1580), Psalm 12, argument; Anthony Gilby's translation was also published in 1580. It should be remembered that many psalms were thought to have been said by David when in exile and not physically at court.
24 That some heard a reply to an imputation of ambition may indicate unease, one result of reading David less typologically – as his kingdom becomes like other kingdoms, political desire unexceptionable in God's son can seem troubling even in God's elect prince. No one I have read thought David power-hungry, but some make a point of denying his ambition or 'policy'. Thus Virgilio Malvezzi's *David Persecuted* (London: John Haviland, 1637), sig. H4, says of David's showing a bit of Saul's garment to prove that he could have killed his king but chose not to: 'That which David doth here out of modesty, is done often by others out of subtilty.' I have never seen serious scepticism about David himself, however; political cynicism is deflected onto his enemies. For a David that would have baffled Wyatt's contemporaries, see Alexandra Halasz's clever 'Wyatt's David', *Texas Studies in Literature and Language* 30 (1988): 320–44. This 'unregenerate David' who 'craftily subverts the psalms to gain material ends' is too much at odds with his time.
25 London: [Thomas Vautrollier,] 1580.
26 Amsterdam: Ian Fredericksz Stam, 1629.
27 London: William Aspley, 1617.
28 London: E. Brewster, 1640.
29 Many recollected that David was 'advaunced from the sheephooke to the scepter', from 'a kings page … to a kings personage' (Richard Robinson, preface to Victorinus Strigelius, *A Proceeding in the Harmonie of King Davids Harpe* [London: John Wolfe, 1591], sig. A2v). Malvezzi's conclusions on class and

power in *David Persecuted* are particularly bold. As Hannay notes in *Philip's Phoenix*, English sermons frequently deduce politically relevant parallels between David's history and modern times. My own favourite is an admonishment to the queen by Edward Dering in a 1569 sermon on Psalm 78:70 ('He chose David his servant also, and tooke him from the sheepfolds'): once Elizabeth was '*Tanquam ovis*, as a Sheepe appointed to be slayne' (Psalm 44:20), but now with 'the Sterne and Helme' in her hands, 'Take heede you heare not nowe of [Jeremiah]: *Tanquam indomita iuvenca*, as an untamed and unrulie Heiffer.' 'Search your raines', he urges, to check up on yourself. The thought of Elizabeth searching her reins for signs of an untamed heifer is mindbending (*A Sermon Preached before the Quenes Majestie* [London: James Roberts, 1596; first published London: J. Awdely, 1569?], sig. A7v.

30 *Divine Fancies* (London: John Marriot, 1632), sig. Z4v.
31 On Marot, see my 'Musical Strains: Marat's Double Role as Psalmist and Courtier', in Marie-Rose Logan and Peter Rudnytsky, eds., *Contending Kingdoms: Historical, Psychological, and Feminist Approaches to the Literature of Sixteenth-Century England and France* (Detroit, Mich.: Wayne State University Press, 1990). Herbert criticism has explored the points of contact between religious and courtier-like energies: see Marion White Singleton, *God's Courtier: Configuring a Different Grace in George Herbert's 'Temple'* (Cambridge: Cambridge University Press, 1987); Richard Strier, *Love Known: Theology and Experience in George Herbert's Poetry* (Chicago, Ill. University of Chicago Press, 1983); and idem, 'Sanctifying the Aristocracy: "Devout Humanism" in François de Sales, John Donne, and George Herbert', *The Journal of Religion* 69 (1989): 36–58. On related complexities see Gary Waller, '"This Matching of Contraries": Calvinism and Courtly Philosophy in the Sidney Psalms', *English Studies* 55 (1974): 22–31.
32 I quote the 1606 translation by Joshua Sylvester in his *Works*, ed. A. B. Grosart ([Edinburgh: T. and A. Constable,] 1880; reprint Hildesheim: G. Olms, 1969), 2:3–7.
33 *A Preparation to the Psalter*, sigs. N4–N5v.
34 *Exercises upon the First Psalme Both in Prose and Verse* (London: Edward Griffin, 1620, reprint in Publications of the Spenser Society no. 34, 1882, and New York: Burt Franklin, 1967; I quote 128, 148–49).
35 I quote J. C. A. Rathmell's edition of the Sidney Psalter (Garden City, N.Y.: Doubleday, 1963).

5

Musical strains: Marot's double role as psalmist and courtier

In about 1519 Clément Marot wrote to Francis I to request a place. He is a young 'Rimeur', he says in verses that equivocate on words for 'rhyme', and hopes to find 'par sa rime heur' (success through rhyme).[1] The style and stance are those of a late Medieval court poet: smiling, gracious, clever, one arm held across the bending waist, the other outstretched to support the upturned palm. Marot's 'heur' was at first service with the king's sister Marguerite, but in 1527 he became one of Francis's valets de chambre. By the time he died at Torino in 1544, he could reckon up what he had won: fame, favour, some money, a house, and occasional royal protection against the guardians of Catholic orthodoxy who twice imprisoned him and sought to kill him. And, because of his reputation as a Lutheran, he had twice fled France, terrified, he wrote Francis from Ferrara in 1535, of his prince's 'oeil obscur' (darkened eye) and punished, he wrote from Savoy in 1543, 'De plus ne voir vostre Royalle face' (no longer to see your royal face).[2] He had also translated forty-nine psalms, which together with the translations of Theodore Beza were to form the influential Huguenot psalter. Marot had not begun work with this in mind, though, and Protestant enthusiasm made his situation in France more delicate.

In this essay I will trace some of the difficulties Marot found in being a courtier psalmist with two patrons, both of them givers of reward and punishment but one of them beyond the reach of kings and theological faculties. I will also suggest how those complexities intersected at times with Marot's situation as the protégé of a king who was not only a minor poet himself but, depending on circumstances, sometimes the object of humanist or reformist hopes and at other times the persecutors' ally. Marot must have recognized the potential contradiction between his roles as courtier and psalmist, for his detractors told him about it. I suspect he also sensed that the king too had a double part, being both the protective father of his people, a potential David, but also the unpredictable and terrifying Saul. As a psalmist in trouble, Marot might have to play David to the king's Saul, soothing his suspicious anger even while stressing the safer role of Ovid courting Augustus. Yet to play David to the king's David might require even subtler evasions and deflections of voice.

It is true that the life of a court poet at a time of cultural upheaval could never have been easy, but Marot's position was, I think, particularly poignant, and had become so in part because of Reformation concerns with scriptural language and Renaissance concerns with the source and transmission of the poetical impulse. Arguments over scriptural translation touched on the very bases of thought and society, on how meaning inheres in or is constructed by words, on how revelation might survive rewording, on whether exposing holy meaning directly to the multitudes might vulgarize the words while misleading the many, and on who is authorized to control or read the meaning and the words. Even before the Pléiade's more strident assertions, poets had sometimes claimed a special status; and since merely to read the psalms correctly was to make them one's own, translators could in this case acquire a *furor* caught, so to speak, from David's own. If the translator was also a courtier, was his position more ambiguous than that of any good man doing his best in a fallen world? Good men and good poets can serve even bad rulers, or so many have believed; yet for Marot to be a servant and an inspired poet impersonating the impersonator of Christ remained tricky, not least because both he and his enterprise had been called heretical.

In any case, as the attacks on Marot make clear, many disliked the notion of a valet de chambre who presumed to imitate and interpret David. Their disgust was perhaps due to jealousy or was simply assumed because it was polemically convenient; but it owed something, I think, to the Reformation's necessary interest in how words relate to power and how authors relate to both power and the Word, a Word that seemed to some to be escaping from traditional social controls and seemed to others to be so uniquely precious that only good and serious men should dare wrest it from one set of words to another. To conservative Catholics, Marot could seem a dangerously arrogant vulgarizer and distorter who typified new threats to the realm; but some Protestants thought him too worldly for his task, too courtly. And although Catholics might hesitate to say so out loud, one more reason for their irritation with Marot's combined role as courtier-psalmist was distrust of the king himself, so much less reliable than the Sorbonne or Parlement. Marot's situation, in sum, was complex in ways not quite anticipated by the ancient Christian tension between World and Word.

Renaissance psalm translation incorporated aims ranging from liturgical reformation to the discovery of magically 'effective' settings, but Marot's own scriptural poetry, probably begun in the 1530s, had started at least in part as courtiership.[3] His first published psalm, after all, was a rendition of Psalm 6 included in a 1533 edition of Marguerite's *Miroir de l'âme pécheresse*, a 'Lutheran' addition that seems to have offended the Sorbonne but not the king.[4] At court it was fashionable to sing his efforts, and in 1540 they were even presented to an appreciative Charles V. Although they later appeared regularly on lists of officially forbidden books, publishers in the capital continued to print them with the royal privilege.[5] Marot's problem was that an activity many in a calmer time would have thought innocent, an activity that evidently pleased the people who mattered to him, was rapidly coming to appear heretical; and Francis, a patron of the new learning and not personally opposed to his sister's evangelical fervour, found heresy enraging: it offended his religious sensibilities, and its more radical implications threatened his job. When he was frightened, pressured, or allied to other Catholic powers, the climate would worsen for those who, like Marot, were suspected of Lutheranism. When he was courting German princes or upset by insolent theologians and parlements, Marot was freer to laugh at those he could claim were rebels to throne and muses alike.

One further irony of Marot's position was that he was translating texts believed to have been written by a courtier subjected to royal persecution and by that same courtier after he had become a king. David had seen courts from both sides, a fact that drew increased attention as biblical exegesis turned more often from allegory to philology and history. Thus Marot's headings, probably modelled on those of Martin Bucer, do not merely mention but emphasize David's responses to his adventures both before and after his accession.[6] The heading for Psalm 5, for instance, says that 'David en exil ayant beaucoup souffert et s'attendant souffrir davantaige par les flatteurs qui estoient autour de Saul dresse sa priere à Dieu' (David in exile, having suffered much, and expecting to suffer more, from the flatterers who were around Saul, addresses his prayer to God). Commentators disagreed on the specifics, to be sure. For Marot, Psalm 4 concerns 'la conspiration d'Abschalom' (the conspiracy of Absalom), but the Geneva Bible of 1560 says that David refers to the time 'when Saul persecuted him'. Marot and other translators agreed, though, that the psalms record David's sufferings at court or in exile.

David, then, knew from experience the evils of court life. Indeed, despite the significance to Christian pastoral poetry of his earliest occupation, the Renaissance David was much less a shepherd poet than one might expect. He was a giant killer, courtier, poet in many genres, sinner, soldier, and shepherd amazingly turned anointed king – a *royal* poet, his own laureate, and eventually his own patron. His complaints thus seemed to anticipate the Renaissance anti-courtier sentiments that flourished alongside flattery of the great, especially as there is much in the psalms on slander and mockery. In truth, the story of David as recounted in 1 Samuel has very little on evil tongues, but the increased effort to tie the psalms to events recorded elsewhere in the Bible allowed for the simultaneous politicizing of the psalter and the projection onto Saul's court of the psalms' preoccupation with language. Thus in Marot's Psalm 12, Saul is surrounded by sycophants with 'levres blandissantes' (flattering lips) who say, 'Nous serons grans par noz langues sur tous; / A nous de droict noz levres appartiennent; / Flattons, mentons; qui est maistre sur nous?' (By our tongues we will be great beyond everyone; by rights our lips belong to us: let us flatter and lie – who is master over us?) Court poets also want to be 'grands par [leurs] langues', and the question of to whom one's lips belong is a complicated matter for a poet pensioned by a king but speaking in the voice of God.

But since David was a king as well as a courtier, Medieval and Renaissance courtiers could flatter monarchs by calling them David (which also recalled their priestly role). Such compliments became conventional, even if few writers achieved the dazzle of Christopher Watson on Henry V's Davidic kingship: 'This warlike Captaine was a sincere shepherd, whom his fawning flocke faithfully favored, and obediently obeyed', such a 'just justiciarie, that no facinorous fact was pretermitted unpunished, or faithful frendshyp destitute of due desert'.[7] When a king was also a poet (though Francis himself favoured the amatory rondeau), such flattery took that in. James I, Bishop William Cowper told him, was, like David, the 'heart, the tongue, and the pen of the first King' [i.e., God] (*Two Sermons*, 1618, sig. A4). Eventually any Protestant or even potentially reforming monarch could be seen specifically as a David overthrowing Goliath, to whom the pope was regularly compared, or replacing Saul, the pseudo-father of his people now miscalling himself 'papa', patron only of insolence and repression. Every new reign, like any other birth, precipitates both hope for renovation and fear of change; in a time of rapid religious shifts such hope and fear are projected onto a monarch/patron/*pater patriae* with particular force.

Was Francis a David? Marot was not alone in saying so. In 1547 Marguerite told God that the dying king was 'vostre vray David' (your true David), who 'Pour malladye et pour prison, / Pour peine, doulleur et souffrance, / Pour envie ou par trahison, / N' a eu en vous moindre esperance' (in sickness and in prison, in pain, grief, and suffering, and despite envy or treason, had no less hope in you).[8] Several years earlier, however, she had been more concerned to persuade the brother himself. For New Year's Day 1543, she sent him an image of David aimed, I suspect, at recalling a Davidic role she feared he might neglect in her absence.[9] According to the accompanying poem, the hero has heard of Francis's problems with modern Philistines and has come to help. All naked and unarmed like that? Yes, says David, demonstrating a 'Lutheran' reliance on faith rather than on the armour a king had given him. He has already slain the 'geant espouvantable' (terrifying giant), symbol of anyone 'qui veult estre / Du roy Françoys ou ennemy ou maistre' (who wishes to be enemy or master of King Francis). God loves the king for recognizing his nothingness before his 'vray pere' (true father), and Francis forgives 'son injure passée' (past offences). God has told David that the king honours each 'psaulme / Que mon esprit par vous a composé' (each psalm that my Spirit has composed through you), so the psalmist gives Marguerite his sling, a stone, and a psalter. Perhaps ominously, at a time when Francis was pursuing heretics, Marot had just arrived in Geneva, and Marguerite was not quite in her usual favour, her brother responded modestly that 'Poinct je ne suis au bon David semblable / ... Je suis pecheur' (I am not at all like the good David ... I am a sinner). He sends Marguerite a Saint Catherine, who drew her power from the same God who helped Jael drive the 'clou deshonneste' (vile nail) into a 'royalle teste' (royal head) (there may be a trace of acid in the brotherly humour here). Has the king missed the point? David was himself a sinner, after all, which is one reason his psalms are so therapeutic. Or is Francis making a subtler point, nimbly refusing the part that Marguerite, like Marot, Calvin, and many others, still hoped he would play? As the English diplomatic records show, he himself fed those hopes when it suited him; but here he sends his sister a Catholic saint for her thoughtful scrutiny.[10]

David was a king but not, like Francis, through inheritance. His upward mobility caused little overt anxiety, for unlike Tamburlaine he was God's beloved, not his scourge. Still, his was a story apt to move the imagination of those impressed by vertical political movement, and future Levellers would have enjoyed certain passages in Virgilio Malvezzi's *Davide perseguitato* (trans. R. Ashley, 1637): 'He that bringeth David from the sheephooke to the scepter, and exalteth him from the stable to the Kingdome, it is hee that humbled himselfe from his Kingdome to the stable: Hee that is both a sheepheard and a King, maketh him a King who was but a sheepheard' (sig. B8). And if God can translate a shepherd from fields to court, he can lead others to greener pastures. Thus Calvin says in his commentaries on the psalms that as David found a throne, so he himself had become 'from base and slender beginnings' a 'preacher and minister of his Gospel' (trans. A. Golding, 1571, sig. *7). David's career thus shows God's willingness to exalt the valleys or make the mountains low, and nothing could counteract the power of that image in revolutionary times. So it is not surprising that within a few years Marot's translations were sung by those who despised hierarchy itself. In June 1551, for instance, an armed crowd of 'menu peuple' (humble folk) including women and children gathered in Lyons singing 'les pseaumes de David traduicts par Clement Marot, le tout en scandalle et blasphème de Dieu et de sa saincte église catholique' (the psalms of David translated by Clement Marot, the whole matter a scandal and blasphemy against God and the Holy Catholic Church).[11] As Calvin told the readers of his 1543 *Forme des prières* (containing thirty psalms by Marot), Chrysostom himself had hoped that 'tant hommes que femmes et petits enfans' (men, women, and small children alike) would sing psalms.[12] But the mixing of genders and ages and the excitement of 'little people' who speak only the 'vulgar' suggest a tension, finally, between inspiration by a God who is 'tousjours elevant les humbles et restablissant les miserables' (always raising the meek and restoring the wretched) (Psalm 113, argument) and royal patronage; indeed, there is tension between *sola Scriptura* and the entire patronage system of kings and magnates as power brokers of language. God is the final patron, mysterious in his methods and favours but at least beyond corruption or vanity. Omniscient, he must be a good reader (a disquieting as well as consoling thought) and impervious to slander. This very fact, though, raises uncomfortable questions about his earthly counterparts.

An alert court psalmist like Marot might have felt the pressure of other problematic energies inherent in his enterprise. One area of unease and possibility was the question of what poetry owes to earlier texts and to inspiration.[13] Whom does a translator of the psalms imitate? God? If the Lord favours such poetry, does he also lend a hand? If so, does the help travel through tradition and exegesis? Perhaps it works through the power of scripture itself, or maybe the aid comes directly from the Spirit – or from the Father, for within this complex of issues lie potent images of sonship and fatherhood. David was not Saul's child, but he married his daughter; and twice after David spared his life, Saul called him 'son' (1 Sam. 24, 26). Other sons, even without benefit of Freud, might have sympathized as Saul's envious javelin came hurtling at him. David's harping could, at first, calm Saul's evil moods, a talent many sons and court poets might envy. And, of course, David was beloved by the most important Father of all, was indeed a type of that Father's own Son. Yet David was also a parent, weeping for the rebel Absalom ('would God I had died for thee') and consoled by Solomon ('Beholde, a sonne is borne to thee, which shalbe a man of rest', 1 Chron. 22, Geneva translation, 1560).

Also difficult, as well as inviting, is the matter of voice.[14] Many or even most of the psalms, it was believed, are spoken by David in the person of Christ. Readers differed on the degree to which David knew he was speaking for the Son of God as well as for the son of Jesse; Lefèvre d'Etaples, much admired by Marguerite, thought he was exactly aware of his impersonation. May a translator, remouthing David's words, also speak the Word that created him? If he does his work well, the translator's voice will be intensely personal, yet he may hope (or fear?) that it also belongs to David and Christ, his cospeakers, and to God, his coauthor and patron. Concepts like the anxiety of influence do not begin to address the complexity of his situation.

It is because of situational and psychological tangles like this that we cannot say if Marot turned to the psalms because he hoped that being a David would resolve the tension in his position as a sometimes serious and courageous poet with a constricted role in a hierarchal and dangerous court, or whether he translated the psalms to please God, Francis, and Marguerite only to find himself more like David than he had anticipated – exiled, slandered, hounded (though without the prospect of a throne). In other words, was David a precedent for combining roles or was imitating him a *cause* of tension? Perhaps his relation to David, like that to Francis, was a mixture of service and identification (and even rivalry, although hardly consciously). We will never know how all this worked itself out in Marot's personal depths, but its impact on his poetry is not impossible to hear. And if, as Gerard Defaux has argued, Marot was led eventually by a distrust of mere human words into a search for a style that resonates with silence, then that silence may have as a source not only fidelity to God's Word but the impasse into which the mazes I have described can lead.[15]

Robert Griffin has argued that Marot remained a court poet to the end, his vocations as courtier and Christian poet uniting in a single sensibility.[16] Yes; yet it is possible to feel more unease in Marot's verse than Griffin allows, even in the early work. Sometimes the tensions seem all the more intriguing precisely because although Marot and Francis were radically unlike in their worldly positions, they shared several roles. Both had been, or would be, Davids; and both had, in effect, inherited their posts. Furthermore, Marot tried throughout his career to persuade the king that he and his 'serf' were bound by mutual understanding. Hence tactics such as the faked impudence of concluding a request for funds with a parody of court flattery ('mon stile j'enfleray, / Disant ... / Roy plus que Mars d'honneur environné, / Roy le plus Roy qui fut oncq couronné' (I will inflate my style, / saying, / 'O King, whom more than Mars all honor does surround, / O King, more of a king than any ever crowned') (Epître 25). Such surefooted movements, common in Marot's poetry to Francis, posit a reader who can recognize urbanity, and hence imply that patron and poet share a culture too subtle for the agents of envy and obscurantism. So it is significant that even within this pleasant myth, this assumed conspiracy of wit and insight, cracks appear.

Thus Marot's charming Epigram 246, of uncertain date, touches lightly on topics that, particularly in the context of psalm translation, generate modulating overtones: identity, role, paternity, and Rome.

> Si mon Seigneur, mon Prince & plus que Pere,
> Qui des François FRANÇOYS premier se nomme,
> N'estoit point Roy de sa France prospere,

> Ne Prince avec, mais simple Gentil-homme,
> J'irois autant dix fois par dela Rome,
> Que j'en suis loing, chercher son accoinctance,
> Pour sa vertu qui plus fort le couronne
> Que sa fortune & Royalle prestance.
> Mais souhaiter cas de telle importance
> Seroit vouloir mon bien particulier,
> A luy dommage, & tort faict à la France,
> Qui a besoing d'un Roy tant singulier.

If, says Marot, my lord, prince, and more than father, Francis the first of Frenchmen, were neither king nor prince of his flourishing France but a mere 'gentilhomme', I would go ten times as far beyond Rome as I am now distant from it just to meet him, whom virtue crowns more than does his fortune and royal excellence; but in such a great matter to wish for my private good would hurt the king and wrong France, which needs so singular a king. Griffin remarks that, after Marot separates the man Francis from his role, he circles back to destroy 'the presumptuously individual wish of the narrator' (144). True, but he has also temporarily dethroned and decentred his 'plus que pere' ('more than father', a phrase Mayer's note says echoes the 'Testament' of Villon, Marot's elder). He sends his king well beyond Rome, city of the Holy Father as well as of Augustus Maro, a city from which the poet is now 'loing', restoring him only from statesmanlike solicitude for the public 'besoing'. And the poem's witty move from Francis 'premier' to Francis 'singulier' ('outstanding', but with a suggestion of 'unique') renders more problematic a Francis II, biological continuation of the doubly patronymic 'Francis'. Here is a singular father indeed. To read this spirited compliment as a complaint would be preposterous; the king was doubtless charmed by the implied play with his own separation of monarch and man in his favourite oath, 'foi de gentilhomme'. Yet to think thoughts like those Marot here records discloses, however endearingly, the subversions and power possible to the imagination, to the conditional tense.

Not surprisingly, then, similar dissonance concerning role and fatherhood qualifies Marot's more sustained courtships. In 1527, all humility and smiles, he asked to succeed his deceased father in the king's household (Epître 12), joining the 'brebis' (sheep) in the king's 'parc': 'Et ne falloit, Sire, tant seulement / Qu'effacer Jan & escrire Clément' (and all this needs, Sire, is to erase 'Jean' and write 'Clément'). To suggest effacing the father's name and inserting the son's raises thoughts of generational replacement for both poets and kings (and a modern reader may recall the famous story of Freud's faint when Jung described similar erasures).[17] But then, having asked for the 'bien Paternel' (patrimony) as though poets too could rule by the death of fathers (or at least of predecessors like Saul and Louis XII), Clément revives

Jean long enough to quote the latter's dying advice. There are other curious touches. Francis 'cherit & practique ... ce noble Art Poëtique' (cherishes and practises the noble poetic art) and his 'Dire est ung divin Oracle' (his speech is a divine oracle), but the poem ends with a demotion: Marot's father had a double 'bien': his art was his 'bien Spirituel, / Et voz Biensfaictz estoient son Temporel'; Jean has left Clément his spiritual goods, may Francis order his temporal. A royal oracle might do better than that. Marot says engagingly of the benefits he wants: 'Vray est aussi que pas ne les merite, / Mais bien est vray que j'ay d'iceulx besoing' (true, I do not merit them, but beyond question I need them). How suavely modest. But in a man recently let out of jail for, as seems most probable, a 'Lutheran' breach of Lenten rules, this seems an unrepentant way of relating merit to reward.

It is possible to hear similar jars in much of Marot's major poetry to Francis, not because he was a malcontent (although he would have had cause) but because he was human, because this is how words work, and because the entanglements and angers of the developing Reformation made his elegant poise hard to sustain on all levels of language and suggestion. Here I will focus on a few slippages in the courtier's stance, particularly as they relate, directly or indirectly, to psalmody. Doubtless some of the resulting tension is unconscious, but as Marot became more seriously interested in scriptural poetry, the ironies of his situation were bound to occur to him. His hints, deliberate or not, seem to gesture particularly at a disquiet concerning fathers, patrons, and words.[18]

In October 1534 posters attacking the mass went up in Paris, Blois, and even Amboise, where Francis was staying. Although uninvolved, Marot fled; he was accused of heresy and his papers, probably including some psalms, were burned. He sought refuge with Duchess Renée of Ferrara, daughter to Louis XII and Francis's sister-in-law; and there in the summer of 1535, he composed Epître 36, designed to show that he was not a Lutheran (his slippery denials convinced few), not a rebel, and not out of touch. His noble and moving poem, however, has implications that modify the flattery and even deflect, a little, Marot's overt meaning. Written to a ruler by a poet in exile, the epistle has been called 'Ovidian'.[19] Certainly Ovid was on his mind. Epîtres 44 to the king and 46 to Marguerite, both composed in the summer of 1536, paraphrase the *Tristia* and *Ex Ponto*, although Marot consistently revises out Ovid's admissions of guilt. But Ovid was not the only exiled poet Marot knew; David too had fled an angry king, and muted Davidic touches show even in his Ovidian letters, particularly and explicitly in that to Marguerite, but in those to Francis as well. Thus when in Epître 37 his enemies say that his master has abandoned him, he prays, 'O Sire, donq renverse leurs langaiges' (O Sire, then, overturn their words). Compare Psalm 3, on which Marot had been working, where it is God who 'renverse' the enemy mouths that sneeringly say his Lord will offer David no help. And in Epître 44 he baptizes Ovid's reference to singing Jove a poem on the gigantomachia with the claim that God is pleased if one 'Loue ses faictz' (praises his deeds), which is just what the psalmist often does – indeed, in David's case it is the singer himself who has conquered a giant.

Moments like these, and even a few verbal parallels, provide an ambiguous Davidic subtext for Epître 36, one quite as important as the Ovidian and, I think, too seldom fully heard. Marot fled, he says to Francis, because he feared corrupt and inhumane judges, happy to 'ne tomber en leurs mains' (not fall into their hands). The wording closely recalls (or anticipates) Marot's translation of Psalm 7, 3–4, which according to Renaissance exegetes is David's protestation of innocence in the face of false accusation and Saul's persecution (see Marot's headnote). Francis, says Marot, has protected him in the past against mutual enemies who hate learning and thus defy the 'vueil celeste' (heavenly will) of a patron as great as the Caesars. The strategy of the argument is like that of Psalm 5 ('Pseaulme propre contre les calumniateurs', Marot's headnote was to say): David asks God for protection against liars, 'Car c'est contre toy qu'ilz se prennent' (for it is against you that they aim). Now Marot is slandered with 'bruyt plein de propos menteurs' (noise full of lying speech), phrasing that recalls many psalms. May God sustain him if he must burn. More on evil judges, on the ransacking of his library, closet of the muses, in which a poet should be free to read anything and test it against scripture. Knowing his innocence, he would have gone first to Francis, but he was warned by someone (somewhat like David hearing of his danger from Jonathan) to fear a king's darkened eye. So he went, not to a foreign prince (as David had done, although Marot does not say so), but to the king's own sister. France is ungrateful. He misses his children. Now he is with the daughter of Louis XII, father of his people. May the king please understand him.

The poem is not, as it may seem, a jumble of brilliant digressions. I would call it a triptych centred on a martyrdom. Each outer panel is crowded with arguments; pagan references (Caesars, Muses); echoes of, or references to, scripture; and complaints and narratives of injustice, slander, and flight. Rising up in the poem's approximate middle is the narrow panel in which the bustle ceases and Marot speaks directly to God, setting off his discourse further by a shift to 'vous' (Francis is 'tu'). O Lord, he prays, may I believe I am reserved for your glory; though you have not had my body burnt, allow me to write in your honour. But if you have predestined my flesh to the flames, may it be for you and your 'parolle', your Word. And, 'pere', in such torment may my soul trust only in you, invoking you to my last sigh. In a time of persecution this last sentiment was hardly singular, if seldom expressed with such brilliant fervour, but in their context the invocation's concluding lines specifically suggest Psalm 146. In that cry of fear and faithful hope, David tells his soul 'to praise the Lord during my life: as long as I have anie being, I wil sing unto my God'. Marot did not translate this psalm, but in his work on the psalter he would have discovered that scholars read the verse I have quoted as saying, literally, that David would praise God to his last *breath*; for example, the notes to Robert Estienne's 1546 psalter, drawn from lectures by the great Hebraist Vatablus, whom Marot may have consulted, say that the Hebrew means 'Exibit spiritus eius' (his spirit/breath will leave). The famous following verse says, 'Put not your trust in princes', for only God keeps his word and sustains us with true help. Had Marot in truth been burned alive, he might have remembered to his comfort that in this same psalm God takes care of the widow and orphan. Marot retains David's statement of faith in God alone and his vow to sing till the breath leaves him, but he naturally omits the bit on princes.

Marot's prayer is also an ecstasy, for in a traditional postraptural confusion, he asks, 'Que dys je? où suys je? O noble Roy Françoys, / Pardonne moy, car allieurs je pensoys' (What am I saying? Where am I? O noble King Francis, pardon me, for my thoughts wandered).[20] Marot may need pardon, for his imagined immolation could take place only with the permission of some ruler, most likely Francis (later in the poem he hints at the world's amazement over the executions of 1534 and 1535). And though any ruler might admire such prayerful fidelity to a Lord who has 'predestined' the fire – just the sort of 'serf' a monarch wants – there is little room for Francis in this image of the literally inflamed poet who has been writing God's praises. Little room for Francis in what Marot says overtly, that is, but if indeed the prayer invites us (and the king?) to hear an echo of Psalm 146, then there is plenty of room in the subtext, the complex underplot, for Saul. The scene's ecstatic verticality excludes the broad world of patrons, courts, cities, yet they are responsible as secondary causes for the stake and reaching flames. In that fire Marot suffers for the 'parolle' whose written form he had begun translating, by which he judges other texts, and whose words he has echoed. Furthermore, the God for whose Word the poet dies and whose honour he has been singing is no mere patron but a 'pere'. Griffin has rightly remarked the hopeful logic behind Marot's references to Louis XII as 'pere du peuple', but in fact Francis's own paternity, of nation or princelings, goes unmentioned.[21] The poem's fathers include God, Louis XII, and Marot himself, not Francis – and to compare him to the Caesars is hardly reassuring in this regard.

Was Francis reassured? Marot can hardly have hoped to repair his fortunes with Francis by comparing him to Saul, even if the logic of his poetry points that way. If he consciously intended the king himself to hear the echoes of the psalms – and Francis, who intermittently encouraged such piety, was a fellow poet and no fool – he may have been attempting something both cannier and nobler than self-dramatizing reproach; he may have hoped, rather, to appeal from one Francis to another, summoning the king to remember who he was before he began to be Saul. But he cannot, or does not, say this clearly, so the poem remains curiously, if only implicitly, divided between a flattering overt attempt to re-establish a courtly role as a pious, urbane, unheretical supporter of the king and good letters, and a pained, maybe even angry, movement away from confidence in princes. I do not mean that Marot had given up on Francis; he would not have tried so hard to get home if he had. But the multiplicity of paternal references and the silent refusal of the title 'father' to *this* king, the adaptation of David's supplications to God and the careful dissociation of Francis and Jehovah, are worth pondering for the ambivalence, to say nothing of the hurt and courage, that they imply.

Marot's enemies struck, anger guiding their aim.[22] Enraged by the attack on the Sorbonne and Parlement, Parisian protectors of orthodoxy, they scorned his religious presumption and sneered at his talents as a court poet. The Sorbonne, says Francis Sagon, knows more about scripture than Marot, who muddles 'le texte aevangelicque' (the biblical text). And he is a clever sneak, says the pseudonymous 'General Chambor', who with 'elegance' and 'termes affables' converts scripture to fables. Note that it is his *style* (elegant, friendly, but – such is the cruelty of good manners – doubtless readable by noncourtiers as exclusionary) that distorts truth and scripture. Yes, he is bright, for 'ton esprit maling saulva ton corps' (thy wicked spirit/wit saved thy body), but who does 'Clement qui ment' (Clement the mendacious) think he is? He is not France's great 'pere'. 'Chambor' senses, I think, that in Epître 36 Marot indeed has in some fashion shunted the king aside and adopted a prophetic stance: there is more than a touch of David's prophet Nathan to this valet. No wonder, then, that 'Chambor' refers angrily to Marot's 'oblicque escript' (oblique writing). But by the spring of 1537, Marot was back in court, having been recalled ('rapellé' – his enemies called him 'rat pelé'); he wrote Francis to thank him for being more moved by just pity 'Que ne fut pas envers Ovide Auguste' (than Augustus ever was toward Ovid) (*OL* 78).

That year saw Marot's pamphlet war with Francis Sagon and his friends, an affair fuelled by a quarrel in 1534; the attacks on Marot's epistle from Ferrara; professional rivalry; and continuing anger at Marot's 'heresy' and distortion of scripture.[23] Marot, says Sagon, once accused him of being in Mosaic darkness. This, if true, was no arbitrary insult: Sagon lingers in the old 'Judaizing' legalism. Hence Marot's running joke that Sagon is 'Sagouin', simian, for his religion, like his verse, is apish imitation with no inward renewing Word: 'le babouyn / Ne fait rien synon contrefaire' (the baboon does nothing but imitate) (Épigramme 195.8–9). Indeed, themes of supplantation and renewal affected the quarrel, for during Marot's absence one of Sagon's allies, Charles de la Heutterie, 'voulut voler la place / De l'absent' (wanted to steal the place of the absent) (*OS* 6). Marot had once suggested that Francis 'efface' the name of Jean Marot; now he struggled to find the back wages lost when his own name was cancelled, 'rayer' (Épigramme 193.4).

Marot's technique in taking on Sagon was to jump the argument down a level by writing in the person of his own valet 'Frippelippes' (*OS* 6). The servant has kept up with his master's psalmody, for he says Marot

> Avecques David peult bien dire:
> 'Or sont tombez les malheureux
> En la fosse faicte par eulx;
> Leur pied mesme s'est venu prendre
> Au file qu'ilz ont voulu tendre'. (11. 32–34)[24]

The text resembles a manuscript version of Marot's Psalm 9. So 'zon!' on this Balaam's ass: Sagon has a valet named 'Nichil valet' (Nothingworth), but I am valet to the Maro of France. Marot, himself a king's valet and glad of it, is thus promoted out of the modern court system, although not beyond patronage.

At this point Marot wisely stopped fighting, but his rivals and allies continued the battle. Taunting him for his exile, Sagon and his friends complained of his heresy, womanizing, pseudoprophetic arrogance, stink, wrongful theft of the name 'Maro', ugly children, bad rhymes, bulging eyes, halitosis, disloyalty to France and Parisian institutions, offence to ladies he kissed, and envious hoarding of favour.[25] There is one especially notable moment in Sagon's denunciations. Hatred can bring insight, and like a deconstructionist with an eye for hidden contradictions, he sees through to a significant self-betrayal in the text. In calling him 'l'asne de Balaan', says Sagon, Marot misreads the Bible. First, Balaam's ass was an 'asnesse', as Marot should know. Furthermore, it is the ass who triumphs. Balaam was in the 'faveur publique' (public favour) and declared the meaning of God's word (like Marot?); but, because he was stubborn and a public danger, when an angel appeared it was the 'asnesse ... / Qui vit bien l'ange, et le prophete non' (the she-ass who saw the angel, not the prophet). Thus God confutes 'L'orgueil trop hault de Balaan prophete' (the too lofty pride of the prophet Balaam) by a 'simple beste' who understands angelic 'propos' (speech). This is no mere 'pédantisme', as Mayer calls Sagon's comments.[26] Marot has indeed misread, and he has also snarled his own play with hierarchy: associating the fictive 'real' Marot with David and Vergil, even while humbling his voice to that of his valet, he demotes Sagon even lower, to monkeydom, and calls *his* valet 'Nichil'. Sagon is also, here, an ass. Marot's friends might agree on Sagon's asininity – but the biblical tale Marot calls on says that *this (female) ass sees angels!* Where are we now? One can imagine a hundred reasons why Marot forgot who was the heroine of the story, but Sagon thought he glimpsed some careless pride. That he was a dreadful creature does not make him wrong.

In 1539 Marot wrote his exquisite 'Eglogue de Marot au Roy, soubz les noms de Pan & Robin' (*OL* 89). One recent critic has connected Pan's 'vert cabinet' (green private room) with Marot's 'cabinet des muses' (his library, that is) in Epître 36.[27] Maybe so, even if these are not Marot's only cabinets, but Eglogue 3 may have less of the tension I have remarked elsewhere, recording rather a moment of reconciliation and recollection: Francis was protective and generous, the gibbering 'Sagouin' had fallen silent. There remain situational gaps, though, into which ironies could fall, gaps between Marot as Robin, a Robin who echoes Maro, and Marot as a once exiled psalmist whom his enemies called 'Maraud' (thief). And there is one odd touch. For Marot, Pan is 'souverain', his pipe signifying 'l'armonye / Des cieulx' (the harmony of the heavens). Yet when the poet allegorizes his trip to court, he claims that 'le blond Phebus' (yellow-haired Phoebus) can witness how difficult it was to cross the rocks and torrents. Apparently there is another god besides Pan, one who from above keeps an eye on sufferings of this world. Robin himself makes no explicitly Davidic claims. Why not? This was the year in which Marot presented a manuscript of his psalms to Francis. Perhaps he relied on implication; or perhaps he hesitated to confuse the eclogue's poet–patron hierarchy by recalling that this shepherd was translating the work of 'le bon Roy David' (good King David).[28]

In 1541 Marot published a collection of thirty psalms and prefaced it with a long poem to Francis that is remarkable for its effort to keep Marot's roles as psalmist and courtier from splitting apart.[29] Much of it celebrates David in terms familiar from patristic commentary and Luther, but it also honours Francis with, I think, a Gallican subtext: to praise the king was, often, to denigrate disgruntled papists, and to compare him to a prophet-king could, in contexts specifically like this, indicate hopes for an at least moderately reformed church of France looking more to the monarch and less to the Pope. God, says Marot, gave David to the 'peuples Hebraiques' and Francis 'aux Galliques'. There is more than flattery here, as there is in Marot's suggestion that Hebrew scholars, like the 'hons espritz rusez' (clever souls) who restore ancient inscriptions, have clarified the obscurity into which time has brought the psalms. To those who still clutched the Vulgate, this must have been infuriating.

Yet accompanying these invitations to remember the old alliance against obscurantism is a peculiarity in the situation: the psalms are both Marot's and the king's. So much is this work '& Royal & Chrestien', that 'il se dit estre tien' (it declares itself thine); and Francis is like David, we hear, in having suffered adversity, loved learning, honoured the muses, and with the same hand that bears the sceptre written 'escriptz' not 'subjectz à la mort' (writings not subject to death). This parallel associates the king with divine *furor*, for David did not have to study: by drinking the waters of Grace, 'il devint Poete en ung moment' (he became a poet in an instant) even though he was also learned in 'toutes sciences bonnes' (all good learning); evidently the ancient indecision about the place of inspiration and imitation in poets was, in him, resolved. But if all this is true, then the king's valet de chambre, too, has made a 'royal' work as he unites his voice to David's (and Christ's), and since Marot also says that the psalms' profundity derives from their subject, he himself participates in the conquest of Orpheus (who, we are told, would hang up his lyre after hearing David), Arion (who would fall silent), and Phoebus (who would de-laurel himself). Celebrating the psalms had long involved such indications of literary rivalry and aggression; here Marot's logic elevates *himself* as well as the king and does so through seemingly modest piety and praise.

There are other faint reminders of the translator's complex position. David, whom God raised 'de bergier en grand roy ... / Et sa houlette en sceptre luy changea' (from shepherd to a great king and turned his crook to a sceptre), calmed Saul's mania, and even appeased with his lyre 'de dieu courroussé l'yre' (the wrath of an angry god). Francis, Marot may have thought, might remember that this poet had done the same to him. Another moment of possible tension comes when the poem turns from the king to the noble hearts who have languished in 'prison, peché, soucy, / Perte ou opprobre' (prison, sin, care, loss, or shame) and who can find remedy in this 'jardin, plain d'herbes & racines' (garden filled with herbs and roots). Francis too had known prison, but Marot does not mention that in his reference to the king's troubles. Neither tact nor the recollection that David was never in jail required avoiding the topic; Marguerite mentioned it in her 1543 New Year's poem to Francis and again when she compared her dying brother to the psalmist. Marot deflects the more detailed description of suffering away from the king, to whom almost all the poem is addressed, and, as he had in Epître 36, signals his shift by an apostrophe and a new pronoun ('vous'). Didactic strategy might require that he arrange matters like this, yet the passage provokes thought: in whose name, finally, are 'gentilz cueurs & ames amoureuses' (noble hearts and loving souls) held in prison? At whose court can some suffer 'Perte ou opprobre'?

One day in the fall of 1542, Marot went home and was warned that he was in danger of arrest (perhaps he remembered David's similar experience): his psalms had recently been listed among forbidden books and the king was away. Once more he fled, this time making his way to Geneva. There, in 1543, more of his psalms were published, although for reasons yet unclear he left after some months. It is true that he had dared play dice in Calvin's city, but despite his appearance in an official report, he was not in legal difficulties, not like 'Master William the Cantor' a few years later, troubled by the authorities for playing dance music 'et austres mondanité' (and other worldliness); (oh no, he said, that loud ruckus was really the sound of holy songs and, he assured his interrogators when caught once again, what looked like dancing was little girls jumping to psalms).[30]

From Chambéry, in 1544, Marot wrote his last major piece of occasional verse, 'Eglogue sur la Naissance du filz de Monseigneur le Daulphin', a paraphrase of Vergil's Messianic eclogue. Griffin notes how the source gives the offering from a still hopeful courtier an evangelical resonance: Vergil's golden age is the same myth that haunts the author's 'Aux Dames de France', published with the psalms in 1543.[31] The poem has, moreover, another specific connection with the psalms. In 1559 one Villemadon wrote Catherine de Medici, mother of this 'gracieux Enfantin' (gracious baby), recalling the days when she appeared infertile and in danger, some said, of repudiation.[32] Hearing that she and the dauphin Henry sang psalms in their distress, Marguerite de Navarre prophesied the birth of a baby; or so Villemadon says. The birth, when it came, reinforced the position of Catherine and Marguerite, with whom the dauphine got on, and encouraged a faction somewhat more sympathetic to evangelical piety; indeed, it could be read as a response to such piety. Marguerite herself, after a few months of declining influence, seemed to be regaining stature; and Marot was not misguided (merely wrong) in having hopes for this baby, born after so many prayers and psalms made all the more fervent for the worldly desires they also carried.

Minor revisions incorporate Marot's own 'adversitez', but as in his earlier reworkings of Ovid, he refuses to allow guilt, changing Vergil's 'sceleris vestigia nostri' (traces of our crime) to 'la malice aujourd'huy manifeste' (the malice one sees today). He also adds a hope for peace, perhaps because Francis was once more at odds with Henry VIII. Unlike Vergil, furthermore, Marot must praise not two but three generations. Francis is treated with the utmost respect – he is the 'grand Berger de France' (great shepherd of France), who now sees his youth reborn – but he is inevitably upstaged by the new parents and their child; even the prayer that his days be multiplied and increased, an echo of Proverbs 11, is Old Testament and patriarchal. It is a bittersweet compliment to tell a man that the golden age arrives with his grandson; the touching image of royal renewal, as though the baby were Francis's right self reborn, may conceal a faint disappointment (perhaps not intended but inherent in the logic) that this old shepherd had not done more for his sheep. The poem backs out of the royal presence with a bow, but its eyes are on the rising sun. A few months later Marot died.

In the years that followed, Marot's career drew the unloving attention of those who tried to discredit Protestantism by denigrating the 'chants qui s'appellent vulgairement Marotines' (songs popularly called Marotic).[33] The potential split between his roles as courtier and psalmist gave his critics a tempting opening. True, the 'cygne Royal de Judée' (royal swan of Judea) had been a courtier, harping for distracted Saul, but he wrote him no humble flattery.[34] Nor, despite the Uriah business, which he repented, did David combine singing to Jehova with singing to girls. But even during his last months of life, an unregenerate Marot could write,

> My hearty thanks I give you, Ma'am,
> For having turned my offer down.
> You think I care? or that I am
> Inclined to muster up a frown?
> No, no. And why no grief, no curse?
> The six *écus* you'll go without
> Are lodged far better in my purse
> Than in the hole you know about. (Épigramme 230)[35]

Readers like Marguerite took this sort of thing calmly, but some eyebrows went up at what one critic called 'escriptz voluptueux' (sensuous writings). In England, George Gascoigne, defending his own mild indecency, thought Marot's 'Alyx' subject to 'impeach of crime'. He was referring to verse like this:

> For giving quite enough to Alice,
> *Hic jacet* Martin: ten times over,
> To fill her up, he'd ply his phallus
> In woods, in coppice, or on clover.
> Pray God, O Reader standing here,
> That He will the departed keep
> Wherever Alice can't come near:
> Poor Martin then may get some sleep.[36]

Beza had written like that, but not after he became a psalmist.

Beza, in fact, said in 1553 that Marot was a 'docte' poet whose death left David speechless; but in his later *Icones*, he remarked that even when old the poet kept the unchristian habits he picked up at court, that worst teacher of piety and decency (Geneva, 1580, sig. Y4).[37] Scepticism about Marot in this regard continued a long time; Protestants could say he was libertine and 'nourri de vanités dans une cour souverainement corrompue' (brought up with vanities in a court utterly corrupt); and Voltaire thought, perhaps with admiration, that Marot sang of God on a 'lyre incrédule' (an unbelieving lyre).[38] Furthermore, it was all the easier to 'cast in the teeth of the Professors in France, that they sing the Psalms translated in meter by Clement Marot, a courtly Gentleman' because of slander by writers like Florimond de Raemond and the recusant Thomas Harrab, who wrote in his *Tessaradelphus* (1616) that Marot 'was a wanton Courtier, a Poet, and a Musition', who seduced his hostess in Geneva and was publicly whipped.[39]

It is this discomfort with a courtier psalmist, I think, that made it hard to 'place' Marot; other court poets, like Wyatt, had translated the psalms, but most of these were gentlemen or scholars. Catholic polemicists might call Marot 'scurra' (clown) or 'bouffon', unfit to translate the texts he had 'si mal Marotté' (another pun on 'marotte', a fool's sceptre); but even the sympathetic John Wodroephe, a French teacher living in England who quoted the Huguenot psalter in his *Marrow of the French tongue* (1623), could half contemptuously joke that 'Clement Marot se cacha dans la malle grasse du Roy de France, estant dans ses malgraces' (an approximate translation of the pun might be 'Clement Marot hid in the king's big suitcase, being in his case unsuitable').[40] Even an English envoy could treat such 'malgraces' (disfavour) with a curious lack of sympathy, as though Marot's position as valet de chambre and producer of *étrennes* made his sufferings seem not Davidic but imprudent: John Wallop writes Henry VIII in January 1541 to report that he hears Francis is sending an expedition with the explorer Jacques Cartier; the captain of the footmen is 'Clement Marotte, who has been an exile for Lutheranism, and his men are malefactors and vagabonds, who can well be spared'.X[41] The notion itself is ridiculous, and so far as we know, Marot was in good odor at that time. Is Wallop, too, making a Marot/Marotte joke? Was it the king's joke? Wallop also reports that Francis says he hears Wyatt is arrested and wonders if he too is Lutheran. They thought so in Spain, he says, and Charles V had once tapped his head as though he believed the Englishman 'fantastic'. Henry should watch those Lutherans. A bunch of them turned up in Dauphiné recently; they would assemble in the dark, preach by candlelight, and cry, 'Dele candelam, crescite et multiplicamini' (Put out the candle, increase and multiply). Francis hated heresy, but his image of Lutherans shouting for darkness and presumably plunging into procreative fornication justified by scripture is so funny that the tone of his remark about Marot is hard to gauge.

Many who translated the psalms felt no tension between Christian vocation and the comforts of polite or mercantile society. One can find traces of this worldliness even in Geneva, in Matthieu Malingre's 1542 praise of Marot's 'ryme élégante'; in Paris, Clement Janequin assured those who bought his settings of Marot's psalms that 'pour gaingner temps' ('to gain time', a thrifty touch) they could at once instruct their spirit, polish their language, and content their ear.[42] Nor was Marot alone in attempting to fuse the roles of psalmist and courtier; David himself provided a model of both the attempt and its partial failure. Understandably, moreover, most Christians prefer comfortable coexistence to hard choice.[43] So it was in a not uncommon spirit of easy refinement that George Sandys published his attractive *Paraphrase upon the psalmes of David* (1636), prefacing it with a smooth poem to Charles ('our graver Muse from her long Dreame awakes, / Peneian Groves, and Cirrha's Caves forsakes') and an even smoother one to the queen:

> Urania your chast eares invites
> To these her more sublime Delights.
> Then, with your zealous Lover, daigne
> To enter David's numerous Fane.

The prefatory poem to Sandys by Lucius Cary, Lord Falkland, is smoother yet, the very Osric of prefaces. Some deplore cosmetic eloquence,

> Yet, as the Church with Ornaments is Fraught,
> Why may not That be too, which there is taught?
> And sure that Vessell of Election, Paul,
> Who Judais'd with Jewes, was All to All.

Better this verse than the amatory, for those who write to gain 'Damnation, and a Mistres' forget 'How constant that is, how Inconstant she'. The queen to whom this volume is in part dedicated was the descendant of Marguerite de Navarre. It seems fitting that Marot's kindest patron is thus distantly associated with the volume, for the distinction between constant damnation and inconstant ladies seems to revise a related argument in Marot's 'Aux Dames de France'. Marot, however, had located the constancy not in Hell but in Christ:

> Commencez, dames, commencez,
> Le siecle doré avancez,
> [...]
> Afin que du monde s'envole
> Ce Dieu inconstant d'amour folle,
> Place faisant à l'amyable
> Vray Dieu d'amour non variable.[44]

France has yet to become that golden world of changeless love, and the Englishmen who attempted their own version of it relied on sterner troops than court ladies when the implicit contradictions in Marot's position were recapitulated in actual civil wars.[45]

Marot's psalms or others he affected were on the lips of queens and regicides, pilgrims to Massachusetts and Parisian musicians, Dutch Calvinists, Navarre's infantry, and James I. In Marot's own self (or at least in the poetry associated with it) such disparate realities were as interlocked as one courtly psalmist could make them. Here, though, I have tried to locate and provide a context for a few of the cracks, sometimes hairline thin, in that stressed and beleaguered unity.

Notes

1 I quote Marot in the edition of C. A. Mayer: vols. 1–5 (London: Athlone Press), *Les Epîtres*, 1958; *Oeuvres satiriques*, 1962 (*OS*); *Oeuvres lyriques*, 1964 (*OL*); *Oeuvres diverses*, 1966 (*OD*); *Les Epigrammes*, 1970; vol. 6, *Les Traductions* (Geneva: Slatkine, 1980), has the psalms, also available as vol. 3, ed. S. J. Lenselink (Assen: van Gorcum, 1969), added to Pierre Pidoux, *Le Psautier huguenot du XVIe siècle*, vols. 1–2 (Basel: Baerenreiter, 1962). My numbers refer to items, not pages, and all translations are mine. Marot's letter asking for a job is Epître 1. On Marot's career see P. M. Smith, *Clément Marot* (London: Athlone Press, 1970) and C. A. Mayer, *Clément Marot* (Paris: Nizet, 1972). A good recent study of the king is R. J. Knecht, *Francis I* (Cambridge: Cambridge University Press, 1982).
2 Epître 36.176; Épigramme 229.10.
3 The material on Renaissance psalm translation is vast. See, in particular, Orentin Douen, *Clément Marot et le psautier huguenot* (1878–79; rpt. Nieuwkoop: de Graaf, 1977, 2 vols.), and Michel Jeanneret, *Poésie et tradition biblique au XVIe siècle* (Paris: Corti, 1969), who is particularly helpful on the motivations involved; see also his 'Marot Traducteur des Psaumes entre la Néo-Platonisme et la Reforme', *Bibliothèque d'Humanisme et Renaissance* 27 (1965): 629–43. Marot's religion is much debated. P. Leblanc, *La Poésie religieuse de Clément Marot* (Paris: Nizet, 1955) underplays the 'Lutheran' Marot. C. A. Mayer, *La Religion de Marot* (Geneva: Droz, 1960), proves that Marot was thought 'Lutheran' (then a slippery term), but he may make Catholic and Protestant views in the 1520s and 1530s too distinct. Michael Screech, *Marot évangélique* (Geneva: Droz, 1967), notes many biblical echoes, echoes Mayer tends to ignore. Probably wisest is Robert Griffin's nuanced *Clément Marot and the Inflections of Poetic Voice* (Berkeley: University of California Press, 1974), ch. 5.
4 Pierre Jourda, *Marguerite d'Angoulême* (Paris: Champion, 1930), vol. 1, recounts the queen's difficulties with the Sorbonne.
5 Francis M. Higman, *Censorship and the Sorbonne* (Geneva: Droz, 1979).
6 In *The King's Progress to Jerusalem* (Malibu, Calif.: Udena Publications, 1976), Edward A. Gosselin traces the shift in exegesis. In his introduction to Marot's psalms, Mayer denies that the arguments are based on Bucer's and doubts they are Marot's. They appear, however, in an edition published with his knowledge, and Bucer's arguments do resemble Marot's.
7 Quoted by David Evett in 'Types of King David in Shakespeare's Lancastrian Tetralogy', *Shakespeare Studies* 17 (1981): 142–43. On David and Elizabeth,

see Margaret P. Hannay, '"Doo What Men May Sing": Mary Sidney and the Tradition of Admonitory Dedication', in *Silent But for the Word* (Kent, Ohio: Kent State University Press, 1985); her *Philip's Phoenix: Mary Sidney, Countess of Pembroke* (Oxford: Oxford University Press, 1990), ch. 4, further explores the politics of psalm translation.

8 *Poésies du Roi François Ier*, ed. Aimé Champollion-Figeac (Paris, 1847; rpt. Geneva: Slatkine, 1970), 54–57; this edition conveniently puts the poetic correspondence of Francis and Marguerite together.

9 Ibid., 63–69; Francis's reply is on 69–72; my text is from the edition of the king's poetry ed. J. E. Kane (Geneva: Slatkine, 1984), 340.

10 On March 25, 1542, for example, Paget reported that Francis had spoken to him of possibly breaking with Rome but had asked him not to mention the conversation to his sister (*Letters and Papers*, Henry VIII, ed. James Gairdner, 1905, vol. 17, no. 200). A Saint Catherine, patroness of childbirth, was especially appropriate for the pregnant Marguerite; see Kane's note to Francis's poem.

11 Pidoux, *Le Psautier huguenot*, 2, 51. Werner Gundersheimer, 'Patronage in the Renaissance: An Exploratory Approach', in *Patronage in the Renaissance*, ed. Guy F. Lytle and Stephen Orgel (Princeton, N.J.: Princeton University Press, 1981), 3–23, reads some iconoclasm as 'symbolic eradication of a past' associated with parental figures. What he says of artists and 'status dissonance' applies to psalmists too.

12 Pidoux, *Le Psautier huguenot*, 2, 21.

13 See, e.g., David Quint, *Origin and Originality in Renaissance Literature* (New Haven, Conn.: Yale University Press, 1983), and John Guillory, *Poetic Authority* (New York: Columbia University Press, 1983), although neither discusses psalmody. Marot's situation has analogues with Ronsard's as a vatic polemicist; see Ullrich Langer, 'A Courtier's Problematic Defense: Ronsard's "Responce aux injures"', *Bibliothèque d'Humanisme et Renaissance* 46 (1984): 343–55.

14 Many commentators noted the multiple voices and our obligation to respond both as individuals and as members of Christ's body. See Barbara Lewalski, *Protestant Poetics and the Seventeenth-Century Religious Lyric* (Princeton, N.J.: Princeton University Press, 1979).

15 Gérard Defaux, 'Rhétorique, silence et liberté dans l'oeuvre de Marot', *Bibliothèque d'Humanisme et Renaissance* 46 (1984): 299–322. It is a measure of the subtlety of Marot's voice, and also of the subjectivity of modern criticism, that whereas Defaux's bravura piece sees Marot as subversively suspicious of mortal words, a Marot equally divided but now with 'a textuality that is never oppressed by the incapacity of words to mean' appears in Annabel Patterson's 'Re-opening the Green Cabinet: Clément Marot and Edmund Spenser', *English Literary Renaissance* 16 (1986): 44–70.

16 See especially 157–58: the 'degree of symbiosis between Marot's religious calling and his court vocation is ... astonishing', and 'there is no intrinsic sense of tension, no feeling of tragic disproportion between the evangelical impulse and court life'. Although insisting more on Marot's dedication to a courtier role ('Faith in the court remained as essential to Marot as faith in God'), George

Joseph comes to something like the same conclusion; see his *Clement Marot* (Boston, Mass.: Twayne, 1985), 141 and preface.

17 Carl Jung, *Memories, Dreams, Reflections*, trans. Richard and Clara Winston (New York: Vintage, 1961), 156–57.
18 Defaux eloquently associates a father–son tension with Marot's move away from the rhétoriqueur style, 306–8; more than Defaux I also find such tension in Marot's response to Francis.
19 E.g., Griffin, *Clément Marot*, 53. Joseph, *Clement Marot*, 131, plays down the poem's religious impulse, seeing it 'as primarily concerned to re-establish his contract with power'. It is certainly that – but not only that. I do agree that the poem attempts to 'turn back the clock to the pre-1534 court evangelism of a tolerant, enlightened Francis I'. Marot was not alone in such hopes.
20 The prayer, ll. 103–120, says:

> O seigneur dieu, permettez moy de croire
> Que reservé m'avez à vostre gloire.
> Serpentz tortuz & mostres contrefaictz,
> Certes, sont bien à vostre gloire faictz.
> Puis que n'avez voulu doncq; condescendre
> Que ma chair ville ayt esté mise en cendre,
> Faictes au moins, tant que seray vivant,
> Qu'à vostre honneur soit ma plume escripvant;
> Et si ce corps avez predestiné
> A estre ung jour par flamme terminé,
> Que ce ne soit au moins pour cause folle,
> Ainçoys pour vous & pour vostre parolle;
> Et vous supply, pere, que le tourment
> Ne luy soit pas donne si vehement
> Que l'ame vienne à mettre en oubliance
> Vous, en qui seul gist toute sa fiance;
> Si que je puysse, avant que d'assoupir,
> Vous invocquer jusque au dernier souspir.
>
> Smith, *Clément Marot*, calls this passage 'worthy in its intensity of the Hebrew Psalmists', 118.

21 Griffin, *Clément Marot*, 53–54. If Marot's lines about Louis XII recall Jean Marot, then, as Griffin says, we have another father. I do not agree that Francis is compared to Augustus; elsewhere, playing exiled Ovid, Marot insists on the parallel, but here he refers to the Caesars, plural.
22 Their responses are excerpted in Mayer's notes.
23 Mayer gives excerpts in his notes to *OS* 6. More may be found, with title pages, in Georges Guiffrey's edition of Marot (1911; rpt. Geneva: Slatkine, 1969), vol. 1, and almost the entire verse war, but no pictures, in vol. 6 of the 1731 edition. I have seen, but been unable to work with, the facsimiles, edited by Emile Picot and Paul Lecombe (Rouen: Laine, 1920).

24 'With David he can say, / Now stumble wicked men / In that same ditch they dug: / With their own wire taut / Their own feet have been caught.'

25 Marot's literary pretensions inspired sneers at his claim to be 'Maro'; Sagon says in his *Coup d'essay* (1536; 1731 ed., 6: 22) that Maro with no T is a fine poet, but with one is utterly corrupt; 'Il prent de T. Marotte pour houllette / Et peult sans T. ce que plusieurs n'ont peu', a clever image of a would-be Maro holding his 'T' like a 'marotte' (a fool's sceptre) instead of the shepherd-poet's crook. The implication is that Marot claims a Vergilian pastoral role, but there may also be a glance at presumptuous theologizing. The replies of Marot's friends, in turn, anticipate the Pléiade's view of poetry; see especially Bonaventure Des Périers Charles Fontaine and François Calvy de la Fontaine, *Les Disciples de Marot* (1731, 146–201). For them he is a 'vray Maro': 'un vray Poëte est tant digne, / Et de nature est tant noble & insigne, / Qu'en luy est Dieu, qui par son mouvement / Le faict parler, comme ung vent l'instrument', and so forth (A true poet is so worthy and by nature so noble and outstanding, that in him is God, who moves him to speak as wind does an instrument). This Maro is closer to the *vates* who wrote the *Aeneid* as well as the Messianic eclogue. Sagon and his allies complain of Marot's 'chewing' the Scriptures (1731, 73), and Sagon says grimly that the fragment of Ps. 9 that Frippelippes quotes will apply to Marot himself when he is hanging 'hault en l'air' (1731, 89). But Marot's friends tend not to specify his biblical translations, still in progress. They do associate him with poets, pagan and Israelite both, who wrote in their vernaculars: Homer, Vergil (writing in 'italique'), Isaiah, David (who spoke good verse 'en l'hebraique'), and now Marot, who solicits from French 'Ung milion de sentences abstruses, / Prinses au fons de la sourse des muses' (a million learned sayings, drawn from the bottom of the muses' well'; 1731, 151–53).

26 *OS*, 106.

27 Patterson, 'Re-opening the Green Cabinet'.

28 Calvin's phrase, 1543, in Pidoux, *Le Psautier huguenot*, 2, 21. David's songs could on occasion be those of an at least allegorical shepherd: Beza's long prefatory poem of 1553 (Pidoux, *Le Psautier huguenot*, 2, 63) tells shepherds to hear 'd'un berger la musette sonner" (a shepherd bagpipe sound), but he refers to clergymen.

29 I follow the text in *Traductions*, ed. Mayer, 309–14.

30 Pidoux, *Le Psautier huguenot*, 2, 76–77, 1555, and 89, 1556.

31 Griffin, *Clément Marot*, 160.

32 See V.-L. Saulnier, 'Autour de la lettre dite de Villemadon', *Bibliothèque d'Humanisme et Renaissance* 37 (1975): 349–76; he does not mention Eglogue 4.

33 Pidoux, *Le Psautier huguenot*, 2, 22, an Imperial ordinance of 1543 against heresy.

34 The swan is in Pidoux, *Le Psautier huguenot*, 2, 143 (a poem in a Paris 1564 edition of the Geneva psalms). On David as a courtier in the Renaissance, see my 'Evil Tongues at the Court of Saul: David as a Slandered Courtier' (see Chapter 4 in this volume), a companion piece to the present essay.

35 Ma dame, je vous remercie

> De m'avoir esté si rebourse.
> Pensez vous que je m'en soucye,
> Ne que tant soit peu m'en courrousse?
> Nanny, non. Et pourquoy? & pour-ce
> Que six escuz sauvez m'avez,
> Qui sont aussi bien en ma bourse
> Que dans le trou que vous sçavez.

36 Sagon quoted with *Espitre* 36. Gascoigne criticizes Marot in the 1575 preface to his *Poesies*. Marot's original is in *OD*, 274, and is perhaps spurious:

> Cy gist, pour Alix contenter,
> Martin, qui souloit plus que dix
> A la rengette culeter
> Par champaignes, boys & taillis.
> Prie Dieu, toy qui cecy lys,
> Mettre l' Ame du trespassé
> En quelque lieu bien loing d' Alix,
> Affin qu'il repose *In pace*.

Beza lived to regret his early indecency; see my 'English Writers and Beza's Latin Epigrams', *StRen* 21 (1974): 83–117.

37 Pidoux, *Le Psautier huguenot*, 2, 64.
38 Walther de Lerber, *L'Influence de Clément Marot aux XVIIe et XVIIIe siècles* (Paris: Champion, 1920).
39 Scoffs at Huguenots were heard by Zachary Boyd; see John Holland, *Psalmists of Britain*, 2 vols. (London, 1841), 1, 257–58. I cite Raemond's Latin version of his *Historiae de Ortu, Progressu, et Ruina Haereseon* (Cologne, 1614). Ch. 16 attacks Marot for both fettering and dismembering David. Harrab, sig. D2v–D3, borrows from Raemond.
40 'Scurra' is Raemond's word; 'bouffon' is from Michel Coyssard (1600), quoted by Jeanneret, *Poésie*, 193 n. 'Marotté' is from Artus Désiré's *Combatz* (1550), quoted by Jacques Pineaux in his introduction to Désiré's 1560 *Contrepoison* (Geneva: Droz, 1977), 17. In the latter work Désiré, sig. A3v, tells the duke of Savoy that this heretical and rebellious psalmist had ignored 'Parens, Parreins, Peres, Predecesseurs' (family, godfathers, fathers, predecessors). Désiré writes with hatred, but he is right to sense ambivalence in Marot's understanding of paternity and precedent. For other images of Marot as a court fool, see my *French Poets and the English Renaissance* (New Haven, Conn.: Yale University Press, 1978). I quote Wodroephe in the 1625 ed., sig. B6. C. A. Mayer, 'Notes sur la réputation de Marot au XVIIe et XVIIIe siecles', *Bibliothèque d'Humanisme et Renaissance* 25 (1963): 404–07, describes a jestbook starring him, concluding that Marot lived in popular memory as a 'symbole du rebelle', but one can also see a confused demotion of a courtier in periodic trouble.

41 *Letters and Papers*, Henry VIII, ed. James Gairdner, 1509–47, vol. 16, no. 488. Mayer, *Religion*, discusses the reference to Marot, dismissing the rumour but reading the passage more solemnly than it perhaps warrants. For another unadmiring comment, see a dispatch from R. Jones on Sept. 30, 1559. He has been reading Marot, and a companion 'has burned him for a heretic, as they would do the writer [i.e., Jones] if he were no wiser than his book'. But he has bought a new Marot and will 'study his follies, and so shall be out of danger, for vice is not so much punished here as virtue' (*Calendar of State Papers*, Foreign Series, vol. 5, no. 1413). Thus I cannot agree with Annabel Patterson, 'Cabinet', that 'Marot's status as an early supporter of the Reformation in France virtually guaranteed him Spenser's admiration.' Whatever his own views (I find them mixed), he could not rely on even Protestants' full appreciation of Marot. Patterson's already good case for 'December's' political subtext would in fact be strengthened by recognizing the complexity of Marot's reputation.
42 Pidoux, *Le Psautier huguenot*, 2, 12 (1542) and 45 (1549).
43 In 'Sanctifying the Aristocracy: Devout Humanism in François de Sales, John Donne, and George Herbert', (*The Unrepentant Renaissance from Petrarch to Shakespeare to Milton* [Chicago, Ill.: University of Chicago Press, 2011], 187–203), Richard Strier describes well some tempting and polite accommodations.
44 Begin my ladies, let it start –

> Hurry along the age of gold,
> So that from off our world will fly
> This foolish god of faithless heart,
> Yielding the place we see him hold
> To steadfast Love that will not lie.

45 W. Stanford Reid describes how the psalter stirred French and English soldiers in 'The Battle Hymns of the Lord: Calvinist Psalmody of the Sixteenth Century', *Sixteenth Century Essays and Studies* 2 (1971): 36–54.

6

King David as a 'right poet': Sidney and the psalmist

Shortly after Philip Sidney's death, an epitaph appeared in St. Paul's; as quoted by John Elyot in his *Ortho-epia gallica* (1593), it begins,

> England, Netherland, the Heavens, and the Arts,
> The Souldiors, and the World, have made six parts
> Of the noble Sydney: for none will suppose,
> That a small heape of stones can Sydney enclose. (sig. X2)

The epitaph is a useful way to start discussing Sidney: even its derivation from a poem by Du Bellay suggests an element of *translatio* in both Sidney's life and, despite his disclaimers, his work. Moreover, it anticipates a recent sense that his life and work are each more subject to diverging energies than the older image of an ideal courtier-poet had allowed. In his epitaph Sidney is given a post-mortem dispersal, as though he were a medieval king or saint, whereas in modern criticism the stress has been on the divisions within his imagination. During the past several decades, for example, the fractures within the *Apology* have become so apparent that for some readers the arguments it offers can be unified only by recourse to salvific notions of paradox, self-subversion, and play-notions, I hasten to add, that I too use gratefully.[1]

This complexity shows in Sidney's treatment of David, who in the *Apology* appears among the divine poets, distinguished by their inspiration from the second category, that of philosophical poets, and the third, that of the 'right' poets Sidney proposes to defend. Sidney has added him and other biblical authors of metrical poetry to the exclusively pagan list of poet-prophets he found in Scaliger, whose tripartite division was the model for his own.[2] Why this addition? Perhaps from an admiring piety, perhaps to lend further support to poetry. But not for company. Indeed, Sidney may have aimed to protect *himself* by thus shunting David and his poems to one side where their inspiration and occult metrical harmonies could not complicate his arguments. He thus manages, as others have said, to 'set ... apart' divine poetry, 'to bracket off religious matters'.³ One might even dare to say that in Sidney's *Apology* the Holy Ghost has been respectfully pigeonholed.

Or has he? With casual inconsistency, if to considerable rhetorical effect, Sidney uses David as an example of what the Romans meant by their word for poet, *vates*, granting the Holy Spirit a little breathing room in the preliminaries to an argument that otherwise privileges a secular if ideal imitation (99). Since, as Sidney admits, no one was attacking divine poets, whether David was a *vates* or not is immaterial. Yet by mentioning him in this fashion Sidney can transfer some of the glamour surrounding his name and the mysterious power of his supernatural verse through the seemingly impermeable barrier of the argument's logical divisions or the lines of its categories. In the same passage we are also told, as evidence of David's status as a poet, that he wrote in meter, which Sidney elsewhere says the true poet need not use (121).⁴ And David is remembered once more, even after the discussion has settled firmly on the third category of right poets, to remind us that sometimes kings have been known 'not only to favour poets, but to be poets', sharing this distinction with Francis I and James VI (131).

There must have been any number of reasons for this desire to set David's psalms aside and yet to recall them and logic be damned: reasons including an ambivalence rendered even more intriguing by the fact of Sidney's efforts to translate the psalter, and reasons including also the pressure of a forensic rhetorical tradition, whether used straight or paradoxically, that encouraged the summoning to court of all possible witnesses, the marshalling of all possible arguments, no matter how they might quarrel or clash in the vestibule afterwards. Had Sidney been willing to allow ordinary poets divine inspiration, he could have said with Skelton (paraphrasing Jerome), 'I call to this rekenyng / Davyd, that royall kyng' and used his 'warblynge' as evidence against those who have 'disdayne / At poetes, and complayne / Howe poetes do but fayne'.⁵ It is 'feigning' that Sidney needs to defend, although David of course 'feigned' allegories and metaphors, to say nothing of fore-conceits. Or if he could have resisted the temptation to adduce, as particularly persuasive testimony, the poetry we know he loved, Sidney could have kept his categories less fluid. It was his wish to defend uninspired if excellent poets *and* to subpoena the world's greatest poet (so many called him) that led to this peculiar tangle. In this essay, however, I would like to identify yet one more possibility, one more reason for the tension and illogic in Sidney's handling of a fellow poet whose words he could translate but who also wrote (and typologically foreshadowed) the Word beyond emulation.

In more precisely mapping Sidney's tactics, both the main lines of his argument and his gingerly sidestepping around David, it might be useful to remember a way of praising the psalms begun, so far as I know, by Athanasius and Basil in the fourth century and very much alive through translation and imitation in the sixteenth. Almost never discussed by literary historians, to a startling degree it anticipates and parallels Sidney's arguments on behalf of right poetry (and some of Scaliger's as well). Indeed, nowhere else are these parallels so exact; nowhere else that I know of does one find this particular argument in praise of speaking pictures that outdo in motivating energy both precept and history combined with this particular cluster of metaphors. I am not claiming a 'source' for the *Apology*, exactly, for this tradition was itself heavily indebted to classical rhetoric and psychology, and in any case Sidney's mind was both eclectic and alchemical. I do argue that since Sidney unquestionably knew some of the texts involved and, I suspect, knew all the central ones (without dates for the *Apology* and his psalms it is hard to be sure), some of the push and pull one can feel in his treatment of David can be traced to an awareness of a rival tradition in which the psalmist, besides his other advantages, was also in his fashion a right poet. According to this tradition of commentary and celebration, David was, like the poets of Sidney's third category, an imitator of an invisible excellence (in this case Christ and his kingdom), the creator of a lively and moving image that teaches goodness and self-knowledge to both old and young more effectively than the bare precepts of moral law or the specificities of history. This David, again like Sidney's poet, steals upon us like a doctor offering medicine hidden in sweetness and works curatively on our imagination and will through mirror and speaking picture. His work does not so much mediate between precept and history as include both. True, the psalmist did not engender sustained fables of the sort Sidney (and Christ) made up, but except for the crucial disability of his divine inspiration and authority, David makes a very presentable right poet.

Because the theologians in question write significantly of how David's infolded voices express Christ and ourselves as well as his own circumstance, this tradition has not gone altogether unnoticed by those concerned with Protestant poetics, typology, and the seventeenth-century lyric.[6] What I refer to, however, is a distinct if overlapping set of metaphors and claims somewhat less relevant to Herbert or Vaughan but very relevant indeed to Sidney's poetics. Sidney could have found the chief ancient texts, together with others touching on metrics, conveniently excerpted in the 1567 metrical psalter of his father's friend and correspondent Archbishop Matthew Parker. Parker's translation, printed with great care in a variety of typefaces and accompanied by collects, headnotes, and eight tunes that Thomas Tallis created to suit the different moods of the psalms and readers, combines a plain, serviceable diction with metrical schemes that on occasion shake off the dreary fourteener or poulters' measure for patterns of almost diabolical cleverness. Without literary merit of the sort modern readers are likely to appreciate, Parker's psalter nonetheless was a significant venture with greater interest than it has been allowed; I believe that Sidney probably used it for his own translations. This is not the place to argue the matter, so I will say only that Sidney's rhymes, and to a lesser extent his sister's, owe as much to Parker as to Sternhold and Hopkins, and that he uses the Archbishop's metrical schemes on occasion. The coincidence of rhyme goes beyond what one would expect from the obviousness or inevitability of certain words and a common debt to prose translations.[7] None of this proves, to be sure, that Sidney read the prefatory material before sitting down to the *Apology*, but it does render even more likely his familiarity with the tradition I am describing.

In the latter part of the fourth century, Athanasius wrote his friend Marcellinus about the psalms, quoting a wise old man on their nature and uses. They are, he reports the aged father as saying, an epitome of the Bible, incorporating the essence of other books of law, history, and prophecy, to make up a 'pleasant garden of all deliciousnes' (I quote the translation in Parker's psalter, sig. B4v).[8] Furthermore, the psalter 'hath this[,] in a marvelous consideration proper to himself alone', that it shows us ourselves: 'the motions, the mutations, the alterations of every mans hart and conscience described and lively paynted out to [our] owne sight, so that if a man list, he might easely gather out thereof certaine considerations of himselfe as out of a bright glasse and playne paterne set before his face, so therby to refourme himselfe as he red therin'. In other words the psalms offer not mere information or exhortation but what Sidney calls 'the knowledge of a mans selfe with the end of well dooing and not of well knowing onely' (161).[9] And they do so through a pattern, an image.

In extolling the psalms' architectonic efficacy, Athanasius cannot of course denigrate Moses or the prophets the way Sidney can laugh at the historian or philosopher. Nevertheless, his arguments contain a reverent version of the ancient competition with which Sidney plays: elsewhere in the Bible, says Athanasius, 'onely we heare the preceptes of the law, what ought to be done, and what undone, we heare the matter of prophecy ... furthermore, we reade the histories, wherby the actes of kynges and holy fathers might be knowne and brought to remembrance, but in the bookes of the Psalmes, over and above that, we learne and heare all these foresaid things sufficiently: there every one may see and perceive the motions and affections of his owne hart and soule' (sig. C1). The psalms, in other words, not only incorporate what the rest of the Bible contains but also teach us about ourselves. And because the psalms give us a 'fourme' of curative prayerful life, what one learns in the psalms one learns deeply, not letting it 'fal from his consideration, assoone as he have hard them'. Knowledge breeds desire for reformation, for healing the 'affections and passions, by worde and by deede', and although 'there be in other bookes wordes and sentences which forbid divers vices and enormities', here in the psalter a person may find a 'fourme, how a man may be cleare of them, and how to avoyde them'. (That this 'fourme' or image affects the will, *moves* us, is even clearer in the original.)[10] It is true that whereas Sidney speaks primarily of the poet, historian, and philosopher, claiming reforming power for the first of these, Athanasius has four terms: precept, past event, prophecy, and the mediating, inclusive, motivating, and pattern-giving psalms. But since the coming of Christ and hence the fulfilment of the prophecies, one could argue, these terms have been reduced to Sidney's three: what should be done, what has been done, and that discourse which includes and transcends these, poetry. (The book of Revelation is prophetic, but it points beyond time.)

In the translation of Athanasius that Parker had printed with his psalter there follows a rather confusing passage – the Greek is apparently hard to disentangle – which says that other books of Scripture can also in a fashion move us through images: when we 'recite or rehearse them' our hearers at once 'conceive in their imagination that they be other mens words and deedes that they heare, and in such sort are they enflamed ... that they bend themselves to be as followers to them to counterfayte the like'.[11] What we read affects our mental images and inspires us to copy what we see. Compare Sidney's remark that in heroical poetry 'the lofty image of such worthies most inflameth the mind with desire to be worthy, and informs with counsel how to be worthy' (119), a comment that combines the inflammatory image with something like Athanasius' praise for the psalms' how-to-do-it 'forms'.[12]

Such imitation of historical figures does not greatly impress Athanasius, however, for the models to be copied are too specific, too limited by both their actuality and their otherness. When we read of Moses or the patriarchs, or the prophets, we think of those admirable individuals, but David also describes general figures: 'for as much as the psalme[s] without respect of persons' express both 'the righteous man' and the sinner (sig. C1v). Consequently, the psalms achieve more effective and inclusive variety, since 'all manner of men must needes be comprehended in them', not just those of whom they make 'plaine mention'. This capacity to be both varied and general makes David's reader feel as though the words were that reader's own creation, 'first by him conceyved and pronounced'. To a sinner who recites Psalm 51 ('historically' said by the individual sinner David after Nathan rebuked him for murder and adultery), 'so speaketh he the words of a penitent contrite harte, as they were his in deede' (sig. C2). Thus the psalms are relevant universally, offering as many patterns of a better self as there are readers, and working not merely 'in a singuler respect'.

The psalter's impact is dynamic, moreover, for as we sing the psalms they are for us a 'glasse' which when 'uttered' become a source of effect on others as they too are 'compunct and styrred'. The inner image, the introjected mirror, then, is almost literally reforming. Indeed, in a passage Parker omits, Athanasius speaks of Christ himself as an image for imitation by his followers. This is a seemingly innocent concept with much resonance in Byzantine poetics and Greek orthodoxy, but Parker may have felt that it was subtly alien or potentially dangerous and so leaves it out.[13] Compare, however, Sidney's claim that poetry can give ideas or examples that in turn create copies, an image of Cyrus that will 'make many Cyruses'. True, the 'real' Cyrus was historical, like the figures Athanasius finds less effective as models than the David/Christ/reader mirrored in the psalms. But Sidney's Cyrus is not, after all, the actual man — whoever *he* was, for the mouse-eaten records are not clear; he is, rather, the ideal image of Cyrus that can generate new versions of itself (101).

The latter part of Athanasius' letter is a guide to the psalms that was also published in some editions of the psalter of Sternhold and Hopkins. The guide praises the effect of the psalms on the individual soul, but its poetics are less fully developed and it makes no mention of a mirror or speaking picture. More significant for Sidney is the homily of St. Basil on the first psalm, often ascribed during the Middle Ages to St. Augustine.[14] Parker includes it and at his suggestion it was printed with the psalter of the Bishops' Bible. Tremellius and Junius, whom Sidney cites on scriptural poetry, incorporate most of the homily into their preface to the poetical part of the *Biblia Sacra* (first English edition, 1580). As Jan van Dorsten justly writes, here is a stress on moving and pleasing similar to Sidney's and in a text we know he read. Van Dorsten, however, does not identify the argument as Basil's (although Tremellius and Junius make the origin of the passage quite clear, saying 'adducemus' what that father says). The text he says Sidney echoes, in other words, is found elsewhere than here, being famous, influential, and often attached to the Bible authorized for public worship.[15]

For Basil, too, the psalms epitomize the books of history, prophecy, and precept, comprehending 'the whole commoditie of all these doctrines aforesayde', serving as a 'treasur house' or 'common storehouse of all good doctrine, which doth aptly distribute matter to every man peculiar to himselfe', and having 'a speciall peculier grace above all other partes of scripture' (I quote 'A Prologue of saint Basil the great, *upon the Psalmes*' that prefaces Part III of the Bishops' Bible, 1569, sigs. S1v–S2). The psalter works on our souls through 'agreeable delectation, instilling pleasauntly into our heart all sober honestie', for the Holy Ghost charitably mixes his 'fourme of doctrine' with music so that it might 'secretly steale into us'. Like the doctor who puts honey on the rim of a child's medicine cup, the psalms give delight to those who are 'either by age or children by manners': 'And for this ende be these sweete and harmonious songes devised for us, that such as be instructed, though for the tyme they seeme but to sing only'. This is quite close to Sidney's description of the poet who 'steals' (114) to us with doctrine hidden within a fable or the doctors who hide bitter drugs with sweetness, a trick that he, like Basil, says works for adult children too (113).[16] The psalms, adds Basil, are useful for beginners as well as for the experienced (something Sidney claims is true of right poetry), for they are 'high in mysterie, and profounde in sense: but yet familier and ready to be understanded of the true christen heart'. 'The psalme is an introduction to beginners, it is a furtherer to them whiche go forwarde to vertue, it is to the perfect man a stable foundation to rest on.' Through singing psalms God's doctrine is 'the deper printed in us', for pleasure, including the pleasure of song, both moves us and makes us remember: 'O wyse and marveylous devise of our heavenly schoolemaster who coulde invent that we should both pleasauntly sing and therwith profitably learne, whereby wholsome doctrine might be the deeper printed in us: for that which with violence and force is learned of us, is not wont to abyde long: but that whiche entreth into us with pleasure, and by loving grace, it continueth the longer in our heartes, it sticketh the faster in our memories.' On numbers, delight, and memory Sidney (like many others, to be sure) agreed, calling music 'the most divine striker of the senses' and poetry 'the only fit speech for music', the 'fittest for memory', and bearer of a delight that helps us remember (122). Much of what Basil says, then, finds a parallel in the *Apology*. Missing from his famous homily, however, is Athanasius' conception of the psalter as an inner image, a speaking painting or mirror.

Also in Parker's psalter the reader would find Chrysostom on how 'David was wont to aswage Saules fury with his harpe' and on how in his poetry he told 'not onely of things that were to come, but ... of those visible creatures, & of the invisible forme of the firmament', giving inspired information about such subjects as astronomy, earthquakes, and the reason for wine (to make us 'more mery and joconde'; sigs. E3v–F2). Here too are Augustine's caveats concerning song and, from Basil's epistle on how to study pagan literature, a comparison of David's musical power over Saul to the story of Timotheus first exciting and then calming Alexander ('Such strenght & vertue is set in the true use of music') and to the tale that Pythagoras once sobered some drunks by 'playeng to them the Dorian harmonie' (sig. G1v). And here are Josephus and Jerome on the psalter's metrics, and Eusebius on music and on David as the creator of patterns for emulation and avoidance: 'David inspierd with the grace of gods holy sprite so described a blessed man in his Odys and songes longe before these dayes, teaching who is truely a blessed man, and who is contrary' (sig. G1).

As I have indicated, this tradition was by no means obscure in the sixteenth century; to read praise of David is often to hear echoes of Athanasius, Basil, and later commentators who freely borrowed their imagery. Martin Luther's moving preface to the psalms, for example, makes similar claims if also some crucial revisions. The psalter, he says, uniquely and efficaciously incorporates what we read elsewhere in Scripture concerning history, prophecy, and precept. This argument clearly derives from Athanasius' and Basil's praise of David's poetry as an epitome of the Bible, but Luther minimizes their perhaps inadvertent implication that the books and genres of scripture are in some way rivals, competitors for a laurel garland awarded to the best book. He keeps the notion of competition but changes the arena, contrasting the psalter not to other voices in the Word of God but to saints' legends, and adding a Protestant emphasis on hearing. 'No books of moral tales and no legends of saints are to my mind as noble as the Book of Psalms; and if my purpose were to choose the best of all the edificatory books, legends of saints, or moral stories, and to have them assembled and presented in the best possible way, my choice would inevitably fall on our present Book.'[17]

The reasons for Luther's choice are quite like those that led Athanasius and Basil to single out the psalms so particularly. In the psalter, he says, we may see a general truth or pattern: 'We find, not what this or that saint did, but what the chief of all saints did, and what all saints still do.' The psalms, furthermore, incorporate what in his more secular context Sidney called philosophy and history – 'precepts' and a record of 'what the saints [i.e., the regenerate] did and said'. And since they also show the causes of action, the inwardness of men, the psalms are more relevant to our condition than those legends that display images without the models' words and hence (like Sidney's philosophers) 'advocate works that no man can imitate'. Thus the psalms are more moving, more effective, but for Luther this also means (as it did not for the Greek fathers) more vocal: ordinary 'legends of saints and other exemplary matter, depict holy men all with their tongues tied; whereas the Book of Psalms presents us with saints alive and in the round. It is like putting a dumb man side by side with one who can speak.' To be sure, the psalter is also something that we can 'see', for it is not only a garden and a treasury but also a painting, one in which we can observe 'the holy Christian church mirror' that gives us 'the true *gnosci teauton*' by which we can know ourselves and God. There, as one contemporary French translation put it, one can see 'le visage et face du roy David'.[18] And, like Sidney but unlike Athanasius, Luther insists that these marvels of the psalter are available only to the faithful (cf. the *Apology*, 99).

Calvin repeated much of this ancient praise together with its Lutheran modifications: in the introduction to his commentaries on the psalms he says that unlike scriptural books on how we should behave, the psalter is a treasury, a pedagogical and moving 'glasse' in which we see men's minds, both the evil and the good within us, 'lyvely set out before our eyes' and all the more effective because we hear the saints' very words (trans. Golding, 1571, sig. *vi). The psalms almost literally give us a speaking picture, and thus move beyond abstraction to provide us with remedies (sig. *vii). As Golding suggests in the preface to his translation, although without quite stating it, this effectiveness involves a sort of feigning or *poesis*: whereas other books make 'plaine declarations', the psalms present figures and 'borrowed personages' to show the faithful 'the unspeakable and inestimable comfort of their souls'. Compare Sidney's wording in his claim that David showed the coming of God and his 'unspeakable' beauty through 'the often and free changing of persons, his notable *prosopopeias*' (99). In fact, though, Golding shows some ambivalence toward *enargia* and commends Calvin's refusal to employ 'rhetorical enlarging of painted sentences' (sig. *v); again a Protestant withdraws a little from the seductive dangers of the image.

Theodore Beza in turn echoed Calvin: the psalter takes pride of place because it includes the precepts and prophecies that we find in other books of the Bible and has in addition its own particular property of presenting us with a model of how to talk to God. The psalms are like paintings, too. Psalm 22, for example, 'so painteth foorth the abasing of the sonne of God, that we may almost see him with our very eyes, and heare him with our very eares as yet hanging upon the Crosse' and 'wrastling' with Satan (trans. Anthony Gilbie, 1580). And at some point Sidney doubtless read Clément Marot's contribution to this tradition, the subtle 1541 epistle to Francis I that prefaces his *Trente Pseaulmes de David*. Marot, too, positions the psalms into a version of the old *paragone*. Playing down the *intra*scriptural rivalry at which Athanasius and Basil had hinted, he claims that David is not merely like the great pagan writers in technique and genre but so much better that after hearing him Apollo, for example, would break his own lyre and Orpheus would hang his on a tree. The psalms' power is seen in how they epitomize the 'loy' and God's 'faicts' found elsewhere in the Bible, make up a medicinal garden, form a crown of rhetorical gems (an image that revises for a king the ancient comparison of the psalter to a treasury), teach self-knowledge, and through figures paint Christ a thousand years before his coming more vividly than anyone has done since – not even 'Le tien Janet ne le grand Miquel l'ange'.[19] (Some years later a German commentator, Victorinus Strigelius, said something similar but changed the artists to Apelles and Dürer.)[20] Here, says Marot, Christians will 'trouvent leur amant', anticipating Philippe de Mornay's view of the psalms as 'songs of the very Love itself" (*Trewnesse of the christian religion*, trans. Sidney and A. Golding [1587] sig. Dd5) or Sidney's reference to David making us see

'God comming in his Majestie' and showing himself a 'passionate lover' (99). Sidney's lover, however, is the speaker of the psalms, not the divine object of his passion – although since Christ speaks the psalms through David the distinction is hard to keep clear.

Even without turning to these Genevan or French works, though, English readers could find this complex of metaphors in the preface to Anthony Cope's *Godly meditacion upon xx ... psalmes* (1547). According to Cope, David is a 'celestial Orpheus' who reforms us with 'strength and force' (what Tremellius, following Basil, calls 'vim et efficacitatem', sig. Aaa3, and Sidney calls *energia*). Psalms, says Cope, give a 'myrroure' and 'perfecte image' of ourselves and Christ, 'as lyvely as they were in colours set forth before oure eyes, and so many tropes, figures and allegories, that there is almoste no worde which lacketh an hidde misterie' (sig. *iii). In them David made a 'perfecte patron [pattern]' for teaching us to honor God. Nor was it only Protestants who adopted arguments and images that descend finally from Basil or Athanasius or their readers, for Cardinal Bellarmine himself uses some of them in the preface to his commentaries on the psalter. For him, too, the book of psalms both epitomizes what the Old Testament says elsewhere of precept, history, or prophecy and seizes the soul (*rapit animos*) not with mere narrative but with song and metaphor (more conscientious than many, Bellarmine cites his sources, Basil and Chrysostom).[21]

In sum, Sidney would have known much of a traditional set of *topoi* praising the psalms of David as a garden, treasury, mirror, and painting: a repository of lively images of an otherwise invisible excellence that inspires imitation, creates sweetness that 'steals' upon us, and conceals medicine good for children of all ages. Above all, the psalms outdo as efficacious teachers other works concerning abstract precept and particular event, in part because they give patterns, generally applicable forms that move the will and show the way. They even include images for avoidance as well as emulation. All this, including the metaphors, is in Sidney's *Apology* and applied to 'right poetry'. This tradition of praise was undoubtedly known to other Renaissance critics, especially after translations of the letter to Marcellinus began appearing, but Sidney had particular cause to know about it because of his interest in the psalms (he may have begun his own translation after writing the *Apology*, but his citation of Tremellius and Junius shows he was reading that part of the Bible with particular care). To other English critics such as Richard Wills, for instance, the notion that what one could say concerning Vergil or Horace might apply also to David would seem natural and welcome. Only someone who rejects the possibility of poetic inspiration, either because of the Protestant piety usually ascribed to Sidney or because of a more subversive desire to make room for his uninspired self, is likely to feel uncomfortable about the psalms as poetry one can praise in terms akin to those used for secular literature (although, to be sure, David's relation to the source of his inspiration was both closer and less problematic than, say, Homer's). It was, I think, precisely the peculiar status of the psalms – so like 'right' poetry and yet so beyond emulation, so central to parts of his case and yet finally so irrelevant to a defence of merely secular verse – that encouraged Sidney both to keep David under house arrest in the temple of divine poets and yet to subpoena him from time to time to testify on poetry's behalf.

Sidney's discomfort might also illuminate one other anomaly in his defence, the failure in his passage on divine poets to cite any biblical prose (101–02). In 1934 Israel Barroway explained this omission by arguing that Sidney is here following his source in the preface to Part III of the Junius-Tremellius Bible, for elsewhere he cites the stories told by Nathan (115) and Jesus ('not historical acts, but instructing parables') as examples of the 'feigned image' poets make up (108–09).[22] But perhaps Sidney simply felt happier omitting parables from his list of divine poems. Extended fictions, he may have thought, consciously or not, were what he himself could create, whether feigning Arcadia or Stellifying a lady. He could not of course be a Christ, but he could be a Nathan, not king of kings but advisor to a monarch. Further insulating his argument from the divine status of biblical prose, moreover, when he describes Nathan he puts him with the Roman statesman Menenius Agrippa, separating him by some pages from the incomparable narrator of the prodigal son parable, the only poet for whom divine inspiration and personal creation were the same thing.

The prophet Nathan, it will be remembered, is the effective fabulist who recalled David to his moral senses by inventing a story of a stolen lamb ('the discourse itself feigned' although 'the application most divinely true') and thus showed the royal murderer of Bathsheba's husband 'a glasse to see his own filthines' (II 5; Figure 6.1). The situation is in fact a bit tricky and touches on difficult issues of source and free will. The Bible is inspired; but *within* the history that the inspired text describes is Nathan directly inspired, perhaps like his master in the psalms? If not, he has a degree of autonomy that does not subvert but certainly complicates the divine status of this providentially arranged text-within-a-text, and he risks being secularized out of his prophethood. If he is inspired, then he is not a right poet by Sidney's definition and his presence here creates another slippage in the *Apology*'s logic. Sidney evidently sensed a problem, for he not only separates Nathan from his fellow (and self-inspired) poet Christ but rescues him for right poetry by identifying his influence on David as a 'second and instrumental cause' (the primary cause is God, but this can be said, theoretically, of all other reformations inspired by poetry). In any case, as Margaret Ferguson has observantly remarked, Nathan achieves his effect only by explaining

King David as a 'right poet' 171

⁋ For this cruell synne Nathan the pro=
phete
Dauid reproued: and blamed gretely.
Wher fore Dauyd with heuynesse replete.
Tenderly wepyng cryed: Peccaui.

Figure 6.1 Nathan enlightens David. He holds no glass, but the scene itself is a mirror shape. From a 1533 Sarum Primer, STC 15891, fol. cix.

his fiction.[23] It is not the reflecting fable but the exegetical nonfiction that shocks David into self-recognition. This is an exciting thought for critics and professors, even if poets might argue that, as Sidney himself says, the stricken monarch responded to Nathan's admonition by shaping his repentance into 'that heavenly psalm of mercy', almost certainly the penitential Psalm 51, set in the Christian liturgy for Ash Wednesday as a pattern for all sinners (the penitential psalms were regularly read as referring to the Bathsheba affair; Figure 6.2). Indeed, in the Sternhold-Hopkins psalter Sidney would have read that David composed his great poem specifically as what Elizabethan English liked to call a 'moniment', an aide-memoire not unlike those structures raised by more secular poets such as Horace and his 'monumentum aere perennius' (*Odes*, III.30). Persuaded by Nathan, says the psalter (1576 ed., STC 2446), the psalmist not only repented 'but also left a memoriall therof to his posteritie'. The Geneva Bible says the same. Sidney, however, here memorializes the instrument of the repentance, not the penance or the penitent.

Ferguson astutely ties the scene to Sidney's political anxieties and to his hope in the *Apology* to turn the reader's own gaze inward. I agree, but there is even more to be said about Nathan's mirror for a magistrate. To call language a looking glass was, by Sidney's day, so much a cliché that even Stephen Gosson grudgingly said a play might be a reforming 'glasse'.[24] Nevertheless, it is hard to imagine Sidney forgetting the specular power of the psalter that had so moved Christians from Athanasius to Calvin, so it is interesting to see him displace the mirror metaphor from the king's inspired numbers to the advisor's 'right' poetical fable. Did John Harington sense something odd in Sidney's treatment of the episode? When he paraphrased this passage for his own essay, he put the parables of Christ and Nathan together in his argument, a logical move that renders even more significant Sidney's separation, and he dropped the mirror image altogether.[25] But how satisfying for Sidney to have wrested the looking glass away from the king, and not just from any king, but from David: the out-of-towner whose military prowess was the subject of enraptured female song, the *successful* adulterer who must have had more 'skill of a sonnet' than Astrophil, the exiled courtier who did not merely rusticate and scribble elegant fantasies but collected an army and – in God's good time – replaced his politically powerful father-in-law, the spiritually advantaged harpist who was brought up short by a moving fable composed by an advisor seeking to save him from the consequences of a degrading love affair. Poor Sidney.

Sidney himself would, I imagine, reject such a reading with contempt and dismay, insisting that Nathan and David are beyond a rational man's envy. So let me end with a less problematic similarity between the *Apology* and the tradition I have described. In its later development the ancient

King David as a 'right poet'   173

Figure 6.2 Rebuked by Nathan, David prays in repentance. From the Ash Wednesday section of the 1555 Sarum Missal, STC 16217, fol. xxxviiiv, illustrating Psalm 51.

wonder at the psalter's power to address and reflect us individually and inwardly on occasion became the conviction that a given psalm has no one tonality: each person reads, says Archbishop Parker, 'as God shall move him', completing the psalter for himself in his own depths.[26] Sidney's *Apology*, too, has something of this openness, which perhaps explains why it seems to reflect so many outlooks and why readers have held such different images of it. We may be collectively confused, but then as Sidney's anonymous epitaph writer might have put it, no heap of stones – scholarly, speculative, or merely commemorative – can enclose a really lively text.

Notes

1 E.g., Catherine Barnes, 'The Hidden Persuader: the Complex Speaking Voice of Sidney's *Defence of Poetry*', *PMLA* 86 (1971): 422–27; Ronald Levao, 'Sidney's Feigned *Apology*', *PMLA* 94 (1979): 223–33; and Martin Raitiere, 'The Unity of Sidney's *Apology for Poetry*', *Studies in English Literature* 21 (1981): 37–57. O. B. Hardison, 'The Two Voices of Sidney's *Apology for Poetry*', *English Literary Renaissance* 2 (1972): 83–99, suggests two stages of composition; D. H. Craig, 'A Hybrid Growth: Sidney's Theory of Poetry in *An Apology for Poetry*', *English Literary Renaissance* 10 (1980): 183–201, points to Sidney's use of incompatible traditions. Margaret Ferguson, *Trials of Desire: Renaissance Defenses of Poetry* (New Haven, Conn., 1983), explores the political and personal anxieties behind Sidney's rhetorical manoeuvrings. Two recent studies find order beneath argument's fractures. John Ulreich, '"The Poets Only Deliver": Sidney's Conception of *Mimesis*', *Studies in the Literary Imagination* 15 (1982): 67–84, reprinted in *Essential Articles for the Study of Sir Philip Sidney*, ed. Arthur F. Kinney (Hamden, Conn., 1986), stresses the dynamism both Plato and Aristotle give to 'form' as model and energy (a concept relevant to the tradition I will describe). And John Hunt, 'Allusive Coherence in Sidney's *Apology for Poetry*', *Studies in English Literature* 27 (1987): 1–16, notes a syncretic method that works by implied reference and context.

2 I have used Geoffrey Shepherd's edition of the *Apology* (Manchester: Manchester University Press, 1973); my citations refer to his page numbers. For Scaliger's division of poets, see 161. Perhaps Sidney followed Jean de Serres in adding David to the divine poets, although Serres does not mention David by name. See S. K. Heninger, 'Sidney and Serranus' *Plato*', *English Literary Renaissance* 13 (1983): 155; he does not note this revision of Scaliger but does make a good case that Sidney knew Serres' text.

3 Levao, 'Sidney's Feigned *Apology*', 224; Alan Sinfield, 'The Cultural Politics of the *Defence of Poetry*', in *Sir Philip Sidney and the Interpretation of Renaissance Culture*, ed. Gary F. Waller and Michael D. Moore (Totowa, N.J.: Barnes and Noble, 1984), 128. Sinfield finds some divisions caused by Sidney's Protestantism, but opinions were sometimes less strict than he suggests. He says, for example, that Du Bartas 'rejected secular poetry altogether' (cf. his 'Sidney and Du Bartas',

Comparative Literature 27 [1975]: 8–20); true, the muse in Du Bartas' 'Uranie' does so, but elsewhere Du Bartas himself was happy to praise Petrarch, Ariosto, and Ronsard.

4   Katherine Duncan-Jones and Jan van Dorsten, Miscellaneous Prose of Sir Philip Sidney (Oxford: Oxford University Press, 1973), 188–89, note this inconsistency.
5   John Skelton, The Complete English Poems, ed. John Scattergood (New Haven, Conn., 1983), 382–84, from 'A Replycacion'.
6   Annabel Patterson, 'Bermudas and The Coronet: Marvell's Protestant Poetics', English Literary History 44 (1977): 478–99, outlines the significance for the lyric of one aspect of these patristic commentaries and cites the psalter by Parker that I discuss below. See also Barbara Lewalski, Protestant Poetics and the Seventeenth Century Religious Lyric (Princeton, N.J.: Princeton University Press, 1979), 39–53. However, in thinking that the extract Parker calls 'Athanasius in Psalmos' was reprinted by Sternhold and Hopkins, Lewalski confuses it with another extract he calls 'Of the use and vertue of the Psalmes'. Ira Clark, Christ Revealed: The History of the Neotypological Lyric in the English Renaissance (Gainesville, Fla.: University Presses of Florida, 1982), argues with some justice that the poetics implied can be as much Counter-reformationist as Protestant. In her invaluable study English Metrical Psalms: Poetry as Praise and Prayer, 1535–1601 (Cambridge: Cambridge University Press, 1987), 27–34, Rivkah Zim touches on this tradition but does not tie it, as such, to the more secular aspects of Sidney's Apology (see 154–55, 159).
7   Hallett Smith, 'English Metrical Psalms in the Sixteenth Century', Huntington Library Quarterly 9 (1945–46): 249–71, puts Parker's psalter 'in a middle position between the Puritans and the courtiers', just where Sidney himself was placed, one might add. Margaret Hannay, who has seen the correspondence, informs me that Parker wrote Henry Sidney and even sent him a book (although not this one), and there is no reason to suppose that the psalter's rarity prevented Sir Philip from seeing it. Estimating its impact on his own translations, if any, is difficult. The editors of Sidney's psalms, both William Ringler and J. C. A. Rathmell, think it had none; nor does Zim consider the possibility. Recently the list of Sidney's possible sources has been growing longer, however. Seth Weiner, 'The Quantitative Poems and the Psalm Translations: The Place of Sidney's Experimental Verse in the Legend', in Sir Philip Sidney: 1586 and the Creation of a Legend, ed. Jan van Dorsten, Dominic Baker-Smith, and Arthur F. Kinney (Leiden: Brill, 1986), 193–220, suggests some additional scholars and commentators, and Richard Todd, '"So well Attyr'd Abroad": A Background to the Sidney–Pembroke Psalter and Its Implications for the Seventeenth-Century Religious Lyric', Texas Studies in Language and Literature 29 (1987): 74–93, persuasively argues for the Dutch Souterliedekens. Parker (I call him 'Parker', although it is not clear who made the translation), Sternhold and Hopkins, Robert Crowley, and Sidney all derive much of their language from the Bishops' and Geneva translations. That fact and their fairly simple style with obvious rhymes like 'might' and 'right' produce an inevitable similarity, although Sidney is more imaginative metrically and less flaccid in diction. After comparing the rhymes, however, I am convinced that Sidney read Parker. Excluding those

also in Sternhold and Hopkins, he and Parker share at least one pair of ending sounds, and often more, in twenty-nine of forty-three psalms, which seems more frequent than chance and common sources require. In Psalm 34, for example, both translators rhyme the opening quatrain on *always*, *high*, continually, and *praise* (Sternhold and Hopkins have 'always/ praise') and both have the same rhymes in the ninth, sharing none with Sternhold and Hopkins:

Parker:	Sidney:
O feare the Lord: ye sainctes of his,	Feare God ye saints of his,
therin your travayle plant:	For nothing they can ever want
For they that feare: the Lord of blis,	Who faithfull feares in him do plant;
shall nothyng ever want.	They have and shall have blisse.

Parker opens Psalm 10 with 'Why stondst so far: and art no star', Sidney with 'Why standest Thou so farr, / O God our only starr'. Sidney's Psalm 43 shares Parker's rhyme scheme (*aabccb*) together with five rhymes, and his Psalm 19 has Parker's favourite scheme (*aabaab*), meter (fragmented fourteeners), and at least nine exact or related rhymes.

8 Levao, 'Sidney's Feigned *Apology*', 228, says that for Sidney poetry is not a mean but an inclusion of opposites. The tradition I describe is similar in this regard. On poetry as mediation and hence as a sort of equity, however, see Kathy Eden, *Poetic and Legal Fiction in the Aristotelian Tradition* (Princeton, N.J.: Princeton University Press, 1986). She does not discuss the Aristotelian line that branches off into the commentary I treat, but on Augustine's view of images and on how Aristotelian tradition related poetry to equity, mediation, and the New Law, she is very helpful. A. Leigh DeNeef, 'Rereading Sidney's *Apology*', *Journal of Medieval and Renaissance Studies* 10 (1980): 183 also discusses Sidney's conception of poetry as mediation; and on Sidney's conception of metaphor as 'bridge-building', see Judith Dundas, '"To Speak Metaphorically": Sidney in the Subjunctive Mood', *Renaissance Quarterly* 41 (1988): 268–87.

9 Cf. A. E. Malloch, '"Architectonic" Knowledge and Sidney's *Apologie*', *English Literary History* 20 (1953): 181–85, and Neil Rudenstine, 'Sidney and Energia', in *Elizabethan Poetry: Modern Essays in Criticism*, ed. Paul Alpers (New York: Oxford University Press, 1967), 210–34. A. C. Hamilton, 'Sidney's Idea of the "Right Poet"', *Comparative Literature* 9 (1957): 51–59, says Sidney's emphasis on motivation to action goes beyond what he found in Scaliger and adds, 'no critic, so far as I am aware, anticipates Sidney's vigorous emphasis upon the end of moving'. Basil and Athanasius do just that, although as Hamilton would point out, much must remain distinct between a celebration of divine discourse that includes some fictions and an argument in defense of secular fictions that teach moral truths.

10 Or so I deduce from the translation in Robert C. G. Gregg's edition of *The Life of Antony and The Letter to Marcellinus* (New York: Paulist Press, 1980), 108: the reader of the psalms learns right action because he understands 'the emotions of the soul, and, consequently, on the basis of that which affects him, and by which he is constrained, he also is enabled by this book to possess the image deriving from the word'.

11 Sig. C1v. Gregg, *Life of Antony*, 145, says the Greek presents many difficulties.
12 Praise of an art's power to create vivid images was of course common; cf. Amyot's claim that history can do so better than philosophy (although he does not use the flame metaphor), quoted by Shepherd, *Apology*, 171. See also DeNeef, 'Rereading Sidney's *Apology*', especially 185, who suspects a link with Augustine. For a recent study of Sidney and Amyot that cites and extends earlier work by Margaret Hearsey and Elizabeth Donno, see Anthony Miller, 'Sidney's *Apology for Poetry* and Plutarch's *Moralia*', *English Literary Renaissance* 17 (1987): 259–76. There are, incidentally, striking resemblances between Sidney's argument and that on 'the use and profite of histories' prefaced to Thomas Cooper's *Chronicle* (1560 ed., STC 15218). Writing before North's translation, Cooper closely parallels Amyot: history is a 'treasure' of effective 'paynted' examples, for 'Even as in every arte paternes be gyven to folowe ... yet in examples and deedes it is more evidently perceived, what the dygnytee of vertue, and agayne, what the basenesse of dishonestee and vices bee, than in bare preceptes, because the examples, set as images before us, do not onely openly teache, but also both warne and stirre our myndes, so that therby with a certayne delite and desire they be kyndled towards vertue and honestee' (sig. h1). As one such story he names that of Nathan and David, cited as a picture of divine forgiveness – Cooper focuses on the imaginable historical event and not, like Sidney, on the prophet's moving fiction.
13 Since images derive from or are uncomfortably close to the mind's capacity for fantasy, they may mislead as well as motivate us and may dazzle our sight while deafening us to the Word. On this complicated and ambiguous matter see, e.g., Virginia Riley Hyman, 'Sidney's Definition of Poetry', *Studies in English Literature* 10 (1970): 49–62, Eden, *Poetic and Legal Fiction*, 62–175, and William Rossky, 'Imagination in the English Renaissance: Psychology and Poetic', *Studies in the Renaissance* 5 (1958): 49–73. Ernest B. Gilman, *Iconoclasm and Poetry in the English Reformation: Down Went Dagon* (Chicago: University of Chicago Press, 1986), 37, suggests that if the Bible paints lively pictures of Christian truth, then language has 'vanquished the image entirely'. Gerhart B. Ladner, 'The Concept of the Image in the Greek Fathers and the Byzantine Iconoclastic Controversy', *Dumbarton Oaks Papers* 7 (1953): 1–34, describes the iconophile assumptions with which Athanasius and Basil began; St. Methodus of Olympus, for example, said in about A.D. 300 that Christ himself was like a painting that God made so we could see what to imitate (10). Thus when theologians like Luther and Calvin adopt their comments on the psalms they modify the terms (e.g., Luther's claim that only believers 'see' Christ in the psalms) or allow the potential, at least, for some logical tension. Andrew Weiner, *Sir Philip Sidney and the Poetics of Protestantism: A Study of Contexts* (Minneapolis, Minn., 1978), 28–50, shows how these issues affect Sidney (although without reference to the Greek fathers). I share his disagreement (45) with Forrest G. Robinson, *The Shape of Things Known: Sidney's Apology in Its Philosophical Tradition* (Cambridge, Mass.: Harvard University Press, 1972), who argues that 'There could be no speaking picture, no delightful teaching, of wisdom received through grace' (101). Like Basil and others, Sidney knew better.

14 Saint Basil, *Exegetic Homilies*, trans. Sr. Agnes Clare Way (Washington, D.C.: Catholic University of America Press, 1963), 151.
15 Jan van Dorsten, 'Sidney and Franciscus Junius the Elder', *Huntington Library Quarterly* 42 (1978–79): 1–13. Shepherd also cites the *Biblia Sacra* on 161 and 182 and he too ascribes to it what is Basil's. I note this because the passages are not merely the opinion of two Reformation translators but part of a continuum, a tradition with its own arguments and images that need not always be read as inherently Protestant. In *Language and Meaning in the Renaissance* (Princeton, N.J.: Princeton University Press, 1987), which I read after completing this essay, Richard Waswo says perceptively that 'The fundamental dynamic of Sidney's defense ... seems to proceed much more directly from reformed ways of treating Scripture than from Italian theoretical debates about literature. Reading and interpretation, for both Erasmus and Sidney, were to 'inflame our souls' (228). Yes. But we should hesitate to call 'reformed' what had an ancient ancestry and considerable appeal to Catholics: claims for the inflammatory effect of the psalter go back centuries, whatever Sidney's other Protestant assumptions.
16 Mark Roberts, 'The Pill and the Cherries: Sidney and the Neo-Classical Tradition', *Essays in Criticism* 16 (1966): 22–31, finds Sidney caught between thinking that poetry works 'with the kind of deception appropriate for getting children to take pills' [although Sidney could be referring to a liquid], a 'Christian' concept, and the more 'pagan' image of something both pleasant *and* medicinal. Here is another disjunction in Sidney's argument, and Basil's honey-smeared cup is certainly closer to Sidney's first thought. But since the more than pagan Lucretius uses the identical comparison (Shepherd, *Apology*, 182), and to serve what Sidney would call 'a full wrong divinity' (102), I would hesitate to insist on its Christianity. Basil has an ambivalence of his own, for in his famous epistle on how to study secular learning (trans. William Berker, 1557) he remarks that wicked men can take us in with evil like 'a poyson tempered with honye' (sig. B2).
17 Martin Luther, 'Preface to the Psalms' (1528), trans. Bertram Lee Woolf (1956), in *Selections from His Writings*, ed. John Dillenberger (New York: Doubleday, 1961), 37–41.
18 Pierre Caroli [?] translated Luther for his own *Livre des Psalmes* (Alençon, 1531 or 1532); printed in *The Prefatory Epistles of Jacques Lefèvre d'Etaples and Related Texts*, ed. Eugene Rice (New York: Columbia University Press, 1972), 517–23. Athanasius' Letter to Marcellinus was well known in circles like Lèfevre's; Lèfevre's *Quincuplex Psalterium*, ed. G. T. Bedowelle (Geneva: Droz, 1979), II, 87–88, cites some Renaissance translations beginning with Politian's and including that by Reuchlin.
19 Clément Marot, *Les Traductions*, ed. C. A. Mayer (Geneva: Slatkine, 1980), 309–14. Marot includes both the visual and oral by alternating verbs: 'orrez ... verrez ... oyt on ... verrez ... orra' (II.73–91).
20 *A proceeding in the harmonie of King Davids harpe*, trans. R. Robinson (1591), sigs. B1–B1v, on Psalm 22 (said to prophesy the crucifixion and quoted by Jesus on the cross), which shows Christ 'better than what Apelles or Dürer could

do', for David has 'so great light of wordes and efficacie of meaning' that he sets the passion 'before our eyes'.
21 *Opera Omnia* (Paris, 1874; repr. Frankfurt, 1965), X, 3–5.
22 Israel Barroway, 'Tremellius, Sidney, and Biblical Verse', *Modern Language Notes* 49 (1934): 145–49.
23 Ferguson, *Trials of Desire*, 159–62, explores the psychodynamics of the passage and the relevance of Sidney's political frustration over the Queen's possible French marriage and her foreign policy. I would add to her list of Sidney's subtextual anxieties those relating to David himself. For another closeup view that reveals snags in the argument, see Lawrence C. Wolfley, 'Sidney's Visual-Didactic Poetic: Some Complexities and Limitations', *Journal of Medieval and Renaissance Studies* 6 (1976): 240, who points out some confusions in Sidney's use of Lucrece as an *image* of constancy and the *actor* of a suicide.
24 Cited by Arthur F. Kinney, 'Parody and Its Implications in Sidney's Defense of Poesie', *Studies in English Literature* 12 (1972): 17, as evidence that Sidney was mocking Gosson. Incidentally, there is one other possible explanation for Sidney's opening story of Pugliano to add to Kinney's suggestions. When Sidney wrote that under the spell of the horsemaster's self-loving arguments he almost wished himself a horse, he may have hoped that his readers would smilingly remember that according to his name he could hardly help himself: Philip *means* lover of horses (although as 'a piece of a logician' Sidney would know that one cannot be the thing one loves without serious identity problems; as a horse he would be Hip, not Philip). Since the horse is an ancient symbol of passion, Philip's name and self-defense, Pugliano's expertise, and Nathan's rebuke of David's criminal sexuality take on added poignancy – as do Astrophil's wry comments on various sorts of ridership.
25 John Harington, 'A Brief Apology for Poetry' (1591), in *Elizabethan Critical Essays*, ed. G. G. Smith (Oxford: Clarendon Press, 1904), II, 205.
26 Sigs. VV2v–VV3; Smith, 'Metrical Psalms', plausibly sees a 'concession to Protestant individualism', although Parker's sense of human 'diversitie' is already implied by ancient praise of the psalms' personal relevance.

7

The countess of Pembroke's *Ruins of Rome*

An interest in architectural ruins must be very old, older than cities and temples. In broken towns and monuments, in barely legible foundation stones and mossy walls, we read the past and, so the thoughtful can imagine, also read our future. Some of the most compelling Renaissance poetry and painting treats images of ruination, from Shakespeare's sonnets to the damaged masonry in the backgrounds of Nativity scenes, from Joachim du Bellay's *Antiquitez de Rome* (1558) to the eroded stones framing title pages like that in Arthur Golding's 1571 translation of Calvin's psalm commentaries.[1] Unsurprisingly, a fascination with ruined walls and Time's curious mineral appetite (as though Kronos had actually enjoyed the stone his wife fed him in place of Zeus) was often tied to thoughts on the pride of ancient and modern Rome: *translatio imperii* served as a tragic or hopeful warning against earthly arrogance.

In later Elizabethan England a fairly coherent complex of words and images gathered around this matter, one major source, although by no means the only one, being Spenser's translation of du Bellay's *Antiquitez*, published in his *Complaints* (1591) as 'The Ruines of Rome'. The complex includes allusions to blood, falling or eroded walls, Time's speedy consumption or gradual erosion, urban pride, civil war, and rebellion punished either by shocks from above or by Time's ingestion and wearing, and – sometimes – the persistence of poetry despite all this. 'Manent scripta', reads the hopeful motto to one of Geoffrey Whitney's 1586 *Emblems*, placed defiantly above a picture of collapsing towers and a pile of impressively bound tomes (Figure 7.1).[2]

Relevant phrases and images are not missing from Anglo-Saxon and Medieval poetry, but it is far easier to find them, often clustered together, in the later English Renaissance, particularly in the 1580s and 1590s, as a long process was completed by which Fortuna's blows and wheel were replaced or joined by a newly energized Father Time. Although Chronos/Kronos/Saturn had never disappeared, the old god was now even better equipped to devour as *Tempus edax* or to fly with faster wings as *Tempus*

IF mightie TROIE, with gates of steele, and brasse,
Bee worne awaie, with tracte of stealinge time:
If CARTHAGE, raste: if THEBES be growne with grasse.
If BABEL stoope: that to the cloudes did clime:

Figure 7.1 Towers falling. Engraving from Geoffrey Whitney's *A Choice of Emblemes and Other Devises*, F2r.

fugit and showed more interest than ever in wearing down and messing up whatever human beings build. The verbal and conceptual cluster – self-replicating and contagious, like a lexical virus – is not entirely coherent, for writers who blame ruins on mutability can in virtually the same breath blame the same ruins on civil war, external enemies, the victim's criminal stupidity, or God's admonitory wrath. The sonnets in Du Bellay's *Antiquitez*, for example attribute Rome's collapse variously to time, civil strife, hubris, and Germans.

As Kent Hieatt showed some years ago, Shakespeare probably read Spenser's *Ruines* before applying its vocabulary to the future of his sonnets' time-disdaining or time-threatened young man (although not, perhaps significantly, to that of their sexually available dark lady).³ There is similar imagery in his *Lucrece* and early history plays, often serving in the latter case to warn against civil war. Some poets, including those associated one way or another with Mary Sidney, countess of Pembroke, likewise found the cluster moving, as witness many passages in the poetry of Samuel Daniel and Michael Drayton. Others, however, show little attraction to this cluster. Philip Sidney ignores it, as do Christopher Marlowe and John Donne. Writers, that is, seem either to have been deeply moved by this discourse or to have found it uninteresting.

In her part of the Sidney Psalter, Mary Sidney shows a real if intermittent commitment to this particular language of ruination. Why? She was doubtless touched and impressed by Spenser's *Complaints* and by the verse of Daniel and Drayton. Her translation of Garnier's *Antonius* (1592), moreover, reproduces in English his own use of the French version of what one might call the 'ruinish' lexicon (one Garnier almost certainly derived from du Bellay).⁴ Wherever she found it, thereby helping to perpetuate it, Sidney's protégé Daniel noticed that the Countess was taken by what was later to be called the 'ruins aesthetic', for he applied it not only to Delia, Rosamond, Stonehenge, and Cleopatra, but to Mary's own estate. Thanks to her hymns and psalms, he tells her in 1594, Time 'shall never pray upon her': she will still be famous 'When Wilton lyes low levell'd with the ground: / And this is that which thou maist call thine owne, / Which sacriligious time cannot confound'.⁵ Nor was he alone. Nicholas Breton, another poet whom Sidney encouraged, turns the conceit in a more godly direction, indeed the same direction to which she turns her psalm translations, telling his patroness in the preface to his *Pilgrimage to Paradise* (1592) that even if she finds his poetry inadequate, 'thinke not of the mines of Troie, but helpe to builde up the walles of Jerusalem'.⁶ Sidney, I think, hoped to do just that. Her interest in the language of ruination was likely to have been the result not just of brooding over Troy (or Rome, or England's own bare ruined choirs) but of a concern for God's city and for hopes of a re-edified and renewed Jerusalem, the peaceful city lying beyond the ravages of time and sin.

Sidney's gentle nudge of English biblical vocabulary in the direction of 'ruinish' allows her more strenuously to contrast images of waste and collapse with the God who has 'timeless raign' (Ps. 64:37), whose name his servants will 'love and prize' and 'eternize' (Ps. 69:110–14), of whom we can say 'Tyme in noe terms his mercy comprehends' (Ps. 100:13; Geneva has 'his mercie is everlasting'), whom 'tyme nor force can shake' (Ps. 104:18), and 'whom no times enfold' (Ps. 116:49). How unlike mortality: 'nay all be thousands here, / ten thousands there decay: / that Ruine to approach thee nere, / shall finde no force nor way' (Ps. 9:21–24). True, the sinner has his or her own eternity, but it is not God's: 'yea to eternall tyme / synne of his mother and his mothers side / may in his mind, who is eternall, stand.' God has destroyed many evil nations, and

> Therefore ô Lord, thy name is famous still,
>   the memory thy ancient wonders gott,
> Tyme well to world his message may fulfill
>   And back retorne to thee, yet never blott
> Out of our thoughts ... (Ps. 135:36–40)

God's favourites do not always escape:

> by my support all threates of time shall scorne.
> and lord, as running skies with wheeles unworne
> cease not to lend this wonder their commending
> ...
> While circling time, still ending and beginning,
>   shall runne the race where stopp nor start appeares:
> my bounty towards him, not ever linning,
>   I will conserve nor write my league in years
> ...
> And yet, ô now by thee abjected, scorned,
>   Scorcht with thy wrath is thy annointed one:
> Hated his league, the crowne him late adorned,
>   Puld from his head, by thee, augments his moane.
>   Raz'd are his fortes: his walls to ruine gone. (Ps. 89:12–13, 73–76, 97–101)

The relevant phrases are not in the English biblical translations I have seen. The psalms declare the eternity of God, of course, but Sidney's vocabulary is more likely than that of scripture to use a now fashionable vocabulary describing a Time that wears away mortality and a divinity that transcends or restores it.

Sidney also makes slight but detectable use of this complex when describing not God's transcendence of time but earthly structures' vulnerability to ruination, temporal or violent. In order to add something of the 'ruinish' tonality to her translation she did not need to intrude imagery about battered towers and walls, for of course that is already in the psalms. Rather, on a number of occasions she uses variants of 'ruin' where her English sources are more likely to use some version of 'waste' or 'destruction'. Sometimes, moreover, by adding the language of time's effects, she could complete her version of a now culturally significant ruination vocabulary. Thus in Psalm 66 'the rebell who against him bandeth, / of Ruins cup shall quickly tast', whereas in Geneva rebels should merely 'not exalt them selves'. Worldlings ignore mutability: 'A second thinkes his house shall not decaie, / nor time his glorious buildings overthrow, / nam'd proudlie of his name ... (Ps.

49:19–21; Geneva has 'Yet they thinke, their houses, and their habitacions shal continue for ever, even from generacion to generacion, and call their lands by their names'). Sometimes enemies vainly threaten ruination like that of Rome: 'hee whose forehed Envies mark had sign'd, / his trophes on my ruins sought to reare' (Ps. 55:34–35; Geneva says 'Neither did mine adversarie exalt him selfe against me'). Or compare the psalmist's anguished question in Psalm 77, 'Doeth his promes faile for ever more?' to Sidney's: 'could rusty teeth of tyme / to nought his promise turne?' (Spenser's *Ruines of Rome* 13 has 'rust of age', and his *Teares of the Muses* 433 the 'rust of time'; the ultimate source is Ovid's *tempus edax*, but Ovid's Time, whatever his problematic diet, has clean teeth).[7] Nor is holiness always exempt:

> Thy most holy seate
> the greedy flames do eate,
> and have such ruthlesse ruyns wrought,
> that all thy house is raste,
> So raste, and so defast,
> that of that all remayneth nought.[8]

If even the sacred can be razed and defaced, what hope for the secular?

Indeed, what of Babylon? Rome was not the only ruined city. As Sidney puts it in her translation of Psalm 137, the psalmist – in this case not possibly David, as some exegetes admitted – says 'downe, downe with it at any hand / make all platt pais, lett nothing stand. / And Babilon, that didst us wast, / thy self shalt one daie wasted be' (31–34). The 'platt pais', or flat countryside, seems even worse than the devastation in the Geneva Bible ('Rase it, rase it to the fundacion thereof. O daughter of Babel, worthie to be destroied, blessed shal he be that rewardeth thee, as thou hast served us'), for Sidney imagines, as does Spenser in the *Ruines of Time*, an annihilation so extreme that not even foundations are visible. True, Jerusalem is another earthly city subject to ruin, but if it falls God can restore it.

We could call Sidney's approach to the psalms in crucial ways typological. If she minimizes the explicit mentions of Christ that even after the Reformation may be found in much psalm translation and commentary, her added details and turns of phrasing show that she nevertheless perceived that David's angry threats to his enemies of temporal decay and violent ruination expressed a prophetic understanding that the Rome of Antichrist would fall again and the New Jerusalem rise above the ruins to live like the bride she truly is. Hence Sidney can say, 'for lo the lord againe to forme doth bring / Jerusalems long ruinated walls', whereas the Geneva says tersely, 'The Lord doeth buyld up Jerusalem' (Ps. 147:5–6). Her 'ruins aesthetic', then, is what one might call Protestant urban typology, Reformation hope. Doubtless she knew the

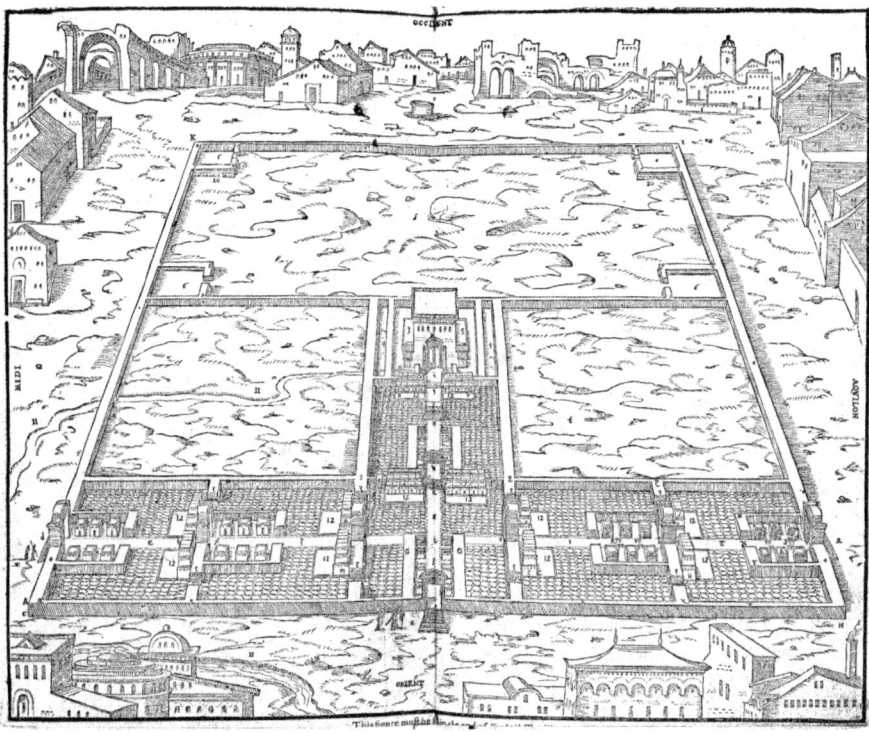

Figure 7.2 Layout of temple and city, Ezekiel. Folding plate between leaf 3T2 verso (folio 356v) and leaf 3T3 recto (folio 357r). The restless translation of empire has achieved stability and peace, whether in this world thanks to Reform or, if that is impossible, then in the next. God's temple in His city is restored against the ruined City of Man.

picture of the re-edified Temple and its City with which the Geneva Bible illustrates Ezekiel. Its bold and rectilinear lines stand against a background of jumbled and incoherent ruins (Figure 7.2).[9]

Something like that pattern is operating when Sidney elaborates on a passage in Psalm 102 that imagines the restoration of Zion:

> eternall thou eternally dost bide,
>   thy memory noe yeares can freat
> ...
>   Thy servauntes waite the day
>   when she, who like a Carcasse lay
>   stretch'd forth in Ruines beare
>   shall soe arise and live,

> that Nations all Jehovas name shall feare,
> all kings to thee shall glory give.
> Because thou has a new
> Made Sion stand, restor'd to view
> thy glorious presence there?
> ...
> But thou art one, still one:
> tyme interest in thee hath none
> (42–43, 49–56, 85–86)

In the Geneva version, God is unchanging, but not in quite these terms:

> But thou, ô Lord doest remaine for ever, and thy remembrance from generacion to generacion. Thou wilt arise & have mercie upon Zion: for the time is come to have mercie thereon, for the appointed time is come. For thy servants delite in the stones thereof, and have pitie on the dust thereof. Then the heathen shal feare the Name of the Lord, & all the Kings of the earth thy glorie, When the Lord shal buylde up Zion, & shal appeare in his glorie. But thou art the same, and thy yeres shal not faile. (verses 12–16, 27)

Unlike the psalmist, perhaps inevitably, Sidney thinks of Roman as well as Israelite ruins and adopts the appropriate lexicon. (Indeed, the 'Carcasse' stretched among ruins but now reviving parallels the resurrecting 'corpse' in Spenser's *Ruines of Rome* 5 and 27.)

Several times, moreover, Sidney stresses or adds the claim that Time can chew cities but not words. After all, she might have reflected, ancient Roman boasts about brass-outwearing verse are mere pagan bluster, whereas similar claims in the mouth of God's prophet have real credibility. Her translations thus occasionally edge into celebration of authorship itself, whether we read the (human) author as David, Sidney, or somebody writing/singing in a melded voice.[10] The psalms' chief author, she would in any case have believed, is God. Indeed, because she tends to apply the 'ruinish' complex to affirmations of divinity's immunity to time, she has in a sense written a companion piece to Spenser's *Ruines of Rome* and his *Visions of Bellay*: the earthly city is in ruins, but the words of the God of Israel will last. If the psalmist says (in the Geneva version) 'I wil declare high sentences of olde ... That the posteritie might knowe it, and the children, which shulde be borne, shulde stand up, and declare it to their children', Sidney says more robustly,

> A grave discourse to utter I entend;
> the age of tyme I purpose to renew
> ...
> That while the yong shall over-live the old,
> and of their brood some yet shalbe unborn;
> these memories in memory enrold
> by freating tyme may never thence be worn

> that still on god their anchor, hope may hold;
> from him by no dispairefull tempest torn. (78:1–2, 17–22)

This is not the only way, furthermore, in which Sidney suggests that writings outlive brass or stone, for she often favours the verb 'record' – which etymologically can mean draw upon the heart's retrieval system (re-cord) but in recent centuries has strongly connoted writing. In the Geneva version of Psalm 140, 'the righteous shal praise thy Name', but for Sidney 'the just may glad record the honor of thy name' (29–30; there are parallels with Spenser's *Ruines of Rome* 28 and 33). Where the Geneva translation gives some version of 'praise', 'remember', or 'survive', then, Sidney can prefer a term suggesting script or print. 'And the trueth of the Lord endureth for ever', says Geneva's Psalm 117, which she translates as 'Like as the word / Once he doth give / Rold in record / Doth tyme outlive' (9–12). Just whose 'record' is unclear, and 'rold' could suggest a scroll or 'enrolled', but in this passage the translator is more than half way to being what one might call graphocentric. The perdurable and timeless *Logos* is a text, if a text engraved on the heart: 'Record', says Sidney's David, 'in speciall memory / the miracles he wrought, the lawes he gave' (Ps. 105: 9; Geneva just has 'remember', which requires no pen or stylus, not even metaphorical ones).

What encouraged Mary Sidney to write like this? Her brother Philip had not introduced this lexical pattern in his share of the Sidney Psalter (Psalms 1–43), if only because Fortune, although not Time, had killed him before the fashion took full hold. Perhaps Mary was simply drawn to a vocabulary with which Spenser, Daniel, and Drayton were then increasing – or shortly after Philip's death were about to increase – the pathos of their ruminations on mutability. I suspect, though, that Sidney was also attracted to this complex of images precisely because it was now, thanks to Spenser's *Ruines*, religious polemic, and perhaps the plays by Garnier popular in Sidney's circle, so often associated with Rome, with translation of empire, and with Protestant (and even some Catholic) disgust at the way modern popes laid claim to the eternal city's in fact problematic glamour and rule. Sidney might also have been struck by pictures in the great 1568 Bishops' Bible, published under the auspices of her father's friend, Archbishop Matthew Parker. Some illustrations in Daniel and Ezekiel position figures in landscapes with ruins resembling those in more secular texts: an image of Daniel in the lions' den is set in a landscape with the broken arch and tufts of moss familiar from any number of Renaissance woodcuts showing the ruins of Rome (Figure 7.3).

It is the case that the discourse of ruin was also applied to more secular matters. It helped Shakespeare, Daniel, Drayton, and others, to articulate

Figure 7.3 Daniel in the lions' den (lower right). Bishops Bible part 3, Daniel, leaf Y5 verso (folio clxxiij.v).

earthly loves. Minor poets, too, could adopt the language: when Richard Tofte, for example, writes a *carpe diem* poem to his lady, Alba, that threatens her with an old age like that of the not-so-eternal city, he paraphrases Spenser's *Ruines of Rome* 7.[11] And yet, just as those thundering at Babylon or Jerusalem could allegorize civic sin as whorishness, so behind the erotic and private language of a Shakespeare or Drayton may lie a memory of public and urban significance: *Roma summus amor*, as the old palindrome went, and of course – palindromes being what they are – vice versa. Shakespeare was not alone in imagining the body as a city or kingdom at war with time or subject to parietal breach or decay, whereas both Petrarch and du Bellay seem on some imaginative level to have associated Rome with a woman, whether harlot or simply a desired mistress.[12] More important for my purposes, though, is the way some who attacked the papacy likewise found this lexical pattern useful, relishing the thought of Rome's once and future ruination, its walls collapsing into its bloody soil, its pride humbled and its empire divinely abbreviated. Time, in this understanding, is on God's side. Needless to say, this rhetoric intensified, with or without du Bellay/Spenser's stress on Time, in the years following the Armada.

An early example is a sermon Robert Humston preached on 22 September 1588, recalling how God saved the Jews and reduced Babylon and its walls to a heap of stones. Our own cities were in danger, he says, but God defeated our enemies and foiled 'gold-thirstie Babell' (Spain, of course). Let us fear our own bloodiness, however, or, as the prophet warns, the very 'stone shall crye out of the wall'.[13] A *Treatise, touching Antichrist* by Lambert Daneau, a distinguished Calvinist theologian, expert on witches, and (I suspect) reader of du Bellay, owes even more to this lexicon, at least in John Swan's translation. True, he stresses the role of violence in Rome's fall and minimizes that of time. The old Rome, he says, was 'quite defaced,... brought to utter ruine' with 'her walles beaten downe' so that 'such as are not well acquaynted with the Citie, might seeke for Rome, beeing in the middest of her'. Alas, Rome is now 'repaired out of the dust and mines of the old overthrone Citie', for the city of the Antichrist, built upon the 'grave, mines, and ashes of that aunciet and famous Rome ... is seene to be re-edified and inhabited again ... Re-edified, I say, but to a cleane contrarie purpose to that of the restoring of the second Jerusalem.' There is hope: Rome might raise again 'her courage to the Skie', but 'Armageddon', when read backward – it is Hebrew, after all – as 'Geddon-Harma', means 'where the high place was cut downe: as if ye should terme it, the Ruine of Rome'.[14] We end with some translations of Petrarch's verses on Rome as Babylon by Thomas 'Hovell' (perhaps Sidney's Thomas Howell).

Only somewhat less triumphalist is Lodowick Lloyd's *Consent of Time*, an attempt at universal chronology. Lloyd asserts that just as 'the dignitie of the empire, and the glorie of the olde Romanes was quite defaced', so now 'the pompe of the Pope beginneth to quaile'. Rome, he notes, has plausibly been compared 'to Babylon, whose glorie for a thousand and odde yeeres ... excelled al the kingdoms of the world: and even so Rome, who seemed to be a whole worlde of it selfe, is nowe brought to nothing'. Rome is the fourth beast, the trampling iron-toothed monster, that Daniel saw in his vision, and the time of its monarchy is coming to its end. As is typical in this post-Armada discourse, Lloyd ends with the reminder that just as ancient Rome was not to be subdued except by Romans, 'even so the Brittaines were not to be overthrowen but by Britaines'.[15] Civil war, as David knew, is no way to keep the walls of Jerusalem – or Rome or London – intact.

Reading the history of ancient Rome, then, can give one hope that aggressive and serpentine papal Rome and its recently defeated but still hugely rich and powerful Spanish ally might suffer the same fate. (English post-Armada talk is an odd mixture of abject fear and smug triumph.) Thus the preface to one E. L.'s *Romes monarchie, entituled the globe of renowmed glorie* informs readers that this history of Rome will tell how like many other great 'Monarchies, Kingdomes, Cities, and Countries' she 'fel to ruine and decay' through civil discord, ambition, hate, insurrections, and sneaky politics. Now, 'in these thundring dayes', we may observe 'the great threatnings of our mightie and mortal foe, the insatiable Monarch, whom the worlds Empire will not suffice' and who strives to 'kindle the fire of strife and civill discension among us, the easier to prevaile, to [our] utter ruine'.[16] Let such powers beware, E. L. adds, turning to verse: 'So worketh time of everything the change ... / Whom Time hath rais'de, and likewise made to fall', and he exclaims 'O pride of Rome, Ambitions patterne left, / Which never will from following race be reft'.[17] Listening for just such a mixture of current worry and prophetic satisfaction gives further resonance to Sidney's echoes of this same post-Armada language.

The opposite of ruination is of course edification: the edification of the person, the re-edification of Jerusalem's walls and the restoration of the Temple. The Bible is, needless to say, the major source of such language (although Ovid's claim that the first man was the first creature to stand erect and see the stars is a reminder that the association of verticality with excellence is widespread and ancient). We are all buildings, and if subject to time's consumption and ravaged by the effects of sin, also capable of being rebuilt, individually as godly members of Christ's church and collectively as that Church itself. The Temple, as the margin of the Geneva Bible explains, can be read metaphorically as Christ's body (John 2:21 and note). No Protestant, indeed no Christian, needed reminding of this set of metaphors and hopes. Anne Lock, author of the first sonnet sequence in English (a set of meditations on Psalm 51 printed in 1560), writes in a 1590 dedicatory epistle to the countess of Warwick, printed with her translation of a French religious work by Jean Taffin, that because 'Everie one in his calling is bound to doo somewhat to the furtherance of the holie building', she has 'brought my poore basket of stones to the strengthening of the walles of that Jerusalem, whereof (by grace) wee are all both Citizens and members'.[18] Lock is humble, but the belief that we are all citizens of Jerusalem entails a conviction that the walls of God's holy city include both male and female stones.

One of the most detailed deployments of such biblical metaphors comes in Nicholas Byfield's sermon on 1 Peter 2, published posthumously in 1623. Admittedly too late for Mary Sidney to have read before translating the psalms, his discussion is nevertheless useful. (Peter's very name of course means 'stone', not a point Byfield exploits, perhaps because the papacy made its claim for primacy partly on Jesus' punning words to Peter that upon this 'rock' he would build his church). The relevant passages are on verse 5: 'Ye also, as lively stones, be made a spirituall house, an holy Priest-hood, to offer up spirituall sacrifices, acceptable to God by Jesus Christ.' Byfield devotes several pages to the phrase 'As lively stones', expatiating on them with what reads like Ramist 'method' of tracing ramifying meanings and submeanings and locating many, many biblical texts relevant to his branching definitions. Stones may be bad (for example, stonily insensible hearts or sinners astonished by God) and may be used in bad architecture (e.g., the stones of a leprous house or 'Jerusalem when it was made a heap of stones'). The good are also like stones: the anointed stones of Bethel, 'pillars, consecrated to God', the onyx on the breast of the High Priest, and, in the passage being explicated, 'the stones of the Temple'. How are the godly like stones? They are unmoved in the storm, are durable, are 'digged out of the quarry of mankinde', and 'If you consider their union with Christ, and Christians in one body, they are like the stone of the house compact in themselves, and upon the foundation.' May 'all the servants of God take pleasure in the stones of this spirituall Sion'.[19]

On spiritual Zion, Byfield cites Psalm 102, the relevant verses being 13–16:

> Thou shalt arise, and have mercy upon Zion: for the time to favour her, yea, the set time is come. For thy servants take pleasure in her stones, and favour of the dust thereof. So the heathen shall fear the name of the Lord, and all the kings of the earth thy glory. When the Lord shall build up Zion he shall appear in his glory.

Sidney would doubtless agree with Byfield that such re-edification requires us to be 'lively stones' and indeed 'cheerefull' ones (K8) individually 'built up' (L1). We must, he adds, build on a rock, and build coherently so that we raise Zion and not Babel. We must have proportion, as in Psalm 122, and the help of the Lord, as in Psalm 127, and we should not be arrogant stones who will not hear reproof.[20]

Closer to the time when Sidney was working on her translations, and less relentlessly in search of every possible biblical rock, pillar, or stone, is a sermon preached in 1589 (probably 1590 new style) before Queen Elizabeth by the great preacher Lancelot Andrewes on Psalm 75:3: 'The earth, and all the Inhabitants thereof are dissolved: but I will establish the Pillars of it.'[21] Andrewes applies the metaphor, which as he says 'runneth in the termes of *Architecture*', to 're-edifying the State new againe', for the state's pillars 'were all out of course, by the misgovernment of *Saul*'. Andrewes, too, writes at a time when the scare over the Armada had produced a rush of agitated and often scoffing anti-Spanish and anti-papal polemic, so his words are in part directed at what many still feared: external enemies and internal dissension, the latter danger increased by dilapidations recalling King Saul's refusal to treat God's enemies harshly enough. David, says Andrewes, 'sweetly' sings of the duties of court (Ps. 101), of the Church (Ps. 45), of judges (Ps. 82) and of the Commons (Ps. 144), but if even he 'offended in ought', it was 'that hee used *Dicam* ['I will speak'] too much, and *Frangam* ['I will break'] not often enough'. Andrewes often accentuates the positive, the *'Power to edification*, ([as] saith Saint *Paul*) not to destruction: that is, to build up, not to decay the Building', but he still recalls that David did in fact at times say 'Take off his head' (the margin cites Psalm 58). 'Thus did David repaire Sauls ruines', says Andrewes, and 'these are his steppes, thus did hee shew himselfe as good as his promise (here) a skillful *Upholder* of these two maine *Pillars*, which beare up and give strength to every Land.' How better to rebuild the Temple than to imitate the stone that the builders rejected and make Him our own cornerstone?

If Sidney heard or read this court sermon, she would doubtless have understood and probably shared its agenda. (Elizabeth could not have mistaken the rigorous advice it offered – unless she heard it as admiration for the execution of Mary Stuart – for Andrewes' mention of 'conspirators' was all too relevant to the queen's circumstances, real and imagined). To voice hopes for rebuilding the walls of Jerusalem, whether one can threaten 'frangam' like a queen or merely sing 'dicam' like a lady, and whatever many Protestants' irenic hopes for a less fractious Christendom, had in the 1590s a geopolitical and anti-Roman significance. Time and God will crush Babylon. In the meantime we can bring stones and mortar to His city, if only by translating the psalms.

The Countess's techniques in her part of the Sidney Psalter are a reminder that a 'Protestant poetics', as far as the psalms are concerned, was not as inward as is sometimes thought, for the psalms of David – expressing one person's thoughts and yet also spoken on behalf of the Church or in the person of Christ – had long provided a model for discourse at once private and public. This became even more the case when after the Reformation the psalms were read with increased interest in David's political problems, first as a persecuted courtier and then as a beleaguered king. Mary Sidney's use of a metaphoric pattern, often applied to ancient and papal Rome as well as to recalcitrant lovers, is also further evidence of her quiet capacity, one that Margaret Hannay has noted, to work relevant political overtones into her religious verse. In sum, if as a scholar she looked back to see what David's Hebrew might have said, she also sometimes chose to adopt a very current tonality that remembered the ruins of ancient empires, ones with monitory significance for Babylon by the Tiber and even, maybe, for Troynovant by the Thames.

Notes

1 The ruins, identifiable as such by the conventional plants growing on broken stones, form an arch. In this essay I cite the hugely influential 1560 Geneva

Bible, although I have also looked at the Bishops' and the Great. I quote Mary Sidney from Mary Sidney Herbert, Countess of Pembroke, *The Collected Works*, eds. Margaret P. Hannay, Noel J. Kinnamon, and Michael G. Brennan, 2 vols. (Oxford: Clarendon Press, 1998), vol. 2, citing psalm numbers and lines. By the time Mary Sidney began work there had been so many published commentaries and translations of the psalms that it is virtually impossible to determine in every case if she was following sources we have not yet found or working from her own imagination. For some of my own suggestions concerning her possible sources, see my 'Evil Tongues at the Court of Saul: David as a Slandered Courtier', *Journal of Medieval and Renaissance Studies* 21 (1991): 163–86 (Chapter 4 in this volume). It seems safe to say that a *pattern* such as the one I explore here was her own doing. I quote Geneva for contrast, not to suggest that all her sources lack ruination imagery, although in no other translation I have read is there such a wealth of it. On her psalms see also Mary Beth Fiskin, 'Mary Sidney's *Psalmes*: Education and Wisdom', in *Silent but for the Word: Tudor Women as Patrons, Translators, and Writers of Religious Works*, ed. Margaret P. Hannay (Kent, Ohio: Kent State University Press, 1985), 166–83; Hannibal Hamlin, *Psalm Culture and Early Modern English Literature* (Cambridge: Cambridge University Press, 2004); Kathleen M. Swaim, 'Contextualizing Mary Sidney's Psalms', *Christianity and Literature* 48.3 (1999): 253–73; Suzanne Trill, 'Sixteenth-century Women's Writing: Mary Sidney's *Psalmes* and the 'Femininity' of Translation', in *Writing and the English Renaissance*, eds. William Zunder and Suzanne Trill (London and New York: Longman, 1996), 140–58; and the essays by Margaret Hannay noted below.

2   Geoffrey Whitney, *A Choice of Emblemes, and Other Devises ...* (Leiden: Plantin. 1586), R2. The volume, which includes an image of Philip Sidney on a rearing horse (E3v), is dedicated to Sidney's uncle Robert, earl of Leicester; figure 2 shows a penitent David.

3   A. Kent Hieatt, 'The Genesis of Shakespeare's *Sonnets*: Spenser's *Ruines of Rome: by Bellay*', PMLA 98 (1983): 800–14. Professor Hieatt tells me that he would now modify his claim because some phrases cited as evidence are found elsewhere before 1591 or in poets other than Spenser. Nevertheless, nowhere before Shakespeare's 1609 *Sonnets* is the complex so concentrated as in Spenser's 'Ruines'. For a postmodern take on *Sonnets*, time, textual ruins, and hermeneutic ruination, see Roger P. Kuin, *Chamber Music: Elizabethan Sonnet-Sequences and the Pleasure of Criticism* (Toronto: University of Toronto Press, 1998), ch. 2.

4   See, e.g., phrases in the Chorus, Pembroke, *Collected Works*, I: 175–76.

5   See Samuel Daniel's *Cleopatra, Delia and Rosamond, Augmented Cleopatra* (London: Waterson, 1594), H6–H6v. Compare George Whetstone's *Aurelia: The Paragon of Pleasure and Princely Delights* (London: Richard Jones, 1593), T4: Mausolus' widow dries and powders her husband's heart, then drinks it with wine so as to bury him 'in her owne bowels: & to crowne his fame with an everlasting memorie, for that the ruine of his Sepulchre was subject to the injurie of time'.

6   Nicholas Breton, *Pilgrimage to Paradise, Joined with the Countess of Penbrookes love* (Oxford: Barnes, 1592), ¶2. Cf. Sir John Harington, who says that Sidney restores a matter 'rude and ruinous before', probably a reference to the Psalter of Sternhold and Hopkins (quoted by Trill, 'Sixteenth-century Women's Writing', 157: she also notes Harington's doubt that a woman could have authored the translations).
7   *Metamorphoses* 15. 234–36 and *Ex Ponto* 4.10, II. 4–8.
8   Ps. 74:31–36; Geneva has 'They have cast thy Sanctuarie into the fyre, and rased it to the ground, and have defiled the dwelling place of thy Name.'
9   Geneva Bible (1560), Ttt3. The line at the top of the illustration reads, 'The forme of the Temple', and at the bottom, 'This figure must be set in the end of Ezekiel Ttt.iii.'
10 Renaissance views of the psalms' voice and authorship are too complicated to explore here. Whatever Sidney's thinking, though, there are traces in her translations of pride in somebody's verses, whoever that somebody might be. Cf. Trill. 'Sixteenth-century Women's Writing', 151: Sidney 'self-consciously draws attention to the fact that [her psalms] are poetic'. On voice and gender see also Margaret P. Hannay, '"House-confined maids": The Presentation of Woman's Role in the *Psalmes* of the Countess of Pembroke', *English Literary Renaissance* 24 (1994): 44–71.
11 Richard Tofte, *Alba: The Months Mind of a Melancholy Lover* (London: Lownes, 1598), C3.
12 See my '*Translatio Lupae*: Du Bellay's Roman Whore Goes North', *Renaissance Quarterly* 42 (1989): 397–419 (Chapter 10 in this volume) and Wayne Rebhorn, 'Du Bellay's Imperial Mistress: *Les Anitquitez de Rome* as Petrarchist Sonnet Sequence', *Renaissance Quarterly* 33 (1980): 609–22. There is another complaining city in Sir John Ogle, *The Lamentation of Troy, for the death of Hector* (London: Peter Short, 1594; ascribed on the title page to 'I. O.'), a poem owing much to Spenser's *Ruines of Time*, it too apparently mourns Philip Sidney.
13 Robert Humston, *A Sermon preached at Reyfham in Norff ... in 1588* (London, 1589), A2v, C6, D1.
14 Lambert Daneau, *Treatise, touching Antichrist* (London 1589), K1–L2. The parallels with du Bellay are striking (1589, too early for Spenser's influence, unless read in MS). Not finding Rome in Rome is the conceit of a famous neo-Latin epigram by Janus Vital reworked by du Bellay as *Antiquitez* 3; Rome's raising her 'courage to the Skie' recalls *Antiquitez* 6: 'courage aux cieux'.
15 Lodowick Lloyd, *Consent of Time* (London, 1590), Pp4–4v, Bbb1v.
16 E. L., *Romes monarchie, entituled the globe of renowmed glorie* (London, 1596), A3.
17 E. L., *Romes monarchie*, B1v, G4v (the margin explains that 'Romes ambition still continueth').
18 Jean Taffin, *Of the markes of the children of God*, trans. Anne Prowse [Lok] (London, 1590), A3v–A4. On this preface see Margaret P. Hannay, '"Strengthning the walles of ... Jerusalem": Anne Vaughan Lok's Dedication to the Countess of Warwick', *ANQ: A Quarterly Journal of Short Articles, Notes and Reviews* 5 (1992): 71–5.

19 Nicholas Byfield, *A Commentary: or, sermons upon the second chapter of the first epistle of Saint Peter*, ed. William Gouge (London: Lownes, 1623; published posthumously), K6v–K7v.
20 Byfield, *A Commentary*, L1v–L3. There is a less exhaustive but eloquent discussion of stones elaborating on Ps. 51's phrase 'Build the walles' (likewise 1623) in Archibald Simson's *A Sacred Septenarie, or, a godly and fruitful exposition on the seven Psalmes of repentance* (London: Jones, 1623), Ll8–Mm1.
21 Bishop Lancelot Andrewes, *XCVI Sermons*, eds. Archbishop William Laud and Bishop J. Buckeridge (London: R. Badger, 1632; 2nd ed.), 263–71 (easier to locate than signatures in this case). Geneva reads, 'The earth and all the inhabitans [sic] thereof are dissolved: but I wil establish the pillers of it.' Despite the hint in Geneva's gloss ('Thogh all things be brought to ruine, yet I can restore & preserve them'), Sidney passes up the opportunity for 'ruinish'; perhaps her ear told her that dissolution differs tonally and conceptually from ruination, so she has 'The people loose, the land I shaken find'. While the narrator's vow to praise God in 'never-dying rhymes' (26) recalls phrasing with which poets sometimes consoled themselves, Geneva has only 'I wil declare for ever, and sing praises unto the God of Jaakob', which differs subtly from Sidney's more Ovidian or Horatian claim.

Part III

Imagining gender

8

Male lesbian voices: Ronsard, Tyard, and Donne play Sappho

John Donne's 'Sapho to Philaenis' is a startling poem, an erotic 'lesbian' epistolary elegy by one of English literature's most famous male heterosexual love poets (if, to be sure, one also able in his younger days to write a male friend with a fervour that may go beyond ordinary male bonding).[1] In very recent years, after long neglect punctuated by snorts of disgust or chaste refusals to think that Donne could have written such a poem, it has won attention from a number of Donne scholars. I will not engage current debates over what 'lesbian' meant in the early modern period, whether it was visible or invisible, how it related to dildos and cross-dressing, or how women's cooler anatomy was understood as a reversed and undeveloped version of the male. It might be wise to recall, though, that in those days dildos and cross-dressing sometimes seemed less 'Sapphic' than more generally transgressive. The crime was not same-sex love so much as the inversion of hierarchy and confusion of gender. Women wielding dildos, puffing pipes, prancing around the capital in doublet and hose, or – an extreme instance – playing the husband in a supposed marriage, are pretending to be men. And that was all the more dangerously criminal because women, should they increase their vital heat or grow into their disguise, might actually become male and so produce little eddies of social chaos.[2] By 'lesbian' I mean a woman's passionate fondness for another woman with feelings that transcend even a generous definition of friendship, that take precedence over attachments to men, and that may hint at physical desire.

In these terms, Donne's poem sounds 'lesbian'.[3] In his elegy, my readers will recall, Sappho addresses her beloved Philaenis, celebrating their now broken love for each other as the love of like for like, so different from the more penetrating 'tillage' by a 'harsh rough man'. At least, nearly everybody assumes that Sappho is the speaker and that Philaenis, a lascivious courtesan and possibly fictional author of a how-to-do-it book on sex who figures in several ancient texts, is the reluctant beloved who has deserted Sappho for heterosexual companionship and the pleasures of sexual difference.[4] We assume this because of the poem's title and because of a fleeting reference to Phaon, the faithless ferryman whom, said a late and dubious legend, Sappho loved so dearly that she killed herself when he failed to reciprocate and to whom, in Ovid's *Heroides*, she writes a pleading letter. (Phaon was younger than Sappho; the introduction to a paperback edition of Sappho's verse quotes one scholar's irritating remark that she had reached 'woman's most tragic age, when beauty wanes but longing is not gone'.[5]) Yet nobody knows who first gave the poem its title as it is found in the 1633 edition of Donne's poetry. Without this clue, as George Klawitter has pointed out, and even with the mention of 'Phao', the poem would be homoerotic but need not specify Sappho herself as its speaker.[6] And, I would add, the poem would not so insistently claim Ovid's heroic epistle from Sappho to Phaon as its chief intertext. For Klawitter, in fact, the lines suggest male-to-male passion. I do not find the claim plausible, although one modern critic has wittily noted 'an ongoing tendency among Renaissance authors to slip from femininity to effeminacy – from Rosalind to Ganymede'.[7] Klawitter's argument, though, is a helpful warning not simply to assume that Donne means his reader to think hard about Ovid or to read this poem against what little was then known of Sappho's poetry.

Here I will, though, assume that the title is, if not Donne's, then a probable index of how the poem was read in 1633 and follow that early edition in taking the speaker as Sappho and her friend as Philaenis, whose name indeed means 'friend'. Much as a human body has bilateral symmetry, thinks Donne's Sappho, so the love of two women for each other has erotic symmetry. Philaenis is perfect, a 'naturall Paradise', just as she is, and needs no masculine attention, no Adamic digging and plowing – and hence, Donne may suggest, no need for that other curse, the labour of childbirth. The two women's dalliance, moreover, leaves no criminal trace behind it. No footsteps in the snow to mark the thief, no more signs than fish leave in water or birds in the air. Not only safe sex, one might say, but hardly sex at all – sex without consequence in every sense, if presumably offering a little pallid pleasure, for Renaissance writers tended to assume that lesbian sex was mere imitation of the real thing and thus neither truly satisfying nor to be counted as fornication or adultery. Then, in lines that some critics have found disturbing (for squeamishness is not dead in Renaissance studies, even when it takes the curious form of arguing that Donne makes autoeroticism into a symptom of verbal failure), Sappho asserts that the two women mirror each other to such a degree that in touching herself it seems to her that she is touching Philaenis. Oh may Philaenis return to her, she begs, and thus keep sickness and change far away.

Reaction to Donne's 'Sapho' has provoked both admiration and cold dislike, even irritation. Does it subtly denigrate a narcissist claustrophobia that diverts love to autoeroticism? Or is the poem, rather, a sympathetic experiment in imagining an alien sexuality, and a safer sexuality, too, with no scratchy beard to hurt one's soft skin and no trace left on the body of what one has been doing, if indeed it counts as 'doing' at all? Like many poets, Donne was probably intrigued by imagining other voices, other rooms, other stanzas, other stances. But some find his Sappho's self-speculating image of sex without trace or sign a deliberate comment on the failure or inadequacy of poetry that literally does not signify. Lesbianism as Donne constructs it is inert, its egalitarian mirroring parallel to a flat, onanistic and repetitive language that means only itself. (I might add, although I am reluctant to take too solemn an approach to Donne's exploration of sameness and erotic identity, that if he *is* commenting on masturbatory, unpregnant and unsignifying language, then what he says is relevant to post-Reformation arguments over the Eucharist and over how signs relate to the things they point at, in whose nature they participate.[8])

Despite occasional statements to the contrary, Donne was not the first Renaissance male poet to imagine love from a lesbian perspective, although he is the first I know of to do so sensuously and (probably) to make his lesbian speaker Sappho herself.[9] At least three French elegies written between 1565 and 1585, two by Pierre de Ronsard (1524–85) and one by Pontus de Tyard (1522–1605), an aristocratic cleric with Neoplatonic leanings best known for his *Erreurs Amoureuses* (1549) and *Solitaire Premier* (1552), adopt the voice of a female speaker who yearns erotically, or at least passionately, for another woman. None mentions Sappho, perhaps because the authors were still under the sway of Sappho's Ovidian reconstruction as a heterosexual poet, a merely partial reconstruction, however, thanks to a medieval tradition of commentary on Ovid, and the myth that there had been two Sapphos: one a fine and decent poet, the other a degraded courtesan. (True, Jean Dorat, who taught Ronsard Greek, wrote a sweet poem to his newborn daughter hoping she would use the pen as well as the needle and vowing that although Sappho was 'depraved' his child would be 'better behaved'.[10]) In an essay on 'Sapho to Philaenis', Janel Mueller does very briefly note the elegy by Tyard and its relevance to Donne.[11] So far as I know, however, Ronsard's more ambiguously 'lesbian' poems, epistles that could, with a little nudging and coaching and historicizing, be read as expressing more *philia* than *eros*, have gone unnoticed by those who write about Donne. For that matter, the few *seiziémistes* who mention even one of these French poems ignore 'Sapho'.

For the rest of this essay I will set Donne's 'Sapho' next to these 'lesbian' – at a minimum equivocal – precedents. The context, the cultural forcefield surrounding and sustaining the poem, should include Continental verse that Donne could have known, and that, even if he did not know, was part of the world in which he wrote. I beg my reader's indulgence for devoting so much space to paraphrase: early modern representations of female same-sex desire are sufficiently rare to make any instance worth getting to know better.[12]

The first pseudo-lesbian poem is an elegy by Ronsard, whose love poetry I am sure Donne knew and to whose taste for green-eyed girls he refers.[13] It first appeared in Ronsard's *Elegies, mascarades et bergerie* (1565), a collection that also addresses Elizabeth I, gives Merlin a rapturous prophecy of her future grandeur, and in very fancy language praises Lord Burleigh, who must have been amused and perhaps mildly flattered to see himself called the 'Docte Cecille, à qui la Pieride / A fait gouster de l'onde Aganippide'.[14] (Some years later, angered by England's treatment of Mary Stuart, Ronsard revised the poem so that the English 'Cecille' becomes a nameless 'Sicilian'.) The 'Elegie' in question supposedly accompanies the gift of a portrait sent by one lady to another. Since the speaker describes the image and its setting in detail, interpreting its little allegories as she goes, the elegy should interest those concerned with Renaissance portraiture and how pictures might be 'read'. Whatever is the case in Donne's Sappho's pleading epistle, moreover, *this* poem imagines a crowd of signs and signifiers, with no suggestion that same-sex affection might put meaning and language at risk. The ladies are Anne and Diane; the speaker points out that 'Anne' lives 'in' 'Diane', but they are otherwise unidentified. In a pinch – a strong pinch – we could read the lines as the expression of powerful friendship: Cicero's *De amicitia* for girls. Even some decades ago, however, Ronsard's editor Paul Laumonier did not scruple to call the speaker's effusions 'lesbien' or to associate them with rumours circulating at the court of Catherine de Medici about the tribades and dildo-happy goings-on among her ladies-in-waiting.[15] Perhaps thanks to a belated worry about the change in cultural tone under the bisexual but showily pious Henri III, Ronsard withdrew it from the 1584 edition of his works; or perhaps he came to regret its uncharacteristically flat and repetitious language. It was, though, posthumously reprinted in 1609 and thereafter.

I offer a condensed paraphrase with some running commentary. My 'you' translates the speaker's more formal 'vous', not an intimate 'tu'. 'Vous' preserves a slight difference in social position, although its use is also common in French Renaissance love poetry.

'This portrait is a sign of how much I wish to serve you.' Note that there is nothing here of Donne's ambivalent interest in female erotic equality or similarity; rather we find the old system of erotic service merged with the more egalitarian custom of exchanging portraits among friends. 'The impression on the gold setting that shines like the faith kindled in me by your holy flame parallels the love for you that your virtue has imprinted on me,' a telling detail, in this age of print, and a metaphor usually applied to the impress of masculine form on female matter; Ronsard maintains a sort of gender difference for his two female friends.

> On each side is a temple; one, to Apollo, shows Coroebus dying of love for Cassandra.[16] Oh happy death! May I die yours! Nothing shall part us: not storm, war, or the envious. And around the image is some Latin that means 'My love and yours so chaste / Shall overgo loves past'.

Ronsard gives only the French translation, a decision worth considering in terms of the two languages' social meanings. Did he think, despite imagining a lady who appreciates and understands Latin posies, that quoting one would make her seem too 'learned', too 'masculine'?

> The other Temple is for Diana, where we see Orestes and Pylades, the pair that won fame for the blood each shed for the other. Such friendship, although perfect, is surpassed by mine, for I would die for you a hundred and a hundred thousand times. So I have used a Latin verse showing that there is no parallel to our love and that Orestes and Pylades yield place to our fidelity, which can surmount them ['les peut surmonter']. Below the temple is the altar on which the Greeks vowed to die for one another and kill the youth of Troy. On this altar I swear to serve you, Mistress, for whom I would shed my blood in immortal sacrifice. In the raised centre is my image: pale, silent, grieving at your absence. Alas that it is mute and cannot tell you of my pain.

As in much elegy, and certainly in Donne, love-longing, absence, and the threat of silence are connected: love torments us into poetry but also into inarticulate grief.

> It would tell you at leisure my anguish when apart from you, my all. I live only on memory and on your reputation, written on my soul. But what need of a picture when you are the mistress of my body and spirit? So that you will at least grieve for me as I languish because I cannot see your face before me, for I can have no greater pleasure than to serve and see you.
>
> Because I so much wish to be within you ['dedans vous'], I have put this Roman verse around the portrait: 'Anne lives fervently in her Diane, Diane in Anne, and Time, which breaks empires and kings and subjects everything, cannot untie two such lovely names.'[17] The greatest good God can give us here below is a friendship that effaces all else. Without friendship, a person would die, unable to live whole in the world, for blood and heart do not make one live as much as faithful friendship when one has found again one's other half.
>
> Having experienced this love in me, Mistress, you have found me sure within your love, for you and I are one; and if we share one common body, then your thought is mine and my life entirely follows yours. We have one blood, one soul, one faith; I am in you and you are in me with a knot so tightly made that you can never forget me without forgetting yourself; and thus I have no fear, so much do I find myself wholly in you, Madame, and my soul is utterly in your soul.

> This good comes to me, as I acknowledge, without illusion, from the favour it has pleased you to show me, knowing myself to be much less than you. For you deign to join your greatness to me, most lowly, and such honour makes me equal to you through good fortune: that is why I dedicate to you my blood, my heart, my picture, and my life.

Catherine Yandell has noted that despite Ronsard's attempt to express close female friendship or erotic affection (French *amitié* can slide into either meaning), he cannot escape the dominant – and dominating – heterosexual tradition in which he worked: for example, this lady's love will 'surmount' all others. Indeed so: the speaker's love, like her portrait, dazzles, glitters, deserves fame, recalls lovers of old, defeats the jealous, conquers, outdoes. The old competitive paradigm, the laurel-grabbing, temple-building, race-winning, my-lady-is-better-than-other-ladies swagger, still shapes the poet's attitudes even when he plays the almost-lesbian. This poem, unlike Donne's, could be fairly easily heterosexualized by shifting the pronouns and unfeminizing some parts of speech while leaving the poetic and erotic assumptions intact. Nobly born women can of course serve even nobler women, and the social context for the poem is the hierarchical Valois court in which many a lady waited on those yet higher on the social pyramid, even when mutual love, as in this poem, partly overcame social difference. The stress on self-sacrificing bloodshed and service unto death, however, is more male and feudal than Sapphic, more Loire valley than ancient Lesbos. True, for all we know, court ladies did imitate feudal love service when doing whatever it was that court ladies did when generating the rumours of tribadism that Ronsard (and, later, Tyard) may have been exploiting.

The second 'lesbian' poem is an extraordinary elegy that Donne could not have read unless he had access, which it is not beyond possibility, to the often risqué poetry circulating in late Renaissance French manuscripts. It comes from a seventeenth-century collection that ascribes it, not implausibly, to Ronsard, whose most recent editors make room for it at the end of his *Oeuvres*. In several regards it is worth juxtaposing with Donne's 'Sapho'.

The elegy records an energetic if long-winded lament by a widowed female dove, moping on a dry tree and mourning the loss of her female mate, snatched away by a young male fowler and now held captive in a dark cage. Ronsard presumably chooses doves to allegorize parted friends because those birds are said to be faithful lovers and because Venus favours the dove. But there may be a further implication in this context: what modern Americans call 'French kissing', something that Brantôme quotes Lucian as saying lesbians enjoy, in Ronsard's France was called kissing 'en pigeonne'.[18] The fowler might represent a father or brother and the cage simply some château, but it seems likely that he is meant specifically to suggest a husband and that the cage is an avian equivalent of what Blake was to call a 'marriage hearse'. (True, the dove's status as a 'widow' makes marriage in this poem a puzzle; evidently, in these woods, forest laws permit same-sex marriage, at least for birds.[19]) Her day is now night, weeps the widowed bird, the streams keep harmony with her plaints, and even the flowers are tainted by her grief. The poet then turns to a human addressee, switching from 'tu' to the more respectful 'vous', and imagines for her an equally impassioned complaint to be said to that lady's female friend, with whom she had shared both a body and a soul, as the latter leaves for the Alps and marriage. She will lament, says the poet, that she feels eviscerated, paralyzed, lifeless, sustained only by memory. May the new husband receive only a very cold kiss while in thought the two women still enjoy amorous heat, games, and pleasures, and the bereft lady, even as she curses the man who has taken her beloved (may rocks and brigands trouble his journey), anticipates nocturnal visions in which she will hold her friend in her arms, consoled by her empty image.

Donne's Sappho would sympathize: two women, once sharing an identity, have been torn asunder, although in this case by male force, not by one woman's sexual reorientation. Then, at the very end, in a sudden swerve to a heterosexual economy and rhetoric, the speaker tells the desolate recipient of his poem that as consolation for her loss she can reflect that she has gained a servant – the poet himself. He will drink one of her tears, make room in his heart for her sighs, and his unfeigned love will assuage her anguish. We are back to the normal course of things: male poet bowing gallantly to a lady and the lady's friend destined for marriage, babies, and the upward-pointing Alps. I do not know who these ladies are: nobody in Pierre de Brantôme's gossipy stories of French court life and ladies quite fits. The poem nevertheless reads less like Donne's gendered thought experiment than an ingratiating intervention in an actual lady's grief over a separation entailing marriage in another country.

Ronsard, if indeed he is the author, again shows a genuine sympathy for a female erotic bonding that is more than *philia*. And again same-sex passion is interrupted by and absorbed into the ordinary world. Has the world once more been made safe for patriarchy? Perhaps. But Ronsard, it is worth stressing, is at no pains whatsoever to make that world appealing. Nor does he offer either birds or ladies any alternative. Perhaps he agreed with Shakespeare's Benedick that the world must be peopled, although being in minor orders himself he could not himself help people it, or not legitimately. And, yes, the poem relies on explicit ventriloquizing. That is, although within the poem's fiction the sad dove has her own elegiac language, the sad woman has only the words given her by the poet as he scripts her complaint. With what has to me come to seem an endearing arrogance (not everyone agrees), Ronsard plays the voluble dove's audience, the so far silent lady's speechwriter, and her talented and faithful servant.

Ronsard was a great writer, one who, it has been observed, adopts female voices to access a part of his own psyche or verbal capacity otherwise subdued or even mute.[20] Seldom in the poetry he wrote in a male voice, not even in his love poetry, and not even at his most powerfully moving, does he show the sheer passion, the overt emotionality, of – for example – the lovesick prophetess in his *Franciade*, that incomplete epic with a twit of a hero and two compelling women. Perhaps he thought, and he would not have been alone, that unrestrained tears and storms of affect are womanish, diagnosable as a touch of the mother, perhaps. In a strange reversal of anatomy, when it comes to emotion men keep everything tucked in and women let it all hang out. For whatever reason, Ronsard's empathy for the voluble dove and bereft lady seems worth sustained pondering. As witness his frequent excuses for failing to finish his epic, he too had seen his desires and preferences blocked or deflected by those more powerful than he. Getting very far outside his own head, though, was not among Ronsard's talents. His reversion to a traditional stance – humbly wheedling but *au fond* imperative – is not astonishing.

Tyard's 'Elegie pour une dame enamourée d'une autre dame' is more explicitly homoerotic. Although mentioned briefly by several scholars writing on homosexuality in early modern France and by at least one Donne scholar, it deserves more attention even from English professors (it is getting somewhat more from the French). Tyard published it in his *Oeuvres poétiques* (1573). It was possibly written considerably earlier, and in any case seems mystifyingly unlike his other poems.[21] Like Donne's 'Sapho', a poem of seduction, it shares with that elegy some entertainingly sophistical logic concerning desire and honour. It also shares with 'The Canonization' the dream of a love that might live on in story as an example to the nation, although I suspect that a closer parallel is with a poem by Ronsard.[22] Janel Mueller, one of the very few Donne scholars even to mention the poem, remarks that its 'lesbian longings are altogether checked in the implied plot' because the 'beloved lady is disdainful and unresponsive'. True, yet more precisely it is not the lesbian longings but the lesbian hopes that are 'checked'. It is also the case, moreover, that much compelling love poetry by poets of whatever sexual orientation expresses loss, not gain, and frustration, not enjoyment. Few poets have had their desires so 'checked' as Petrarch. In 'The Tower', Yeats asks, 'Does the imagination dwell the most / Upon the woman won or woman lost?' and never quite gives an answer. Experienced readers can supply it for him. That is why, I think, one should not make too much of the speaker's failure, like that of Donne's Sappho, to win back her lady.

Although one can think of many exceptions, especially in real life, lovers of any gender are especially interesting when vexed into poetry by pain, desire, betrayal, distance, and memory. Happy lovers, if not all alike, are often too busy *doing* something to grope around for pen and paper.

Tyard's lovelorn speaker, perhaps thinking that unhappy lovers should all be unhappy in their own way, calls her desire for another woman unprecedented. Nobody, she claims, has written like this before or loved like this before – common claim in love poetry, of course, and almost always false. Indeed, Tyard is here more or less paraphrasing a passage from Ariosto's *Orlando furioso* in which Fiordispina expresses her supposedly unheard-of love for Bradamante.[23] Does Tyard hope we will remember this precedent – or forget it? Maybe his lady's insistence on novelty is the reason Tyard avoids naming Sappho, unless he so tightly associated that now famous name with Ovid's heterosexual poetess that he forgot, or (despite the evidence that other Renaissance poets were well aware of her proclivities) did not want to know, that Sappho's passion had preceded his speaker's, and Ariosto's, by two millennia. A unique passion, moreover, makes the love in question more 'monstrous' – 'queer', but not in any good sense. Indeed, monstrosity is just what many thought tribadism must imply, for a discouraging number of medical authorities, including the great Alopius himself, supposed that women given to lesbian sex must have enlarged clitorises (for them, apparently, the answer is yes – size matters).[24] Tyard is not unsympathetic, certainly not denunciatory, but it is hard to find in his poem the sort of imaginative empathy that Ronsard and Donne could intermittently sustain, whatever their lapses into a more traditionally 'masculine' poetics.

What follows is a somewhat condensed paraphrase. I apologize for the convoluted language: like Donne, Tyard had a taste for curly syntax and compressed logic. It is impossible in English, moreover, exactly to replicate the impact of the gendered adjectives and participles: one can hide a speaker's gender in French, but doing so takes effort and attention.

> I had always believed that Love and honour, the only two flames that burn my heart, would kindle so beautiful a blaze that nothing lovelier would shine in the soul. But I was unable to think how one should light these two fires together: for however much beauty might be matter for Love, and utter beauty be in utter honour, it did not seem to me that the same beauty should pertain to both Love and Honesty. I said, 'My honour's beauty is in myself, but not so the beauty that I must love: because to judge beauty by myself would be only to love my honour, and a [female] lover must seek outside herself for the beauty that Love claims as a conquest. Will honour's flame find place only in me? Must I flee the other god's flame?
>
> 'Alas! I will choose Love's beauty from men! Wait – no. Nowadays a man loves beauty and scoffs at honour; the more beauty pleases him, the more

honour perishes.' Thus dearly caring only for honour I scorned all amorous flame until Love, offended by my liberty, spreads for me a subtle trap. He enriches thy wit; he sugars thy mouth and eloquent speech; he lurks in thine eyes; in thy hair he coils an unprecedented knot that binds me to thee. He makes burn a flame (alas, who will believe me?) of such a novel fire that he enamours me of a woman – alas, of another woman.

Never more softly had Love glided into a heart: for unwounded honor retained its beauty unspoiled and Love enjoyed a beloved beauty in the same person. Ah, what happiness! If only, light one, it had pleased thee not to love lightly. But cruel Love, having seen me wounded to the quick has breathed all himself into me and left thee empty ... Where are thy promised faith and thy proffered vows? Where are the beautifully devised words of thy speeches? Like a counterfeit and persuasive Pythia[25] thou hast known how to chain me, captivated, by the ear.

Alas that I have vainly poured out my speech! That I have vainly fled all other loves! That vainly I have chosen thee, disdainful one, as my only joy! That vainly I had believed that in times to come we would be thought a miracle down the long centuries and that, as a unique exemplum, we would live in memory to prove that a woman's love for a woman can snatch the prize from male loves. A Damon for Pythius, an Aeneas for Achates, a Hercules for Nestor, Chairephon for Socrates, a Hopleus for Dymas,[26] have shown that the love of a man for a man has been known: and proof that men can love women is so ample that there is no need for an example.

The male couples are provocatively chosen. Tyard's lovelorn speaker implies that Aeneas and his 'fidus Achates', as Virgil calls him, are a loving couple, not just good friends; perhaps she was not alone in Renaissance France. But why link Socrates to Chairephon? Figuring in several Platonic dialogues, he reported that the oracle at Delphi had called Socrates the wisest man in the world; but it was Alcibiades who, according to the *Symposium*, attempted to seduce Socrates. Hercules and Nestor make an odd couple, not least because Hercules killed Nestor's brothers. Does Tyard laugh a little at the lady's way with classical example, winking at his male readers? Or does he, rather, grant her a share of classical learning and please his female ones?

> But as for love of a woman for a woman, there has not yet been seen so rich a treasure in Love's empire, oh too light one, since in return for my faith thine has proven a liar. For never was there such great purity in Heaven, greater ardour in fire, more sweetness in honey, greater goodness in the rest of nature than in my heart, where Love is nourished. But thine is harder than a rock in the sea; crueller than a Scythian barbarian; and the Bear Callisto [that is, Ursa Major, that compliant nymph who was first ursified, then stellified, and lastly condemned to paw her way around the North Pole] does not see so much ice as thou hast in thy breast; nor has the mobile face of Morpheus so many forms as your inconstant spirit has variable thoughts.

Alas! Desire transports me far from myself! Open thou to Love, thankless one. Allow the sweet shaft that pierced our hearts once more to pierce thine; let thy language show the old feeling; retie the sweet knot laced together by common liking, and rejoin these hands that swore inviolable faith. But if Love enflames thee with a new fire, I pray Anteros that before my heart's pain can change me so that only my sad voice remains as I wander the forest or my anguish distils into a flower or flows as a spring, and while alone in this dense forest I tell the deer of thy disdain, that thou, consumed by passion for someone unworthy, languish in love and never be loved.

As an exercise in queering Cupid this poem has problems, if only because the speaker's desire is merely what Tyard can but suppose a woman's might feel like. Granted the psychological effect of literary and cultural traditions and the flexibility of the human spirit, it seems reasonable to assume that somewhere a woman has experienced just such feelings as Tyard imagines. Nevertheless, the emotions and their expression seem too familiar for a supposedly novel sort of passion. Generic expectations, the resort to the usual personifications and imagery, and the magnetic tug of traditionally male attitudes, inherent or cultural, make for familiar rhetorical moves that enter the poem like old friends knowing where to hang their hats and find the whiskey: I love you but you betray me; make things as they used to be or I will be an echo, flower, or running water (see Ovid), and if you *won't* love me, may you suffer. Some readers will remember, among many other poets, the most unlesbian Wyatt threatening his reluctant lady with her future sexual frustration under the cold moon of old age.

What might be the use of these three poems to Donne scholarship? First, very simply, remembering more often and more attentively that other early modern poets, although for any number of reasons not naming Sappho herself, had also adopted a passionate and, in the case of Tyard, an unabashedly homoerotic female voice. Donne (maybe) stars Sappho and Philaenis, but his plot – girl loves girl, girl loses girl to boy – parallels that of Ronsard's unpublished elegy and, although only if we take the beloved's infidelity as implying a new love for a man, that of Tyard's elegy as well. In Donne's London, Ronsard and Tyard were not obscure poets, and if in his day the height of their vogue was passing or past in France, in England they still enjoyed fame and prestige. Their poems allow us to see near contemporary male poets, one a writer of international fame whose career seemed stellar to the outward eye (although given to gloomy laments that he was underappreciated by rich magnates and underfunded by his several kings), experimented with adopting the voice of an 'other' who for once loves the 'same'. That is to say, a male poet imagines a female 'other' writing not in response to some male like the poet's self but to yet another female 'other'.

Questions that Donne scholars raise concerning 'Sapho to Philaenis' can be raised about Ronsard and Tyard as well. To what extent do their poems escape a male subjectivity, granted that anatomy probably ensures that there is such a thing? Are not their voices, perhaps in spite of their authors' efforts, still 'masculine', as their culture tended to define 'masculine'? If so, then it is here that Donne's originality shows most clearly, for there is little in his 'Sapho' that parallels Ronsard's and Tyard's lapses into quasi-feudal hand-kissing service on the one hand or bragging competition with other lovers on the other. To be sure, Ronsard and Tyard might argue, everybody knows that lesbian love must entail masculine behaviour on one lady's part, which is why a tribade must use a dildo, when not equipped with an enlarged clitoris, so as to imitate heterosexual intercourse.[27] A woman who makes love to another woman must be pseudo-manly. Donne's Sappho, then, fails to follow standard expectations inherited from centuries of (male) assumptions concerning lesbian sexuality. The self-mirroring symmetry, the literal *homosexuality*, that so disturbs some readers, and is perhaps meant to do so, is unsurprising in recent times but could have seemed a striking departure in Donne's own culture. Sappho wants only to love Philaenis, not to serve her, and although she prefers a lovely self-resembling and unplowed woman to any hairy and trace-leaving man, she nowhere boasts that her passion outdoes that of famous lovers past.

Should we, moreover, perceive in these French poems the 'anxiety' that so many now see in – or, I suspect, often project onto – Renaissance male writers? Do they appear sympathetic to same-sex love between women in part so as to sidle quietly up to same-sex 'sodomitical' love between men? Neither Ronsard nor Tyard seems to have been drawn to male homoerotic poetry, but their social and personal circumstances – literary, ecclesiastical, academic – encouraged masculine camaraderie quite as much as court life encouraged the wooing or flattery of women. Do the three French elegies, that is, serve male homosociality? Is the sparkling group of poets called 'The Pléiade' further constellated, so to speak, by Ronsard's and Tyard's slightly naughty flirtation with lesbianism? After all, Donne's fancied Sappho, more truly Sapphic than Ovid's epistolary ferryman-lover, may have helped a young man-about-Lincoln's Inn look urbane, and doubtless all the more jauntily urbane if he could also look somewhat French, somewhat proto-*libertin* as well.[28]

Do the French poems, beneath their show of empathy, satirize the tribade bonding taking place in the closed chambers of Catherine de Medici's ladies? Or is Ronsard trying to *please* court ladies named Anne and Diane and one other whose dearest friend had been caught, caged, and transported to the snowy mountains? How do all four poems, three by unmarried Catholics well inside the Church and one by a Catholic somewhere near its exit

('Sapho to Philaenis' is undated, so it is hard to know just how near), relate to shifts in attitudes toward marriage? Would scholars who claim, in a pleasantly Donnean paradox, that Sappho's lesbian autoeroticism signifies failed signs as well as narcissist flaccidity say the same of Ronsard's and Tyard's 'lesbian' poems? Is Ronsard's lady's imagined portrait a sort of narcissist looking-glass? Or, as Lacan might ask, is he reflecting on an extended mirror stage? Compared to the poets' other works, moreover, Ronsard's 1565 elegy and Tyard's 'Elegie pour une dame' can seem insipid, with uncharacteristic verbal repetition. Is this an effort to sound feminine? Or an indication that the poets' hearts are not really in what they write? Does such flatness hint at condemnation?

If critical response to Donne's poem is any guide, a consensus on answers to such questions is unlikely. The topic itself is likely to provoke a more than ordinarily subjective reaction, consciously or not, and the texts in question are more than ordinarily unstable and ambiguous. In thinking about Donne's 'Sapho', however, it is well to remember that although the first in England to write in the person of the famous lesbian poet and to insist on her lesbianism, he was not the first to impersonate a woman loving – and in the case of Ronsard's moping dove married to – another woman. Does this matter? Yes, because the French poems can help us more accurately to disentangle what is unique and what merely unusual in Donne's poem, to set his elegy in one more literary and cultural context. To read him simply as attempting to rival, undo, overgo, imitate, revise Ovid is useful, although without its title the poem might seem less insistent in soliciting such a reading. But Donne may also have hoped, although I cannot prove this, to show his friends that an English wit could rival, overgo, imitate or otherwise equal the risqué French. The map of his social world included the Continental literary scene as well as that of ancient Rome and, more faintly drawn, Sappho's Lesbos.

At the very least these French analogues can reinforce our awareness that good poets, like good people, can envision, inadequately or with mixed motives, more possibilities than they wish to or could act out, more lives than they can live. 'He do humanity in different voices' is not the only way to be a fine poet, to be sure, and, like Ronsard, Donne was too much himself to range through as many octaves as, say, Browning, let alone Shakespeare. Negative capability was not his strong suit. Nevertheless, and taste in such matters is of course very personal – anything to do with gender and sex must be – many might prefer these three poets' treatment of women's same-sex desire to the sniggering of the slightly later *libertins* who wrote about tribadism, with or without dildos, sometimes noting its supposed effects on the health (no hair on the palms, one gathers, but pallor, sunken eyes, bad breath, and lassitude).

Those displeased by Ronsard's and Tyard's efforts to appropriate or 'ventriloquize' lesbian voices, and I assume that those who distrust Donne would distrust the French poets as well, might compare these sixteenth-century poems to a sonnet by Denis Sanguin de Saint-Pavin (1595–1670), a distinguished cleric and reputed atheist, which says that

> Two belles love each other tenderly, one drawn to the other, and each suffering equally from the same arrow-wound. Without complaining of their torment, both sigh ceaselessly: sometimes the lover ['amant', the masculine form] is the mistress, sometimes the mistress is the lover. Whatever they do to please themselves, they cannot satisfy their hearts and lose their best time of life. In such sort of love, these 'innocent' [naive, that is] ladies who abuse themselves ['abusent' also means delude, fool] vainly seek the pleasures that they refuse to us [that is, us men].[29]

The tribades themselves might retort that it is likewise surprisingly *innocent* on the part of a libertine poet, hardly a promoter of family values, to assume that their mutual pleasure is unreal, but such innocence was (among men) common. Donne, had he lived to read this poem, might have been intrigued by the ease with which the ladies reverse roles: this behaviour is not quite Sappho-in-the-mirror, but it does have symmetry. Historians of sexuality and gender will note that these 'belles' evidently must include one 'amant' and one mistress, not two female 'amantes'. And any reader can detect the hostility behind the speaker's mock resentment at the denial of sexual favours to the appropriate sex.

Ronsard could also snigger at times, as witness his sonnet on a woman who, to preserve a purely notional virtue, prefers fooling around with a dildo to going to bed with men – not even bed with Ronsard, who, if the lady really is Hélène de Surgères, had asked for it so prettily and so often.[30] But whatever their moments of misogyny, of accusatory cynicism, Ronsard, Tyard, and Donne could also imagine, or try to imagine, or think they were imagining, a sexual subjectivity other than their own and to do so with what strikes some readers as real if limited sympathy. Their poems, moreover, perform a love that was culturally subversive, however we take it. If such love is physically sexual, it may not be adulterous but it is at least ostensibly repugnant to respectable early modern imaginations. If it is intense but purely emotional, with no dildos or genital monstrosity, no *doing*, it proves that whatever Platonic tradition holds to be the case, even women (anatomically too cool for perfection, mentally too hot for rationality) are capable of a love that transcends the body. Even those who perceive these poems' limitations, then, or catch the verse's negative overtones and biases could, in a generous mood, find it moving to hear Ronsard and Donne – those imperiously masculine poets – and the less cocksure Tyard attempting to up their vocal register, if momentarily, from commanding baritone to melting soprano.

Notes

1 See George Klawitter, 'Verse Letters to T. W. from John Donne: "By You My Love Is Sent"', in *Homosexuality in Renaissance and Enlightenment England: Literary Representations in Historical Context*, ed. Claude Summers (New York: Haworth Press, 1992), 85–102. On Donne's probable knowledge of Sappho, see Stella Revard, 'The Sapphic Voice in Donne's "Sapho to Philaenis"', in *Renaissance Discourses of Desire*, ed. Claude J. Summers and Ted-Larry Pebworth (Columbia: University of Missouri Press, 1993). On the performance of cross-dressing in verse and its consequent blurring of gender lines, see the sympathetic and thoughtful introduction to *The Routledge Anthology of Cross-Gendered Verse*, ed. Alan Michael Parker and Mark Willhardt (London: Routledge, 1996), which includes Donne's 'Sapho'. I quote Donne from his *Complete English Poems*, ed. C. A. Patrides (New York: Knopf, 1991). This essay derives from a talk first given at Victoria College, Toronto, in January 2000. I thank Konrad Eisenbichler for inviting me and for showing me his paper on the love between Laudomia Forteguerri and Margaret of Austria.

2 See, for example, Stephen Greenblatt, 'Fiction and Friction', in *Reconstructing Individualism: Autonomy, Individuality, and the Self in Western Thought*, ed. Thomas C. Heller et al. (Stanford, Calif.: Stanford University Press, 1986). On a criminal case noted in Henri Estienne's *Apologie pour Hérodote* (1566) that involved a woman with an unsuspecting bride, see C. Annette Grisé, 'Depicting Lesbian Desire: Contexts for John Donne's "Sapho to Philaenis"', *Mosaic* 29 (1996): 41–57. Critics of theatrical cross-dressing feared the effeminization of men, argues Laura Levine in *Men in Women's Clothing: Anti-Theatricality and Feminism* (Cambridge: Cambridge University Press, 1994).

3 This is not the only poem by Donne with an interest in lesbian or, to use the once preferred term, 'tribade' relations: a poem to 'T. W.' suggests that the poets' muses have engaged in a 'chaste and mistique tribadree' and that T. W.'s muse then 'gott this Song on mee'; see Grisé, 'Depicting', 49.

4 Philaenis appears in the Greek anthology, the epigrams of Martial, and dialogues by Lucian and pseudo-Lucian as the author of a sexual manual or as a lady confused with her. On how Donne might have come to link Philaenis to Sappho, see Elizabeth Harvey, 'Ventriloquizing Sappho, or the Lesbian Muse', in *Reading Sappho: Reception and Transmission*, ed. Ellen Greene (Berkeley and Los Angeles: University of California Press, 1996), 79–104. Lucian's possible role in Donne's view of tribadism and Philaenis has been obscured by faulty citations and a misplaced trust in available translations. Usually cited is the pseudo-Lucianic 'Affairs of the Heart' (*Amores*) in Lucian's works, trans. M. D. Macleod (Cambridge, Mass.: Harvard University Press, 1967), vol. 8, which has a passage on tribadism that mentions Philaenis. Lillian Faderman's useful and

oft-cited *Surpassing the Love of Men: Romantic Friendship and Love between Women from the Renaissance to the Present* (New York: William Morrow, 1981) solemnly ascribes the latter's refusal to say what goes on between lesbians to male ignorance; but it could be knowing humour. A girl in the less often noted 'Dialogues of the Courtesans' by Lucian himself will buy red beads like those of Philaenis with her first earnings (*Lucian*, trans. MacLeod, 7:387). But especially relevant to Donne, one would think, is 'The Mistaken Critic' ('Pseudologista'), which asks those who use fancy terms where they get such words as 'bromologous' or 'anthocracy'. From a composer of dirges? 'Or from the Tablets of Philaenis, which you keep in hand?' The mention of 'hand' – 'cheiros' – may hint at what the tablets are good for. If so, Lucian links Philaenis, failed language and autoeroticism. See *Lucian*, vol. 5, trans. and ed. A. M. Harmon (London: William Heinemann, 1936), 401.

5 Arthur Weigall, quoted in *The Love Songs of Sappho*, ed. Paul Roche (New York: New American Library, 1966). Roche denies that Sappho was a 'pervert'.

6 George Klawitter, *The Enigmatic Narrator: The Voicing of Same-Sex Love in the Poetry of John Donne* (New York: Peter Lang, 1994), 47–61.

7 Maria Prendergast, *Renaissance Fantasies: The Gendering of Aesthetics in Early Modern Fiction* (Kent, Ohio: Kent State University Press, 1999), 126; Prendergast's book is not without error (for example, mistaking François I for Henri II), but it can be clever.

8 On Donne's implied links among lesbian egalitarian erotics, flatness of style, and failures of signification, as well as on the 'tolerant patriarchalism' that reduces lesbianism to a preliminary erotic stage and, by means of the name 'Sapho', to the classical past, see James Holstun, '"Will You Rent Our Ancient Love Asunder?": Lesbian Elegy in Donne, Marvell, and Milton', *English Literary History* 54 (1987): 835–67. Harvey, 'Ventriloquizing', also focuses on Donne's effort to imitate a female voice, an effort she reads rather frostily as an effort to overgo and cannibalize his rival Ovid as well as a homosocial commodification, erasure, and colonization of a threatening female writer. William West, 'Thinking with the Body: Sappho's "Sappho to Philaenis," Donne's "Sappho to Philaenis"', *Renaissance Papers 1994* (1995): 67–83, associates the poem's lack of metaphor (and hence its minimizing of difference) with this voice; but West reads Donne's move positively, finding it fruitfully ambiguous because it is itself metaphoric. Writing in a female voice was, of course, an old story; for many examples and a learned survey, see John Kerrigan, *Motives of Woe: Shakespeare and 'Female Complaint': A Critical Anthology* (Oxford: Clarendon Press, 1991). For Barbara Correll, 'Symbolic Economies and Zero-Sum Erotics: Donne's "Sapho to Philaenis"', *English Literary History* 62 (1995): 487–507, who seems to find the poem irksome, Donne produces a backfiring and 'programmatically failed poem' about 'a crisis of signification', one that 'voids signification and paints the ventriloquizing poet into a corner' and responds to what Correll calls an 'economically embedded cultural masculine crisis'. A heavy load for one paradoxical elegy to carry. More sympathetic is Paula Blank, 'Comparing Sappho to Philaenis: John Donne's Homo-poetics', *PMLA* 110 (1995): 358–68, who argues that Donne calls into question not 'lesbian desire' itself but 'the

homoeroticization of desire, the effort to re-create the other as the self and the self as other' (364). Blank's essay is refreshing for its judicious and crisply expressed empathy, although I am not fully convinced that Donne means to question Sappho's affection rather than imagine it. Cecilia Infante, 'Donne's Incarnate Muse and His Claim to Poetic Control in "Sapho to Philaenis"', in *Representing Women in Renaissance England*, ed. Claude J. Summers and Ted-Larry Pebworth (Columbia: University of Missouri Press, 1997), 93–106, stresses Sappho's onanism. Yet moralists and satirists have long accused male lovers of narcissism. When it comes to misreading passion for oneself as passion for another, Cupid is an equal-opportunity archer.

9 Blank, 'Comparing Sappho', 365. H. L. Meakin, *John Donne's Articulations of the Feminine* (Oxford: Clarendon Press, 1998), whose commentary on 'Sapho' is subtle and sympathetic, calls it 'astonishingly anomalous within classical and Renaissance literature generally' (88). Moderately anomalous, yes. Meakin also thinks the pseudo-Lucian's 'Affairs of the Heart' is innovative in using 'Lesbian' and 'Sapphic' to describe tribadism (195). But these are the translator's words. The fourth-century author has 'tribade' and 'androgynous'. On the terminology for same-sex female eras in ancient and medieval times, see Bernadette J. Brooten, *Love between Women: Early Christian Responses to Female Homoeroticism* (Chicago, Ill.: Chicago University Press, 1996), 4–9; on Sappho and her premodern reputation, see 9–41.

10 *The Latin Poems of Jean Dorat*, trans. David R. Slavitt (Alexandria, Va.: Orchises Press, 2000), 12.

11 Janel Mueller, 'Lesbian Erotics: The Utopian Trope of Donne's "Sapho to Philaenis"', in *Homosexuality in Renaissance and Enlightenment England: Literary Representations in Historical Context*, ed. Claude Summers (New York: Haworth Press, 1992), 103–34. I agree with Mueller that Donne is conducting a quasi-utopian 'thought-experiment' and that his poem has connections with the Renaissance paradox. Faderman, *Surpassing the Love of Men*, mentions Tyard and quotes several lines.

12 Translations of the three French poems appear with commentary in *Same-Sex Desire in the English Renaissance: A Sourcebook of Texts, 1470–1650*, ed. Kenneth Borris (London: Routledge, 2004), pp. 329–36. Joan DeJean, *Fictions of Sappho 1546–1937* (Chicago, Ill.: University of Chicago Press, 1989), traces the ways Sappho was imagined and reconstructed. She does not deal with these French poems, I assume because they do not mention Sappho. She argues that Renaissance poets usually took Sappho to be a heterosexual love poet. Yet thanks to Medieval annotations on Ovid, the heterosexual Sappho did not entirely erase memories of the lesbian one; for quotations from commentators and relevant Renaissance translations of Ovid, see Harriette Andreadis, 'Sappho in Early Modern England', in *Re-Reading Sappho: Reception and Transmission*, ed. Ellen Greene (Berkeley and Los Angeles: University of California Press, 1996), 105–21.

13 See the chapter on Ronsard in my *French Poets and the English Renaissance: Studies in Fame and Transformation* (New Haven, Conn.: Yale University Press, 1978), and, with caution, various studies by Hugh Richmond.

14 Pierre de Ronsard, *Oeuvres complètes*, ed. Jean Céard, Daniel Menager, and Michel Simonin, 2 vols. (Paris: Gallimard, 1993–94), 2:421–26; for poems to English dignitaries, see 2:51–64, 100–04. From 1567 to 1573 a sonnet (Céard, 1:514) followed the elegy, likewise in celebration of the love between Anne and Diane. On a parallel sonnet by Etienne Jodelle from the same period and perhaps alluding to the same 'lesbian' affair, see Richard Griffiths, '"Les Trois Sortes d'Aimer": Impersonation and Sexual Fantasy in French Renaissance Love Poetry', *Journal of the Institute of Romance Studies* 3 (1994–95): 111–27.

15 On dildos and tribadism at court, see Pierre de Bourdeille, sieur de Brantôme, *Recueil des dames, poésies et tombeaux*, ed. Etienne Vaucheret (Paris: Gallimard, 1991); this includes the memoirs sometimes called the 'Vies des dames gallantes'. *Recueil* 12.1, 'Sur les dames qui font l'amour et leurs maris cocus' has much on tribadism. As is often remarked by those who note his delicious and chatty gossip, Brantôme, who cites Lucian on the matter, assumes that tribadism – love 'donna con donna' (is there a multilingual pun here on 'con'?) – is imitative, that one woman plays the man's valorous part, that the practice came from Italy, that rubbing is harmless but dildos can cause damage, and that lesbianism is a preliminary to heterosexual relations because women will prefer running water to the stagnant and because any doctor can tell you that a wound needs probing, not rubbing.

16 See *Aeneid*, 2.341.

17 When I read a version of this essay at Yale University, Edwin Duval suggested that there may be a pun on 'vit' – 'lives' but also 'penis' – in this line. Such a pun would seem unsuitable for the poem's time, but it would not be unlike a Pléiade poet to make it, especially in so problematic a context. Professor Duval also noted the move from the heterosexual Coroebus and Cassandra to the male Pylades and Orestes.

18 Brantôme, *Recueil des dames*, 363.

19 On some (ambiguous) evidence for lesbian marriages in the ancient world, though, see Brooten, *Love between Women*.

20 Daniel Ménager, 'L'Amour au féminin', in *Sur des vers de Ronsard (1585–1985): Actes du colloque international, Duke University 11–13 Avril 1985* (Paris: Aux Amateurs de Livres, 1990), 105–16. Ménager mentions the 1565 elegy but not this one.

21 Eva Kushner tells me that she and other scholars who work with Tyard are struck by how anomalous the poem seems in its volume.

22 One of Ronsard's love poems foresees a closely similar post-mortem fame and temple (see my *French Poets*, 115). Tyard's poem may be found in *Poètes du XVIe siècle*, ed. Albert-Marie Schmidt (Paris: Gallimard, 1953), 403–05, and in Pontus de Tyard, *Oeuvres poétiques complètes*, ed. John C. Lapp (Paris: Didier, 1966), 246–50. The translation is mine.

23 The passage is quoted by Faderman, *Surpassing the Love of Men*, 35, who notes Fiordispina's assumption that such a love cannot be satisfied.

24 See the quotations from Fallopius and others in Andreadis, 'Sappho in Early Modern England'.

25 Priestess of Apollo, but 'Peitho', the name of the goddess of persuasion and, sometimes, a surname for Aphrodite, makes better sense. The ear-chaining recalls the Gallic Hercules.
26 On the friendship of Hopleus and Dymas, see Book 10, 347–448 of P. Papinius Statius, *Thebaid* (Ithaca, N.Y.: Cornell University Press, 2008), 271–74.
27 Brooten, *Love between Women*, 29–50, describes many classical comments on this point.
28 Meakin, *Articulations*, 107–08, thinks Donne perhaps read Brantôme on tribades: admiring Rabelais and Aretino, he may have, in the 1590s, 'sought out what soft-pornographic writing was available in Europe and England'. Neither Meakin nor, I think, anyone else writing on Donne, notes that Brantôme mentions Philaenis ('Filenes', 363).
29 From *Le cabinet secret du Parnasse ... Théophile de Viau et les libertins*, ed. Louis Perceau (Paris: Cabinet du Livre, 1935), 139. The headnote to Saint-Pavin notes that his nickname was the 'King of Sodom'. I thank Kenneth Borris for sending me these and several similar libertine poems on 'tribades'.
30 'Amour, je ne me plains de l'orgueil endurcy', withdrawn in 1584 from *Les Amours diverses*; in *Oeuvres*, ed. Céard, 1:466. The poem complains of the mistress' 'godmicy', her dildo, and the 'faux plaisir' it gives her all night. She should, says the speaker, be altogether a Laïs rather than employ such means to feign being Portia. For Ronsard, as for Saint-Pavin, the pleasure from a dildo is imitative, unreal. Thomas Nashe, in his notorious 'Choice of Valentines', raises, at greater length and with more self-mockery, the same issue. On Ronsard's poem and its possible relevance to Hélène de Surgères, subject of Ronsard's *Amours de Helene*, see Gregory de Rocher, 'Ronsard's Dildo Sonnet: The Scandal of Poissy and Rasse de Noeux', in *Writing the Renaissance: Essays on Sixteenth-Century French Literature in Honor of Floyd Gray*, ed. Raymond C. La Charité (Lexington, Ky.: French Forum Monographs 77, 1992), 149–64.

9

Family grief: mourning and gender in Marguerite de Navarre's *Les Prisons*

Why would a famous queen, grieved by the deaths of so many she had loved and aware that her own death could not be far away, write 4,928 lines of religious allegory in the person of a male lover? The queen is Marguerite de Navarre, the poem is *Les Prisons*, and her most recent sorrow is the death of her younger brother, François I, on March 31, 1547.[1] In this essay I will explore some of the possible contexts for her not unprecedented but nevertheless unusual decision to write in a male voice. At about this time Marguerite was composing her famous collection of stories, the *Heptaméron*, in which a variety of men speak with what evidently seemed to her a variety of male attitudes, from the suave to the cynical. But *Prisons* is her only long poem with a male speaker. It is impossible fully to understand the pressures and opportunities that guided her decision to narrate her poem's story as 'Ami' and not 'Amie', but to speculate about them is a useful exercise in imagining how poetic cross-dressing, like any other kind, may be multidetermined. Nor can we long forget the narrator's sex, for in Romance languages grammatical gender renders any unisex speaker default-male.

In this essay I will speculate as to some of the reasons for and effects of Marguerite's decision. First, though, a summary of this long poem. Although its cleverly conceived primary narrative does not concern death or mourning, the poem moves toward four deathbed scenes that seem in turn to impel the narrator into rapturous religious comprehension and to at least the prospect of bliss and silence that are the best answer to loss.[2] Before we arrive at the deaths, we follow the narrator as he experiences his consecutive captivity in and release from three prisons, prisons that merely get bigger. If, as has been plausibly suggested, they form a triptych, it is a very lopsided one.[3] The poem is filled with Marguerite's Evangelical piety as well as with the irony at which she was also adept and to which she often joined a charity that comes, paradoxically, from thinking the entire world fetid with sin and pride. If we are all filthy, simple justice requires us to be as forgiving as we can.

Family grief 219

In Book I of *Les Prisons* the narrator recounts to 'Amie' – his female friend/beloved – how he was Love's captive. In Love's tower, darkness seems bright and the stones, chains, and bars seem pleasing: Amie's eyes and speech are his welcome bonds and his harmony. Thinking himself a king ('J'etais donc roy'), he finds that this tower is all his delight.[4] But Time does its work, and he finds that the tower has begun to collapse, so that despite his urgent efforts with mortar and tools, the tower's stones fall, its bars crack, and the lover's health decays. Eventually the tower burns, and the lover turns to blame Amie for the catastrophe until the Sun itself tells him that he is now free from a love that would have held him in the beloved's womb-like prison. God sends light, and the prisoner now can see how his tower had been built on sand, on piles of earth (411–42; the piles recall Adam ['earth'] and hence bondage to the law, to the letter, to the infected will). The lover rejoices in his new liberty, scorning his recent chains and the false pleasure he took in them when he lived with shadows. To God must go the praise: no father or mother or sister or brother or friend could have known the secret; nor was his escape his own doing. So farewell, tower, farewell abyss, fire, ice, and tremblings (he might as well add, 'farewell Petrarch', now extending his power in France). He is free!

In Book II the liberated lover tells Amie of his life in the broad world of men, among creatures to whom alone God gave heads raised high (he has read Ovid's *Metamorphoses*). The lover sees trees, fields, flowers, animals, sailors and voyages, houses, wealth that leads to lawsuits, war, and politics (the progression recapitulates the myth of the Golden Age and its degeneration). He sees altars with rich images, hears organs, builds churches so as to be purged of his sins, buys masses to make up for his adulteries, jousts, drinks, dances, courts witty ladies, sleeps with women – but he has the nerve to assure Amie that she is the only one he ever actually loved, adding with something less than gallantry that thanks to *her* infidelity he will never marry. Ami now goes to court, where kings can kill with a single word, and men scramble for place and power (these pages are not bad anti-court satire, and by one who knew). At last an old man named 'de science Amateur' (1555, 'Learning's Lover') tells Ami that he is still a captive, bound in silk by 'ambition, / Concupiscence et vayne affection' (1207–08). Read some history, he urges, and learn what happens to kings, emperors, and popes; learn to detect the cruelties sustaining splendour; scan the skies, not gold; find good exempla; study books, including the Bible. The sun shines and, citing Dante, the lover tells Amie to beware of the flesh, avarice, and pride.

So in Book III Ami turns to books, building for himself what turns out to be a new prison: piles of reading matter are its pillars, and the capital is laurel. He makes one pillar of philosophy; a grey and ashy one of canons and decretals; another of poetry that he loves so much he forgets to eat;

another of law books he never reads for pleasure and is hard to keep upright; a thorny yet curiously addictive one of maths books with geometric shapes on top; another of medicine, and so forth. Of course there is a theology pillar, not all of it sound; on its summit is a Bible, bound in bloodstained lambskin, closed by seven clasps, and locked to the uncomprehending. The lover is among these last – stuck in the letter and working by candlelight. Finally his eye falls on the passage in which Jesus thanks God that He has revealed his secrets to the humble and not to the wise. There is a burst of radiance as God's voice kills and remakes him with the Word that is both sword and lancet. Realizing that he is nothing and God is All, the lover sees his pillars collapse and the laurel burn; God has delivered his heart from books (2432, 'mon cueur des livres delivra').

The story is effectively over, but the poem is not. Its second half includes, for example, a discussion of allegory.[5] Reading is still valuable; Ami learns that history, law, poetry, and all the other pillars are built upon truths found in Scripture. He now reads the work of a dead lady (in fact, Marguerite Porete, an unorthodox nun burned for her writings, something Marguerite may not have known) whose mystical view of God as 'near' and 'far' impresses him – although his creator subtly changes her source so as to retain some distinction between the human and the divine.[6] Now he is the commander of books, not their slave: his open books make a paved road to liberty. Many lines then explore the paradox that human nothingness gives us access to God's all (mortal zero, as Marguerite does not quite say, can join God's eternal circle). So why fear death? After describing the martyrdom of the French ambassador to the sultan, the lover now recounts to Amie four important deaths. If the scenes make up a small percentage of *Les Prisons*' lines, they made up a large part of Marguerite's meditations during her stay at Tusson and cast a backward light on the poem's earlier narrative. Although their piety entails distaste for worldly illusion and distraction, there is nothing grisly or sadistic in this Evangelical version of a *contemptus mundi*. The scenes' specificity gives narrative vigour and interest, not monitory shudders, and makes them almost novelistic or dramaturgical. What can seem Marguerite's compulsion to recall even small details may be a desire to lend a convincing exemplarity to her theological arguments.[7] Such clarity of memory is also one way we have to work through grief: mourning as memory, as a family photo in the mind, a mental videotape to be played and replayed.

The first death is that of the pious Marguerite de Lorraine, mother of Marguerite's first husband, Charles d'Alençon. Born in 1463, widowed in 1492, she eventually took the veil and died in 1521. The account of her death, says Glasson (364), accords well with other accounts except that Ami omits the dying lady's well-attested invocation of the Virgin and saints.

As she goes to meet her divine 'sweet husband' and 'true sun', in other words, the nun sounds quite Evangelical. Marguerite's affection for her mother-in-law was doubtless genuine, but her resonant mixture of pity and admiration did not stop and probably encouraged her to revise the past. Nor does Marguerite claim for her devout mother-in-law any moral triumph; rather, she has the convent's wise abbess assure her that God will marry her despite her sins.[8]

The next death is that of Charles d'Alençon. Ami mentions the duke's wife, Marguerite, but as one present at the scene, not as one with any relation to the narrator himself. Marguerite's mourning was now long behind her, and in any case the degree of her marital happiness with Charles remains unclear, but the split between past self and current persona is especially curious here, as though such a narrator would enable her to remember as somebody else, to deploy gender difference to indicate or reinforce a temporal and perhaps an emotional gap. On Shrove Tuesday a sick Charles sits listening to his wife read the Bible. She playfully ('par jeu', line 3976) reminds him to confess and take communion; he then retires, calls Marguerite, listens to her read the story of the Passion, and learnedly expounds upon it to five attendant theologians. To his mother-in-law, the regent Louise de Savoie, he laments the king's recent capture at Pavia, begs her pardon (we are not told why, but many thought that Charles had shown himself a coward during the battle), and praises his wife. Despite her mother's orders and unwilling to distress her husband (4043–44: 'non obstant maternelle deffence, / Ne voulu pas au mary faire offense'), Marguerite stays with Charles, who tells his doctor to keep her healthy, gives her final instructions he knows she will obey, and expresses a faith remarkably like Marguerite's own. A chariot arrives to bring the bride, Charles' soul, to her Creator.

And now, says the narrator to Amie, he will recount to her the death of Louise de Savoie. Louise, he says, had always followed virtue's path. Now, at fifty-five and after long sorrows and brief pleasures, she is dying. A brief biography follows: children, widowhood, a refusal to remarry, and charity toward slanderous servants who tried to have her children removed. She was a prudent and powerful regent, so that François praises her for so well managing public affairs. Worn out, she asks God, speaking as a wife to a husband, why he delays; then, too weak to receive the Host, she asks Marguerite to take it for her. In many lines of quoted speech, Louise admits that she has sinned but relies on grace, not virtue, to save her (if hardly heretical, the stress is again Evangelical). She thus showed herself to be God's spouse and daughter (4325, 'se monstrant de Dieu espouse et fille'; in her *Miroir*, Marguerite had also been His mother and sister). So long as she hears Scripture she is pain-free; when the reading pauses, the torment returns.

The king would not have been able to reach his mother in time, we read, but Louise reflects that the sorrow would have been unbearable on both sides. Their love had been too great, she adds, and she must think of it no longer. Indeed Louise sends Marguerite herself away, saying that while she is in the room her mother cannot rejoice at dying and would talk instead of being absorbed by divine love. This is, I think, a particularly interesting touch, granted Marguerite's conviction that silence is where language at its best is headed. Marguerite asks the company to leave, noting that Louise aimed at Heaven, considering power, wealth, children, and honours to be trash. In spite of her desire for silence, Louise praises Marguerite for these words, and, Ami reports, it was Marguerite alone who noticed the exact moment of her mother's passing. Louise dies, then, with praise for Marguerite on her lips and Marguerite's theology in her heart.

It is now the brother's turn to die, the address to Amie reminding us that the person speaking is still the poem's male narrator. Again there is some biography: the noble race, the wars, the captivity (which, says Marguerite implausibly, was nevertheless glorious), the fondness for letters, the learning, the handsome looks, the wisdom. True, those judging from outside would never take him to be another St. Louis in piety, but, says Ami, both he and Amie have heard him say at a feast that were God to call on him to die that dawn he would find the present delights nothing in comparison to Heaven. No one could say that he took his pleasures without the fear of God, and indeed he would weep at the mention of his Creator. His spirit loved God, then, even though his fragile flesh turned to sin. After all, says Ami, such sinning gave him humility. Had he not had such imperfection, so high-soaring a spirit would have been tempted by pride; had Satan not fixed his dart in François's flesh to lower his self-esteem, Pride would have raised him to the heights. (Well, yes. Maybe. A cynic might point out that royal gallivanting, also found, thinly disguised, in the *Heptaméron* and treated with possibly amused or possibly vexed tolerance, can result from rather than preclude arrogance; it's good to be the king – you get girls. Gary Ferguson, moreover, remarks that Marguerite's defence of her brother, whose sins Ferguson says she views with some humour, elides the traditional requirement that penitence entail amendment.[9] Yet Marguerite's defence is not wholly sophistical. She believed that because the world is fallen, has become wordy trash, and because our chief sin is the pride that separates us from God, only awareness of sin, of *naught*[i]ness, can save us. It can also make us charitable. The uncomfortable humour in the *Heptaméron* may come from disillusion, but a disillusion involving not so much moral indifference or misanthropy as a belief that pride, not love of justice, makes us relentlessly judgemental.[10])

The king, then, sinned in the flesh but preserved faith in his spirit, and it was that faith that blessed him in death. Amie witnessed this, Ami reminds her, although he himself was not so happy. (Nor was Marguerite present. Both male narrator and female author, that is, were missing from the book's final deathbed scene, but a lady – 'Amye' – was there. Is she a surrogate for Marguerite? The speaker's soul [*âme*] with an added 'y'?) Ami's absence does not stop him from reminding her what took place (Amie herself, as always, remains silent). We hear at length of the king's humility, receiving of the sacraments, farewell to his son, and recitation of his sins. With no regret for what he is leaving, François is joyful, saying – several times – that no sin is so mortal that Christ's blood cannot wash it, that he relies on divine mercy, and not on his own merit, to forgive his soiled and dirty life (4526: 'vie salle et orde'). The king says farewell to those near him, evidently including Amye, for Ami knows that her heart still feels the pain. So the king passes through the gate of death, finding it sweet, and recovers life in the All because no sorrow or triumph had ever made him doubt God. If he had wandered into sin, repentance always drew him back to Jesus, fountain of penitence. So now he reigns with Christ, as he had reigned in this world. There is nothing about saints, Purgatory, or bequests. Her brother makes just the end Marguerite would wish.

What literary or psychological work does the maleness of Marguerite's narrator accomplish? First the obvious. To the extent that Marguerite wished to show that describing the traditional tower of love does not begin to exhaust the full story of our imprisonment in the Flesh she needs to take account of the more spacious jail, the World (the Flesh writ large, so to speak). In that world, whatever can be accomplished by kings' sisters, queens of tiny kingdoms, or even royal mistresses, for most women there can be little political power, large-scale capitalist enterprise, courtroom fame, or geographic discovery. To demonstrate that the great world is just another prison, then, requires a male visitor to this House of Lucifera, this Vanity Fair. Similarly, although many women in the Renaissance read a good deal, nearly all scholars were of course male. A female captive or two in the poem's third prison would not be inconceivable – Marguerite had read her way through more than one book-pillar – but the population of such captives would be vanishingly small, too small to make satire or exhortation worthwhile. If she wanted her main narrator for the deathbed scenes, she had to continue in the male voice.

Marguerite's family, moreover, offered her food for cross-gendered thought. The family was exceptional in any case because of its political power, wealth, and brilliance. It was also fatherless, with a mother who knew actual rule and a brother who had first the unmanning experience of being captured, then the less than patriarchal experience of being rescued by his sister and mother, then marriage to the sister of his captor and seeing all this sorted out by the so-called Peace of the Ladies. It was also a family much given to writing poems, including verse letters circulated among Marguerite, François, and their mother – a threesome that sometimes, risking at least a little blasphemy, called itself 'la trinité'.[11] Cross-gendering is not absent from this verse (nor, in more complex senses, from the trinity's political life). For a male poet to adopt the voice of a female is hardly unusual, of course. Indeed, to write a verse epistle in the person of an aggrieved woman was more likely to signal familiarity with Ovid's *Heroides* than a genuine and sympathetic curiosity about female subjectivity. Nevertheless, it is intriguing that François, flanked as he often was by powerful women (including some forceful mistresses), chose to experiment with a feminine voice. After all, he might have told himself, he was not unfamiliar with the sex. More surprising, though, is his imagination's pull toward the plight of betrayed or abandoned ones. Perhaps, some might say, what inspired him was a bad conscience. In any case, among the king's poems one finds an epistle in the voice of a lady to Claude Chappuys, her fickle lover ('Ami variable'), whose cruelty has ruined love and loyalty; now she lies beneath a marble monument with an epitaph expressing her innocence, her relief at being dead, and the lover's current discomfort. Other epigrams offer capsule versions of several poems in *Heroides*, verse nuggets of female misery. One finds Medea to Jason, Hero to Leander, and Briseis to Achilles. Most curious is the brief poem said by a suicidal Canace to Macaire, her brother and lover. Only her death, says Canace, can 'declare her great passion'. In Ovid's much longer poem Canace is less interested in the question of concealment than in the ghastly death her father, the wind-god Aeolus, devised for the siblings' newborn baby, and she kills herself not to reveal her incest but in obedience to her father's order.

François's poem is not evidence for the old ridiculous slander that he and Marguerite committed incest. Rather, as one might also say about Marguerite's tale of incest in the *Heptaméron*, somewhere in the royal mind family ties had particular resonance, perhaps as the result of those tensions that can attend a family's otherwise comforting and pleasurably tight emotional bonds.[12] Not that Marguerite would be startled to hear that those bonds had an erotic tinge. Love is Love – in God, *philia*, *eros*, and *agape* all have their function and discourse. By adopting a male voice, Marguerite can relocate desire for her brother (not sexual desire, I mean, but love with the erotic glow derived from power, prestige, and charm) by in some sense *being* him, or the him he should have been, the him who eventually – in her poem – gets things right. To be God's 'ami' complicates the situation yet further, for to seek unity with God rather than with one's family is again to get around the impossibility and pathos of loving any 'other' to the point of full union, to integrate the split self by giving it up in ways not even a vain royal brother would welcome.

The tightness of the siblings' bonds, erotic or not, shows in yet another poem by François, striking for its mixture of adroit charm, affection, and a certain egotism unsurprising in a monarch. The poem is a ballade to Marguerite written in early 1543, when the by now middle-aged queen was again pregnant. François thanks Christ for having given him 'Conqueste, enfans, et defence et pouvoir (conquest, children, protection, and power) and Christ replies with the reminder that His blood alone suffices to protect us.[13] Then the king turns to his pregnant sister: Come back, he says, so I may see and not just hear how much the glory of the 'maison' – the 'house' – has increased in 'conquest, honour, and lineage', and we may together thank the One who gave us conquest, children, protection, and power. But what 'house' does this mean? Valois? Navarre? Probably the former, for the poem seems to suggest that the baby will add to the king's already impressive list of blessings. The Valois dynasty as a family enterprise will have increased and prospered thanks to the birth of Marguerite's child (a futile hope, for it died); Marguerite's own pleasure, and doubtless her relief, were the baby to be a healthy son, is missing. A charitable reader might think that we are to take her joy for granted. To be sure, as the king's nephew or niece, the anticipated baby would in fact have been part of the larger 'house' of Valois, but the siblings' familial self-absorption shows in the poem's indifference to the baby's possible future as a king of Navarre. Maybe Marguerite shared this view of her pregnancy; maybe she would have also welcomed a trace more happiness on her own behalf, or even on that of her husband's 'house'.

Whatever the possible trace of patriarchal tactlessness that accompanies this poem's sunny fraternal warmth, the fact remains that François could occasionally try to imagine a female subjectivity. A striking instance of the Valois family's interest in cross-gendered – or in this case bisexed – performance is a portrait of François combining the attributes of Mercury, Athena, Cupid, and Diana. Is it, as Edgar Wind says, an emblematic Platonic portrait of political and cosmic wholeness? Or is it, as Raymond Waddington says, a quasi-friendly mockery of François's taste and that of the Fontainebleau school of painting that sometimes exploited Greek mythology's interest in divine gender-ambiguity? Witness, Waddington notes, some remarkable paintings that show nymphs fondling each other (a sort of cross-gendering in early modern thinking about lesbianism), and one of Jove in the guise of Diana seducing a nymph. For Barbara Meyer, the portrait implies less a unified François than a merged François–Marguerite, dyadic remnant of the original 'trinité'. Even those who find Wind's reading plausible might agree with Waddington that the king's body and posture are remarkably effeminized even for a Platonic androgyne.[14]

The portrait, in other words, suggests yet another context for the Valois interest in voicing poetry in the person of the 'other', an interest that even if shared with many poets before and since may have had extra poignancy for so close a pair. This is all the more the case if, as has been recently argued, Marguerite was manoeuvred by the 'trinity''s mythology into taking on the role of being 'feminine' – soft, charitable, sexual, charming, maternal – so that Louise, regent from 1515 to 1516 and again from 1523 to 1527, could more readily take on the phallic role of hard-nosed ruler/adviser.[15] One can push this thought a bit further: freed not only by her mother's death but by her brother's, the surviving member of the 'trinité' could shake off her soft feathers and adopt the masculinity of her phallic mother and the active maleness of her brother, a king with more than his share of 'Amies'.[16] Nor was Marguerite the only important sister of an even more important brother whose task, after the brother's death, was in significant ways to take on aspects of that brother's identity. Young Elizabeth Tudor, who was one day to have the heart and stomach of a king, had many reasons in 1553 to mourn her brother Edward's death, but she also could think, after she mounted the throne and new editions of her translation of Marguerite's *Miroir* saw print, that in a world of gender equality the older Valois sibling would have ruled France. An analogous mixture of love, replacement, and incorporation complicates the sibling relations of Mary 'Philip's Phoenix' Sidney. Here too is sisterly devotion that eventuates in the ambiguities of post-mortem control: Mary edits and completes works by the defunct hero of Zutphen, and Marguerite makes her king her subject, if only the subject of verse.[17]

Such a family dynamic might also explain some of what we find in these death scenes, not least the tendency to give them all an Evangelical look – the sacraments are there, of course, but with the stress thrown on Scripture and salvific faith and the usual saints, masses, bequests, and Purgatory conspicuously absent, more utterly absent than is entirely credible. These are deaths that Erasmus, author of the deathbed dialogue *Funus*, would have applauded. In other words, Marguerite has, at least to some degree, taken the liberty, as the surviving person of the trinity, to remake her now helpless relatives, if not into out-and-out Lutherans, then into something more Erasmian, more Evangelical, more like Marguerite. By giving herself a male narrator she can, in some sense, throw the responsibility for this onto some other person, if only someone inside her own imagination, someone who is the more 'other' for having a different sex. Perhaps the maleness of the narrator, then (although here I may be nearing the margin of legitimate speculation), enabled an increased aggression – and hence in our gender system a masculine attitude – toward those whom she also genuinely loved. Such maleness on the part of a female author certainly further enables a split in consciousness between the loving warm wife/daughter/sister and a narrator who although admiring is nevertheless willing to call a sin a sin.[18]

It might seem odd, granted Marguerite's love for the dead and her insistence on their piety and salvation, to hear aggression in *Les Prisons*.[19] Love, however, is seldom free from ambivalence, and mourning can include anger, if only anger at the dead for dying (blame is a common component of grief, and Marguerite had cause for resentment because her identity and value had for so long been bound to her brother's life and role). It cannot, that is, have been Evangelical theology alone that led the queen to comment so fully on her relatives' failures, from Charles's need for Louise's pardon to François's sins of the flesh. The ambivalence shows, I think, with some poignancy in Marguerite's lines on her mother. It is not to dishonour her grief, only to confess our species' complexity, to observe that after years of being third in the 'trinité', a queen but never a ruler, well-loved but not her mother's chief pride, and bearer of only one surviving child, Marguerite effectively erases the son/brother (loved, but absent) and records maternal praise for the wise daughter/sister. Marguerite and Louise, indeed, join in an intimacy so close that one may take the Host on behalf of the other: in a reversal of the ordinary course of things, the daughter eats that her mother may be nourished.[20]

The voice of the male narrator, on the other hand, also establishes *distance* between Marguerite and this tableau: a memorial narrative in her own voice would bring Marguerite too close to the scene, collapsing author and daughter. Ami gives her cover and perspective; Amye would do so less decisively. It is under such cover and with such perspective that Marguerite can endow her brother with the understanding she hoped he had finally achieved, or would have achieved had she been François. Being François may, in fact, be one of the fantasies haunting this poem. I doubt that Marguerite wanted to be a man, yet to adopt a male voice seems related somehow to her years of serving and advising her brother while also suffering his occasional disapproval and watching his sometimes murderous treatment of those whose religious views she shared. His death gives her the imaginary power, even as she loses influence in the real political world, to make her brother see things her way.

A complicated and ambivalent reaction to loss constitutes much psychoanalytic theory. Julia Kristeva's *Black Sun* may be particularly pertinent to Marguerite's imagination. Depression and mourning, says Kristeva, classically conceal 'an aggressiveness toward the lost object, thus revealing the ambivalence of the depressed person with respect to the object of mourning. 'I love that object', is what the person seems to say ... 'but even more so I hate it because I love it, and in order not to lose it, I imbed it in myself but because I hate it, that other within myself is a bad self, I am bad, I am non-existent, I shall kill myself.' Such logic, of course, assumes 'a stern superego' and a 'dialectic of idealization and devalorisation of self and other, the aggregate of those activities being based on the mechanism of *identification*' (11). Sadness itself is nevertheless a way of maintaining a unity in the self, 'an affective cohesion' in the face of loss (19). As for women and loss, narcissism will demand a large introjection of the ideal so as to satisfy both its negative side *and* a 'longing to be present in the arena where the world's power is at stake' (30). The loss of an erotic object, says Kristeva, produces an inner void, but a void that creates separation can also enable further movement (82–83). Death, a 'dramatic diachrony', creates a needed discontinuity, a hiatus or caesura that enables signification (132–34) and, in Christian terms, can both posit and offer an antidote to depression.[21]

Here is much of what happens in the *Prisons*: the willingness to acknowledge the sins of the dead even while praising them; the identification with the lost brother's gender; the insistence on being 'nothing'; the condemnatory – and masculine – superego; the surge upward toward an idealized 'All' in which the personal 'nothing' can merge, especially after the hiatus of death, to find a new identity/identification; and even a certain *eros* in her feelings for François.[22] Kristeva's observations, moreover, might further explain why Marguerite takes so long to reach that silence in which *Rien* merges with *Tout* – it is hard work to get over death's hiatus, to stop talking and let the unspeakable miracle in the tomb proceed.[23] To apply such thinking to *Les Prisons* must ignore a great deal: the objective reality of her relatives' sins and what for Marguerite (and many others still) is the objective fact of God's judgment and mercy. It is also the case that Marguerite's absence from 'the arena where worldly power is at stake' was historical fact. After her brother's death, her position in the French political theatre had shifted from near centre-stage to somewhere near the exit. This did not make her 'nothing' in French eyes, but a transition from royal sister to royal aunt must have felt like an undoing. One way to respond to an undoing is to embrace it, to turn it into All, not as megalomania but as fulfilled desire.

The psychoanalytically inclined have other theories, of course, as witness Cottrell's Lacanian treatment of *Les Prisons* in *The Grammar of Silence*. For Cottrell, Lacan helps explain why Marguerite used a male speaker.[24] The difference between Ami and Amie marks that split that indicates 'a progression away from the Imaginary' (Ami is growing up, in other words): the fire that burns his tower of love also scatters the self that is constructed in the Imaginary, freeing it (263). But the prisons of the world and of books simply trap Ami in the order of the Symbolic (269, 283). Final liberation is into the silence toward which this long poem strains. Cottrell does not say so, but perhaps leaving the Symbolic behind and unweaving the web of words required Marguerite to repeat to herself, to make even more real to herself, that her mother and brother were dead – behind her in time, if preceding her into eternity.[25]

Are there other reasons for mourning in the voice of a liberated male prisoner?

One, surely, is the gendered body and soul that traditionally find their hierarchal place on the Neoplatonic ladder leading upward to the divine.[26] Marguerite's decision to write as a male is not, however, readily mapped on the usual body/soul division. That division is trickier than sometimes thought in terms of gender, for although in much traditional thinking the material body – *mater*, *materia*, matrix – has seemed feminine (matter is female, form is male), both grammatically and conceptually the soul, *anima*, is, too. A male is made of matter (female in its labile frailty and ability to receive the imprint of form), but he has a female immortal part: 'Ami' has an inner 'Amie'. Like all men, he has a body (material and thus in some sense 'female' even if *corpus* and *corps* are grammatically masculine) that imprisons a lady-butterfly, or *psyche*, that when liberated can flutter its way back to God. The body/soul split is further complicated in much Christian and pagan tradition by the triad of body, soul, and *spirit*. If a man's body is male in shape and function but female in materiality, and if his soul, the part that can marry Christ, is traditionally imagined as female, his spirit (*spiritus*), the force that energizes him and mediates between the senses and the mind, is masculine, at least grammatically.

The problem is that in Renaissance usage 'spirit' and 'soul' are often confused. One writer's 'anima' is another writer's 'spiritus'.[27] After all, our body is *animal*, is *animated* by its 'soul' in a quite secular sense; just as to call teenagers 'high-spirited' need not mean that their immortal parts are levitating, only that their vital 'spirits' are strong. Even when the thinking is dualistic (soul/body, spirit/flesh), then, the availability of both masculine *spiritus* and feminine *anima* to represent – or not represent – what survives death and transcends the flesh can cause confusion. This in turn means that, in gendering the voice of the part of her that longed for God, Marguerite had more than one choice. We can, then, read Ami's love for Amie as the spirit's love for and initial entrapment by the (feminized) flesh. And yet Amie's role in *Les Prisons* seems ambiguous, if only because her name looks suspiciously like 'Ame'. Is it possible that Marguerite is simply uninterested in the spirit/soul's imprisonment in a material body and is instead exploring how spirit relates to soul? In her early poetry having been a sinful 'âme', does she now want to be a temporarily foolish 'esprit'? Or are Ami and Amie, finally, a team? Both find themselves in the flesh of love, world, and books. Not the world, the flesh, and the devil, but another anti-trinity: passion, world, and learning.

I do not wish further to snarl an already difficult and inconsistently used pair of terms, only to remember that the vocabulary and concepts available to Marguerite gave her room to play with gendered voices beyond the dyad of body/not-body. If loss and mourning can produce inner division and fragmentation, and if a switch of gender can seem to indicate that split, then it seems fitting that given a choice of terminology a woman poet might prefer the male voice to represent the spiritual part of herself, her *spiritus*, in a culture that could also imagine a man's immortal part as his *anima*. Marguerite can speak as *spiritus* and can love the *anima*, if we read Amie as that; or the flesh, if we prefer her in those terms. If I am right, and whatever Amie is or means, Marguerite's choice of speaker derives less from an identification with male theological or literary authority than from a desire to make an already cross-gendered psychological and religious tradition even more appropriate to her circumstance. In a strange set of reversals Marguerite, who in her early *Miroir de l'âme pécheresse* had been the 'âme', is now a male speaker, perhaps the author's own *animus* or 'esprit' addressing a female beloved. Her *animus* has an *anima*. And why not? We contain multitudes, and some of the persons in that multitude may well contain yet others.

The terms *animus* and *anima* of course suggest Jung, and indeed, a Jungian take on Marguerite's poem seems inviting.[28] G. Mallary Masters points to her mention of the Platonic Androgyne (Book III, 921–22), a myth of psychic unity that he notes also sustains Jungian psychology. In this view, Marguerite's male voice represents what Jung calls the Animus, a woman's inner 'other' in her unconscious, presenting itself to her as male precisely because 'other' to a subjectively female psyche. Male mystics, longing to join themselves to Christ, notes Masters, sometimes speak from the perspective of the soul, the feminine *anima* (for Jung a male psyche's female 'other' and for others the immortal part of ourselves). So it is only logical for a woman poet to speak as her Animus. Through this intuition, Masters adds, Marguerite finds yet another liberation, that of a feminist psychology that anticipates later psychoanalytic theories. Psychological development depends on a dialogue with the 'other', much as spiritual progress engages the dynamic of Nothing and All. (To be sure, there is no dialogue in *Les Prisons* between Amye and Ami, but maybe Marguerite, a woman, thought that she already knew what Amye had to say.)

Whether or not Marguerite's male persona allegorizes some inner part of herself, and however we read her mourning the loss of her relatives in the voice of an 'other', her writing as 'Ami' does not in itself reverse the usual gender situation in her culture; indeed, she relies on it. But her decision to cross-gender her persona adds a further fold, a wrinkle, to her already multipleated familial circumstance and shifts the terms of her relationship with God. Marguerite's longing to be 'rien', nothing, was by now likely to have been more real to her than ever. Yet, as she seems well aware, a zero can fit comfortably inside the circular God whose centre is everywhere and circumference nowhere. To merge with, to be, that All can annihilate gender as well as death, collapse the distinctions between sister and brother, daughter and mother. The three persons of the Valois 'trinité' can also be a 'unité'. Marguerite's impulse to be an Ami rather than an Amie, to be Spiritus rather than Anima was, as I hope I have shown, impelled by any number of motives – literary, religious, psychological, and philosophical. Merged with, identified with, the *Tout*, Marguerite's *Rien* is a very full 'Nothing' indeed, quite as full as Thomas More's 'Nowhere'. It embraces love, family, prison, liberty, light, anger, envy, memory, resentment, charity, life, death, and, not least, Marguerite herself and God. Hers was not a simple grief. We can be moved by this intelligent and noble allegory even while sensing that in it Death loses its sting in large part because of the author's faith but also because the author has put some of that sting in her poetry.

Notes

1 On François, see R. L. Knecht, *Renaissance Warrior and Patron: The Reign of Francis I* (Cambridge: Cambridge University Press, 1994). Marguerite's influence, still perceptible in 1544 when little Elizabeth Tudor translated her *Miroir de l'âme pécheresse*, had declined and, after her brother's death, effectively ceased. The standard biography is Pierre Jourda, *Marguerite d'Angoulême, Duchesse d'Alençon, Reine de Navarre (1492–1549): Etude biographiqe et littéraire*, 2 vols. (Paris, 1930; Geneva: Slatkine, 1978).
2 The standard edition is *Les Prisons*, ed. Simone Glasson (Geneva: Droz, 1978); no one knows how much was written before François died, but the lines on his death probably postdate the account in the *Oraison funèbre* of Pierre Du Châtel (May, 1547). Composed at the monastery of Tusson, the poem exists in two manuscripts and was first printed in *Les dernières poésies*, ed. Abel Lefranc (Paris: Colin, 1896). The edition by Claire Lynch Wade (New York: Peter Lang, 1989) has a clever English translation, although the introduction has errors (e.g., crediting d'Aubigne's *Tragiques* to Du Bartas) and ignores Glasson. I modernize *Amye* and *Amy* as *Amie* and *Ami*: 'Amy' just doesn't look male in English.
3 Paula Sommers, *Celestial Ladders: Readings in Marguerite de Navarre's Poetry of Spiritual Ascent* (Geneva: Droz, 1989), 84; each section, she observes, is marked by an address to 'Amie'. Sommers points out that the narrator's 'independence, initiative, and aggressiveness', although associated with maleness, 'confer no spiritual advantages' (109).

4 Line 177. The tower's phallic quality – the lover is in a large vertical structure, not in a garden or chamber – cannot have escaped Marguerite.
5 In 2603–06, the lover learns, e.g., that Ovid's Acteon allegorizes Christ: the deer's horns are Jesus' crown of thorns, and he dies surrounded by dogs (cf. Jesus' quotation of Psalm 22; the dogs appear in verse 16). On Marguerite's allegorical poetics, see Carol Thysell, *The Pleasure of Discernment: Marguerite de Navarre as Theologian* (Oxford: Oxford University Press, 2000), 109–16. I agree that her Platonism is inflected by the Christian (and Jewish) belief that God descends when we cannot, unaided, ascend.
6 For Porete, God and soul merge into a 'Loingpres', but for Marguerite they make a 'Loing Pres'; see Thyssell, 22–24, citing Robert D. Cottrell's *Grammar of Silence: A Reading of Marguerite de Navarre's Poetry* (Washington, D.C.: Catholic University of America Press, 1986).
7 So says Olivier Zegna Rata, 'La Preuve par la mort: les récits de morts dans *Les Prisons* de Marguerite de Navarre', *Revue d'histoire littéraire de la France* 92 (1992): 163–77. Rata ignores gender. Cottrell, *Grammar*, calls the death scenes *exempla* (304fn.). Yes; and yet the *Heptaméron* treats *exempla* with some scepticism. One wonders what its more ironic *dévisants* might say about these dying admissions; even these *récits*, if hardly in this context, might be subject to debate.
8 Glasson notes that Evangelical faith welcomed deathbed admissions of sin because knowledge of sin precludes pride (35); such admission, she says on 41, shows a final detachment from edification and moral values. See also Robert D. Cottrell, 'Spirit, Body, and Flesh in the *Heptaméron*', in *Spirit, Body, and Flesh in Marguerite de Navarre's Heptaméron*, ed. Dora Polachek (Amherst, Mass.: Hestia, 1993), 23–37; Cottrell notes that for Marguerite the 'flesh' is sinful, but the body itself is merely human. (Religion, Marguerite might remind promoters of 'family values', is not the same as behaving oneself.)
9 Gary Ferguson, *Mirroring Belief: Marguerite de Navarre's Devotional Poetry* (Edinburgh: Edinburgh University Press, 1992), 46.
10 This is often said in scholarship on the *Heptaméron*. Marguerite's charity does not extend to the regular clergy, roundly condemned for hypocrisy, superstition, and sexual misconduct.
11 *Poésies du roi François 1er, de Louise de Savoie Duchesse d'Angoulême, de Marguerite, reine de Navarre, et Correspondance intime du roi avec Diane de Poitiers et plusieurs autres dames de la cour*, ed. M. Aime Champollion-Figeac (Geneva: Slatkine, 1970). The four deaths make a quaternity, or perhaps a double set of mother–son dyads with Marguerite somewhere near both – a double role in the formation of *two* linked 'trinities'. For Cottrell (*Grammar*, 310), the deaths impose a 'Pythagorean tetrad, the symbol of created matter', on 'the triadic configurations so deliberately stressed throughout much of the work'.
12 Recent treatments of posthumous rumours have focused on Marguerite's adoration and ignored François's less hyperbolic expressions.
13 François I, *Oeuvres poétiques*, ed. J. E. Kane (Geneva: Slatkine, 1984), 6.

14 Edgar Wind, *Pagan Mysteries in the Renaissance* (New Haven, Conn.: Yale University Press, 1958); Raymond Waddington, 'The Bisexual Portrait of Francis I: Fontainebleau, Castiglione, and the Tone of Courtly Mythology', in *Playing With Gender: A Renaissance Pursuit*, ed. Jean Brink et al. (Urbana: University of Illinois Press, 1991), 99–132; and Barbara Hochstetler Meyer, 'Marguerite de Navarre and the Androgynous Portrait of François I', *Renaissance Quarterly* 48 (1995): 287–325. Mayer quotes some loving lines by Marguerite, although none by François, which may explain her reference on 309 to 'unrequited love'. The king is cooler – male reticence? an identity less bound up with the more powerful sibling? – but he could be affectionate. Meyer, too, rejects any thought of actual incest. On François, Marguerite, death, and love see also Collette H. Winn, 'L'Expérience de la mort dans *La Navire*', in *Love and Death in the Renaissance*, eds. Kenneth Bartlett, Konrad Eisenbichler, and Janice Liedl (Ottawa: Dovehouse, 1991), 199–219; in *Navire* the dead François, says Winn, treats death as the pair's recoveries ('retrouvailles'), a sort of 'union amoureuse' (209) that recalls their life together in the world below.

15 Leah Middlebrook, '"Tout mon office": Body Politics and Family Dynamics in the Verse and Epîtres of Marguerite de Navarre', *Renaissance Quarterly* 54 (2001): 1108–41; surprising errors, though, can spoil her clever claims, and she underestimates Marguerite's public role. Middlebrook does not comment on the Evangelical-minded letter that Marguerite sent her brother with the gift of a 'David' (an implicit instruction?) or the king's more traditionally Catholic reply (an implicit rebuke?) that accompanied his return gift of a 'Saint Katherine' (Champollion-Figeac, *Poésies*, 63–72), traditionally an aid to childbirth. François offers Marguerite's baby an almost paternal welcome: come, sweet child, however little we sinners deserve you, and I will hold you in my arms.

16 Cf. Julia Kristeva, *Black Sun: Depression and Melancholia*, trans. Leon S. Roudiez (New York: Columbia University Press, 1989), 45, who notes the presence in female mourning/depression of 'the fantasy of a phallic mother'. Marguerite's 'phallic mother' was no fantasy, however, and the narrator of *Prisons* praises her strength. A 'denial of the father's function', as Kristeva puts it, was easier for Marguerite in that her actual father had died when she was a baby. For a related but distinct view see Lynn Enterline's provocative (if sometimes cryptic) *Tears of Narcissus: Melancholia and Masculinity in Early Modern Writing* (Stanford, Calif.: Stanford University Press, 1995). Does cross-gendering offer escape from narcissism? With a sex change, Narcissus might learn Echo's trick of ventriloquizing, and Echo might take a look in the pool. She would see nothing, of course, but for Marguerite discovering one's 'rien' is a grace.

17 Susan Snyder, 'Guilty Sisters: Marguerite de Navarre, Elizabeth of England, and the *Miroir de l'âme pécheresse*', *Renaissance Quarterly* 50 (1997): 443–58, finds some ambivalence in Marguerite's love for François. On Mary Sidney, see Margaret P. Hannay, *Philips's Phoenix* (Oxford: Oxford University Press, 1990). Elizabeth Harris Sagaser's conference paper, 'Elegiac Intimacy: Pembroke's "To the Angell spirit of the most excellent Sir Philip Sidney"', *The Sidney Journal* 23 (2006): 111–132, suggests that Mary Sidney's mourning for her brother

entailed gestures toward both merged identity (including collaboration in the 'world of words') and maternal loss, the poem being a paradoxical mix of humility and assertiveness. What Sagaser says fits well with Mary Moore's '"This Coupled Work": Mary Sidney's "To the Angell Spirit"', presented at the 2002 Renaissance Society of America conference. Jennifer Vaught reminds me of the likewise complex dynamics in Viola's love for and temporary replacement of her brother in Shakespeare's *Twelfth Night*.

18 What Sylvie L. F. Richards says of male voices in the *Heptaméron* and how they enable Marguerite's comments on the gender system is relevant: 'The separation of the authoritative voice into composite parts allows for a narration with a fractured time frame'; see her 'Politically Correct in the Feminine Voice', in *Imagining Culture: Essays in Early Modern History and Literature*, ed. Jonathan Hart (New York: Garland, 2001), 121–32.

19 Sheri Wolfe Valentine, 'Personal Ties: Book I of Marguerite de Navarre's *Les Prisons*', *Romance Languages Annual* 3 (1991): 126–31, hears anger in the narrator's disabused remarks on love and marriage. The poem 'contains evidence enough of bitterness long held back, at last allowed expression'; no wonder, she adds, that it was not printed. She does not discuss the deaths but does suggest that the narrator's gender helps Marguerite's make use of her Neoplatonism, for in that tradition the aspiring soul is that of a man (indeed; yet the souls themselves can be female).

20 Ferguson, *Mirroring Belief*, 118–19, notes that when visiting her captive brother, Marguerite had taken communion for him when he was too ill to do so.

21 Cottrell, *Grammar*, however, says that Ami comes to see diachrony itself as an illusion (292).

22 The unkind might also note the relevance of Kristeva's claim that depressive speech is 'repetitive, monotonous' (*Black Sun*, 43); Marguerite's *Prisons* is brilliantly conceived but does tend to expatiate where other poets might move on. For Marguerite, furthermore, as for many mystics, silence is less a failure of language than its triumph, the emptiness within the laurel wreath.

23 How speech relates to hiatus in *Les Prisons*, and to the split self that speaks in the voice of the other, is an interesting question. On rupture between human speech and God's Word, between language and Being, see Jan Miernowski, 'La Parole entre l'Etre et le Néant: "Les Prisons" de Marguerite de Navarre aux limites de la poésie exégétique', *French Forum* 16 (1991): 261–84. Marguerite's narrator is one response to the dilemma Miernowski notes: 'La creature ne peut parler de sa propre voix' (the creature cannot speak in its own voice), for speech presupposes being, and being is from God. By ventriloquizing a male voice in so intimate a poem (a voice unlike the fictions in the *Heptaméron* or the persons in her drama), Marguerite separates her voice from herself, dis-*owns* it.

24 Cottrell, *Grammar*, says that 'The seeming reversal of roles in *Les Prisons* is an illusion that disappears if we examine the functions that Marguerite assigns Amy and Amye within the text' (249). Amie is not a Beatrice, he adds, because Ami has the authority, which as usual is male.

25 Although he never mentions Marguerite, the Lacanian arguments of Bruce Thomas Boehrer's *Monarchy and Incest in Renaissance England: Literature, Culture, Kinship, and Kingship* (Philadelphia: University of Pennsylvania Press, 1992) are suggestive.
26 On Marguerite's Platonism see, e.g., George Mallary Masters, 'Marguerite de Navarre's "Prisons"', *Renaissance Papers* (1973): 11–21.
27 For a complaint to this effect (and the problem it causes in studying Renaissance magic), see D. P. Walker, 'Ficino's *Spiritus* and Music', in *Music, Spirit and Language in the Renaissance*, ed. Penelope Gouk (London: Variorum Reprints, 1985), 146–50.
28 G. M. Masters exploits Jungian theory in 'La Libération des prisons structurées: Les Prisons de Marguerite de Navarre', in *International Colloquium Celebrating the 500th Anniversary of the Birth of Marguerite de Navarre*, ed. Regine Reynolds-Cornell (Birmingham, Ala.: Summa, 1995), 111–22. For more on the Androgyne and the union of Rien and Tout, see Matthew Morris, 'Diotima Liberata', 53–61 in the same volume.

Part IV

Italy, France, England

10

Translatio lupae: Du Bellay's Roman whore goes north

In 1609 Gervase Markham, England's leading authority on horses, Sir John Harington's cousin, and not a truly bad poet, invited readers of *The Famous Whore* to give the prostitute 'a kind welcome out of Italy'. According to the headnote of this long poem, the elderly woman who here makes her 'lamentable complaint' was 'Paulina the famous Roman Curtezan, sometimes M[istress] unto the great Cardinal Hypolito of Est'. Since Markham seems so confidently to direct our eyes to Rome, it is understandable both that the entry on him in the *Dictionary of National Biography* posits an unknown Italian model and that neither the modern bibliography of his works nor the revised *Short Title Catalogue* can identify his source.[1] In fact, Markham's work is a fairly close imitation of Joachim Du Bellay's 'Vieille courtisanne', first published in 1558 as part of a collection somewhat misleadingly entitled *Divers jeux rustiques*. That same year a printer in Lyons, Nicolas Edoard, produced a probably unauthorized edition that he called *La Courtisane romaine*, adding commentary and a long note on how this 'plaisant et delectable' poem is 'tresutile ... à l'un et l'autre sexe'. In this 'moral miroir', he says, we may see 'l'instable estat' of those who from lust, avarice, laziness, gluttony, or vainglory sell their flesh and blood.[2] While reading these lines, adolescents will be warned by the 'sage Calypsonne' herself (wording that recalls the ancient association of prostitutes with the sirens and nymphs who delay men on life's epic pilgrimage). It is not clear, says Du Bellay's modern editor Henri Chamard, that Edoard knew the name of his Roman courtesan's creator. Did Markham? His phrase 'the famous Roman Curtezan' and a few details in the text faintly suggest that he used the Lyons edition, so, although Du Bellay's poem was published a number of times during the sixteenth century, sometimes together with Aretino's dialogues and *La Celestina*, Markham may not have known who wrote the original.[3] He worked from a French text, to be sure, but his fascination with Roman lifestyles of the once rich and infamous may have encouraged him to imagine an Italian source for his own model.

The *Famous Whore* is a translation punctuated by passages of expatiation or commentary in which Markham elaborates Du Bellay's meaning and alters his tone, moralizing overtly where his original prefers irony and implication, crowding in corroborative details that sometimes jostle aside the French poem's psychological insights to make room for travelogue or reportage, and nudging the verse a little closer to the mirror tradition and complaint as they had developed by the very late sixteenth century. Didacticism and information now further obscure Du Bellay's already half-hidden meditation on Rome, empire, and epic. The result is no masterpiece of narrative structure or compassionate analysis, but Markham's always competent and sometimes sharply energetic lines are certainly readable as a detailed if unsalacious description of a prostitute's career, a sort of chastened and univocal cousin of the dialogues of Aretino (to which, of course, Du Bellay himself was indebted). There is nothing here like Nashe's brilliantly obscene if less educational *Choice of valentines*; a review board would rate this performance PG – it entangles the reader in adult situations, but it proffers no nudity and its vocabulary is embarrassing only because of the knowledge it assumes the reader has picked up somewhere.[4] Nevertheless, the poem's attitudes toward women and sexuality should intrigue a variety of readers, as should the anti-Italian additions and marginalia.

Moreover, the poem comes near the end of one line of narrative poetry (after the sensuous and delicately witty epyllion had largely given way to a clearer and more satirical tonality, to put the matter oversimply); it both extends and in certain ways retracts that line.[5] The complaints written by William Baldwin's crowd of mirror-holders for Magistrates in the 1550s and by their later imitators, although still a popular and even growing collection in 1609, had been joined in the 1590s by poems like Daniel's *Rosamond* and Shakespeare's *Lucrece*, works that recount some sexual degradation with a luxury not found in, say, Churchyard's first *Shores Wife* (in the 1563 *Mirror for Magistrates*) and that belong to a fashion showing signs of exhaustion – at least among good poets – by the time Markham published his own contribution to the genre. His prostituted and urban street-wise speaker suits a darker and more cynical Jacobean tone, even though some of what she says recalls the more languid and embroidered anguish of Elizabethan courtesans repenting the doomed glory of life spent pleasing the sexual taste of kings.

No royal mistress, although at first no mere whore, 'Paulina' would have found plenty of company in the England of 1609, for the Jacobean stage had seen a population explosion of bawds, tarts, and courtesans, as though to signal the end of Diana's reign in 1603.[6] Markham must have sensed that the time was right for his translation: fashion in erotic poetry had a few years earlier shifted from the sometimes quiet wit and the metaphoric intensity of the Elizabethan sonnet sequence or epyllion to the flashily problematic cynicism of Marston and his like, while increased numbers of Kate Keepdowns and Doll Commons were entertaining theatre-goers. And yet the poem is not in its origin a late complaint, a satirical revision downward to the gutter from the palaces of Lucrece, Elstred, and Rosamond. It is not a narrative analogue to the dramatic explorations of prostitution by Middleton, Dekker, and others. For Markham's model had been there since the time of the first *Mirror for Magistrates*. In fact, the changes Markham makes in the whore's story are gently retrogressive, as though the complaints of Baldwin's day were exerting a slight magnetic attraction, reinforced by that of Daniel, Lodge, Chute, Drayton, Shakespeare, and others who wrote of women's sexual misconduct, voluntary or forced. Markham's Jacobean poem thus translates a work from a much earlier decade, one that saw the start of the Elizabethan complaint tradition, and his own poem is itself modified by that tradition. In the remainder of this essay I shall first describe the poem Markham read and apparently enjoyed (if seeing opportunities for revision) and then explore what the English text does to the French. Markham's translation may not be self-aware enough to deserve the currently fashionable and useful terms 'intertextuality' or *imitatio*; it does show one not unintelligent imagination at work responding to a greater poet during the later stages of a cultural moment when thoughts about degraded cities or empires mixed with those concerning women's bodies in a particularly intense and poignant manner.

If, as is by no means certain, Markham read 'La vieille courtisanne' in its original setting he would have noticed that it is a long climax to and an extended commentary on two preceding poems translated from the neo-Latin verses of Du Bellay's friend Pierre Gillebert (*Divers jeux*, 36 and 37). Since the Latin poems are now lost, it is impossible to know how closely Du Bellay followed them. It is quite clear, however, that passages in the French verse relate ironically to other moments in the poetry that Du Bellay wrote during or just after his visit to Rome. The first, 'La courtisanne repentie', bids farewell to the 'faulx plaisirs de Venus', to all the paraphernalia and techniques of her former trade, to the 'Troppeau romain, qui la grand' Louve suit' – that is, followers of the wolf who, patriotic legend said, suckled Romulus and Remus but who others said was in fact a lactating adulteress the local shepherds called by the Roman slang term for whore, 'lupa', or she-wolf.[7] (The twins' mother, Ilia, identified the father as Mars, who she said begot the boys while raping her; the brothers showed their paternity and foreshadowed the city's civil wars by their fratricidal dispute, soaking the very foundations of Rome with blood.) So now good-bye make-up, aphrodisiacs, drugs, deodorants, lutes, Petrarch and Ariosto, the open window, the little signs of invitation, the silk dresses and fancy jewels.

In 'La contre-repentie', second thoughts urge the courtesan once more wolfwards. Welcome back liberty and the old fire. If life brings uncertainty and pain, who can forbid love? So rest well in the Elysian Fields under urns of lilies and red roses, you ancients who deified Venus, leader of our troop. No wonder the Romans, descended from Venus, immortalized the courtesan Flora with games in her honour and celebrated Ilia. But why has Pope Paul IV enacted his new law expelling prostitutes? He should realize that only through us can Rome regain its lost greatness; we are what remains of that ruined magnificence:

> Des monuments par le temps devorez
> Nous sommes seuls ornemens demeurez,
> Seuls ornemens de l'antique memoire,
> Et de ce lieu la renaissante gloire.
> Rome, qui sceus tout le monde domter,
> Tu le peulx bien encores surmonter
> Par le moyen des armes Cypriennes,
> Et regaingner tes palmes anciennes. (11.69–76)

In his *Antiquitez*, and with a related vocabulary, Du Bellay makes a similar claim for Roman texts, the 'brave writings' as Spenser called them in his translation (*Ruines of Rome*, 5). Here the verse suggests that Rome survives not in books read around the world but in the trade and the contagious diseases generated by Flora's heirs: a *translatio morbi*. So farewell to unnatural prayers, cells, silence, and solitary nights; the courtesan re-enlists 'aux guerres amoureuses', the only kind, Du Bellay implies, through which Rome can now conquer other nations. So much for the imperial tradition and epic poetry, although from another point of view this is Venus' final triumph over her rival Juno; her Roman descendants now have their priorities straight.[8]

It is in this context that Du Bellay offers his long sequel. Old, poor, and ill, the courtesan once more repents, hoping that her 'complainte vaine' will give exemplary warning and thus provide some restitution. So she tells how, spoiled by an immodest mother, seduced by a servant, and sold to a series of lovers (always 'vierge comme devant'), she is eventually bought by a great prelate for a high price – after all, she is a virgin once more. He first teaches her the arts that make the courtesan ('Toucher le luth, et proprement parler', to dress well, to improve beauty with artifice) and then palms her off on a youth unlearned in Rome's false subtleties ('peu rusé aux finesses de Rome'), assuring him of her wealth, family and, of course, chastity. After discovering her past, the young husband tames and then robs her. When he is killed after joining the army, the desperate widow sets herself up in business and soon is famous throughout Rome. She is very good at her job, leading each client to think himself her chief love. Without appearing mercenary, she knows how to extract money by announcing that she is to be married, to be a nun, to go to Venice, to have a baby, is feeling sick. It is not her concern if young men pauperize themselves to give her jewels, perfumes, dresses, soap, make-up, mirrors, pictures, coaches, masks. When she gets flesh from the butcher she pays for it with her own ('Affreux calembour', says Du Bellay's editor V.-L. Saulnier) and banks what she saves. She takes care of herself, avoiding Spanish clients for the 'liberal François', drinking little, eating soberly, behaving herself in public, using 'honneste' speech, smelling good, and postponing company until she has put on her face. With friends in high places, she fears no prison and even avoids taxes, although she does have to put up with lovers' jealousy, unwashed armpits, bad breath, fear of the pox, and time lost fussing with her hair.

Hearing a sermon, she repents (a cross-reference to the 'Courtisanne repentie'), but because her true will is unchanged she relapses with athletic enthusiasm. Now she sleeps with the likes of Rome's executioner (*carnifex*, 'fleshmaker', in Latin, as Du Bellay of course knew and perhaps wants us to remember, so that in his way the man parallels the butcher who figures earlier in the whore's career), and now no paint can hide her years and disease. Still, she has her charms, her chess and primero, her lute to which she sings Petrarch like an angel, and she can ride through the streets of Rome as fiercely proud as Ariosto's Bradamante. Her house is a school of 'honnesteté, où il falloit venir / Pour bien sçavoir dames entretenir'. In this 'school' are found 'bons mots' and laughter; there, even fools try to speak well. They had better read allegory well, too, for her door has on it the golden shower of Danae, 'Voulant par là honnestement monstrer / Que par l'or seul on y pouvoit entrer.'[9] Du Bellay's sly implication is that such clever indirection is 'honneste' in Rome; the sign that invites guests to pause and interpret is itself a model of translation, an initial lesson in elegant mendacity that revises the house from the 'brothel' some might call it into the school of social wit the courtesan claims it to be. There may even be an anatomical hint, as well: the shameless gold-demanding passage-way leads up to a pleasure-filled house or *mons veneris*.

But now the courtesan falls in love, raging though Rome like a Maenad, even consulting a sorceress. In vain. Despite a love potion that would send Macbeth's witches staggering off the stage in nausea, and despite a steady downpour of gifts (no Danae he), the young man is cold. Now old, rheumy, without taste, voice, or repartee, she can only cough and spit, earning a little by needlework, laundering, and peddling. Oh, how am I changed, she says, from that which I was – a paraphrase, as Edoard points out, of Virgil's 'quantum mutatus ab illo / Hectore', and thus one more step in the persistent subversion of Roman epic.[10] Scorned, she remembers the crowds of those who sought her and frets over the new laws chasing whores from

Rome. Who will visit the city? Without whores, men will simply use boys. Alas for Rome – spoiled by civil strife, it regrets its vanished freedoms even more than its 'palais antiques, / Dont nous voyons les poudreuses reliques'. (Du Bellay's language echoes *Songe* X and the prefatory poem to the king, once more juxtaposing his courtesan poetry to his ambiguous lament for ancient Rome.) Worst of all, the courtesan has a daughter and can only dread the child's future. The girl, more beloved to her mother than her eyes (a cliché from Catullus), will be prey to a mere artisan, losing the flower of her virginity and destroying her mother's 'baston de vieillesse'. So in her daughter is her own youthful pain reborn. She has now finished – would her life would end too.

As Du Bellay's little gestures towards his Roman poetry indicate, his courtesan's monologue inscribes, presumably without her awareness (that is to say, her *voice* seems not to include the ironies her *language* suggests), a fairly savage comment on Roman history. Her complaint sets up an association between her autobiography and a city founded in blood by a pair who drew life from an adulteress and milk from a shewolf/whore, a city later torn by civil strife and swollen with pride, a city now sunk into a degradation best symbolized by the arrogant courtesans Du Bellay also describes in his *Regrets*. The association relies on an ancient equation between female body and city that Du Bellay was of course not the first to exploit; indeed, his *Antiquitez* has been plausibly read as displaced Petrarchan poetry that substitutes Rome for the unobtainable Laura: in both cases the poetry grows from absence and loss, although Du Bellay more harshly settles part of the blame for that loss upon the very object of his ambivalent desire.[11] Nor was Du Bellay alone in connecting a ruined woman to the ruins of a specifically ancestral city, for behind the ruins of Rome, city of Ilia and a lupa's nurselings, lie the ashes of Ilium, its topless towers burnt to retrieve an adulteress.[12] And from Troy come modern dynasties (or so a poet may politely agree, especially if his friend Ronsard contemplates writing the *Franciade*). Such a legend is the stuff out of which a modern dynastic epic could be made, but the same legend allows for equally forceful and satirical dissent from the epic imagination. In her own way, the Roman courtesan embodies a *recusatio* even more compelling than those Du Bellay attached to the *Regrets* to explain his refusal to write like Ronsard.

The possibilities for irony in such a context are virtually limitless. Marlowe was to have his Leander argue that 'Who builds a castle and rams up the gate / Shall see it ruinous and desolate'. The whore's gate is open to all – to all who rain gold like the Jove whom Ronsard told Cassandre he would like to become (*Amours* I, 20). Her walls rot anyway. So much for plucking the roses of life: time has eaten her as it ate ancient Rome, as it eats everything. Her autobiography is thus also an archaeology, a restorative performance not wholly unlike that which Du Bellay enacts in the *Antiquitez* when summoning the shades of Rome from the darkness beneath, just as scholars and antiquarians had been bringing texts and stones to light.[13] And here too we see exhumed not only lost glory but past grief and sin. This archaeologist of the self turns up little to be proud of, although what she shows is a 'moniment' in at least one Elizabethan sense: a warning, or, as Edoard said, a mirror; she herself sees it as restitution, a commemorative and monitory act that another courtesan, Rosamond, told Samuel Daniel might 'redeem the time' lost to moral and physical decay.

Such restitution can only be individual, furthermore, for the courtesan's daughter will probably follow her mother into moral ruin. To see whores as matrilineal was a common way to intensify the pathos, satire, or anxious and even guilty anger with which Renaissance prostitution was treated. Aretino provided a model, and George Buchanan's verses on whores (one of them, Elegy 3, an ironic defence of bawds doubtless known to Du Bellay) stress their tainted origins.[14] This negative version of the Persephone legend (get down there in the dirt, daughter; at least you'll pick up some gold and jewels from the king of the muck) is all the more hateful and yet oddly enticing, I suspect, because of its exclusion of men. Perhaps just because of male authors' uneasy awareness that men after all play a role in prostitution, the imagined feminine continuity writes out the masculine, suggesting a secret tradition handed down from mother to daughter and now revealed by the likes of Aretino as though he were reporting on some shabby but still potent Eleusinian mystery. At once exploiting and rejecting this sexually intriguing tradition, Du Bellay makes his own courtesan distraught to see her daughter repeating her own life's pattern.

Behind this sad prospect may lie another comment on Imperial cycles of corruption and descent. The *imperium* has moved elsewhere, but here in Rome the old generates a repetition of itself; the child, the new life, is already launched on the downward path in this perpetually falling and flesh-selling City of Man. In this regard, too, the 'Vieille courtisanne' parallels Du Bellay's 'Songe'. As in those visions of earthly extension and collapse, soaring structure and decay, so here time merely pulls down the whore's pyramid of wealth and celebrity back to the earth whose intestines once hid the gold and whose streets echo with no lasting rumours or fame. There is a further complexity here, for her career, like Rome's, shows the inevitability of metamorphosis. Ovid was right and Virgil wrong: there is no endless empire and our moments hasten to their end like ocean waves. And yet, again like Rome, the courtesan is unable to mutate into true newness, and this despite a hopeful period when she (like Rome) heard a Word that nearly reformed her. Like the solipsistic city of the *Antiquitez*, resembling only itself, conquering itself, being the whole world to itself, the whore is promiscuous without sharing, giving only through futile passion for what she cannot and should not have. She can fornicate but she cannot well nor truly marry. And she and Rome both bring moral and worldly ruin on themselves, even if their physical decay is the work of time. Her very age signifies her refusal to put on the new woman. She now suits her city: fallen, nostalgic, mistress to no one, and the mother of a daughter whose imitation of her source suggests not *translatio* but false promise.

'La Vieille Courtisanne' is, I have suggested, an ironic commentary on Du Bellay's own Roman poetry, echoing its vocabulary and deepening the irony through phrases drawn from Roman authors. But Du Bellay may also encourage us to remember very different texts, texts to which his *Antiquitez* and 'Songe' also point, if never obviously, and in which city harlots are threatened with the destitution and ruin we see in this whore of Rome. To Isaiah, Tyre is not only a relapsed and neglected harlot but, like Du Bellay's, a musician: 'Take an harpe, and go about the citie: (thou harlot that hast bene forgotten) make swete melodie, sing mo songs that thou maiest be remembred' (23:16). In Lamentations, too, errant Jerusalem could be Du Bellay's courtesan, with 'filthines ... in her skirtes', a 'menstrous woman' [and hence 'unclean'], sneered at by passers-by, who in regret 'sigheth and turneth backewarde' (Lam. 1:9, 17; 2:15). Elsewhere God tells her, 'Thogh thou clothes thy self with skarlet, thogh thou deckest thee with ornaments of golde, thogh thou paintest thy face with colours, yet shalt thou trimme thy selfe in vaine: for thy lovers wil abhorre thee ... O daughter of my people, gird thee with sackecloth, and wallowe thy self in the ashes' (Jer. 4:30, 6:26; cf. Hosea). One may hope that Du Bellay's courtesan is like this whorish wife – adulterous, but welcome back if she will turn to her true husband. It seems likely, though, that in the interstices of his Roman whore's complaint lie hints of an Augustinian subtext: although the courtesan compares herself to Bradamante, as she rides boldly through the streets of Rome there is also a whiff, here and in the *Regrets*, of that other whore on her seven-headed beast, the one who, although called the Whore of Babylon, was even by Catholics often thought to figure forth the seven-hilled city.

Markham could have pushed his translation in just such a direction; especially so soon after the Gunpowder Plot, many writers would have found Du Bellay's half-hidden invitation to allegorize his whore as Rome impossible to refuse. After all, as an old palindrome insisted, Rome is the greatest love: *Roma summus amor*. As long ago as the 1540s the Protestant John Bale, who rejoiced scoffingly in Rome's derivation from 'a professed nonne to Venus' and its debt to a harlot nicknamed 'Lupa', had explained how this half-magical phrase is in a significantly perverted way true: 'If ye spell Roma backwarde, ye shall fynde it love in this prodygyouse kynde, for it is preposterous *amor*, a love out of order or a love agaynst kynde';

hence the propensity of English Catholics to play the sodomite or whoremaster.[15] More recently, one J. Baxter had advanced his own arguments for Rome's whorishness by asking in his *Toile for two-legged foxes* (1600), 'Roma quid est? amor est. Qualis? praeposterous' (H5). Paulina could have been a new Duessa, or at least a little more like the villainess of Dekker's *Whore of Babylon* (1607), a play treating the 'continual blody strategems, of that Purple whore of Roome' against England's Fairy Queen, Titania.[16]

Or, if such a revision seemed too polemical and 'Puritan', Du Bellay's perception of a young girl's limited choices in a predatory society might have encouraged Markham to treat Paulina with the amused tolerance bawds and whores were on occasion finding in the theatre. On the other hand, by elaborating on her disease and sorcery he could have pushed his translation closer to a series of poems that extends back at least to Horace in which old women are treated with fear, contempt, and disgust.[17] He could also have more energetically followed Daniel or Shakespeare, for example, who used the complaint not only to address feminine desire, anxiety, or regret but also to explore more fully than Du Bellay (if in a vocabulary learned partly from him or Spenser) the analogies between cities prey to time, pride, or war and female bodies lacerated by age or sexual violation.[18] All these possibilities lie in Du Bellay's poem and all survive the transition to English. None is privileged.

Instead, Markham edges his version closer to the *Mirror for Magistrates* tradition (perhaps encouraged by Edoard's reading), raising his courtesan somewhat in social origin so she might fall further and allowing her to recite some redeeming exhortations. All through the text, in fact, Markham adds didactic exclamations and summations. Since he puts them into the mouth of his courtesan, she thereby acquires an insight that modifies Du Bellay's satirical implications, to say nothing of his subtlety: in Du Bellay's world, moral comprehension is not so easily come by, nor is it so glibly expressed. The result is a mixture of two mirror traditions: early Elizabethan gnomic moralizing after a fall and later Elizabethan analytic reflection (still condemnatory but sympathetic) on female sexual disarray. The two traditions had always overlapped, but Daniel, Drayton, Lodge, Chute, and Shakespeare, whose Lucrece is at least ostensibly free from blame, had to a large extent replaced finger-wagging and head-shaking with psychological anatomy and elegiac pathos. Yet Markham's changes are not altogether reactionary, for if his smugly closed couplets suggest a closed morality, a ponderous but packed and endstopped sententiousness, they also often anticipate the better expressed if still oft-thought commonplaces of heroic couplets yet to come.

Markham's most obvious changes, however, are his conversion of a nameless courtesan into Paulina, the identification of her 'prelate' friend as the cardinal Hypolito of Este, and the addition of marginal comments with more information on Italy, most of it bad news. The prelate in question cannot have been Hypolito, although that loathsome cleric was a notorious womanizer, for the dates do not work out. I do not know the source of Markham's additions on the prostitution business and perhaps, after all, he spoke from the personal experience of himself or his friends. What is certain is the shift from an anonymity that allows the reader more room for symbolic projection and naming *ad libitum* to a specificity that makes Markham's poem closer both to the complaints by known heroines and to travellers' accounts of sin's capital like, say, Anthony Munday's 1582 description of Rome. Markham's poem thus becomes more 'historical' than Du Bellay's even as its satirical relevance to Rome's larger history fades.[19]

Let me now run through some of the deflections that bring the courtesan's lament closer to a less ambiguous *de casibus* tradition, harden its ironies into a sterner if still sympathetic moralism, and reinforce, particularly in the margins, an already deep if somehow pleasurable anxiety about what awaits the innocent Englishman should he venture south of the Alps.

Although following Du Bellay closely, Markham's opening lines glance at a familiar company of the fallen victims of pride, chance, time, and misplaced desire. It is his courtesan, for instance, who worries about reputation. Du Bellay's old woman grieves for the 'mal duquel je suis atteinte', Paulina for the 'deepe scars which on my fame remain'. Fame, of course, was a matter of no small interest to Du Bellay and indeed to all mankind; including Dante's damned and the *Mirror*'s dead, but the particular relation of female sexual errancy and reputation stimulated in English writers a complex of thoughts touching also on time, devouring mouths, burial, earth, and cities. Daniel's Rosamond, like Du Bellay (and Spenser) meditating on Rome, hopes that, even if once proud and sinful, she will not forever lie like a ruined city beyond the glare of memory, her name unconjured by poets from the earthy dark where time stores the relics of its meals (see, e.g., *Rosamond*, 705–21). But does sexual sin deserve fame? To emerge from the past like the ashy ghosts of Rome might merely reopen to sight the wounds that caused the 'scars' of notoriety. Paulina's archaeology, in other words, bears with it the same ambivalence Daniel and others imagined for the damaged woman they resurrected, an ambivalence analogous to the contradictory feelings that shaped Du Bellay's visions of ancient Rome and that a number of English writers, too, showed in their mixed admiration and repulsion toward that city. So powerful was the set of associations between a potentially resurgent empire and a buried but demanding body or voice, in fact, that to assault whoredom could invite exorcising just this myth of fame-hungry but shame-fearing revival. Preaching just a few years after Markham wrote, Thomas Adams threatened whores with what cities and the proud fear most – being forgotten – and does so in a vocabulary familiar from poets who, like Du Bellay or Daniel, claimed to be urging lost names back into the light: 'This is the mischiefe, which sinne in generall, as whoredome in particular, workes to the name; a rotten reputation, an infamous fame, a reproach for a report: that their silent memories are never conjured up from the grave of oblivion, but … for their own disgrace…. It were well for them, if Time, which unnaturally devoures his owne brood, could as well still their mention, as it hath staid their motion: or that their memoriall might not survive their funerall' (*The divells banket*, 1614, X2–X2v). Adams adds that whores can cause inflammations, plague, and haemorrhoids; they are, he says, more merciless than the Spanish Armada (X3v–X4), that now reversed monstrosity that the age's polemic sometimes equated with fallen giants and Roman pyramids.

Du Bellay's courtesan hopes that the reader will profit from her lamentation and so does Paulina; but the latter holds the usual glass: 'My woes to others may as myrrors stand, / And my life give example to our land' (A4). Typically, Markham then adds useful reflection:

> That by my wretched hap they may beware:
> Prevention ever should precede our care;
> And this is all the good my fate can tell,
> To shew to beauties haires how beauty fell.

Note also, besides the pun on 'hair', the mirror tradition's old uncertainty about what causes a 'fall': 'hap', fate, or fault. And the courtesan now has a slightly higher origin in 'ancient worthy blood'. Markham, unlike Du Bellay, makes her explicitly fatherless, perhaps to explain how 'A wanton mother breeds a daughter light' (or as Edoard's marginal comment puts it, 'Fille suit mere'; cf. Ezekiel 16:44). There is no paternal hand to keep the family under control. The additions suggest such concern, for when the girl prostitutes herself to 'one of the meanest and basest drudges of her mothers house', the result of a young life spent too much in mirth, idleness, and 'Garments as rich as star-light', of allowing the 'glutton soule' to be a 'slave unto my sence', Markham elaborates on the danger of bad governance and uppity servants: 'Fit time and place makes peasants apt to dare.' (Compare Edoard's margin: 'Serviteurs larrons d'honneur domestic.')

Du Bellay's courtesan is already a Roman, but Paulina travels from Fano (famous for lovely women, reports the margin) into Rome's lethal interior, a spatial movement with more resonance in England than in urbanized Italy. Markham is particularly taken by the courtesan's amazingly regenerative virginity, for she says dryly that after being sold to 'sundry peares' she 'still returned as pure as when I came. / As if my Hydra maiden head had sprung, / And by the losse of one, two new begunne' (B1v).[20] Now she is bought by the cardinal, and Markham adds some Protestant thoughts on how the clergy ('you Churchmirours') should set a good example and might manage this better if allowed to marry (B2). Even the oldest bawds look to Paulina in admiration, although in retrospect she now exclaims, in depressing lines not derived from Du Bellay and emphasized by quotation marks in the margin:

> O liberty thou serpent subtil vile,
> How many of my sex dost thou beguile!
> Thou mak'st us seeke the soveraignty of will,
> And of our selves to be selfe monarchs still.
> When we so vaine are and unreasonable,
> As our owne selves to rule we are not able.
> Wise are wee when we in obedience stand,
> And best we rule when others us command. (B3)

Indeed, as though to show again the value of male guidance, Markham makes the courtesan's young husband a little kinder. Despite this patriarchal affirmation, though, he constructs for Paulina, now bereft of her cardinal and (Markham's own touch) her mother, a vigorous denunciation of men that invites at least a moment of imaginative sympathy:

> O cruell men, worse then the Crocodile,
> Bred of the poisonous slime of muddy Nile;
> You raile on us poore women, and our kind,
> Calling us false unconstant as the wind:
> And yet theres none so wavering as your selves,
> Which strikes our ships gainst sorrowes swallowing shelves.
> You say that wee are full of all deceipt,
> When you alone does us of glory cheate,
> Our faultes are veniall of simplicity,
> But yours proceede of inward villanie.
> Wast not enough, I bore my husbands blowes,
> And mixt his sullen frownes with greater woes?
> But he must take all the world gave to me,
> And leave me nought but hatefull beggerie?
> May heavens worst plague his ingrav'd bones torment,
> And all besides that hold his president.

Her final wish, though, provokes sharp marginal comment: 'A right passion of a woman and it is called amongst the Italians a curtezans blessing' (B4v–C1).

The story continues, the margins sometimes exclaiming at her technique: 'Another trick of an Italian Curtezan to force liberalitie from her favorites' (C1), and 'A common trick of such curtezans as are most skilful in their trade' (C1v). Markham keeps Du Bellay's pun on her selling her own flesh to the butcher to pay for his, and he adds in words that stress not simply her wickedness but her decline, 'Such was my base and more then muddie minde, / That I forgot myselfe and staind my kinde' (C3). As in Du Bellay, more money is to be had from the French than from the Spanish ('For all the gentlemen of that brave nation, / Are curteous, free, and of a courtly fashion'). In the absence of an acknowledged French author, some of the irony is lost, but in recompense the margin spells out the trouble with the Spanish from a whore's point of view: 'The Spaniard is a right bragadochio, and nothing so liberall as the French man amongst curtezans.'

Markham also elaborates on the courtesan's life, somewhat curiously adding as a further example of ill-gotten luxury her Italian nightgowns – doubtless a sign of elegance and success if worn in England, but hardly remarkable in Rome. Paulina reads, but reads the wrong books, for she 'knew all Aretine by rot / And had him read and in acquaintance got, / So that his booke-rules I could well discover / To every ignorant, yet wanton lover' (C4v). The margin explains: 'Aretine a most famous impudent wicked Italian Poet, who publisht certain strange, and most immodest rules for lust.' Thus taught, Paulina can follow the old advice to be lady when vertical and a harlot when not. Markham almost captures Du Bellay's compression, translating 'rien qu'honneur ne sortoit de ma bouche: / Sage au parler, et follastre à la couche' as 'Abroad by wisdomes rule my course was led, / And lovely I could wantonize in bed' (D1). Du Bellay's courtesan herself moralizes a little at this point, as anyone would, but by expanding the reflections, Markham blunts their point. 'Tant la vertu plaist en celles qui l'ont, / Si-non au cueur, pour le moins sur le front' (251–52) becomes:

> Such vertue is in vertue, where t'is plac't,
> That all desire with her beames to be grac't:
> Which thogh not in their inward harts doth grow,
> Yet outwardly thei'le give thereof a show. (D1v)

Prudence gives mobility and the margin tells why this is noteworthy: 'Although it be lawfull for curtezans to walke abroad in the day time, yet in the night they may not, unlesse they have some extraordinary warrant for the same.'

Seven years of pleasure pass, if, says Du Bellay's courtesan sadly, 'plaisir fault nommer / Un peu de doulx meslé de tant d'amer'. As Saulnier remarks, 'Notre courtisane pétrarquise'. Either Markham knew this and found it out of key where placed, or else this touch of mockery got by him (unlike Du Bellay, he had not had to forget the art of Petrarquizing), so Paulina merely says, 'if I may that call / Pleasure which hath no pleasing thought at all' (D1v). The distress is the same for her as for her model: the loss of a coherent identity after having 'soubmis mes membres ehontez / A l'appétit de tant de voluntez'. But Paulina, reluctant self-fashioner, feels a keener psychological revulsion at being 'forc't gainst nature and gainst kinde, / New to create my selfe to every minde' (D2). Both courtesans fear disease; Du Bellay lists only two of these, the pox and the 'pellarelle', a symptom of syphilis, but Markham afflicts Paulina with the risk of the 'french disease', the 'Leprous curelesse skale, / The Gonorea or the sharp Sarpego, / The Pellirigo and the Malcaduco' (D2).

Sensibly, Paulina repents, and the margin clarifies the social context: 'The curtezans & Jewes in Rome are forced once or twice a weeke every lent to heare certaine sermons, the one at S. Ambrose, the other at La Trinita, in which they disswade and dehort, both the one and the other from their bad lives, and worse religion, & many times divers of both of these kinds are converted & become honest women and good christians' (D2v). But 'Soule-sick to see my goods and riches waste' (D3), a shabbiness Du Bellay spares her model, Paulina sinks back into the old delights, including poetry: 'Was never Lady yet that could rehearse / So much as I of learned Pet[r]arcks verse.' According to Markham, 'This Poet many Italians both men and women have at their fingers ends, singing most of his sonnets, as they go openly in the streets' (D3v). Like her original, Paulina also knows Ariosto (so did Markham, who translated Desportes' expansion of Rodomont's final battle), for besides strolling through the streets of Rome dressed like a man she mounts a 'warlike courser, proud as ire, / With plumed crest, and eies that sparkled fire', and so 'as proudly up and downe did ride, / As faire Marfysa, or Rogeroes bride' (D4).

Fascinated by Paulina's sexual trickery, Markham expands this section. He also adds marginal matter on the men a typical courtesan keeps, such as the 'Bravo', who 'is her champion & swaggereth everywhere in her behalfe, & in all her quarrels, seeketh to defend her small honour with his no little shame', and the 'Bello', a 'neat, spruce & well turned youth, on whom she commonly doateth, being mad for lust' (E1). As for what Du Bellay calls his courtesan's school of 'honesty', of wit, Markham drops that metaphor and adds one more suitable to his echoes of the *de casibus* mirror tradition: 'My house was like a Princes royall court.' Then, to render the place even more shocking and increase its sensuality along the lines of the Ovidian poetry he also remembers, Markham furnishes her chambers with that notoriously Italian product, dirty tapestries: 'Hangings of arras, or of needleworke, / In which did many a wanton story lurke' (E1). And he keeps Du Bellay's liminal lesson in allegory: 'And painted ore my gate, men might behold, / Joves stealing unto Dione in gold: / Which unchast moral ever seemd to say, / None entred there but with a golden key.' How 'la fille d'Acrise' has become Dione I do not know; in the Lyon edition she is called 'Dane corrompue par Jupiter en forme de pluye d'or.' Paulina is educated enough to sigh that 'those Saturnian daies are past and gone', an elegiac moment not in the French, but when she turns to her destructive passion for an indifferent youth, she compares herself to Medea running crazed through the streets, not to Du Bellay's Maenad. This confusion, like that between Danae and Dione, is surprising. Perhaps the printer misread or perhaps Markham preferred an angry witchqueen to a Bacchic madwoman (Du Bellay's own description recalls Dido, another pseudo-epic touch). In any case, the margin elucidates: 'The madde tricks which such foolish women that doate in love, will play, especially the Italians, no women in the world being like unto them to shew true passions' (E1v). Poor Paulina. In the French original she keeps the neighbours awake as she searches for the beloved who she fears is in another's arms; in the English version she is held prisoner by Markham's Petrarchist cliché, dreaming the youth into her own arms and awakening to find herself deluded.

What can she do? Consult a sorcerer. Du Bellay thus sets his whore in a cruel cultural and literary tradition that ties old and unattractive women to witchcraft; Paulina's potion may even recall cup-bearing biblical harlots. To Markham, though, her reasons are unmysterious and her action no symbol: 'It is a common course amongst Italian dames when they are in love and cannot obtain their desire to run to wise women, to sorcerers and such like to help them' (E1v). Such occult behaviour evidently intrigued him, though, for to her love potion he adds owl blood and 'the nostril-haires of cats' (E2). Narrative now ceases while the courtesan advises us to avoid foolish love, especially love for pretty young men like the one for whom she lost her fortune:

> Beware the Catamits, these gallant slaves,
> Who lie to swallow you, like open graves ...
> For sea-nymphs like, if you but heare them wooe you
> They first inchant, and after doe undoe you.[21]

Stick to cash:

> No friend is firme but riches, for they never
> Forsake their owners, but support them ever:
> Gold is to riveld age, the onely crutch,
> She that is wealthy, still is loved much. (E2v)

Du Bellay's Roman says she started her career when Leo XIII was pope, so she is now pushing sixty. She shows it. In the French version her eyes are hidden 'depeur de voir lejour'. In Markham's English they 'now inward sunke, lie coffind in their shame' (E3), an image of burial within the self closer to Daniel's 'Complaint of Rosamond' (cf. 670–72) and Shakespeare's sonnets, but also curiously reminiscent of the *Antiquitez*'s Rome, a once splendid town now withdrawn into its original matter. (Applying this thought to his own lady, Daniel warns the still fresh Delia that in Italy his 'eyes ...

/ Have seene those walles the which ambition reared, / To checke the world, how they intombd have lyen / Within themselves ...', no. 37.) And Markham, too, is struck by the pain of memory. He keeps Du Bellay's echo of Virgil's line on Hector, 'O que je suis differente de celle / Que j'estois lors' (501–02), and for once his own version tightens Du Bellay's connection between a fallen woman and a fallen structure:

> O what a hell is it unto my sence,
> When I but ponder on the difference,
> Betwixt my present state and former glory,
> And but recount the ruines of my story? (E3v)

The diction ('glory') and the mention of a narrative ('recount') echo the *Mirror*, and since Paulina has sat 'towred up in Princes state', spatially higher than where Du Bellay situates her, she can now fall like one of the little kings in older pictures of Fortuna's wheel. Markham has understood Du Bellay's image of ruin, but he nudges its implications away from urban and cultural mutability and toward a more vertical and individually political tumble. In the poetry's inner life, so to speak, the Whore of Babylon residing in Virgil's city is now a shadier Shore's Wife.

Now come grief for her daughter and anger at papal edicts against prostitution. Markham comments in the margin that 'Shee was in hope her yong daughter might have maintained her by her former trade, but it fell out otherwise' (E4; the margin also identifies the various popes). The note suggests that the daughter will be unable to follow her mother's career, but the poetry itself is less certain and Markham's running commentary on Italian habits offers scant hope of reform. In any case the daughter is doomed to defloration by a mere artisan, so the 'torments' of the mother now 'Renew in her that should be all my blisse' (F1v). Markham keeps Du Bellay's satirical argument that Rome needs whores, faced otherwise with depopulation or homosexuality ('horrid, damn'd the spewe of time'), and he also preserves both the mischievous echo of Cicero ('O times, O manners, O unluckie age, / O Rome once master, now worse then a page!') and the evocation of the city's 'antient monuments which now to dust / Are turnd' (F1).[22] Soon Du Bellay stops his poem; his courtesan weeps and asks to die but gives us no concluding *significatio*. Like her city she persists in that which flows (cf. *Antiquitez*, 3). Markham could not allow the reader to depart unedified or his poem to halt unsummarized. Paulina says to her fellow courtesans, just as a fallen king might say to his fellow statesmen, 'Then you faire creatures of my sister-hoode, / I wish this my discourse may do you good' (F1v). The admonitions sit uneasily after the naughty paradoxes a few lines earlier, but her remarks do suit Du Bellay's implications concerning time, origins, and fame:

> Beware in time, give over whilst you may,
> Night will aproach, how long so ere is day.
> Ill gotten goods are seldome long enjoid,
> And ill foundations quickly are destroid ...
> Remember that a spotlesse youth still beares,
> The noble markes of honourable yeares ...
> When we are dead we leave behind our shame,
> And cary with us nought but our good name. (F2)

Markham's conclusion typifies his revision of Du Bellay. While remaining true to some of his model's deeper concerns, he makes his courtesan talk more like Elstred or Rosamond on the dangers of misdirected eros and more like any number of magnates in the *Mirror* bewailing 'the uncertaynty of glory' (Salisbury) or telling us to 'Learne godly wisedome which time nor age can rust' (Blacksmith). In thus converting his corrupt Roman into someone even a keeper at Bridewell could pity, someone who mixes shamefully acquired worldly wisdom with a belated moral sense, he diminishes both Du Bellay's sense of sin's curious tendency to produce psychological stasis and his own tonal consistency: his Paulina is too repentant for a cynic and yet too ironic for a Magdalene. And, more than her French double, Paulina invites us to an ambiguous territory (Moll Flanders country) somewhere between exemplary fiction and a history Markham's additions and marginalia insist is 'real'. Our attention is no longer on a whore who in some ways *is* Rome, epitomizing its history and paradoxes, but on one who *inhabits* the city and illustrates current and particular corruptions. Markham translates Paulina from symbol to symptom, removing her from an anonymity open to symbolic association and naming (Babylon, Rome, maybe Jerusalem) to a specificity that while adding some mild prurient interest also shifts the poem closer to complaints by named characters like Buckingham or Matilda. The trip from Italy to England seems short by contrast.

Markham's poem, then, is flatter than Du Bellay's, less dense and less multivocal. In recompense, however, it contributes in its fashion to a perennial but perhaps recently increased interest in what might be going on in the minds of women, even fallen women. Much of this interest is found on the stage, which is not surprising. Perhaps it was even wise. After all, as Ovid says in his *Fasti*, Rome once neglected to venerate the ex-courtesan, Flora, now settled down as the bride of Zephyr; although not normally 'severe' and indeed 'apta ... deliciis', Flora withdrew her favours until a worried Senate voted to dedicate the Florales games to her (V. 333–49). A good move. English playwrights, too, knew better than to neglect Flora, even if their focus was less on her garden of delights than on the bone ache contracted there, for the goddess retained her ancient connection with festival; the prostitute's self-creative role-playing and the playhouses' proximity to brothels maintained it. Even with a few hearts of gold and a reformation or two, Jacobean stage harlots are a bedraggled lot; yet the cool contempt with which authors often treat the whores and 'honest' courtesans warms on occasion to a more subtle awareness of sexual and social complexity. This tentative compassion shows also in the vogue for complaints with a female narrator, even when, after the mid-1590s, some poets sharpen their voices or impersonate more degraded complainers. It is to that half-sympathetic tradition, no matter what the other generic pressures on him or the pull of his model's other concerns, that Markham most notably contributes. Despite a taste for improving *sententiae*, despite a residual misogyny, Markham may have encouraged a few readers to imagine the possible stories behind the ruins of a face or a shattered life.

Notes

1 Frederick N. L. Poynter, *A Bibliography of Gervase Markham, 1568?–1637* (Oxford Bibliographical Society, 1962), 51–52, suspects the poem is a translation but thinks it 'a short novel of the Italian type'. He calls it 'wise, humane, and even sad, with few or none of the vulgarities to which some of his contemporaries were tempted when treating similar themes', in part a tribute to the work's hitherto unidentified ancestry. The edition by Frederic Ouvry (London, 1868) has no critical apparatus.
2 Edoard printed 'Courtisanne' with Villon's 'Belle Heaumière' and Terence's 'Pornegraphie'; for his comments see Chamard's edition of the *Divers jeux* (Paris: Librairie M. Didier, 1947). I have also used V.-L. Saulnier's edition (Geneva, 1947). A 'courtesan' was an accomplished woman whose sale of sexual favours to an elite was officially condemned but widely accepted among the sophisticated; as J. Sharpham's *Fleire* (1607) has it, 'your whore is for every rascall but your Curtizan is for your Courtier'. Since Du Bellay's courtesan ends as a whore, I use both words. See also Lynne Lawner, *Lives of the Courtesans* (New York: Rizzoli, 1987); in *The New York Review of Books*, 28 May 1987, Charles Hope disputes her methods but her book remains informative and refreshingly sympathetic toward these morally marginal if culturally central women.
3 Chamard, ed., *Divers jeux*, i–v.
4 Michel Glatigny, 'Du Bellay traducteur dans *les Jeux rustiques*', *Information littéraire* 18 (1966): 33–41, notes a 'certaine pudeur' in this collection, although he does not mention the 'Courtisanne'.
5 Heather Dubrow, who read this essay with a friendly but eagle eye and to whom I owe some stimulating suggestions, objects reasonably that later epyllia can be satirical. I agree, and indeed William Keach, *Elizabethan Erotic Narratives* (New Brunswick, N.J.: Rutgers University Press, 1977), notes a satirical element even in the older epyllion. But by the same token the Jacobean narratives further mute or undercut the elegiac sensuosity found in long poems by Daniel, Drayton,

and Shakespeare. To translate Du Bellay's ironic but still nostalgic lament *after* the decline of this late Elizabethan style (a style kept alive, to be sure, by new editions of older verse and by its occasional emergence in Shakespeare's plays) creates a minor swirl in generic chronology. Markham also wrote after some had been searching for new female lamenters. Peter Colse remembered a wife (*Penelopes Complaint*, 1596), but fashion soon made mild depravity desirable. Thus in 1607 William Barksted said leeringly of *Mirrha the Mother of Adonis*, 'Muse be not affraide, / Although thou chauntest of unnaturall love. / Great is my quill, to bring forth such a birth, / as shall abash the Virgins of our earth' (A5). Clark Hulse, *Metamorphic Verse: The Elizabethan Minor Epic* (Princeton, N.J.: Princeton University Press, 1981), finds early Jacobean narrative poems few, mediocre, and written in a style closer to the 1560s (75; he does not mention Markham); slightly later erotic narrative 'changes to the simply lascivious or the simply passionate' (33). Markham is not quaint, but neither is he lascivious or passionate, and although Paulina complains in an older manner, Daniel would have found her too shabby for his grieving elegance. So Markham is hard to place: he has an older foreign model; he sidles closer to Elizabethan patterns; and, as Professor Hulse wrote me after kindly reading this essay, any 'diagnosis' of Paulina's case is complicated by the minor epic's 'generic breakdown'. For more on cross-generic patterns, see Hallett Smith, 'A Woman Killed with Kindness', *PMLA* 53 (1938): 138–47.

6 Alexander Leggatt, *Citizen Comedy in the Age of Shakespeare* (Toronto: University of Toronto Press, 1973), ch. 6, describes stage whores and their connection with economic disease. Anne Haselkorn, *Prostitution in Elizabethan and Jacobean Comedy* (Troy, N.Y.: Whitston Publishing Co., 1983), finds moments of sympathy. Official views were harsh, enforcement often lax; see Ronald Bond, '"Dark Deeds Darkly Answered": Thomas Becon's Homily Against Whoredom and Adultery, Its Contexts, and Its Affiliations with Three Shakespearean Plays', *Sixteenth-Century Journal* 16 (1985): 191–205.

7 Livy's *History*, I.4. Du Bellay's wolf joke connects whorishness to urban foundation, a comment on Rome's source and a hint, perhaps, that whores symbolize or in some sense are the slippery and flawed stuff out of which human structures rise: all cities are grass. For speculation on wolves and archaic Roman religion, see Agnes Kirsopp Michels, 'The Topography and Interpretation of the Lupercalia', *Transactions of the American Philological Association* 84 (1953): 35–59.

8 Du Bellay's epic allusions are satirical, but Markham's complaint tradition had its own connections with the epic as well as with older Boccaccian notions of tragedy: regretful magnates had played roles of national moment, and lamenting females incorporate Ovidian (and hence semi-Virgilian) themes, political subtexts, and epic subplots; as Hulse, *Metamorphic Verse*, ch. 1, shows, the word 'epyllion' is quite appropriate.

9 Danae recurs in English complaints; Lawner, *Courtesans*, 151–59, explores her legend in Italian images of the courtesan.

10 The allusion is also Petrarchan ('Quanto cangiata, oimé, da quel di pria', *Rime* 33) and thus serves a satirical strain that helps unify the *Divers jeux*.

See Yvonne Hoggan, 'Anti-Petrarchism in Joachim Du Bellay's "Divers Jeux rustiques"', *Modern Language Review* 74 (1979): 808–19, although she does not mention this line. Helen O. Platt, 'Structure in Du Bellay's *Divers Jeux rustiques*', *Bibliotheque d'humanisme et renaissance* 35 (1973): 19–37, argues that Du Bellay has positioned this poem so as to balance 'Le Combat d'Hercule et d'Acheloys'; if so, that too subverts the epic mode.

11 Wayne Rebhorn, 'Du Bellay's Imperial Mistress: *Les Antiquitez de Rome* as Petrarchist Sonnet Sequence', *Renaissance Quarterly* 33 (1980): 609–22.

12 The comparison of a body to a building is common and of a woman's body to a city scarcely less so. For particularly relevant comments on sexuality, urban subtexts, and complaints, see Heather Dubrow, *Captive Victors: Shakespeare's Narrative Poems and Sonnets* (Ithaca, N.Y.: Cornell University Press, 1987). See also D. C. Allen, 'The Rape of Lucrece', in *Image and Meaning* (Baltimore, Md.: 1968). The lady as a besieged town was found everywhere: 'Then say you yea, or say you no, / I'le scale your wals, before I go', says a lover in *Willobie his Avisa*, 1594, an anonymous poem that jests at this tradition (ed. G. B. Harrison, New York: Barnes and Noble, 1966, 67).

13 Thomas Greene, *The Light in Troy* (New Haven, Conn.: Yale University Press, 1982), 220–41, eloquently treats Du Bellay as ambivalent archaeologist, although he may underestimate the recoil and negation in Du Bellay's feelings about ancient Rome. On Du Bellay and modern Rome see Gladys Dickinson, *Du Bellay in Rome* (Leiden: Brill, 1960).

14 Buchanan, who made *lupa*/wolf/Lupercalia jokes ('In Romam', *Poemata*, 1615, sig. B5), shepherds a flock of classical allusions into his defence of bawds. Philip J. Ford and W. S. Watt, eds., *George Buchanan, Prince of Poets* (Aberdeen: Aberdeen University Press, 1982), 61, call this 'playful erudition', but the ironies do not leave the ancient city unscathed. Buchanan's Leonora is the mother and daughter of whores: Lena tibi est genitrix, tu matris filia paelex, / et tua suscipiet filia matris onus' (146).

15 *The actes of Englysh votaryes* (1546; 1551 ed.), A6v, A3.

16 I can find no influence of Du Bellay on Dekker's *Honest Whore* plays (1604, 1608?) but they sometimes show a semi-serious empathy not unlike his.

17 The Pleiade contributed notably to this vile tradition; see Jacques Bailbé, 'Le Thème de la Vieille femme clans la poésie satirique du seizième et du début du dix-septième siècles', *Bibliothèque d'humanisme et renaissance* 26 (1964): 98–119 and, although not on the old courtesan, V.-L. Saulnier, 'Sur deux poèmes des "Jeux rustiques"', *Revue universitaire* 59 (1950): 265–71. Bailbé, who traces an increasing humanity in such poetry, points also to its sadism. This sadism shows in some Protestant attacks on Rome as a biblical harlot, hatred merging with sexual anxiety. In foretelling what male theologians will do to the Whore of Babylon, John Bale outdoes his biblical source in ferocity: Luther, Erasmus, Tyndale, Calvin, and 'others', doubtless including Bale, will desert her, chase her, strip her, 'eate her fleshe', and 'Finally with fyre shall they burne her' (*The Image of bothe churches*, 1548? ed., sig. s8).

18 Although the association of woman and city is common, the diction and the emphasis on devouring time show, I believe, the impact on Daniel and Drayton

of Du Bellay's *Antiquitez* especially as translated by Spenser; see also A. K. Hieatt, 'The Genesis of Shakespeare's *Sonnets*: Spenser's *Ruines of Rome: by Bellay*', *PMLA* 98 (1983): 800–14. My own essay owes much to conversations with Professor Hieatt on Spenser, Shakespeare, and Rome.

19 I cannot find a real 'Paulina'; nor can Lynn Lawner, who generously tried to help me. True, Du Bellay's friend Olivier de Magny refers to an old Roman whore 'La Paule', who now suffers neglect and the pox: *Les Souspirs*, ed. David Wilkin (Geneva: Droz, 1978), no. 115. Nicholas Goodman's *Hollands leaguer* (1632), set in 'the Kingdome of Eutopia', describes how the proud atheist Britanica Hollandia becomes a prostitute, inspired partly by a devilish Jesuit and Puritan named Ignatius who describes such role-models as 'Lollea Paulina, the greatest Courtezan, the basest Whore, and the deceitfullest Bawde, that ever Rome did acknowledge' (C3); Ms. Hollandia is fascinated by the tales of Paulina's wealth, but Ignatius is careful not to follow 'the truth of the Story' and omits mention of her sad decline. Many details parallel Markham's poem and I assume that Goodman has no independent information on 'Paulina'.

20 Compare Middleton's *A Mad World, My Masters*, I.i.149–51: a bawd tells her daughter, 'Fifteen times thou know'st I have sold thy maidenhead / To make up a dowry for thy marriage, and yet / There's maidenhead enough ... still' (ed. Standish Henning, Lincoln, Ne.: University of Nebrask Press, 1965).

21 A reversal of tradition: Edoard's 'sage Calypsonne' is now the victim.

22 Poynter, *Bibliography*, says the daughter will now *marry* the artisan. I see no such indication.

11

Housing chessmen and bagging bishops: space and desire in Colonna, 'Rabelais', and Middleton's *Game at Chess*

Compared to time travel, space travel looks easy. But each move we make is pressured, if only in our understanding, by how we and our culture conceive – or, as we say nowadays, construct – that space. Cultural pawns much of the time, we move on a board (space-time or Einstein's projected 'unified field') divided and defined – if not by straight lines into squares, then by laws, assumptions, and metaphors – into often overlapping personal and social places; how we think, feel, and talk models and remodels our sense of the three-dimensional world. In this essay, moving spatially from Catholic Italy to Protestant England and temporally from the late quattrocento to 1624, I will examine three chess games and how they eroticize or politicize the space in which the pieces move and the game is played.[1]

The first is a dance performed to the intense pleasure of Polifilo, lover of Polia and dreaming protagonist of Francesco Colonna's *Hypnerotomachia Polifili*, written in the 1460s and published by Aldus at Venice in 1499. Polifilo's dream takes him through a landscape in which ancient and enigmatic buildings, monuments, and gardens appear with Vitruvian clarity and mathematical specificity against a spatially indistinct background. Not much happens in the dream's narrative; rather, psychological struggles take place within Polifilo in what one critic aptly calls 'the frozen space of ekphrasis.'[2] Some such visually activating space asks with particular urgency to be read, covered as its architecture often is with hieroglyphs and partially erased – but hence all the more emotionally compelling – inscriptions. Polifilo obliges by studying the structures carefully, deducing from them evidence of lost architectural wisdom and on one occasion adding his own voice to what they might mean – entered into a recumbent colossus, he makes the ancient statue resound again by breathing forth a love complaint for his Polia. Never, though, does he write graffiti or responses on the building's esoteric but not quite incomprehensible walls. Mostly he looks and longs.

Eventually Polifilo comes to the palace of Queen Eleuterilida ('Free Choice', or 'Free Will'), where after examining the architecture, gardens, and nymphs, and after a good feast complete with an ingenious portable handwashing machine, he watches enraptured as thirty-two costumed damsels dance out a fast-moving chess game on the banquet room's coral- and red-flecked green chequered floor. The gold and silver 'kings' direct the action, ordering their pieces here and there to the music's Greek modes. The flower-crowned and loose-tressed dancers make 'high Capers and Turnes, without affectation of straying, as it should seeme with facilitie and careles ease at pleasure and sweet jestures' (I quote the 1592 English translation by Robert Dallington).[3] Even those taken 'did presently kiss their Conqueror, and voyded the place'. Nor do the kings play with chivalric prowess alone, for Polifilo reports that as the dance proceeded, 'the lesser number that there was, the more pleasure it was to perceive the pollicies [Colonna has 'deceptione'] of either sides to overcome the other'. The game is loving, but like most games – especially chess and love – it inscribes a power struggle requiring strategy. Silver wins this game and the next, but the third victory goes to the gold. Presumably on some other occasion, at some other happy feast, the silver will have another chance.

To say that Colonna's work at times shows a remarkable and luxurious sensuality thanks to its loving gaze at arches, obelisks, and fountains may sound bizarre, but this extraordinarily beautiful book embellished with a multitude of strikingly lovely woodcuts is uncommonly stirring in its languid and leisurely way, even before we and Polifilo finally meet Polia (Figure 11.1). In a recent article, Donald Hedrick has explored this 'erotics of Renaissance urban design', as he puts it.[4] The new interest in perspective and the techniques required to create its illusion, he suggests, accompanied a newly focused 'visual mastery', perhaps because 'When perspective space is applied to the body ... it invites novel and therefore erotic points of view, depersonalizing the subject as it personalizes the viewer, whose active participation and judgement are required in the viewing of difficult foreshortenings.'[5] This is, as he says, the dynamic at work in a disgracefully clever building by Bracelli that imitates a supine woman spreading her legs and a witty illustration in Durer's *Painter's Manual* showing a man sketching on squared paper as he responds to his female model with an interest indicated by the stiffly vertical perspective rod in front of him. As an example of this 'relationship between erotic obsessiveness and visual perspective', Hedrick cites the *Polifilo* and the embrace of the lovers 'on the expanse of an empty architectural grid'.

Hedrick does not mention Colonna's chess game, but the picture he reprints from the *Polifilo* may explain the effect of the dance on the dreaming lover. The floor is eight squares wide; perhaps (we cannot quite tell) it is also eight squares long.[6] My suggestion is that Colonna was encouraged to imagine his chess dance, unillustrated in his book, by the similarity of

Figure 11.1 Colonna's lovers shown against a chequered floor. *Hypnerotomachia Poliphili.*

chessboards to the chequered floors that Renaissance artists like to depict precisely because, I assume, their squares diminish so neatly along the lines of perspective, giving an illusion of an exactly perceived spatial depth and guiding the viewer's eye into that depth, those penetralia. A chessboard, in fact, is not unlike the Albertian 'window' that S. K. Heninger has associated with the development of secular and autonomous narrative.[7] Like the implied lines of vision in a strictly calculated Renaissance painting, the board's demarcations are necessarily fixed. But even more than Alberti's pictorial and perspectival 'window', a chess window's play space (its fenestral frame, so to speak) gives onto – visually contains – human activity: the figures we see through or in the window actually move, and their movements tell a story of advance, retreat, feint, victory, and loss. The parallel is not exact, to be sure, for in a chess game each player has his or her own point of view on the squares and along the lines of play. Looking at or through *this* window, observers can be participants.

As Polifilo watches the chessladies dance, his mind does not go to politics and war, despite the invigorating Doric and Phrygian modes to which the pieces move and despite the twists and developments of a performance mimicking a battle. Perhaps the female gender and waving hair of the dancers has something to do with what happens next, or perhaps the experience of perspective, of a sharpened spatial sense and focus, has given him even more practice in gazing, in the forward motion of sight and imagination. For soon Eleuterilida sends him, guided by her nymphs Reason (Logistica) and Will (Thelemia), to the land of Queen Telosia, in whose misty kingdom he may choose his telos, his aim and end, among the several offered him. To Reason's disgust but Will's delight, Polifilo prefers the way of sexuality, love, and pleasure. Soon he will see Polia, the love he has freely sought and for whose sight an energetic but spatially contained chess dance in a closely observed and mathematically proportioned Vitruvian palace has in part prepared him. He will eventually marry her, although whether a ceremony performed by Venus counts as obedience to family values is doubtful.

Colonna's chess dance drew the appreciative attention of the person or persons unknown who wrote the fifth book of *Gargantua et Pantagruel* (1564). For want of a better name I will call the author 'Rabelais'. This 'Rabelais' could even include François Rabelais himself, who enjoyed Colonna.[8] Whoever 'Rabelais' was, he knew how to play chess, and not any chess but the early modern kind. To understand his reworking of Colonna's dance it helps to recall what had been happening to the game.

The most significant change – established certainly in the late fifteenth century and probably in Italy – was to allow the bishop to sidle on his own colour as far as he could along uninhabited squares and to allow the queen to move in any straight line with the same restriction.[9] This shift in the rules meant that play could proceed sooner to what had been the endgame, making games shorter and also requiring, for good play, a faster and cannier eye on the opponent's strategy. Bishops and queens no longer needed to take their time in working out their tactics while sauntering thoughtfully at the back of the field; they could now rush forward and penetrate deep into enemy territory, killing as they went, perhaps, but also taking new risks. Long a game of the elite, chess became more than ever a game of the brainy, the cunning, and the aggressive.

There is a gender issue here, too, or so thought those bemused by the new chess. Some even called it and its newly empowered queen 'rabiosa', or 'echés de la dame enragée': crazy-queen chess.[10] Arthur Saul, author of a useful *Famous game of chesse-play* (1614), fusses a bit, not very seriously, over how the new rules for chess do not parallel those customs rightly governing the sexes. In a preliminary poem describing the various pieces, he reassures us:

> Through all the houses of the field,
>   the Queene may take her pleasure,
> And use her power to helpe her King,
>   still in a modest measure.
> If in her march shee prove severe,
>   and taketh all she may,
> Tis for the safegard of the King,
>   that shee makes cleare the way.
> For this she may not blamed be,
>   that seekes her King to save,
> It is her glory for to strive[,]
>   her King in peace to have.[11]

But, in his often translated mock-epic chess poem, *Scacchia ludus*, the humanist Vida calls the queen an Amazon, a potentially troubling epithet that 'Rabelais' and Saul adopt.[12] In Vida's Olympian chess game blood flows fast, partly thanks to the new rules, and the kings who direct the action are accomplished at trickery and deception. True, Vida retains chess's ancient connection to the erotic as well as to military discourse, for he tells how Mercury is much taken by a lovely nymph, Scacchis, whom he has observed feeding her swans; to repay her for her lost virginity, the god gives her a chessboard, pieces, and directions for play.[13]

Added at the last minute (they are missing from the manuscript), chapters 23 and 24 of 'Rabelais's' *Cinquieme livre* describe a chess ballet derived in large part from Colonna (with a touch of Vida) but expanded and revised so as to conform to the new game, the one with the crazy queen.[14] The scene has been little commented upon, perhaps because it is so derivative and because its function in this sharply satirical and seemingly anti-Catholic (or at least anticlerical) text is hard to determine.[15] It will be recalled that Pantagruel and crew are en route to the Oracle of the Bottle to see if Panurge should marry despite the probability (or even certainty) that he will be beaten, robbed, and cuckolded. In Colonna's terms, he must finally decide what his Thelemia, if not his Logistica, tells him should be his telos. The voyagers, island-hopping their way to the Oracle, have landed in the kingdom of Entelechie, whose very name, indicating the realized will, seems to point to some combination of Eleuterilida and Telosia. At the very end of the book we return, in a sense, to the kingdoms of those two queens, for the Oracle of the Bottle lives in a cave owing (as has been noted) a great deal of its architecture and decor to Colonna, not least the inscription 'TOUTES CHOSES CE MEUVENT A LEUR FIN'. Nor is this universal movement wholly deterministic, despite another inscription that says the destinies move the willing and drag the reluctant. As David Quint has argued, the Oracle's wine tastes different to each drinker so as to suggest the role of choice, of freedom, of individual *teloi* in life, in faith, in hearing or reading the Word.[16]

How does a chess game fit a movement toward a willed choice that is also in some sense destined? If it prepares Panurge for his final ecstatic decision to marry, it does not do so directly, for there will be other islands and more anticlerical and antilawyer satire before the ship reaches the Oracle. Nor does the whole scene's implied criticism of frenzied ingenuity and novel inventiveness, although entertaining, seem crucial for this particular trickster to grasp. The dance itself does come, however, in the exact centre of the book if one goes by chapters, and the entire chess section is central if one counts the book's prologue (it is typical of Renaissance texts to have at least two ways of centring or shaping a pattern). Indeed, the chief activity of the island – abstracting the fifth essence – seems pertinent both to a fifth book and to conceptions of space and its relation to the four elements. The structural centrality of the scene and the heavy indebtedness of the *Cinquième livre*'s concluding chapters to Colonna's architectural passages indicate not mere 'borrowing' but full intertextual incorporation and recollection. Is there also a touch of friendly parody, such as may shimmer about the abbey of Thélème, a structure much affected by Polifilo's dream? Perhaps. Much of the language is from Colonna: 'Rabelais' retains the dancers' politesse as they remove each other from play, the ancient modes to which the three games are danced, the admirable speed and grace of the 'mille ruses, mille assaulx, mille desmarches', and the granting to each side a victory or two. The humour, though, depends chiefly on delight and hyperbole; outright satire is reserved for the island's officials hard at work manipulating space and matter so as, for example, to make something out of nothing, toss houses out their own windows, catch wind in nets, and rejuvenate hags.

Small but telling changes in the chess dance, however, show thought about how to encourage Panurge onward to his own kingdom of Telosia. Because 'Rabelais' modernizes Colonna's game, his gold queen, together with her knight and archer (bishop), can scour the board like the Amazon Penthesilea; yet she is soon ambushed by the silver archer and 'knight errant', and the narrator remarks (as a matter of immediate strategy, or is there also a social point to be made?) that she would be better advised to stay closer to her husband and venture forth, if she must do so, otherwise accompanied. If Panurge is paying attention he might have further cause to worry about wives. Some changes seem less relevant to his dilemma, such as the substitution of a portable cloth board for the chequered floor, although it would be typical of François Rabelais himself, so given to evasion and ambiguity, to replace a permanent and stable parquet with movable and supple fabric. Nor in these chapters is there such an explicit focus on classicized architecture and perspective as one finds in the *Polifilo* and its illustrations. True, regendering the game by making only the queen and pawns clearly female allows a different sort of sexual electricity, especially as the text retains Colonna's stress on the pleasure of the watchers' gaze.

Most significant for the spatiality of desire, I think, and for Panurge's quest to locate his personal Thelemia, is a change in the source of the dancers' wills. The matter of how and why we will is of course central to Reformation arguments, for much if not all Protestant thought presupposes severe limits on the will, specifically the individual will to do good except when it flows along with and is carried by the divine will. As an Erasmian and Evangelical Christian (for so I believe him to have been), the 'real' François Rabelais does not in this regard follow Luther or Calvin all the way to the bound will or predestination; but despite scenes like that in which the baby Pantagruel smashes his confining cradle, neither does he suggest a full-fledged imperial self whose will is law. Although the *Cinquième livre* has struck some readers as more narrowly polemical, perhaps because less richly indecisive, than the first four books, the Oracle of the Bottle's ambiguities seem to me to express a quasi-Erasmian and indeed traditional desire to avoid extremes – although Luther might second the proclamation that our wills are free when they are God's (or what the inscription calls destiny's) and bound when they are not.

In this regard chess is a provocative game to think about when it is turned into a dance, allegory, or even a little girl's looking-glass dream. Who plays Alice's chess? Who plays Colonna's? We are not told. But then, who plays us, for that matter? If God plays, does he play only one side? And does he allow his pieces any will of their own? In the *Polifilo*, pieces move through the space of the board at the command of the gold and silver kings and who or what moves the kings remains mysterious – buried in the *arcana imperii*, perhaps, where many said royal secrets belong. But 'Rabelais's' dancers seem to have two wills, as though they had already read the Oracle's inscription. On the one hand the narrator ascribes feelings and aims to them: they scheme, dissimulate, seek revenge, desire, and, like the reckless queen, blunder. At the same time he is clear that the dancers receive direction from the music. That is, they do not merely move *to* the sounds but are instructed *by* the sounds. Polifilo had been reminded by the chess musicians' changing modes of the old story that Timotheus had governed the spirit of Alexander through changing his music's harmonic proportions. 'Rabelais' retains this touch, although confusing the musician's name; but by giving his chessmen more intentionality, depriving the kings of their command, and locating the directing wills off the chequered cloth yet still arguably in the larger play space, he establishes a paradoxical dynamic of will and destiny exactly suiting what Panurge will find at the Oracle.

It also suits, I would argue, the book's delicate balance between religious claims. Who in turn tells the musicians what to play is not, to be sure, specified, but there may be a vague implication of cosmic and possibly providential harmonies at work. In any case, the dance reminds the narrator of a spatial paradox, for he finds some dancers, whirling on their squares, moving so fast that they are like the tops whipped by small boys: they seem not to move, and yet if you put a spot of colour on one, that bright point will become a continuous circular line as the top spins, just as, he says, Cusanus describes God. Evidently the theological possibilities of chess were not lost on 'Rabelais'. The members of Pantagruel's crew, in fact, not only laugh (which, as the narrator reminds us, is the peculiarity of humankind) but feel elevated to Olympus, drawn outside themselves by this 'plus qu'humain' spectacle, and (in another paradox) are both moved and stunned. Especially since their hostess has by now disappeared, they are free to sail on.

Several generations later, in England, the Protestant playwright Thomas Middleton dramatized a very different game in his *Game at Chess*, an enormous *succès de scandale* in 1624. It too involves marriage, sexuality, the will, and space. A few years ago Paul Yachnin plausibly argued that Middleton's allegorical comedy was in part inspired by the living chess ballet in 'Rabelais's' *Cinquieme livre*; more recently the evidence for this has thinned out as the extent of Middleton's use of the 1618 chess guide by Saul and Barbier has become clearer.[17] The entire play and its purported triumph of truth, however, is presented – as though in a dramatized Liar's Paradox – as the story of Error's dream, and as a dream it sooner recalls Colonna. In any case, a link remains between Middleton and the *Cinquième livre* because Saul and Barbier appear themselves to have been reading 'Rabelais' as well as Damiano and Vida. In a section he added, Barbier says the French call bishops 'archers' and derive 'rook' from 'custode de la roche', which certainly sounds like 'Rabelais'. As for Saul, his opening poem on the various pieces seems to echo the similar list in the *Cinquième livre*, although some overlap in chess vocabulary is to be expected.

Middleton would have been struck by other passages in the *Famous game*. Chess, we read, is a civilized game involving no chance; allegorically 'like unto a well composed Common wealth', it contains 'many morall mysteries'. The promotion of pawns can hearten us all, but the queens' warlike fashion suits women in some ancient 'Utopian countrey' – that is, Amazons are fictitious. Some call rooks 'dukes' (Middleton adopts this notion), but perhaps the *queen* should be a duke, in view of the piece's power to go 'abroad to and fro, with that unlimited commaund' and lead 'men to Battel'.[18] In other words, dukes get around; queens should know their space and, in the terminology of the time, not stray far from their 'houses', as Saul calls squares. Middleton will follow this thought by victimizing and virtually immobilizing his white queen and by advancing his dukes, a strategy that makes for poor chess but more plausible early modern English politics, at least now that Elizabeth – hardly 'enragée' but certainly dangerous – was dead.

A Game at Chess, performed to huge and appreciative audiences for nine days in August of 1624 (Figure 11.2), allegorizes Catholic attempts to undermine or convert the Church of England and, more precisely – if also more allusively – a surprise 1623 trip to Spain by Prince Charles and the duke of Buckingham, an adventure in which, not wholly unlike Panurge, the prince was at least ostensibly in search of a wife (and a treaty). Despite King James's desire for the match, a marriage he thought would serve his policy of détente with Madrid, the projected marriage to the Spanish king's young sister was unpopular in Protestant England, so when Charles returned home, wifeless and by now happy to be so, he was met with rejoicing. Like many other Englishmen, Middleton affected to see what was in fact a shabbily dishonest affair not as a matter of changed Spanish and English wills (the infanta did not want to marry a heretic, while Charles and the duke came home angry and bellicose) but of stout English wits at work in foiling the diabolical plots of a sly Catholic enemy implacably bent on world conquest by any means.

Buckingham seems to have gone along with this fiction. His protection (or that of some other anti-Spanish magnate), together with the public's enthusiasm and Middleton's flattery of a king who could not afford to notice the accompanying hints that he was easily duped, shielded those involved from the worst of the government's dismay and the Spanish embassy's outrage.[19] Chess had long allegorized war and politics as well as love: one medieval Hebrew chess poem has Edomites battling Ethiopians, and in the eighteenth century some chess pieces were carved to represent the 'struggle between the East India Company and the native states'.[20] Middleton's play, though, may be the first work in which chess laughingly evokes a man's escape from wedlock.

In Saul's nomenclature a square is a 'house', thus making the board a town with sixty-four dwellings, but in Middleton's play both the Spanish and English sides are 'houses' in a more dynastic sense: black and white, morally speaking, have long genealogies. In this chess game, pieces venture forth from 'houses' that in the implied allegory are spatially distinct but capable of mutual intrusion. The threat, so legitimate in chess yet so terrifying in geopolitics and – perhaps – religion, is that the black side will further infiltrate, debauch, and deceive the white house, pervert white visitors to the black house, and eventually rule the whole board through trickery, intelligence gathering, and seduction. The world as it seemed to many in

Figure 11.2 Middleton's chessmen play the great game. Title page from Thomas Middleton, *A Game at Chess* (1625).

1624 London, that is, had two sides and one was diabolical. Chess had often been read as a metaphor for human conflict, but the stakes were now higher and the entire world – earthly space – felt divided, segmented, into black and white: them and us, Catholic and Protestant, Spain and England. One side, in this view, wanted all space for itself, permanently, as witness its behaviour around the globe. (That many Protestants wanted the same would not have seemed illogical, not when the alternative was the triumph of an evil empire and the limitation of God's word.) If all the world's a stage, then all the world can be a chess game – even the lines that Mercator and other cartographers projected across the globe might seem to make the whole earth a sort of chessboard, as though Alberti's window had been curved into a three-dimensional perspectival space ready for geopolitical narratives.[21]

The play opens with the recently canonized Ignatius Loyola back on Earth and looking around him for his followers: 'I thought theyde spread over the World by this time / Coverd the Earths face and made darke the Land.'[22] Angry, he awakens Error, who has been dreaming of 'a game of Chesse / Betwixt our side and the Whitehouse, the men sett / In theire just order, readie to goe to it' (Induction, 43–45). After a brief chat about chess (Error has been reading the 1618 Saul), the pair settles back to watch what Error says should be seen as his dream or vision. To the sound of music, the two sides assemble. In fact, Loyola says, he would 'rule my selfe, not observe rule', for he 'would doo anye thing to rule alone, / Tis rare to have the world reignd in by one', but he agrees to 'see 'em anon, and marke 'em in theire playe, / Observe, as in a dance, they glide awaye' (Induction, 73–76).

The play proper begins, expectedly enough, with moves by the pawns, from whom we hear how the Jesuits are at work around the world labouring for 'universall Monarchie'. As the plot proceeds, involving notably the black side's attempted seduction and slander of the white queen's pawn, it is clear that the white house's space is too permeable, subject not only to the intrusions expected in chess but to what one might call 'extraludic' manoeuvring, treachery, and espionage. Some pieces may seem white (with names like Blanche and Bridget), but from their 'sanctuarie' in 'the Whitefriers' and 'the bowells of Bloomsburie' (2.1.233–36) they operate as black moles and black informants. In the first scene the arrogantly witty black knight (representing Count Gondomar, recently ambassador from Spain), had spelled it out: 'The Busines of the Universall Monarchie / Goes forward well now', aided by 'all Intelligences [i.e., reports from spies] possible / Thorough the Christian kingdomes' (1.1.264–68). One source of his 'intelligence' is, shockingly, a seemingly white pawn; not that the black side is grateful, for the black knight secretly scorns this 'Poore Jesuite ridden Soule' for being 'foolde' out of his 'Alleagance' with no safe place on the board: 'Wch path so ere thou tak'st thou'rt a lost Pawne' (1.1.358–60).

Less pathetic and much more comic is the book-scribbling Fat Bishop, representing the portly and prolific bishop of Spalatro – once black, now passing as white, but inwardly blackhearted in his gluttony for food, money, drabs by the 'Holesale', and ecclesiastical preferments: his bulk expands in space as the integrity of this 'greasie turnecoate Gurmundizing Prelate' shrivels (2.2.44, 57). The black knight, whose contemptuous description this is, imagines the Fat Bishop as a sort of miniglobe, the 'mund' in 'Gur-mundizing', maybe:

> Ile make him the Baloom [sic] Ball of the churches
> And both the sides shall tosse him, hee lookes like one,
> A thing sweld up with mingled drinck and Urine
> And will bound well from one side to another![23]

The black knight in fact has globes almost literally on the brain. Aiming at planetary empire and thinking of the Fat Bishop as a balloon, he imagines his own brain as a mapped sphere. If the Fat Bishop pens 'Fat and fulsome Volumes' (2.2.59), the black knight rewrites the world. In a frank conversation with his pawn he explains. The pawn has just told him that a plot of his has been discovered, to which he has merely replied, 'Wch of the twentie thousand and nine hundred / Fourescore and five, canst tell?' The pawn is understandably impressed, if confused, noting that mere peasants have 'but one plot / To Keepe a Cowe on'. To make him understand, the knight asks him to remember the globe in his study. Oh yes, replies the pawn, 'A thing Sir full of Cuntryes, and hard words'. Well, says his master, 'Just such a thing (if ere my Skull bee opend) / Will my Braynes looke like, ... and some M[aster]-Politician / That has sharpe State Eyes will goe neere to pick out / The plotts, and everie Clymate where they fastened.' Readers of his cerebral globe will 'neede use Spectacles' to read the plots inscribed on it, he boasts, but in fact the 'white Knights policie' has just uncovered one of the black knight's treacherous letters (3.1.125–46). This Machiavel is more legible than he thinks.

The following scenes see the black knight planning to 'entrap' the white knight in the 'black house' (a political allusion, of course, to marriage with the infanta and a treaty emancipating English Catholics) and the black side's continued efforts to seduce the white queen's pawn. Even white pieces, though, however reluctantly – 'What a payne it is / For Truth to fayne a little' (4.4.17–18), says the white king sadly to the white duke – must look about them and indulge in 'policy'. As the struggle intensifies, the white queen, who may represent the Church of England, is nearly 'taken' by the Fat Bishop. Luckily, the white bishop (George Abbot, some say) rescues her and thus prevents a 'Master check'. In real chess, queens are fearsome protectors of the king; here, with a compliment to James I as head of the church, the white king tells the still trembling queen that 'The doves house is not safer in the Rock / Then thou in my firme bosome' (4.4.85–86) – a loving sentiment, even if Saul might object that this nesting of bodies breaks the rule of one piece to a square. Foiled and himself taken, the Fat Bishop is put into the off-board bag, the repository of captured pieces sometimes moralized in the Middle Ages and Renaissance as the equalizing realm of death but here a seriocomic version of the older morality plays' Hell-mouth.

Toward the play's end, the white duke and knight are made welcome by the major black pieces and treated to some remarkably open admissions of black voracity for empire, a hunger expressed through metaphors of consumption at 'the large Feast of our Vast Ambition' (5.3.92). Getting the black side fully to acknowledge its evil, the white duke and knight perform a checkmate 'by discovery', a punning reference to a manoeuvre in which one piece moves so that another of the same colour will thereby, without moving, automatically exert a checkmate. Their king captured and with (suggests the buried pun) no black 'mate' for the white side, the black pieces tumble squabbling into the bag that 'like Hell opens / To take her due' (5.3.197–98). The white pieces rejoice with (I think) some common Protestant puns on 'room' and 'Rome': early modern pronunciation encouraging such bitter spatial jokes on Roman expansion; then, thanking Heaven, the white knight orders the bag closed: 'the fittest Wombe / For trecherie pride and malice' (5.3.238–39).[24] Despite defiant black threats, there is no indication either that it is ever to be reopened (Protestants, especially, argued that no one leaves Hell) or that any white pieces are in it. The black house has found its sphere, its room/Rome, for its paths of glory on the chessboard have, in its case, led but to an internal uterine but – so far as we know – infertile cul de sac (or *sac de cul*).

Middleton's play is indeed a game of chess, if a dishevelled one,[25] yet its political wish is something no chess game could survive – that the black and white houses remain apart, not penetrate each other through espionage, corruption, or even sex and marriage. Unlike the *Cinquième livre*, this is implicitly – if only implicitly, for there were limits to Middleton's daring – a drama about *not* getting married, about staying put so as to avoid ideological exogamy. It is the black side that is just as sex-obsessed and penetration-oriented as many English Protestants supposed Catholics to be: the black urge to expand, to tumesce into full spherical imperium, is both expressed and disguised by its discourse of love and desire. For in truth the black house offers not a wife but the great Whore herself; in Panurge's terms, the white knight escapes an entanglement that would get his whole house, particularly its church, beaten, robbed, and cuckolded.

In this regard two other spatial issues are pertinent. First, whereas Pantagruel's crew leaves the mainland to island-hop toward the Oracle of the Bottle, the fear in Middleton's play (and in Middleton's England) is that the island kingdom will be absorbed by the Continent, swallowed by the nation and religion so often, in the Renaissance, symbolized by cannibal giants and in this play by geophagous gourmands.[26] England, that is, perceived its geographical marginality as providential protection against being beguiled and ingested by Madrid and Rome. The island is not the *Cinquième livre*'s Lucianic and fantasy 'other'; the island is a besieged home.

Second, although I hesitate to make too much of this, is the function in some theological disputes of disagreements over the nature of space itself, including how space relates to bodies and eating. Jerzy Limon has made an especially compelling case that *A Game at Chess* thinks about the cosmos, not just about the Spanish marriage, and that it represents larger religious struggles.[27] Even he, though, defines the ideological questions largely in terms of power, of what many Protestants took to be a diabolical Catholic desire for empire under one tyrannical will. Several specifically doctrinal disagreements, however, also involved spatial (and linguistic) issues. For example, can two bodies inhabit the same space and can one body be simultaneously in two places? Modern common sense and Newtonian physics find such questions merely risible. Post-Heisenberg physics is at least a little less sure.[28] The issues are not frivolous. Is the risen Christ's body wholly present on each altar during the mass, and, if so, can he be simultaneously in Heaven? Protestants who deny this simultaneous location, says the Catholic William Rainolds (for example), argue like pagans from mere Euclidian or Aristotelian assumptions about space.[29] Not that all Protestants adopted an Aristotelian view of bodies; Adam Hill, for instance, devotes much effort to showing how on Easter Saturday Christ could be wholly in the grave and wholly in Hell.[30] For the most part, though, it was Catholics who had more stake in what were soon to seem like unscientific conceptions of bodies in space, for if space is quite homogeneous and if bodies are finally distinct, even when apparently merged like water mixed with wine, then certain doctrines become harder – although many would say not impossible – to maintain.

Chess, I hope it is not too trivial to say, is in this regard an unambiguously Aristotelian game. One piece, one space, and no fair having two pieces on one or one piece on two; newcomers to a space must therefore expel the old, while vacators of a space open it to a new occupant. In Eucharistic terms, I suppose, *con*substantiation is quite impossible, whereas *trans*substantiation breaks the rules by having one body in two locations. True, the procedures for checks and checkmates imply that *energy* is less spatially confined by borders. My point may seem impertinent in every sense, but the fact is that chess haunts the mind more than most games and one reason,

I suspect, is how it treats space. Middleton's play wisely ignores overtly theological arguments, but those arguments rendered even more acute the concern it registers about replacement and removal – and even consumption, for Protestant attacks on the mass were often expressed through worried or contemptuous sneers at Catholic 'cannibalism'.[31]

It is this dread of, and relief at so far escaping, hostile takeover and ingestion that energizes *A Game at Chess*. The takeover would mean the physical removal or blackification of white pieces and the rewriting of the planet's surface (to say nothing of Rome's continued scribbles atop God's Word), for the play geopoliticizes the flat chessboard into a sphere at risk of becoming a universal empire of evil. Chess slips outdoors, out of Polifilo's and 'Rabelais's' perspectival and festive architecture of desire, and into the cold shadow war against the hungry 'Other's' inflated will. Far from being inspired to marry by a focused and delighted perspective on an indoors chess dance, the white knight plays in an outdoors game so cleverly, with such suspicious 'wit-wondrous strength, / And *circum*spective Prudency'[32] (my italics) that he avoids losing his virtue and protects his friends from capture.

Is his cleverness his own? He and the other pieces self-consciously play themselves, in a sense; one frontispiece shows them doing so (see Figure 11.2). Unlike Colonna's chessmen, however, they receive scant instruction from their kings, and although there is music the pieces do not seem directed by it. Has the Protestant Middleton discovered free will – liberated his knight's Thelemia if not given it a marital telos? Not entirely, for while the black house appears voluntarily to serve a satanic overlord, the play also hints that Providence plays all the pieces, perhaps inspiring the willing and dragging along the recalcitrant by some inaudible off-board music of its own. Unlike Polifilo's and 'Rabelais's' chess dances, however, this comedy rejoices not in festive, implicitly erotic, and lighthearted games to be replayed with different music and different outcomes, but in a single conflict played just once and for keeps. In real chess, luckily, we can take turns being white or black and challenge our victors to a rematch. But in real history, as it turned out, Protestantism's white knight escaped the infanta only to marry Henrietta Maria, a daughter of the now Catholic and Stuart-friendly house of Bourbon. On the real globe, after all, there are more than two sets of players – and more than two colours.[33]

Notes

1 This essay began as a paper read at the 1992 Sixteenth-Century Conference and the Modern Language Association in sessions organized by my colleague,

Catherine Randall; the topic was Protestant constructions of space. I thank Skiles Howard, who read this essay while finishing a dissertation at Columbia on dance and space, for her challenging queries: when, for example, is space an unbound void (to the extent that Renaissance thinking allowed for a void) and when is it imagined as some sort of matter? Can a void be segmented? Does segmenting it make it more nearly material and hence more subject to power and erotic charge?

2 On the edifice's enigmatic quality and alternation with undefined space, see Gilles Polizzi, 'L'Esthétique de l'enigme: le spectacle et le sens dans le *Songe de Poliphile*', *Rivista di letterature moderne e comparate* 41 (1988): 209–33; 'l'espace pétrifié de *l'ekphrasis*' is on 211. See also his 'Le Songe de Poliphile: Renovation ou metamorphoses du genre littéraire', in *Le Songe à la Renaissance*, ed. Françoise Charpentier (n.p., 1989), 85–97. There is some question about which Francesco Colonna wrote the *Polifilo*. Since the acrostic formed by the chapter headings includes 'Frater', I prefer the traditional ascription to the Venetian monk – and, as A. Kent Hieatt (who read this essay with astute attention) reminds me, internal evidence shows that the author must have lived near Venice for a long time.

3 R[obert] D[allington], *The strife of love in a dreame*, ed. Lucy Gent (Delmar, N.Y.: Scholars' Facsimiles & Reprints, 1973), 137. The translation is sometimes called loose; it is indeed partial, but often (as here) closer to Colonna than Jean Martin's 1546 French translation. Some of Dallington's wording, such as calling his pawns 'nymphs' and the specifying of Alexander as the monarch affected by his musician, seem to recollect *Gargantua et Pantagruel*, 5.23–24. Dallington knew Rabelais well, quoting him several times in his *View of Fraunce* (1604); like Rabelais, he uses a version of chess introduced after Colonna wrote (see below, n. 8) and thus modernizes the dance somewhat.

4 Donald Keith Hedrick, 'The Ideology of Ornament: Alberti and the Erotics of Renaissance Urban Design', *Word & Image* 3 (January 1987): 111–37. I am less persuaded that the lines of sight he traces are 'masculinist' (118) in their ideology and not merely masculine in their erotic perspective.

5 Ibid., 118–19.

6 There are two inverted scallop shells in the arches near the lovers; this was (and is) a common motif in architectural decoration, but it is appropriate here: mythographers called this shell a sign of Venus because she rose from the sea and because 'concha' was Roman slang for vulva.

7 S. K. Heninger Jr., *The Subtext of Form in the English Renaissance: Proportion Poetical* (University Park: Pennsylvania State University Press, 1994), ch. 5 ('Alberti's Window: The Rhetoric of Perspective'). Like those of many other scholars, my own perspectives on space, form, and story in early modern England are much indebted to Heninger's work on Renaissance cosmology, literary structure, and spatiality.

8 On Rabelais and Colonna, see A. Kent Hieatt and Anne Lake Prescott, 'Contemporizing Antiquity: The *Hypnerotomachia* and Its Afterlife in France', *Word & Image* 8 (Spring 1992): 291–321; the article cites earlier work I omit

here. Robert J. Clements, 'The Chess Ballet: A Faraway Vision of Pantagruel and Polifilo', in *Connaissance de l'étranger: Mélanges offerts à la mémoire de Jean-Marie Carre* (Paris: Didier, 1964), 224–39, tries to calculate the degree of borrowing (he may exaggerate) and to sort out the more elaborate game that 'Rabelais' invents; Clements seems unaware that the rules of chess had changed. It is usually said that Rabelais used the Italian original, not Martin's 1546 translation, although the opening of chapter 23 ('Le soupper parfait, fut en présence de la dame fait un bal') seems to me closer to the start of Martin's chapter ('Le banquet prodigue achevé, la royne ... ordonna ... un bal') than to Colonna, who has no parallel introductory phrase and starts the chess game further along in the chapter. Perhaps, then, the author(s) of the *Cinquième livre* had consulted Martin.

9 Henry J. R. Murray, *A History of Chess* (Oxford: Clarendon Press, 1913) gives a detailed history of the game's nomenclature, rules, and social status. For a convenient bibliography, see Karl-Ludwig Selig, '*Don Quixote* and the Game of Chess', in *The Verbal and the Visual: Essays in Honor of William Sebastian Heckscher* (New York: Italia Press, 1990), 203–11.

10 Murray, *History of Chess*, 777. Originally the 'queen' had been the shah's male adviser – his 'farzin'; European players soon regendered the piece, although long retaining the now mystifying name 'fers'.

11 Arthur Saul, *Famous game of chesse-play* (1614), sig. A8v.

12 *The Game of Chess: Marco Girolamo Vida's Scacchia Ludus*, ed. Mario A. Di Cesare (Nieuwkoop: De Graaf, 1975). So, too, Odemira da Damiano in *Ludus Scacchiae: A game, both pleasant, wittie, and politicke* (I give the 1597 title of the English translation; this edition includes 'G. B.'s' fragmentary English version of Vida), sig. A2v, describing modern chess. An anonymous imitation of Vida in *Musarum Deliciae* (1655) calls the queen 'Amazonian', specifically likening her to 'our sixt Henryes Margaret'; see the facsimile edition with an introduction by Tim Raylor (Delmar, N.Y.: Scholars' Facsimiles and Reprints, 1985), sig. D6.

13 Murray, *History of Chess*, 183–85, notes that since in their language 'rukh' – the origin of our 'rook' – is a homonym for 'cheek', Arabic love poets liked to pun by telling, for example, of a shah captured by two smooth and rosy (female) rooks.

14 The touch of Vida shows in calling the queen an Amazon and the bishops archers (in the *Polifilo* they are 'secretaries' or 'counsel-keepers').

15 But see Florence Weinberg, 'Chess as a Literary Idea in Colonna's *Hypnerotomachia* and in Rabelais' *Cinqiesme Livre*', *Romantic Review* 70 (summer 1979): 321–35. This thought-provoking article reads both texts as tracing a Platonic movement from sense to reason (represented by the rationality of chess) to love (Polifilo's choice of a venereal telos and Panurge's Bacchic joy in the Oracle's cave); she also thinks the triumph of gold represents a solar masculine perfection overcoming a more sluggish feminine lunar mutability. The presence of Bacchic Christian ecstasy in these texts' eventual celebrations of love is very likely, yet I suspect that Colonna, especially, is willing to affirm the continuing value of eros in and

of itself, notably in a loyal and noble lover. In other words, progress there may be, but as Polifilo scales Plato's ladder he takes the lower rungs with him.
16 David Quint, *Origin and Originality in Renaissance Literature: Versions of the Source* (New Haven, Conn.: Yale University Press, 1983), 192–206. Quint thinks the *Cinquième livre* by Rabelais; the complexity and insight, not just the extent, of the intertextual gestures toward Colonna do show a subtle imagination at work.
17 Paul Yachnin, '*A Game at Chess* and Chess Allegory', *Studies in English Literature 1500–1900* 22 (Spring 1982): 317–30, cites the prologue's discussion of chess pieces, a stress on the knight's 'ability to plan ahead', and indeed the whole black side's capacity for dissimulation, the role of music, a tripartite structure to the procedure of play (three games in 'Rabelais', two advances for black and a victory for white in Middleton), an allusion to children picking kernels from dung that resembles an earlier passage in Rabelais, and the prologue's comparison of Middleton's play to a dance. N. W. Bawcutt, 'New Light on Middleton's Knowledge of Chess', *Notes and Queries* 232 (1987): 301–2, shows that the prologue's passage on nomenclature and the use of 'duke' for 'rook' (facilitating the allegory, for the white duke represents the duke of Buckingham) more probably derive from Barbier's additions to Saul.
18 Saul, *Famous game of chesse-play*, sigs. C3v–C4.
19 There has been debate as to who protected Middleton, whether he needed protection (few that summer were pro-Spanish, and it may be that what disturbed James was the impudence of representing him on the public stage), whether the last-minute topical allusions distract us from more basic allegory about good and evil, whether the white side escapes Middleton's irony. On such issues I have found particularly useful: T. H. Howard-Hill, 'The Origins of Middleton's *A Game at Chess*', *Research Opportunities in Renaissance Drama* 28 (1985): 3–14; Paul Yachnin, '*A Game at Chess*: Thomas Middleton's "Praise of Folly"', *Modern Language Quarterly* 48 (June 1987): 107–23, who also suggests that Middleton plays an older moralistic allegory against up-to-date diction; and Neil Taylor and Bryan Loughrey, 'Middleton's Chess Strategies in *Women Beware Women*', *Studies in English Literature 1500–1900* 24 (Spring 1984): 341–54, who comment on the usefulness of chess to allegory. Richard Davies and Alan Young, '"Strange Cunning" in Thomas Middleton's *A Game at Chess*', *University of Toronto Quarterly* 14 (Spring 1976): 236–45, hear an irony in the treatment of the white side inaudible to some other critics; Margot Heinemann, *Puritanism and Theatre: Thomas Middleton and Opposition Drama under the Early Stuarts* (Cambridge: Cambridge University Press, 1980), may exaggerate the playwright's 'Puritanism' but makes a good case that strongly Protestant writers were not always antitheatrical. For the political and cultural energies at work behind and in the play, see in particular Jerzy Limon, *Dangerous Matter: English Drama and Politics in 1623/24* (Cambridge: Cambridge University Press, 1986).
20 Murray, *History of Chess*, 526–28, 183–85.
21 Once a world is the play space, furthermore, players lose the rationality and safety of a frame. The Spanish 'house' in Middleton's play is terrifying in part

because its game is literally without limit. On Alberti's window, story, and projections beyond the frame, see Heninger, *Subtext*, esp. 167.

22 I quote the edition by R. C. Bald (Cambridge: Cambridge University Press, 1929), induction, lines 6–7; here and elsewhere, I normalize *i* and *j*, *u* and *v*.

23 2.2.78–81. The bishop, greedy and ambitious though he was, and angry though he made all sides, seems in some regards to have been what later Christians would call 'ecumenical'; nowadays the Vatican and Lambeth might ask him to head an interfaith committee.

24 Uncomfortable in the crowded bag, the Fat Bishop objects that 'The Bishop must have Roome, hee will have roome, / And roome to lye [another pun?] at pleasure', to which the play's 'Jesting pawn' replies, 'All the bagg I thinke / Is roome too scant for youre Spoletta-Paunce' (5.3.211–14).

25 Middleton's knowledge of chess is unclear; for a defence and analysis, sec John R. Moore, 'Middleton's "Game at Chesse"', *PMLA* 50 (June 1935): 761–68.

26 For a psychologically relevant configuration of islands near mainland giants, see a map in André Thevet's *Grand insulaire* (c. 1586) of what is now southern Chile, reproduced in *Art et légendes d'espaces: figures du voyage et rhétoriques du monde*, ed. Christian Jacob and Frank Lestringant (Paris: Presses de l'école normale supérieure, 1981), 10.

27 Limon, *Dangerous Matter*, 98–129. Limon is particularly helpful on English dread of Spain's global ambitions and Jesuit trickery; arguing that the real players of the game are, finally, God and the devil, he too notes the frequency with which the black house thinks in the sexual terms that Protestants often associated with Catholic clergy and the Antichrist.

28 See Richard Sorabji, *Matter, Space, and Motion: Theories in Antiquity and Their Sequel* (Ithaca, N.Y.: Cornell University Press, 1988). On late-twentieth-century views see, although I am not expert enough to judge its accuracy, Paul Davies and John Gribbin, *The Matter Myth* (New York: Simon and Schuster, 1992), particularly ch. 7, 'Quantum Weirdness Space' – at least very small and very large space – is once more nonhomogeneous and unpredictable, with somewhat more room for non-Euclidean geometry and non-Aristotelian logic.

29 William Rainolds, *A refutation of sundry reprehensions, cavils, and false sleightes* ... (Paris, 1583), sigs. M1–M2, which attacks his Protestant opponent for basing arguments against the real presence on Aristotle, Euclid, and rules of nature known even to mere 'prentises and artisans in their shops'. Rainolds is reacting to complaints such as that by William Fulke in *D. Heskins, D. Sanders and M. Rastell overthrowne* (1579), sig. L2v, that Catholic belief 'that one bodie may be in another, and two bodies in one place' is 'against naturall Philosophie and reason.

30 Adam Hill, *The defence of the article: Christ descended into hell* (1592).

31 See Frank Lestringant, 'Catholiques et cannibales: Le thème du cannibalisme dans le discours protestant au temps des guerres de religion', in *Pratiques et discoours alimentaires à la renaissance*, ed. J.-C. Margolin and Rohen Sauzet (Paris: Maisonneuve et Larose, 1982), 233–35. (It may be no accident that the future's understanding of space-time is neatly represented on the TV series *Star*

Trek by the crew's fondness for three-dimensional chess, while Heninger's Alberti might have been amused to know that someday people would play chess in the virtual and mathematical space of 'Windows'.
32 Prefatory poem: 'The PICTURE plainly explained after the manner of the CHESSE-PLAYE', lines 10–11.
33 In turning gold and silver to white and black, is Middleton's play implicitly racist? The Spanish, although not the Hapsburg family itself, were darker than the English, but I think Middleton takes advantage of an old, and not just European, moral division.

12

Imperfect pearls from France: Ronsard's conceits meet Donne's

Anne Lake Prescott and Roger Kuin

There have been many attempts to create a stylistic genealogy for the lyrics of John Donne, and more especially for what are commonly referred to as their 'conceits'.[1] In the present inquiry, we do not propose to add to the English ancestry of these features, but to see if some illumination may be gained by crossing the Channel. It may be useful to remember, for instance, that as far as the term 'conceit' is concerned, the *Oxford English Dictionary* (*OED*) sees its origins as being 'a borrowing probably from French'.

In French it remained as *concept* but is not found as such in Claude Hollyband's (Claude de Sainliens') 1593 *Dictionary French and English*, nor in Jean Nicot's 1606 *Trésor de la langue française*, the earliest French dictionary. Hollyband, however, does list the French *conception* as 'a conceite', and *la conception de nostre entendement* as 'the sense, feeling, or perceiving'.[2] In Randal Cotgrave's 1611 *Dictionarie of the French and English Tongues* the French *concept* is translated into the English 'conception'; while a little later the French *conception* becomes, in English, 'a conceit; also sence, apprehension, iudgement, understanding; also, the conception, or conceiving, of women with child; whence, *La conception de notre Dame*, the conception of our Ladie: a solemne holy day kept by the Church of Rome on the eight of December'. By 1787 the *Dictionnaire critique de la langue française* had this to say about *concept*: '*Vieux mot scolastique, en usage encôre parmi quelques Savans. l'Académie se contente de dire que c'est un terme didactique : Idée, simple vûe de l'esprit.*' ('An old Scholastic word, still in use among a few scholars. The Academy only says that it is a didactic term [meaning] an Idea, a simple view of the mind.') It then quotes the seventeenth-century Jesuit theologian René Rapin (1620–87), who in his *Art de prêcher* ('Art of Preaching') wrote '*Crains, d'un brillant concept cherchant l'eclat trompeur, / De doner pour lumière, une fausse lueur*' ('Beware, in seeking the deceptive glitter of a brilliant conceit, of presenting as light a false glimmer.').

These useful lexicographical facts support the impressive arguments and warnings given by Alexander Parker in his 1982 Presidential Address to the Modern Humanities Research Association. Before turning to the Spanish Baroque texts that were the subject of his inquiry, he discussed the concept, and the term, of 'conceit'. 'In literary history and criticism English has two terms which cannot be translated by a single word in the languages of Western Europe. The first is "romance" as distinct from "novel"; the second is "conceit" as distinct from "concept" ... Italian and Spanish have to use their forms of "concept", *where French has to use the Italian word*, and where German has no recognized equivalent at all.'[3]

Parker goes on to point out the confusion which the English word, used indiscriminately by Anglophone critics of other literatures, has caused in comparative literary studies. He cites K. K. Ruthven's useful 1969 book[4] as reminding us that 'the Italian *concetto* and the Spanish *concepto* meant much more than the modern conceit', and substantiates this, not only through lexicography but by reference to such texts as Giulio Cortese's 1591 *Avvertimenti nel poetare*, Tasso's *Discorsi dell'arte poetica* (1565/1594), and Camillo Pellegrino's 1598 *Del concetto poetico*. Important for us is his point that at some time between Pellegrino in 1598 and Matteo Peregrini's 1639 *Delle acutezze* 'the term *concetto* came to add the idea of "witty" to that of concept and statement' (xxv).

Returning to France and England, we see first of all that for the French the word very much retained its original meaning as an idea, a conception by the mind. Such an idea might of course be the idea behind a poem, but it might equally be the idea behind a sermon, a baby, a political structure, or an expedition to the New World. It seems not to have acquired at any time the English (and Peregrini's) connotation of lightness, exceptional wit, or poetic ingenuity (*OED* III.10.a, b, c). But we also remark that even for Cotgrave, who uses the word 'conceit' in 1611, at the height of Donne's poetic career, it seems not to bear that connotation either: he segues seamlessly into 'sense, apprehension, judgement, understanding'.

Taught by this, we should beware of taking Rapin's glimmer for glitter and of expecting to find 'Metaphysical conceits' in the work of, say, the French Pléiade. While poets such as Donne were definitely aware of their French contemporaries and immediate predecessors,[5] it is likely that neither side of the Channel had the concept of 'conceit' to which Herbert Grierson and Helen Gardner have accustomed a century of scholars.[6] Giles Fletcher, in his *Licia* of 1593, says that too many of his contemporaries have gone to Italy, Spain, or France for their 'best and choicest conceites'. Even a likely Italian such as Pellegrino (1527–1603), writing specifically about poetry, is perfectly in line with Philip Sidney's '*Idea* or fore-conceit' and Edmund Spenser's 'Allegory or darke conceit'.[7] And even when in 1643 Sir Richard Baker (1568–1645), in his *Chronicle of the Kings of England*, described his acquaintance Mr John Donne as, in the time of King James I, living at the

Inns of Court, 'not dissolute, but very neat; a great visitor of ladies, a great frequenter of playes, a great writer of conceited verses',[8] it is likely that by 'conceited' he chiefly meant a highly intellectual poetic that (as Dryden later wrote) affects the metaphysics.

It might, then, be instructive and even delightful to detach 'conceit' from the image and restore to it its wider sense of a clever and original idea, a 'find' or *trouvaille* which brings a pleased smile to the poet's face as it comes to him, and which he hopes will, if not please, at least startle his readers into a greater tension of consciousness. The image, in that case, returns to its proper place as the vehicle for the conceit rather than the conceit itself.[9]

If we do this, and if we approach it by way of the image, new and more useful perspectives present themselves. Let us begin with the notorious term of 'Petrarchism'. This movement, which was for a long time an honoured and approved literary model, consisted chiefly of a certain way of seeing love, and crystallized that way of seeing in a category of images. These, one might say, were characterized by contrast and hyperbole in the service of profound, harmonious, and faithful love for a sometimes sympathetic but always unattainable beloved. For delight as well as instruction we permit ourselves to quote an example from Petrarch's *Canzoniere* (no. 90):

Erano i capei d'oro a l'aura sparsi	*Her golden hairs were loosened to the wind*
che 'n mille dolci nodi gli avolgea,	*that wound them in a thousand gentle knots,*
e 'l vago lume oltra misura ardea	*the faint soft light was kindled beyond measure*
di quei begli occhi, ch'or ne son sì scarsi;	*by those fine eyes, no longer so unveiled now;*
e l'viso di pietosi color' farsi,	*and, true or false, I know not, her face seemed*
non so se vero o falso, mi parea:	*to turn then to the colours of compassion,*
i' che l'ésca amorosa al petto avea,	*I thought; I, with love's bait hooked in my breast,*
qual meraviglia se di súbito arsi?	*what wonder that I flamed in sudden fire?*
Non era l'andar suo cosa mortale,	*Her tread was never once a mortal thing*
ma d'angelica forma: et le parole	*but of angelic form: the words she spoke*
sonavan altro, che pur voce humana.	*sounded unlike a simple human voice*

Uno spirito celeste, un vivo sole	*a heavenly spirit, aye, a living sun*
fu quel ch'i'vidi: et se non fosse or tale,	*was she I saw: if she is not so now,*
piagha per allentar d'arco non sana.	*a loosened bowstring cannot heal a wound.*

The hair is gold thread, the eyes can kindle moonlight into day, love is a swallowed bait, the lover bursts into flame, her walk is an angel's, her voice other than human (presumably angelic also); she was a heavenly spirit and a living sun. These 'compares', though, are not conceits, not even 'Petrarchan conceits'. The *conceit* is her more-than-humanness; the images embody and convey it.

In the century-and-a half that followed Francesco, however, the images became so standardized and the Beloved so identified with the ways of writing about her that contemporary readers may have muddled the two categories as much as later scholars. Be that as it may, by the second half of the sixteenth century, poets such as Pietro Bembo (1470–1547) had so codified the 'Petrarchan' writing of, say, sonnets and *canzoni* about love that a certain reaction began to make itself felt. Nowhere was this more true than in France. As early as 1542 Antoine Héroët from Lyon, in *La Parfaicte amye*, criticized

Tous les escripts et larmoyants autheurs	*All those writings and weepy authors*
Tout le Pétrarque et ses imitateurs	*All of Petrarch and his imitators*
Qui de souspirs et de froydes querelles	*Who with sighs and chilly arguments*
Remplissent l'air en parlant aux estoilles	*Fill the air as they commune with the stars*
Ne facent point soupsonner, qu'a aymer	*Would not make you suspect that in loving*
Entre les doulx il y ayt de l'amer	*Among the sweets there is bitterness also*
Quand vous voyez ces seruiteurs, qui meurent	*When you see those 'servants', who 'die'*
Et en priant hors d'alaine demeurent,	*And are breathless in their beseeching*
Euitez les, comme males odeurs,	*Avoid them like bad smells*
Fuyez ces sots, & lourds persuadeurs,	*Flee those fools, & heavy persuaders*
Pour vous tirer, qui n'ont autre aymant	*Who to attract you have no other magnet*
Que compter maulx, qu'ilz souffrent en aymant.	*Than to count the ills they suffer in loving.*[10]

This was followed in 1553 by Joachim du Bellay, writing as to a lady:

J'ay oublié l'art de pétrarquizer.	*I have forgotten Petrarchizing's art.*
Je veulx d'amour franchement deviser	*I want to talk of love with openness*
Sans vous flater, et sans me deguiser.	*not flatter you, and not disguise myself.*
Ceulx qui font tant de plaintes	*Those who complain and weep*
N'ont pas le quart d'une vraye amitié,	*Don't have a smidge of love that's true and honest*
Et n'ont pas tant de peine la moitié,	*and have no morsel of the hurt they claim*
Comme leurs yeulx, pour vous faire pitié	*just as their eyes, to draw your sympathy,*
Getent de larmes feintes.	*Weep tears that are pretence.*[11]

Instead of comparing elements of her beauty, as the Petrarchists do, to gold, crystal, marble, ivory, lilies, carnations, and roses, he will simply say that her beauty matches her grace and leave it at that. Instead of saying, as the Petrarchists do, that his love is such that, transfixed by ice and fire, he will die of it, he will say only that his love is as perfect as affection for a lovely face can be and leave it at that. (But – he ends, disturbingly – if, having heard this, she still prefers Petrarchizing, he can and will do that too.)

Clearly, a new wave has been building. A group of young men of good family, destined chiefly for the study of law but fond of literature, found itself at the Collège Coqueret in Paris, under the aegis of the great humanist Jean Daurat (1508–88), studying Greek and Latin poetry and writing French. When Du Bellay got there, he found young Jean-Antoine de Baïf (1532–89) and Pierre, the son of the bookish former warrior knight Louis de Ronsard and very much the dominant personality and talent. At least during the moments of Daurat's absence, the atmosphere must have been intriguingly similar to that of young Jack Donne and his literary friends in Lincoln's Inn – with this difference, that lads like Baïf and Ronsard were of a class that could easily frequent the Court.

Even in the third generation of the French Renaissance writing love-sonnets came naturally to literary young men whose grandfathers had known Francis I's Italian campaigns. Ronsard did so with gusto, addressing his first batch to the very young daughter of a banker of noble Florentine descent, Cassandre Salviati. Having fought his father's desire to see him study law and purchase an important Court position, and unapt for a military career through early deafness, he had entered into minor orders[12] in 1543 and decided to make his name as a poet. We are here concerned only with his love-poetry, of which the first collection, *Amours*, appeared in 1552, with Cassandre's portrait on the frontispiece.

Even though his friend Du Bellay had crossly rejected 'Petrarchizing' the year before, a number of the sonnets to Cassandre still carry on, or appear to carry on, that grand old tradition.

Ce beau coral, ce marbre qui soupire	*That coral exquisite, that breathing marble*
Et cet eben ornement du sourci,	*that ornament of eyebrow's ebony*
Et cet albâtre en voûte racourci,	*that alabaster in a shortened arch*
Et ces saphirs, ce iaspe et ce porphyre:	*those sapphires, jaspers and that porphyry:*
Ces diamans, ces rubis, qu'un Zephyre	*Those diamonds, those rubies, that a Zephyr*
Tient animez d'un soupir adouci,	*keeps with a sigh in motion animate*
Et ces oeillets et ces roses aussi,	*and then those roses and carnations too,*
Et ce fin or, où l'or mesme se mire :	*and that fine gold that mirrors gold itself:*
Me sont dans l'ame en si profond esmoy,	*Deep in my soul they live in such emotion*
Qu'un autre objet ne se presente à moy,	*that other subject I encounter none*
Sinon, Belleau, leur beauté que j'honore,	*only their beauty, Belleau,[13] which I honour*
Et le plaisir qui ne se peut passer	*and, yes, the pleasure that can't help itself*
De les songer, penser et repenser,	*but dream them, think them, and think them anew,*
Songer, penser et repenser encore.	*dream them, think them, and then think them still.*

However, in others he already confuses conventional readers with startling twists:

Ces liens d'or, ceste bouche vermeille,	*Those golden bonds – the crimson of the lips,*
Pleine de lis, de roses et d'oeillets,	*carnations, roses, lilies all in plenty,*
Et ces sourcis deux croissans nouvelets,	*and eyebrows like two crescents newly-formed*
Et ceste joue a l'Aurore pareille :	*and ah, that cheek's complexion, like the Dawn:*
Ces mains, ce col, ce front, et ceste oreille,	*Those hands, that neck, that forehead and that ear,*

Et de ce sein les boutons verdelets	and on that breast the lovely lively buds
Et de ces yeux les astres jumelets,	and the twin glowing stars that are her eyes
Qui font trembler les ames de merveille,	and make all living souls in wonder tremble,
Firent nicher Amour dedans mon sein,	made Love for dwelling-place nest in my breast
Qui gros de germe avoit le ventre plein	who, big with seed, had all his belly full
D'oeufs non formez qu'en nostre sang il couve.	of unformed eggs he broods on in our blood.
Comment vivroy-je autrement qu'en langueur,	How can I live other than weak and feeble
Quand une engence immortelle je trouve,	when I discover an immortal brood
D'Amours esclos et couvez en mon cueur?	of Loves bred, hatched, and brooded in my heart?[14]

What are we to make of this? What did Ronsard's readers make of it? It is as if, having mounted a horse of a known and trusted breed, we are suddenly, in the middle of the journey, with a kick of its heels and a cunning twist of its back, thrown into the dust.

First of all, we should probably forget Cassandre. While this sonnet is nominally about her, we may safely assume that it was written, and certainly published, to surprise the poet's friends and rivals.[15] If we retain our distinction between *concept* and image, the basic 'conceit' here is not unusual: love is, if not a poison, then something incurable in the blood. There is, however, in this case a second stage: the decision to embody the basic conceit in a secondary one of surrealistic impossibility – Eros, a young boy, becomes a kind of gravid female insect, brooding and breeding immortal larvae in the lover's bloodstream. This surreal *concetto* is presented in an image lively enough to disgust, retroactively creating the whole sonnet as a *barroco*, a pearl with a great flaw. And that in its turn suggests to readers a dark conceit on the subject of love.

As early as 1552, then, we can see that Ronsard was already experimenting with ways to undermine the outmoded art of *pétrarquizer* by means, not so much of new themes concerning love – love is still the terrible tyrant, the lover his helpless victim, the beloved his heedless and even heartless collaborator – but of new *concepts* in which to dress the lasting themes.

From Cassandre Ronsard's sonnet art (and conceivably his heart) moved on, first to Marie, a simple country girl from Anjou whom, he says, he loved for six years, for whom he wrote sixty-nine sonnets, some *chansons*, and at her death a handsome *Elegie*, of which more below. Clearly, he attempts in a number of these to suit his style to her simplicity, and in the process attains a certain freedom from the visible struggles of the Cassandre collection – struggles between *pétrarquisme* and *antipétrarquisme*, between an ornate idealism on the one hand and its self-consciously provocatory opposite on the other.

Incorporating both, and learning a new simplicity from his celebration of Marie, by 1572 he has moved on to his third and final beloved, Hélène de Fonsèque de Surgères (1546–1618), Gentlewoman of the Bedchamber to Catherine de Medici who, legend claims, suggested to the poet that he celebrate her young protégée. The third and last collection of *Amours*, then, appeared in two volumes in 1578, and it is with these poems, notably the sonnets, and their conceits that we chiefly concern ourselves. What these have suggested to us will be most clearly shown in discussing half a dozen individual sonnets and summing up our findings afterwards.

Maîtresse, quand je pense aux traverses d'Amour,	*O mistress mine, when Love's predicaments*
Qu'ores chaude, ores froide en aimant tu me donnes,	*teem in my mind, how you wax hot and cold,*
Comme sans passion mon cœur tu passionnes,	*how, passionless, you fill my heart with passion,*
Qui n'a contre son mal ni trêve ni séjour :	*so that it knows no cease-fire and no rest:*
Je soupire la nuit, je me complains le jour	*at night I sigh, complaining in the daytime*
Contre toi, ma Raison, qui mon fort abandonnes,	*against you, Reason mine, that flee my fortress:*
Et pleine de discours, confuse, tu t'étonnes	*full of fine words, embarrassed and amazed*
Dès le premier assaut, sans défendre ma tour.	*upon the first assault you quit my towers*
Non : si forts ennemis n'assaillent notre Place,	*O no, those who besiege our citadel*
Qu'ils ne fussent vaincus, si tu tournois la face,	*would flee at once if you'd but turn your face*
Encores que mon cœur trahit ce qui est sien.	*although my heart betrays its own domain*
Une œillade, une main, un petit ris me tue :	*a glance, a hand, a quick laugh, and I'm dead:*
De trois faibles soudards ta force est combattue :	*a mere three soldiers and your force is vanquished:*
Qui te dira divine, il ne dira pas bien.	*who says you are divine is much mistaken.*

This sonnet, no. XLVII in the Premier Livre, opens in a manner that reassures readers with a promise of conventionality. *La maîtresse* is inconstant, she waxes hot and wanes cold; cold herself, she fills the lover with a passion that gives him no rest; all these *traverses* of Love are well known. Then, however, a precocious *volta* intervenes: the addressee changes from the Beloved to Reason, and remains so until the end. The theme, of course, is that reason is no match for love. What, then, is the 'conceit'? We consider it to be unambiguously expressed in the last line: Reason, who is supposedly man's godly faculty, is in no way divine. He is routed without a fight by three pygmy entities: a glance, the touch of a hand, a smile. And as such, the image that expresses the conceit is that of a fortress basely betrayed by a commander quite capable of defending it, one who surrenders when faced with three puny infantrymen.

Such an image, perhaps, might occur to any poet; but is it a coincidence that one finds it again, with a slight variation, in John Donne? 'I, like an usurp'd town to another due, / Labor to admit you, but oh, to no end; / *Reason, your viceroy in me, me should defend, / But is captiv'd, and proves weak or untrue.*'[16]

(Once again, this may make us ponder the question, fundamental to the understanding of both Ronsard's poetic and Donne's, of conceit's relation to image. There will be more to say about this, but for the moment it is useful to bear in mind that in Ronsard's sonnets *concept*, while frequently related to 'comparison' or imagery, is not identical with it and still carries much of the traditional meaning of an intellectual idea.)

Celle, de qui l'Amour vainquit la fantaisie,	*The one whose fancy Cupid bound in thrall*
Que Jupiter conceut sous un Cygne emprunté :	*Whom Jove begot beneath a borrowed swan*
Ceste sœur des Jumeaux, qui fist par sa beauté	*divine Twins' sister, who by matchless beauty*
Opposer toute Europe aux forces de l'Asie,	*made Europe and all Asia enemies,*
Disoit à son mirouer, quand elle vit saisie	*said to her mirror, when she saw her face*
Sa face de vieillesse et de hideuseté :	*deformed and scrawled with age and ugliness:*
Que mes premiers Maris insensez ont esté	*how foolish were my husbands, up in arms*
De s'armer pour jouyr d'une chair si moisie !	*to conquer and enjoy such rotting flesh!*
Dieux, vous estes jaloux et pleins de cruauté !	*Gods, you are jealous and quite pitiless!*

Des dames sans retour s'en-vole la beauté :	Beauty of ladies, with the wind it goes:
Aux serpens tous les ans vous ostez la vieillesse.	yet even snakes are younger every year.
Ainsi disoit Helene en remirant son teint.	So Helen said, examining her skin.
Cest exemple est pour vous : cueillez vostre jeunesse :	Your *story* this: enjoy your youth right now:
Quand on perd son Avril, en Octobre on s'en plaint.	When April's wasted, tears come in October.

In this sonnet, no. XXVI in the Second Livre, the theme is once again traditional: *carpe diem*, enjoy your youth while it lasts, for it lasts not long, and concomitantly enjoy your youth by ceding to your lover's (i.e. my) entreaties. It is the same theme that informs Ronsard's most famous sonnet: *Quand vous serez bien vieille, le soir à la chandelle*.

The *concept*, however, is that of Hélène's putative, conceivable identification, by way of her name, with the beauty who occasioned the Siege of Troy. And this *concept* at once produces a memorable and most disturbing image: Helen of Troy in middle age or beyond, looking in her mirror and wincing at what she sees. The image is pursued with merciless precision – not describing what Helen sees but giving an exact portrayal of the emotion the image evokes. Disgust at the *chair moisie*, the 'rotting flesh', and wonder that such ugliness could have provoked a desire strong enough to lead to arms. The final two lines, aiming Helen at Hélène in a reminiscence of the prophet Nathan's applying his parable to King David – *Cest exemple est pour vous!* – restate the theme which, while unoriginal, has now through the *concept* and its image, acquired a new and disturbing force.

Ny la douce pitié, ny le pleur lamentable	Not gentle pity nor a plaining tear
Ne t'ont baillé ton nom : Helene vient d'oster,	gave you your name: Helene comes from deprive,
De ravir, de tuer, de piller, d'emporter	from ravish, kill, pillage, and snatch away
Mon esprit et mon cœur, ta proye miserable.	my spirit and my heart, your wretched prey
Homere, en se jouant, de toy fist une fable,	Homer for fun made out of you a fable
Et moy l'histoire au vray. Amour, pour te flatter,	my tale's the truth. Love, out to flatter you,
Comme tu feis à Troye, au cœur me vient jetter	like you in Troy, comes, flings into my heart

Ton feu, qui de mes oz se paist insatiable.	your fire, which feeds with greed upon my bones
La voix, que tu feignois à l'entour du Cheval	The voice you charmed and feigned around the Horse
Pour decevoir les Grecs, me devoit faire sage :	to dupe the Greeks should now have made me wise
Mais l'homme de nature est aveugle à son mal,	but man's by nature blind to meet his bane
Qui ne peut se garder, ny prevoir son dommage.	can't save himself nor can foresee his ruin.
Au pis-aller, je meurs pour ce beau nom fatal,	at worst I die for that sweet fatal name
Qui mit tout l'Asie et l'Europe en pillage.	that put all Asia and Europe to the sack.

Sonnet no. IX of the Second Livre takes the *concept* of no. XXVI and turns it into a lethal game. The theme, now distantly perceptible, is the usual one of the lover's suffering; the *concept* takes up all the space and sucks up all the air in the room. What game is this? It is one we shall see again, one of Ronsard's favourite conceits: we might call it the Perverted Connotation. When readers see, at first glance – and we are necessarily intended to suppose that the original, privileged reader was Hélène herself – that the poet will compare her with her Homeric namesake, they (she?) will assume that the purpose of that 'compare' is a compliment to her beauty, a beauty so incomparable that two nations went to war for it.[17]

No. The poet forces us to contemplate not the beauty but the war, and he rubs our reluctant noses in war's ugliness. And in suddenly turning the implied object of the pillage into *mon esprit et mon cœur*, he turns the 'compare' of the two Helens into an identification. This he pursues implacably by telling her what *she* (not a namesake) did in Troy. Love has lit in his, the lover's heart a fire as devastating as those *she* lit in Troy. Hearing *her* voice, the voice of the charmer which the Greeks heard around the Horse[18] should have warned him; but we men are powerless against the evil that seeks us out. Homer wrote fiction; my story is true. And if I die of it [as good Petrarchan lovers must] I will die for a name that put all Europe and Asia to the sack.

Not only is this the Perverted Connotation, it is also what Frank Warnke mentions as a characteristic of Early Baroque: 'extravagance, extremeness'.[19] The relentless asyndeta of lines 2–3, the fire that feeds with greed upon his bones, and the sonnet's ending with 'pillage' as its final word, leave the readers breathless.

Comme un vieil combatant qui ne veut plus s'armer,	*As an old fighter tired of taking arms*
Ayant le corps chargé de coups et de vieillesse,	*His body battered long by blows and age*
Regarde en s'esbatant l'Olympique jeunesse	*Ruefully smiles at the Olympic young*
Pleine d'un sang bouillant aux joustes escrimer :	*Sword-fighting in their jousts with joyous blood:*
Ainsi je regardois du jeune Dieu d'aimer,	*So was I looking at the champions bold*
Dieu qui combat tousjours par ruse et par finesse.	*of the young God of love (he always fights*
Les gaillards champions, qui d'une chaude presse	*by tricks and sleights) hotly competing*
Se veulent en l'arene amoureuse enfermer :	*in love's arena fast to lock themselves:*
Quand tu lis reverdir mon escorce ridée	*when all at once you greened my wrinkled bark*
De ta charmante voix, ainsi que fit Medee	*with charming voice, just as Medea did*
Par herbes et par jus le père de Jason.	*with herbs and juice to Jason's agèd father*
Je n'ay contre ton charme opposé ma défense :	*Against your charm I've entered no defence:*
Toutefois je me deuls de r'entrer en enfance,	*and yet I mourn to be in second childhood,*
Pour perdre tant de fois l'esprit et la Raison	*to lose and lose my Reason and my mind.*

A milder sonnet, this no. XXI of the Second Livre: more melancholy, more rueful, and much less aggressive. And yet beyond the obvious and elegant 'compare' of the octave which reminds readers, as Ronsard does often, of his age and its drawback for one who still aspires to be a player in the lists of love, there lurk two *concepts* with venom in their tails.

First, there is here another example of what we have called the conceit of the Perverted Connotation. As he was feeling old, Hélène 'greened his wrinkled bark' just as Medea did. Now then, the readers say, isn't that a little doubtful? Medea, after all, carries a connotation of bewitching beauty and lethality. No, no, says the sonnet: what I want to call up here is Medea as a dispenser of benevolent magic: when Aeson, Jason's father, could not be present at the celebrations of the Golden Fleece, Medea rejuvenated him through sorcery. This is comforting; but those readers who actually knew the whole story would remember that Medea's sorcery in this case was associated with Hecate, the goddess of night's terrors. She prepared a cauldron of magic liquid, and then cut Aeson's throat, poured out all his blood, and replaced it with the magic potion. And the old man was now once again young and fit.

Well then, we say, here is a connotation *comfortingly* perverted or reversed. We might find the method of throat-cutting a little disturbing, but the result is entirely desirable. Or is it? For there is one more *concept* to come. In the last tercet, he not only cannot defend himself against her charm (and read that noun as a spell: Medea's sorcery?) but no longer tries to; and yet. And yet this yielding to her compelling loveliness makes him grieve, for to be her lover, we discover, is not after all to be a rejuvenated Aeson with greened bark, full of vigour and robustness. To be her lover is by her magic to go back further; or rather, it is to enter into second childhood (remember: he is an *old* fighter, and an *old* poet), and to lose, and to lose repeatedly, on every new occasion, one's wit, one's mind (*esprit* is both) and one's Reason.

The conceit, then, we may say, is that of first perverting readers' partial memory of Medea by evoking a lesser-known episode of her life; and then in turn perverting even that (and thus disturbing even those readers who remembered Aeson) by giving a lamentable twist to the rejuvenation.

Qu'il me soit arraché des tetins de sa mere	Let someone pull him off his mother's breasts,
Ce jeune enfant Amour, et qu'il me soit vendu :	this brat, this Love, and sell the child to me
Il ne faut plus qu'il croisse, il m'a desja perdu :	he must not grow, he's scuppered me already
Vienne quelque marchand, je le mets à l'enchere.	a trader comes, I'll put him up for auction.
D'un si mauvais garçon la vente n'est pas chere,	The price of such a bad boy can't be high
J'en feray bon marché. Ah ! j'ay trop attendu.	I'll discount him. I've waited far too long.
Mais voyez comme il pleure : il m'a bien entendu.	but see how now he weeps: he's heard me talking.
Appaise toy, mignon, j'ay passé ma cholere,	Calm down, my pretty, all my anger's done.
Je ne te vendray point : au contraire je veux	I'll not sell you: instead what I will do
Pour Page t'envoyer à ma maistresse Heleine,	is send you to Helene, page to my lady,
Qui toute te ressemble et d'yeux et de cheveux,	who is much like you in her eyes and hair

Aussi fine que toy, de malice aussi pleine.	*clever like you, as full of tricks as you,*
Comme enfans vous croistrez et vous jou'rez tous deux :	*like children both you'll grow and play together*
Quand tu seras plus grand, tu me payras ma peine.	*and when you've grown you'll pay me for my grief.*

Sonnet no. XLI of the Second Livre is outrageous, and flamboyantly so. 'Extravagance and extremeness', indeed. We see here another of the characteristics Warnke ascribes to the Early Baroque: 'the illusion of thought in the very process of being thought; verse assimilated to the condition of heightened conversation; a diction at once colloquial and capable of embracing an effectively unlimited range of references to human activities, mundane or learned; a private poetry of the greatest intimacy which we, as audience, have the illusion of not hearing but overhearing'.[20]

The *energia* here is initially one of pure exasperation, couching the common theme of protest against Cupid in a new and marvellous *concept*: I, the lover, will buy the blasted child and sell him to the nearest slave-trader, at a discount yet.

Having introduced this, though, the text instantly produces a precocious *volta* halfway through the second quatrain: the 'heightened conversation' now involves the reader, invited in a second conceit to see the boy's crying and thus also the poet's kindly reply – which also has a sting in the tail, as she is like (i.e. no better than) Cupid, and when he grows up he will have to pay.

J'avois, en regardant tes beaux yeux, enduré	*The beauty of your eyes had lit such flames*
Tant de flammes au cœur, qu'une âpre sécheresse	*throughout my heart that drought had settled there*
Avait cuite ma langue en extrême détresse,	*and parched even my tongue that talked so much*
Ayant de trop parler tout le corps altéré.	*it had dried all of me: pain and distress –*
Lors tu fis apporter en ton vase doré	*but then you had them bring me water, cool,*
De l'eau froide d'un puits : et la soif qui me presse,	*straight from the well in your gold cup: my thirst*
Me fit boire à l'endroit où tu bois, ma Maîtresse,	*hurried me, mistress mine, straight to the spot*
Quand ton vaisseau se voit de ta lèvre honoré.	*where your lip drinking gravely honours it*
Mais le vase amoureux de ta bouche qu'il baise,	*ah, but the cup, in love with your mouth's kisses,*

En réchauffant ses bords du feu qu'il a reçu,	so heats his rim with your imprinted fire
Le garde en sa rondeur comme en une fournaise.	it's held within his roundness like a furnace
Seulement au toucher je l'ai bien aperçu.	only on touching it I found this out:
Comment pourrai-je vivre un quart d'heure à mon aise	how can I live a quarter of an hour
Quand je sens contre moi l'eau se tourner en feu ?	when I feel water changing into fire?

We do not know, in the works of Ronsard, when exactly a particular sonnet was written. But this, no. XXXV of the Premier Livre, shows a version of the *concept* or conceit much more recognizable to readers of English poetry. Here we have no clear distinction between the theme, the *concept*, and the image. A remnant of a distinct theme is found in the opening, which reminds us of the lover's traditional state of burning – whether or not the flames are accompanied by icy frost. But instantly the conceit takes over, and it dominates the poem. The cup, touched once by the lady's lip, has become a lover itself, and thus is also filled with unbearable heat: a heat that invades its entire mass, making it a furnace which in its turn, by implication, boils the water within it, and not only boils it but turns the water, impossibly, into fire itself.

The image, here, is at one with the conceit: the conceit *is* the image. And so by the end of the sonnet we are faced with something that begins to resemble an English 'Metaphysical' conceit. Not entirely: it is not a simile or metaphor, it is not a 'compare'. But it is a sophisticated play with Nature and its laws, not based – as, say, the pair of stiff twin compasses – on a *being like* but on a *becoming*, on a transformation that alters a natural fact and, thus, a natural law. The gold cup, contrary to gold's inanimate kind, falls in love; the touch of the Beloved's lips transforms a small vessel of precious metal into a furnace – which, in turn, transforms cool and healing water into a raging and lethal fire.

We think that in one particular sense the reader here begins to see on the horizon the shade of John Donne. There is not, here, the colloquial *energia* that threatens to sell Cupid to a slaver: that energy that Warnke associates with 'Early Baroque' and that one of us, finding it in Donne, traced (at least in England) to Philip Sidney; but there is the intensity of a physical (metaphysical?) transformation that creates a sensory and therefore intellectual confusion, with Love to blame for all.[21]

Cusin, monstre à doüble aile, au mufle Elephantin,	Mosquito, two-winged monster with a trunk,

Canal à tirer sang, qui voletant en presse	bloodsucking channel, that in busy flight
Sifles d'un son aigu, ne picque ma Maistresse,	hums with high sound, don't sting my lovely mistress
Et la laisse dormir du soir jusqu'au matin.	but let her sleep in peace from night till morn.
Si ton corps d'un atome, et ton nez de mastin	With atom body and with bloodhound nose
Cherche tant à picquer la peau d'une Deesse,	if you must pierce a divine epidermis
En lieu d'elle, Cusin, la mienne je te laisse :	I'll offer mine in just exchange for hers
Succe la, que mon sang te soit comme un butin.	suck mine and so let my blood be your loot.
Cusin, je m'en desdy : hume moy de la belle	But no, I take it back: take from that beauty
Le sang, et m'en apporte une goutte nouvelle	some blood, and bring me just one warm, fresh drop
Pour gouster quel il est. Ha, que le sort fatal	to taste what it is like. Ha, why does fate
Ne permet à mon corps de prendre ton essence !	not let my body take your nature on?
Repicquant ses beaux yeux, elle auroit cognoissance	I'd prick her eyes again, and she would know
Qu'un rien qu'on ne voit pas, fait souvent un grand mal.	how unseen trifles may cause grievous pain.[22]

The first thing Donneans reading this will think of is of course 'The Flea'. And doubtless rightly so: a witty poem about a small troublesome insect and a presumably beautiful woman is not only a delight but a singularly recognizable theme. But the same Donneans, instructed in literary history and aware that influences may proceed beyond the Channel, will then think also of Madeleine and Catherine Desroches from Poitiers, and of the following history:

> The 'Grands-Jours' held at Poitiers in 1579 were a new occasion to show off the worth of the Dames Desroches: their drawing-room was the meeting-place for all the city's magistrates called to this solemnity. One day when they were assembled Etienne Pasquier, noticing a flea that had 'settled on the middle of the breast' of Mlle Desroches, pointed to the creature's temerity. A few playful remarks followed, and the incident ended with the exchange of two passages of verse between Pasquier and Catherine Desroches.
>
> That was all it took to set off the poetical humour of all those honest magistrates, who gave themselves to celebrating the flea in French, in Spanish, in Latin,

and even in Greek. Etienne Pasquier assembled the various texts produced in this poetical joust, and it is their collection that produced the volume known under the title of *La Puce de Mme Desroches*. The proper title would have been *La puce de Mlle Desroches*, for it is Catherine who was the adventure's heroine.[23]

Was this, as is sometimes thought, the origin of Donne's flea poem? It might be so; but it may be interesting also to point to Ronsard's sonnet about the mosquito, which appeared in the 1578 volume of *Amours*, a year before the event in Poitiers. Let us first look at that.

The 'Cusin', also and still today spelled 'Cousin', in modern French is technically not a mosquito but a member of the genus *tipulidae*, in Britain called a Daddy Long-Legs and in America a cranefly. It does not bite or sting, but has a long proboscis used for laying eggs. The word does not appear in Hollyband. However, in Nicot it is translated as 'genus insecti, Culex', and in the 1694 *Dictionnaire de l'Académie française* it is a 'Sorte de mouscheron piquant, & fort importun' (*a sort of small stinging fly, most importunate*). So we may usefully translate it as 'mosquito'.

The first thing we notice in Ronsard's sonnet is the Monster with an Elephantine Snout: an image, one might say, under a microscope, an enormous and almost parodic enlargement. The speaker has been looking at the mosquito very closely indeed. Very soon this is confused by its 'atom body' (not, of course, our atom but that of Epicurus) which at once grows a bloodhound's nose. The whole, aiming itself at the sleeping beloved, is wonderfully surrealistic, suggesting wit and humour from the beginning. The lover's proposing his own skin exchange for that of a Goddess continues this vein. A palinodic *volta* similar to that in his sonnet about Cupid and the slave-trader, though here in its proper place, introduces his wish to taste her blood, while a final extension of that makes him long to *be* the mosquito so that his sting of her may teach her a lesson. Noticeable is the participle phrase '(re)picquant ses yeux', which all dictionaries explain as 'stinging or pricking again' but to which Hollyband adds 'to spurre'.[24] To sting her eyes seems unnecessarily cruel, but if we add an overtone of spurring her to see and understand, the phrase, if not strictly logical, becomes not only comprehensible but cleverly apt.

If we look at this mosquito sonnet in the sense of theme and conceit, we can see that the theme is the lady's sleep while the unquiet lover wakes: the sleep is unconsciousness but also uncaring.[25] And here the *concept*, the conceit, and the image coincide: the mosquito, initially reproved, finally envied, becomes the compact vector of this tiny drama of (un)consciousness.

Clearly, this is the moment for our transition. From mosquito to flea is but a small step, and one of John Donne's most famous poems calls us to trace lines and make comparisons.

> Marke but this flea, and marke in this,
> How little that which thou deniest me is;
> Mee it suck'd first, and now sucks thee,
> And in this flea, our two bloods mingled be;
> Confesse it, this cannot be said
> A sinne, or shame, or losse of maidenhead,
>   Yet this enjoyes before it wooe,
>   And pamper'd swells with one blood made of two,
>   And this, alas, is more than wee would doe.
>
> Oh stay, three lives in one flea spare,
> Where wee almost, nay more than maryed are.
> This flea is you and I, and this
> Our marriage bed, and marriage temple is;
> Though parents grudge, and you, w'are met,
> And cloysterd in these living walls of Jet.
>   Though use make thee apt to kill mee,
>   Let not to this, selfe murder added bee,
>   And sacrilege, three sinnes in killing three.
>
> Cruell and sodaine, hast thou since
> Purpled thy naile, in blood of innocence?
> In what could this flea guilty bee,
> Except in that drop which it suckt from thee?
> Yet thou triumph'st, and saist that thou
> Find'st not thy selfe, nor mee the weaker now;
>   'Tis true; then learne how false, feares bee:
>   Just so much honor, when thou yeeld'st to mee,
>   Will wast, as this flea's death tooke life from thee.

The theme is not quite the same as that of Ronsard's 'Cusin': that was a lover's complaint at his lady's indifference, while this is a straightforward seduction poem, challenging the lady's refusal. The image is similar: a troublesome insect stinging, or biting. Yet the *conceit* is quite different. Ronsard's *concept* blended with his image: first offering a substitute target, then imagining himself a substitute predator, the poet-lover concentrates on the insect's aggression. Donne's conceit is far bolder: not only has the aggression been consummated, it has inspired contrasting reactions which, voiced by only one of the two humans, constitute the poem. And, moreover, there are not only words: there are two (re-)actions which we do not see but which take place invisibly in between the stanzas – the first, the woman's reach for the flea; the second, her killing it. And finally, within the poem's conceit there is the lover's own conceit: the flea, biting both, has mingled their blood just as sex is imagined to do, and has thus become their marriage-bed.

Both poems end with a comment on the insect's insignificance: one contrasts that with the importance of such insignificance's potential effects, the other uses it to argue for a similar insignificance in the refused act of love. How, now, may we compare the conceits? Ronsard's is both simpler and less gripping, because he has the lover addressing the insect. Donne's, creating one side of a human conversation, including physical actions offstage, is far more dramatic, and takes an important stage further what we have seen beginning in Ronsard's development.

Comparing Ronsard and Donne, we may begin with what one of us, Anne Prescott, wrote years ago: 'Ronsard's great lines often achieve a classical finality rather than the intellectual compression of Donne at his best ... yet Donne might have recognized in Ronsard a writer particularly fascinating like himself, for a carefully modulated voice and a sense of self, an often dramatic relationship to the hearer within the poems, varying rhetorical poses, and radical inconsistencies.'[26]

It is interesting that Donne never seems to have written a love-sonnet. And yet some of his non-sonnet lyrics could easily fit a sonnet form: 'The Indifferent' is an excellent example, with the third and last stanza reading very like a Ronsardian sestet.

What of conceits? Ronsard's conceits, we have seen, are not Metaphysical. Neither, however, are they Petrarchan, at least in the sonnets we have shown. They seem to bear a different relationship to both literary tradition and intellectual individuality. We may distinguish three types, at least in these texts. In the first place there is the Perverted Reference or Connotation. Readers are flattered by a reference they recognize and gratefully provide from their own memories the supposedly correct connotation. The text, however, then upsets their satisfaction by leading from the same reference to a different, and sometimes opposite, connotation. At his virtuoso best, Ronsard can double this, slipping one perversion inside another: the reference to Medea, above, first surprises readers by providing them with a connotation of kindliness not usually associated with the character, and then surprises them again by making that connotation lead to an opposite and unwelcome conclusion. Another, and harsher, example of the Perverted Reference is what the poet does with what we may call Helenity. Comparing Hélène (de Surgères) to Helen (of Troy) is so obvious a *concept* that it quickly became a topos, involving other poets as well. In itself it bears a possible complexity, since not only was Helen a famous beauty but she was the cause of a classic conflict. As Nagel and others have shown, that allowed a reference both to love's wars and on occasion to the conflicts in Charles IX's and Henri III's France. But in the first of the two texts we have quoted, Ronsard twists the topos into a Perverted Connotation by adding the element of age. Thus

Helen the legendary beauty is followed into age and (self-)disgust, her reflected image made to lead to a harsh *carpe diem* instead.[27]

The second type of conceit we have discerned in the *Amours* for Hélène is what we might call the Outrageous Exaggeration. Clearly, this applies to the proposition to rip little Cupid from his mother's breast and sell him to the lover, who will then resell him at a discount to the first passing slave-trader. This leaves other accusations against the love-god, such as Sidney's 'murth'ring boy' with his bloody bullet, far behind. And again, a second twist is built in: after a palinodic *volta*, he will be joined to Hélène as a new friend or sibling, they being similar not only in eyes and hair but in (appalling) character. A charming example of 'extravagance, extremeness'.

There is, however, a darker side to the Outrageous Exaggeration. In the second of the two Helen of Troy sonnets quoted above, Ronsard first twists the Helen connotation from beauty to war, and then first bludgeons the reader (and let us not forget that the notional privileged reader was Hélène) with verbs of an all-too-real battlefield, then ties those to his own raped heart, then identifies Hélène with Helen in specific guilty deeds in Troy, and eventually shows the appropriateness of dying for such a murderous name. The connotations are perverted beyond decency, and their instrument is an Outrageous Exaggeration no longer amusing. Every now and then, in these later sonnets, there is a darker side to Ronsard's *concepts* than we have found in Donne.

The third conceit may be described as the Scientific Surprise. This we have shown in the sonnet referring to the golden cup. Golden cups, of course, are topically so rich a field that connotations necessarily abound. In this case, however, the object's *inamoramento*, followed by its physical transformation into a furnace, which in turn transforms the water it contains, not into boiling water or steam but into fire itself, is a *concept* of a new kind, edging from the physical into the Metaphysical: here the conceit truly becomes the image-sequence itself.

It may be worthwhile to take three more poems, two longer and one a sonnet, both perhaps more profound, as a final comparison. Nothing could, in the lyric mode, be more serious and have more need of the poet's personal commitment, than a poem of mourning. Accordingly, we shall look at Ronsard's 'Elegie pour la mort de Marie', his sonnet 'Terre ouvre moy ton sein', and John Donne's 'Nocturnall upon St Lucies Day'.

Marie Dupin, Hélène de Surgères's predecessor in Ronsard's affections, was a simple country girl from Bourgueil in the Anjou, whom the poet loved for six years until she died in 1558 at the age of twenty-one. The only one of his three Muses to do so during his lifetime, she became the subject of a series of thirteen posthumous sonnets, some Stanzas and an

Elegy. The latter (see Appendix A) contains twenty-three stanzas of varying length: the first six of eight lines, then one of twelve, one of six, one of four, one of six, one of eight, one of four, three of six, one of eight, two of four, one of eight, one of eight, one of twelve, and two of six. The rhymes are always in pairs, the metre is the alexandrine. There are 158 lines in all, as against 45 for the Donne poem.

Coming to write his grief at Marie's death at some length, Ronsard at first had recourse to Cupid, or Amour. On the day of her death, Love – the Elegy's first conceit – broke his arrows and extinguished his torch, and threw all of them upon her tomb which he then watered copiously with his tears. After a reminiscence of the poet's *inamoramento*, Amour comes back: we are reminded that in order to affect the hard-hearted poet (already famous for the Classical glories he has bestowed upon French verse), Amour has brought Marie with him, and with one shot launches both her and his arrow into Pierre's heart. Reason – the second conceit – does not betray the lover but faints, leaving desire and the senses to steer his ship whither they will. Simple as she was, she was a Goddess – the next conceit – for Divinity, after all, has been known to choose a simple birth. The conceit then moves to her eyes which, even as they are dead and buried, follow the poet still. A memory of his emotion upon learning of her death is followed by a Complaint that blames Heaven and Nature for creating her and so soon calling her back. A brief vision of her as a blessed soul in Heaven leads to the question what he, abandoned lover, now must do. The only answer is to die also, so that he may be buried in her tomb, and a future passer-by will see that he was killed by the twin arrows of Love and Death: 'and so he died, felled by a double grief, / And all for too much love of a young mistress'.

If for a moment we may imagine Ronsard, faced with the young woman's death and contemplating such a poem, it seems hard to believe that he, France's supreme poet of love-sonnets, would not at least have thought of the model of Petrarch. The Italian had, after all, written 103 of his Canzoniere's 366 poems '*in morte di madona Laura*' – after, and in large measure about, Laura's death. And the Petrarchan text that comes closest to the Elegie, in length and importance, is the first of the *in morte* poems, 'I'vo pensando' (no. 264). Yet when we read this, which comprises 136 lines arranged in seven 18-line stanzas and one of 10 lines, the mood, the emotions, and the tone, are utterly different. Cupid nowhere appears except in one brief and bitter reference: 'Love compels me, / he who never lets those who believe / in him too much follow the path of honour.'[28] There is a deep and genuine religious consciousness, which is entirely lacking in Ronsard; and between that and the poet's equally deep and genuine love for Laura there is now, after her death, a powerful inner strife which is, in fact, the poem's chief conceit.

We do not know the relative dates of the Elegie and 'Terre ouvre moy ton sein', so it would be otiose to imagine the sonnet as either earlier or later. What seems to us evident is that it moves readers as the longer poem does not.

Terre ouvre moy ton sein, et me laisse reprendre	*Open your bosom, earth, let me take back*
Mon thresor, que la Parque a caché dessous toy :	*my treasure, that Fate under you has laid:*
Ou bien si tu ne peux, ô terre cache moy	*or if you cannot, earth, hide me as well*
Sous mesme sepulture avec sa belle cendre.	*in the same tomb with her fair ashes now.*
Le traict qui la tua, devoit faire descendre	*The dart that killed her should have laid my body*
Mon corps aupres du sien pour finir mon esmoy :	*beside hers too, to end my care and grief:*
Aussi bien, veu le mal qu'en sa mort je reçoy,	*for now, given the pain her death has brought me,*
Je ne sçaurois plus vivre, et me fasche d'attendre.	*I can no longer live, and waiting hurts.*
Quand ses yeux m'esclairoient, et qu'en terre j'avois	*When her eyes lit my life, and I on earth*
Le bon-heur de les voir, à l'heure je vivois,	*could relish them, I lived from hour to hour*
Ayant de leurs rayons mon ame gouvernée.	*their gentle beams ruling my grateful soul*
Maintenant je suis mort : la Mort qui s'en-alla	*Now I am dead: Death who was on his way*
Loger dedans ses yeux, en partant m'appella,	*to settle in her eyes, took me along*
Et me fit de son soir accomplir ma journée.	*and with her evening ended all my day.*

What moves us? we ask ourselves. We could consult Sidney, who might say that here the speech of grief is used as if by someone who had genuinely felt that emotion. This is quite true, as far as it goes; but even Sidney, if pressed, would have to admit that it merely displaces the question. We might perhaps remember the topic of this essay, and look at conceits. The theme, here, is obviously grief and mourning for a loved one departed. What are the conceits?

The first is wanting to be reunited with her, in life or in death. The second explains the first, in the bleakly complete line 8. The third and last conceit seems to fold into itself a whole three-hundred-year-old Petrarchan tradition, and end that tradition as Death has ended Marie. It is the conceit of the beloved's eyes and their matchless power over the lover. Exceptionally, Ronsard has not ended with an image of their lasting closing, but has magnificently poured the conceit into a final image that unites him with her. (Modern readers, quite as moved as the poet's contemporaries, might have their reading enriched by memories of a similar image in Wilfred Owen's 'Anthem for Doomed Youth', also a mourning sonnet.) Interestingly, the conceits are mainly the same as those in the Elegie; yet here their greater concentration, and the absence of Cupid, create a vastly different effect.

In Donne's 'Nocturnall', the first thing we notice is that a new cerebral context has been added that is both calendrical and scientific. The calendar is announced in the title: the poem is set 'upon St Lucies day, beeing the shortest day'. This places the poem on the feast of St Lucy, 13 December, which in the Julian calendar, still used in England, was the date of the winter solstice. (Catholic countries had mostly already changed to the new Gregorian calendar; but since the latter had been commissioned and promulgated by the pope, Protestant countries took longer to adopt it, and England, indeed, did not officially do so until 1752.)

It is this calendrical peculiarity of the winter solstice which furnishes the poem's first conceit, that of the shortest space of sunlight and the longest night. The sun is spent, the world's whole sap is sunk into the earth, its life is dead and buried – yet all this gloom is laughter compared to the poet's state of mind.

The second stanza provides a new conceit: the poet as the object of love's new alchemy.[29] Love has made him the Quintessence of Nothingness. While she was alive there had been moments of grief that touched on Chaos; now love has made him the Elixir (which all early dictionaries define as 'quintessence') of Nothing. Humans have soul; animals and plants have desires and react to their environment; he has, he is, Nothing.

In a final conceit, he flirts with blasphemy: 'nor will my Sunne renew'. Even if she is only *his* Sun, and quite unconnected with the common Christian pun, he, John Donne, is still not only a Christian but a priest, who daily avers, in the Creed, his belief in 'the resurrection of the dead, and the life of the world to come'. This conceit, surely, is a deliberate risk, shared with readers, to show the extent and the depth of his grief.

The conceits, then, in this Nocturnall have all become what we think of as 'Metaphysical'. They have merged with the images. They are superficially surprising and unlikely, but profoundly apposite and deeply moving. In fact, the surprise may be precisely what makes them moving.

In this comparison, Ronsard at first suffers. While his 'Elegie pour la Mort de Marie' is elaborate and eloquent, it nowhere moves the twenty-first-century reader and seems unlikely to have done so to our sixteenth-century predecessor. In fact, Philip Sidney's criticism in his *Defence of Poesy* applies perfectly, and explains the problem: 'so coldly do they apply fiery speeches …'. Ronsard, in 1558, was still very much the famous poet, the professional poet who depended for any and all advancement and favours upon his poetic reputation. He was also, at that time, still very much the (brilliant) heir of Italian sixteenth-century *Petrarchismo*, the poet of the Cassandre and Marie *Amours*. As a result, however real his grief at young Marie Dupin's death, its expression at least in part followed the codes that had built his fame. And in the terms of our present inquiry, certain conceits are essential component parts of those codes.

The chief one is personified Amour, or Cupid. Whether in poetry or in painting, by the middle of the sixteenth century, this conceit has become so trite as to lack all conviction. That even in an Elegy upon the death of a greatly beloved woman Ronsard turns instantly to Cupid is a measure of the degree to which the codes still rule his work. (It is instructive to see what Donne does with Cupid: in all the Elegies, Songs and Sonnets he is mentioned only in passing, and never as an important conceit.) Another conceit that forms part of the code Ronsard inherited is the beloved's divinity: both the elements of her beauty and her walk are more than merely human. In all these cases, the specific images are component parts of, but not the same as, the conceit.

On the other hand, the mourning sonnet does move readers, and one suspects it did so even at the time. It does so, however, in ways and by means very different from Donne's. What they have in common is conveying a sense of the poet's complete involvement in the death: his grief is total and totally experienced; and that totality is conveyed. In Ronsard's case, the means, the conceits, are in no way surprising or modern: Anne Prescott's words, quoted above, apply completely: 'Ronsard's great lines often achieve a classical finality rather than the intellectual compression of Donne at his best …'.

Donne, on the other hand, represents a major advance in Sidneian *energia*. He does so in part because he is *not* a professional poet, which gives him a greater freedom to experiment. He fuses conceit and image, and infuses both with the element of intellectual surprise which struck both Grierson and Gardner. The combination of *energia* and intellectual surprise means that he can convey both an extremity of wit and a power of convincing emotion, as his theme demands.

If we may now proceed cautiously to a conclusion, we should at once remind ourselves that Ronsard himself progressed well beyond his own powers of 1558. The sonnets to Hélène that we examined earlier show a poet who had gained enormously in independence and strength: a poet who can surprise by an ambiguity of emotion, by a singularity of imagery, and above all by new and original kinds of conceit. The Perverted Connotation, the Outrageous Exaggeration, and the Scientific Surprise all appear in his late *Amours*, and signal a further distancing from the codes of *pétrarquisme*. And in all these, and the style of lyric writing of which they are a part, he shows what we might call a transition to the style of Donne.

Donne, with different influences and in another country, nevertheless continues the development we saw happening in Ronsard. If, as Anne Prescott has suggested, he probably read a certain amount of Ronsard, what did he do with it? Directly, not a great deal. Ronsard was (fairly) long ago, and in another country, and the wench, if not dead, was living out a blameless and unmarried life in the château of Surgères. Donne's use, and interpretation, of conceits is infinitely more pyrotechnic and profuse: every development we see beginning to happen in Ronsard is pushed to new limits by his English successor. But there is a line we can trace. Some literary historians, including Warnke himself in another work,[30] have associated the evolution of the Pléiade and the nascent Metaphysical style with Mannerism: 'The poets quickly left such Platonic idealism behind and adopted other, more troubling forms of the passion of love.... The rather classical Ronsard of the [early] *Amours* and the *Odes*, Marcel Raymond thinks, also incorporated the colours of mannerism at the end of his life. In the last quarter of the century, the poets subject the canonical forms of Petrarchism to deformations reminiscent of Mannerist paintings' treatment of the Renaissance's masterpieces. The change does not imply the abandonment of earlier styles but their subversion.'[31]

While there is always room for exception in such comparisons between different art-forms, we have not really found in Ronsard the extreme polish, the deliberate distortion, between exquisiteness and caricature, that mark the Mannerist style in painting: certain moments in Desportes might come closer to such work. Rather we tend to agree with Warnke's original insight. The elements he describes as characteristic of the Early Baroque correspond almost perfectly with the traits we have discerned in Ronsard's late *Amours* for Hélène and which we have followed into their Donnean successors: 'extravagance, extremeness, asymmetry; the illusion of thought in the very process of being thought; verse assimilated to the condition of heightened conversation; a diction at once colloquial and capable of embracing an effectively unlimited range of references to human activities, mundane or learned; a private poetry of the greatest intimacy which we, as audience, have the illusion of not hearing but overhearing; a syntax ... which concentrates on the present'.[32] The term 'baroque' derives from the Portuguese *barroco*, describing a pearl with a flaw, an imperfect pearl. In following the journey from the Continental *concept* to the English conceit, we have seen again the narrowness of the Channel and the jewel's value.

Appendix A: Elegie pour la Mort de Marie

Le jour que la beauté du monde la plus belle	*The dark day when the beauty of the world*
Laissa dans le cercueil sa despouille mortelle	*left her remains terrestrial in the grave,*
Pour s'en-voler parfaite entre les plus parfaits,	*perfect to take her place among the perfect,*
Ce jour Amour perdit ses flames et ses traits,	*that day Love lost his arrows and his flames*
Esteignit son flambeau, rompit toutes ses armes,	*extinguished torch and broke his weapons all*
Les jetta sur la tombe, et l'arrousa de larmes :	*then threw them on the tomb he drenched in tears*
Nature la pleura, le Ciel en fut fasché	*All Nature mourned her, Heaven itself was sad*
Et la Parque d'avoir un si beau fil trenché.	*and Fate regretted cutting such a thread.*
Depuis le jour couchant jusqu'à l'Aube vermeille	*From gentle dusk unto the golden dawn*
Phenix en sa beauté ne trouvoit sa pareille,	*Phoenix found nothing equal to her beauty*
Tant de graces au front et d'attraits elle avoit :	*such graces in her face, such loveliness:*
Ou si je me trompois, Amour me decevoit.	*if I am wrong, I was deceived by Love.*
Si tost que je la vey, sa beauté fust enclose	*The first time that I saw her, in my heart*
Si avant en mon cœur, que depuis nulle chose	*her beauty reigned, so that I have not since*
Je n'ay veu qui m'ait pleu, et si fort elle y est,	*seen anything to please, and with such power*

Que toute autre beauté encores me desplaist.	that I can like no other loveliness.
Dans mon sang elle fut si avant imprimée,	So much is she imprinted in my blood
Que tousjours en tous lieux de sa figure aimée	that everywhere I go the blessed portrait
Me suivoit le portrait, et telle impression	of her beloved face would follow me:
D'une perpetuelle imagination	the imprint of such an imagination
M'avoit tant desrobé l'esprit et la cervelle,	had so robbed me of wit and of my brain
Qu'autre bien je n'avois que de penser en elle,	thinking of her became my only good:
En sa bouche en son ris en sa main en son œil,	her mouth, her laugh, her hands, yes, and her eyes
Qu'encor je sens au cœur, bien qu'ils soient au cercueil.	are in my heart as much as in the coffin.
J'avois au-paravant, veincu de la jeunesse,	In days before, a victim of my youth,
Autres dames aimé (ma faute je confesse) :	I had loved other ladies, I confess:
Mais la playe n'avoit profondement saigné,	but never had that wound bled very deeply
Et le cuir seulement n'estoit qu'esgratigné,	and on the skin it was but just a scratch,
Quand Amour, qui les Dieux et les hommes menace,	when Love, who gaily threatens gods and men,
Voyant que son brandon n'eschauffoit point ma glace,	seeing his torch had never warmed my ice,
Comme rusé guerrier ne me voulant faillir,	conceived a ruse, desiring not to spare me:
La print pour son escorte et me vint assaillir.	took her along when he assaulted me.
Encor, ce me dit-il, que de maint beau trofée	'True that you have, with trophies grand and lovely
D'Horace, de Pindare, Hesiode et d'Orfée,	from Horace, Pindar, Orpheus, Hesiod,
Et d'Homere qui eut une si forte vois,	and even from Homer's magnificence,
Tu as orné la langue et l'honneur des François,	adorned the tongue and honour of the French,
Voy ceste dame icy : ton cœur tant soit il brave,	now see this lady: now your valiant heart

Ira sous son empire, et fera son esclave.	will crawl at her behest, and be her slave.'
Ainsi dit, et son arc m'enfonçant de roideur,	He said this, drew his bow, and with one shot
Ensemble dame et traict m'envoya dans le cœur.	sent lady and the dart into my heart.
Lors ma pauvre raison des rayons esblouye	So, blinded by such beauty's beams, my Reason,
D'une telle beauté se perd esvanouye,	poor thing, lost consciousness and all his force,
Laissant le gouvernail aux sens et au desir,	left the wheel to desire and to the senses
Qui depuis ont conduit la barque à leur plaisir.	who since have steered the ship just as they please.
Raison, pardonne-moy : un plus caut en finesse	Reason, forgive me: even one more careful
S'y fust bien englué, tant une douce presse	would have been caught, so thick the throng of joys
De graces et d'amours la suivoient tout ainsi	and graces and of loves came with her, very like
Que les fleurs le Printemps, quand il retourne ici.	flowers that come with Spring, when he returns.
De moy par un destin sa beauté fut cognue :	'Twas Destiny that made me know her beauty:
Son divin se vestoit d'une mortelle nue,	her deity was dressed in mortal cloud
Qui mesprisoit le monde, et personne n'osoit	that scorned the world, and barely did one dare
Luy regarder les yeux tant leur flame luisoit.	look in her eyes, so starry was their flame.
Son ris et son regard et sa parole pleine	Her laugh, her glance, yes, and her conversation
De merveilles, n'estoient d'une nature humaine :	were full of miracles, beyond the human:
Son front ny ses cheveux, son aller ny sa main.	So were her face, her hair, her footfall and her hands.
C'estoit une Déesse en un habit humain,	She was a Goddess clothed in human dress,
Qui visitoit la terre, aussi tost enlevée	who visited the earth, and straight was rapt
Au ciel, comme elle fut en ce monde arrivée.	back into heaven, just as she had come.
Du monde elle partit au mois de son printemps	She left the world in the month of her springtime:

« Aussi toute excellence icy ne vit long temps.	'Excellence here does not enjoy long life.'
Bien qu'elle eut pris naissance en petite bourgade,	True, she was born in just a little town
Non de riches parens ny d'honneurs ny de grade,	of folk not rich nor honoured in degree,
Il ne faut la blasmer : la mesme Deité	but blame her not: for Deity itself
Ne desdaigna de naistre en trespauvre cité :	did not disdain birth in a lowly city:
« Et souvent sous l'habit d'une simple personne	'And oft the dress of quite a simple person
« Se cache tout le mieux que le destin nous donne.	Hides all the best that Destiny can give.'
Vous qui veistes son corps, l'honorant comme moy,	You who have seen and honoured her as I,
Vous sçavez si je mens, et si triste je doy	know if I lie, and if I'm right to mourn
Regretter à bon droict si belle creature,	in sadness deep a creature of such beauty,
Le miracle du Ciel, le miroër de Nature.	wonder of Heaven and the glass of Nature.
O beaux yeux, qui m'estiez si cruels et si doux,	O lovely eyes, cruel to me and sweet,
Je ne me puis lasser de repenser en vous,	I cannot ever cease to think of you
Qui fustes le flambeau de ma lumiere unique,	who were the flambeau of my only light,
Les vrais outils d'Amour, la forge et la boutique.	Love's truest tools, his forge and workshop.
Vous m'ostastes du cœur tout vulgaire penser,	Each vulgar thought you chased out of my heart
Et l'esprit jusqu'au ciel vous me fistes hausser.	and made me lift my spirit to the skies.
J'apprins à vostre eschole à resver sans mot dire,	I learnt in your school dreaming without speech,
A discourir tout seul, à cacher mon martire,	murmuring to myself, hiding my pain,
A ne dormir la nuict, en pleurs me consumer :	not sleeping nights, and drowning in my tears:
Et bref, en vous servant j'apprins que c'est qu'aimer.	so serving you I learnt what love is made of.
Car depuis le matin que l'Aurore s'esveille,	From early morning when the Dawn awakes

Jusqu'au soir que le jour dedans la mer sommeille,	*to evening when the day sleeps in the sea*
Et durant que la nuict par les Poles tournoit,	*and while the night turns by the distant Poles*
Tousjours pensant en vous, de vous me souvenoit.	*thinking of you, always remembered you.*
Vous seule estiez mon bien, ma toute, et ma premiere,	*You were my good, my all, my first of all,*
Et le serez tousjours : tant la vive lumiere	*and will be ever: so the lively light*
De vos yeux, bien que morts, me poursuit, dont je voy	*of your eyes, even dead, pursues me, and*
Tousjours le simulachre errer autour de moy.	*I ever see their image all around me.*
Puis Amour que je sens par mes veines s'espandre,	*May Love that's flowing richly in my veins*
Passe dessous la terre, et r'atize la cendre	*under the earth go and revive the ashes*
Qui froide languissoit dessous vostre tombeau,	*that languish cold and dead beneath your tomb*
Pour r'allumer plus vif en mon cœur son flambeau,	*relight more lively his torch in my heart*
Afin que vous soyez ma flame morte et vive,	*that you may be my flame, dead and alive,*
Et que par le penser en tous lieux je vous suive.	*and my thoughts follow you in every place.*
Pourroy-je raconter le mal que je senty,	*Could I recount the pain that then I felt*
Oyant vostre trespas ? mon cœur fut converty	*hearing your death? my heart converted was*
En rocher insensible, et mes yeux en fonteines :	*to senseless rock, my eyes were changed to springs:*
Et si bien le regret s'escoula par mes veines,	*and grief so surged along my veins that utterly*
Que pasmé je me feis la proye du torment,	*shattered I fell, a prey to torment's pain*
N'ayant que vostre nom pour confort seulement.	*with not a shred of comfort but your name.*
Bien que je resistasse, il ne me fut possible	*Resisting was no use, there was no way*
Que mon cœur, de nature à la peine invincible,	*my heart, though naturally strong in pain*
Peust cacher sa douleur : car plus il la celoit,	*might hide its dolour: more it tried to hide it*

Et plus dessus le front son mal estinceloit.	the more the hurt was written in my face.
En fin voyant mon ame extremement attainte,	And when my soul had reached the ultimate
Je desliay ma bouche, et feis telle complainte.	of torture, my mouth uttered this complaint:
Ah faux Monde trompeur, que tu m'as bien deceu !	O world of falsehood, how you have deceived me!
Amour, tu es enfant : par toy j'avois receu	Love, you're a child: by you I came to have
La divine beauté qui surmontoit l'envie,	the divine beauty far beyond desire
Que maugré toy la Mort en ton regne a ravie.	that Death came to your realm and robbed you of.
Je desplais à moymesme, et veux quitter le jour,	I hate myself and want to leave the daylight
Puis que je voy la Mort triompher de l'amour,	now that I see Death's triumph over love,
Et luy ravir son mieux, sans faire resistance.	stealing his precious best, without resistance.
Malheureux qui te croit, et qui suit ton enfance !	Woe to who still believes your innocence!
Et toy Ciel, qui te dis le père des humains,	And, Heaven, you: the 'father of mankind',
Tu ne devois tracer un tel corps de tes mains	your hands should not have drawn such loveliness
Pour si tost le reprendre : et toy mere Nature,	to take it back so soon: nor mother Nature,
Pour mettre si soudain ton œuvre en sepulture.	so soon put what you fashioned in the grave.
Maintenant à mon dam je cognois pour certain,	Now I have learnt for certain and for sure
Que tout cela qui vit sous ce globe mondain,	that all that lives within this earthly globe
N'est que songe et fumee, et qu'une vaine pompe,	is nought but dream and smoke, a hollow show
Qui doucement nous rit et doucement nous trompe.	that sweetly smiles at us and then deceives us.
Hà, bien-heureux esprit fait citoyen des cieux,	Fortunate soul, of Heaven a citizen,
Tu es assis au rang des Anges precieux	you sit now in the rows of precious angels

En repos eternel, loin de soin et de guerres :	in endless rest, and far from cares and warfare:
Tu vois dessous tes pieds les hommes et les terres,	beneath your feet you see the men and lands
Et je ne voy qu'ennuis, que soucis, et qu'esmoy,	and nought but grief and care and grimness,
Comme ayant emporté tout mon bien avec toy.	as if you'd taken with you all I have.
Je ne te trompe point : du ciel tu vois mes peines,	I do not err: you see my pains in Heaven
Si tu as soin là haut des affaires humaines.	if there you care for what we humans do.
Que doy-je faire, Amour ? que me conseilles-tu ?	What, Love, must I do? What is your counsel?
J'irois comme un Sauvage en noir habit vestu	I'd happily go like a savage dressed in black
Volontiers par les bois, et mes douleurs non feintes	into the woods, and tell my honest sadness
Je dirois aus forests : mais ils sçavent mes plaintes.	to all the forests; but they know my dirge.
Il vaut mieux que je meure au pied de ce rocher,	Better were I to die here by this rock
Nommant tousjours son nom qui me sonne si cher,	saying her name that's music to my ears,
Sans chercher par la peine apres elle de vivre,	not seek by effort to live after her
Gaignant le bruit d'ingrat de ne la vouloir suivre.	getting a bad name for my selfishness.
Aussi toute la terre, où j'ay perdu mon bien,	For all the earth, now I have lost my treasure,
Apres son fascheux vol ne me semble plus rien	after that dreadful theft seems nothing worth
Sinon qu'horreur, qu'effroy, qu'une obscure poussiere,	but horror, fear, and a dark realm of dust.
Au ciel est mon Soleil, au ciel est ma lumiere :	In Heaven is my Sun, there is my light:
Le monde ny ses laqs n'y ont plus de pouvoir :	the world and his foul traps there have no power:
Il faut haster ma mort, si je la veux revoir :	Hasten my death, now, if I want to see her:
La mort en a la clef, et par sa seule porte	Death has the key, and only through his door
Je revoiray le jour qui ma nuict reconforte.	can I behold the day that soothes my night.

Or quand la dure Parque aura le fil coupé,	So *when Fate pitiless has cut the thread*
Qui retient en mon corps l'esprit envelopé,	*that holds my spirit snugly in my body.*
J'ordonne que mes os pour toute couverture	*I hereby order that my bones be laid*
Reposent pres des siens sous mesme sepulture :	*simply to rest with hers in the same tomb:*
Que des larmes du ciel le tumbeau soit lavé,	*and that the grave be cleansed by heaven's tears*
Et tout à l'environ de ces vers engravé :	*and these words graven round about to read:*
Passant, de cest amant enten l'histoire vraye,	*O passer-by, hear thou this lover's story.*
De deux traicts differens il receut double playe :	*A double wound he suffered from two arrows:*
L'une que feit Amour ne versa qu'amitié,	*the one, from Love, was dipped in love and kindness,*
L'autre que feit la Mort ne versa que pitié.	*the other, Death's, was dipped in grief and pity.*
Ainsi mourut navré d'une double tristesse,	*And so he died, felled by a double sadness,*
Et tout pour aimer trop une jeune maistresse.	*And all for too much love of a young mistress.*

Appendix B: A Nocturnall upon St Lucies Day, beeing the shortest day

'Tis the yeares midnight, and it is the dayes,
Lucies, who scarce seaven houres herself unmaskes;
    The Sunne is spent, and now his flasks
    Send forth light squibs, no constant rayes;
        The worlds whole sap is sunke;
The generall balm th' hydroptique earth hath drunk,
Whither, as to the beds-feet, life is shrunke,
Dead and enterr'd; yet all these seeme to laugh,
Compar'd with mee, who am their Epitaph.

Study me then, you who shall lovers bee
At the next world, that is, at the next Spring;
    For I am every dead thing,
      In whom love wrought new Alchimie.
        For his art did expresse

A quintessence even from nothingnesse,
From dull privations, and leane emptinesse;
He ruin'd mee, and I am re-begot
Of absence, darknesse, death: things which are not.

All others, from all things, draw all that's good,
Life, soule, forme, spirit, whence they beeing have;
    I, by Love's limbecke, am the grave
      Of all, that's nothing. Oft a flood
        Have wee two wept, and so
Drownd the whole world, us two; oft did we grow
To be two Chaoses, when we did show
Care to ought else; and often absences
Withdrew our soules, and made us carcasses.

But I am by her death (which word wrongs her)
Of the first nothing, the Elixir grown;
    Were I a man, that I were one
      I needs must know; I should preferre,
        If I were any beast,
Some ends, some means; Yea plants, yea stones detest,
And love; all, all some properties invest;
If I an ordinary nothing were,
As shadow, a light and body must be here.

But I am None; nor will my Sunne renew.
You lovers, for whose sake the lesser Sunne
    At this time to the Goat is runne[33]
      To fetch new lust, and give it you,
        Enjoy your summer all;
Since shee enjoys her long nights festivall,
Let mee prepare towards her, and let mee call
This houre her Vigill, and her Eve, since this
Both the yeares, and the dayes deep midnight is.

Notes

1 E.g. Claudia Brodsky, 'Donne: The Imaging of the Logical Conceit', *English Literary History* 49.4 (1982): 829–48; Katrin Ettenhuber, '"Comparisons Are Odious"? Revisiting the Metaphysical Conceit in Donne', *The Review of English Studies* 62.255 (2011): 393–413; Donald L. Guss, 'Donne's Conceit and Petrarchan Wit', *PMLA* 78.4 (1963): 308–14; J. W. van Hook, '"Concupiscence of Witt": The Metaphysical Conceit in Baroque Poetics', *Modern Philology* 84.1 (1986): 24–38; T. G. A. Nelson, 'Death, Dung, the Devil, and Worldly Delights: A Metaphysical Conceit in Harington, Donne, and Herbert', *Studies in Philology* 76.3 (1979): 272–87.

2 Claude Hollyband [Claude de Sainliens], *A Dictionarie French and English: Published for the benefite of the studious in that language: Gathered and set forth by Claudius Hollyband* (London: Thomas Woodcock, 1593), 105.
3 Alexander A. Parker, '"Concept" and "Conceit": An Aspect of Comparative Literary History', *Modern Language Review* 77 (1982): xxii. Our italics.
4 K. K. Ruthven, *The Conceit*, The Critical Idiom (London: Methuen, 1969).
5 See Anne Lake Prescott, *French Poets and the English Renaissance* (New Haven, Conn. and London: Yale University Press, 1978); and, for a more recent example, A. E. B. Coldiron, 'Watson's "Hekatompathia" and Renaissance Lyric Translation', *Translation and Literature* 5.1 (1996): 3–25.
6 Helen Gardner on conceit: 'a conceit is a comparison whose ingenuity is more striking than its justness' and that 'a comparison becomes a conceit when we are made to concede likeness while being strongly conscious of unlikeness' (*The Metaphysical Poets* [Oxford: Oxford University Press, 1961], xxiii). She was to some extent following H. J. Grierson, whose Introduction to *Metaphysical Lyrics and Poems of the Seventeenth Century* (Oxford: Oxford University Press, 1921), did not, however, so tightly tie the concept of conceit to the image.
7 Françoise Graziani 'Camillo Pellegrino: Del Concetto Poetico (1598)', *Nouvelle Revue Du XVIe Siècle* 18 (2000): 157–81 (full French translation and commentary).
8 Sir Richard Baker, *A Chronicle of the Kings of England* (London: for Daniel Frere, 1643), 156.
9 A phrasing we found helpful was this: 'Conceits were not only ornamental devices, fulfilling the rhetorical "office" of *delectare*, but they functioned equally as instruments to think with, as verbal ideas equivalent, indeed superior, to discursive arguments, pursuing didactic or moral intentions (*docere* and *movere*) and guiding the reader through a line of reasoning. It is their complexity and texture that enable them to do this. In a period that admired both concentration of "matter" and rhetorical finesse, they served as vehicles for surprising, often difficult insight. Charged with intellectual as well as affective power, they tend to explore the edges of familiar systems of thought or move beyond the boundaries of well-trodden philosophical ground.' Verena O. Lobsien, 'In Other Words: George Herbert's Metaphysical Textures', in *Spatial Metaphors: Ancient Texts and Transformations*, ed. Fabian Horn and Cilliers Breytenbach, Berlin Studies of the Ancient World 39 (Berlin: Edition Topoi, 2016), 222.
10 Antoine Héroët (1492–1568), *La parfaicte amye*, 8vo (Lyons: Pierre de Tours, 1542), D iiij.v.
11 Joachim du Bellay (1522–60), 'Contre les pétrarquistes', in *Receuil de poésies*, 2nd ed. (1553).
12 The four minor orders are porter, lector, exorcist, and acolyte. In most cases, they preceded entry into the major orders of subdeacon, deacon and priest, or bishop; but they did not involve a vow of celibacy, and someone in minor orders who did not continue to the priesthood could still marry. The minor orders were abolished by Pope Paul VI in 1972 and replaced by the ministries of reader and acolyte, but they are still practiced in traditionalist areas of the Catholic Church.

13 While describing his love for Cassandre, the sonnet (no. 23 in the *Amours*) is addressed to his friend Rémy Belleau (1528–77), also a poet and member of the Pléiade. This fact, and the extreme 'Petrarchization' as well as the slightly dubious repetition in the final tercet, makes us suspect at least a hint of irony.
14 This is no. 6 of the Cassandre sequence.
15 A good example of this critical point of view (though we might not go quite as far) is Alan F. Nagel, 'Literary and Historical Context in Ronsard's Sonnets Pour Hélène', *PMLA* 94 (1979): 406–19.
16 Holy Sonnets, 'Batter my heart, three-person'd God' (1633). Italics ours.
17 Alan Nagel's article goes into the Hélène/Helen topos very thoroughly, yet never specifically examines the surprising brutality of these two sonnets.
18 The reference is to *Odyssey* IV. 270–290, where Menelaus reminisces: 'Three times you made the circuit of our hollow ambuscade, feeling the outside with your hands, and you challenged all the Argive captains in turn, altering your voice, as you called out the name of each, to mimic that man's wife' (trans. E. V. Rieu, [Harmondsworth: Penguin Classics, 1956], 71.)
19 In Frank J. Warnke, 'Baroque Once More: Notes on a Literary Period', *New Literary History* I (1970): 145–62.
20 Ibid., 148.
21 Roger Kuin, 'Sustainable Energy: Philip Sidney and John Donne', *John Donne Journal* 33 (2014): 63–93. The blaming of Love may itself, however, be a sign that both Sidney and Ronsard belong to a slightly earlier poetic generation.
22 *Second Livre*, no. XXII.
23 From the Introduction by D. Joaust, publisher and printer of the 1868 edition of the 1610 original. Our translation.
24 Hollyband, *A Dictionarie French and English*, 356 s.v. *picquer*: 'to pricke, to launce, to spurre, sometime to quilt, to sting'.
25 See, for example, Philip Sidney's characterization of the German princes' attitude toward the Continental Catholic–Protestant conflict as 'asleep'. (Philip Sidney to Hubert Languet, 15 April 1574, in Kuin, *Correspondence of Sir Philip Sidney* [Oxford: Oxford University Press, 2012], I:162).
26 Prescott, *French Poets*, 115.
27 The influential Classical source for such disgust with age and loss of attraction in women is, of course, Horace's Ode I.25 which does not, however, have the *carpe diem* conclusion.
28 'mi sforza Amore, / che la strada d'onore / mai nol lassa seguir, chi troppo il crede', translation A. L. Kline.
29 We have called this conceit 'scientific': it should be remembered that at this time, the practitioners of natural philosophy included not only the Imperial botanist Clusius but also the Imperial alchemist Edward Kelley (1555–98).
30 Frank J. Warnke, *Versions of Baroque: English Literature in the Seventeenth Century* (New Haven, Conn. and London: Yale University Press, 1972).
31 'Les poètes ne tarderont pas à délaisser cet idéalisme platonicien et S'attacheront à d'autres formes, plus inquiétantes, de la passion amoureuse ... Le Ronsard plutôt classique des *Amours* et des *Odes*, estime Marcel Raymond, connaîtra aussi l'influence de colorations maniéristes à la fin de sa vie. Dans le dernier quart

du siècle, les poètes vont faire subir aux formes canoniques du pétrarquisme des torsions qui s'apparentent au travail des peintures maniéristes sur les chefs-d'oeuvre de la Renaissance. La rupture n'implique pas l'abandon des schémas préexistants, mais leur subversion'. T. Gheeraert, *Miroitements de l'infini: Maniérisme et baroque, des arts plastiques à la littérature*, ch. 2.3.3 'Voluptés morbides' (University of Rouen online course, 2018) at http://manierisme.univ-rouen.fr/spip/?2–3-3-Voluptes-morbides (accessed 29 November 2023). See also Marcel Raymond, 'Aux frontières du maniérisme et du baroque', *Baroque* [online], 3 (1969), http://journals.openedition.org/baroque/288 (uploaded 30 April 2012, accessed 6 February 2022).
32 Warnke, 'Baroque Once More', 147–48.
33 The Goat: the sign of Capricorn. St Lucy's Day, December 13, was popularly regarded as the shortest day, though in the Julian Calendar the winter solstice varied between December 10 and 12.

Afterword: Anne as co-author and editor

The joy of partnership

Roger Kuin

Over a period of twenty-some years, I have had the privilege not only of knowing Anne Prescott but of occasionally collaborating with her on articles.[1] Anyone who has worked on joint scholarly projects knows that while division of labor is comparatively easy in the research phase, to write with two pens is a perilous exercise. The first of our essays *à deux* concerned a friend of Sir Philip Sidney's, the polymath diplomat, scholar, and neo-Latin poet Daniel Rogers (1538? –1591), a manuscript of whose occasional verse had come to Anne's notice while working at the Huntington Library.[2] As Rogers had Dutch connections and had been extensively discussed by Jan van Dorsten in his seminal *Poets, Patrons and Professors*,[3] it seemed useful to Anne to bring in the only Dutch *seiziémiste* she knew: myself. She was far more learned in the background of the humanist republic of letters, while I enjoyed not only translating the neo-Latin verse but puzzling over Rogers' genuinely appalling handwriting. The exercise proved thoroughly enjoyable and fruitful for both of us.

Shortly afterwards, when I was working in the French Bibliothèque nationale in Paris, I came across a hitherto unknown manuscript of a curious poem attributed to Rémy Belleau, the Pléiade poet.[4] It was an extremely lively and cheerfully obscene scherzo on the topic of impotence. As it seemed not to be well known in the context of Belleau's *œuvre*, I turned to the author of *French Poets and the English Renaissance*. The text appealed at once to Anne's sense of humor, and she agreed to collaborate on an article about it. In this case, again, her greater knowledge of the Renaissance contexts and genres proved invaluable, and my role was essentially that of translator: more comfortable with Belleau's French than I had been with Rogers' Latin.

A few years later a much more ambitious project presented itself. The editors of a book of essays on Spenser and Milton had asked Anne for a contribution on the book's theme: those poets' 'imagining of Death'. I cannot now remember what made her suggest that I collaborate with her in this effort, but the topic was wonderfully appealing in its scope and potential, and I accepted with alacrity. Now, twenty years later, I have scattered but vivid memories of long hours of discussion, partly in New York and partly by transatlantic telephone. As always, it was Anne's bottomless fund of Renaissance learning that provided the ground bass and the harmonic structure of the work. My own contribution came in part from the fact that, working for several years on French poststructuralist thinking, I had acquired a taste for, like Roland Barthes, asking what *else* something means, and, like Jacques Derrida, not accepting the author, or the scholar, as an anonymously omniscient voice. So while most of the article concerned the appearance of death in the *Faerie Queene* and Milton as Spenser's almost-ideal reader, its final pages challenge the academic scholar to discard her professional distancing and *undergo* Spenser's text and its meanings as a human contemporary.

After that hugely exciting collaboration, each of us was busy with individual projects, though we occasionally discussed the possibility of another joint effort. So it was only recently that Anne, who had been asked to contribute to a project on the Renaissance and Metaphysical Conceit something involving Pierre de Ronsard, very kindly asked me to join her in that adventure. Not having ever done much with Ronsard, I felt a little nervous, but since working with Anne is not only a great human pleasure but also a learning experience, I accepted. Again, the process was a delight. Anne's knowledge of the Pléiade, its contexts and backgrounds, is so deep and so extensive that it has ripened into wisdom; whereas I, who had for over fifteen years been living in France and living mostly in French, could indulge my love of translating French verse.

These four joint projects have, then, been for me a sort of school of philosophy. Working with Anne is, in the traditional sense of the word, awesome. One skips back and forth across four or five centuries of history and literature, and at any given moment some fact or anecdote may pop up and shed completely unexpected light on a corner of the subject in hand. She knows more about, for instance, the French Revolution than many French historians, while one of her own ancestors was a signatory to King Charles I's death warrant.

And when the project reaches the stage of writing and revision, Anne remembers that she comes from a long line of journalists, including her mother and her grandfather, and becomes Anne Lake the perfect copyeditor, whom not a single error or inelegance escapes. Being her partner in several scholarly and textual projects has been a singular privilege and an immense pleasure.

Anne as editor: a small florilegium

William Oram

In her essays, Anne Lake Prescott is a distinctive stylist, learned, witty, generous, and precise. Her style is the cutting edge of a mind large enough to sympathize imaginatively with those she writes about and canny enough to see beyond her sympathies. Francis Sagon was Marot's vicious enemy, but Anne acknowledges that his hatred enabled him to see real weaknesses: 'That he was a dreadful creature does not make him wrong.' 'Getting very far outside one's own head,' she comments elsewhere, 'was not among Ronsard's talents.'

More elaborate sentences can have their surprises. In discussing Marot's *Epître 36* she focuses on how the poem undermines its praise of Francis I:

> The multiplicity of paternal references and the silent refusal of the title 'father' to *this* king, the adaptation of David's supplications to God and the careful dissociation of Francis and Jehovah, are worth pondering for the ambivalence, to say nothing of the hurt and courage, that they imply.

The sentence begins by reprising the evidence she has brought together to suggest Marot's implicit rebellion. But its final member ('for … imply') shifts to the attitudes she posits in Marot. The first, ambivalence, follows from rest of the sentence. But 'hurt' abruptly stresses his vulnerability, and the subsequent 'courage' reminds us that the courtier's graceful stance conceals an unexpected steel.

In Anne's editing, all these traits are apparent – the learning, the wit, the clarity of perception, the generosity, and the passionate attention to the language that binds them together. Here are a few excerpts from the dozens of reports in the *Spenser Studies* files.

> Within the fiction, dragons aren't 'supernatural' are they? In Spenser's day many still believed in them. Most of the educated who did, placed them in, say, India, but one turned up in Sussex – a baby spitting dragon with bumps on its back that observers said would someday be wings….

> Some sweeping generalizations need modifying. It is not the case that the sixteenth century viewed women in a binary way as whores or virgins. That's an older feminist cliché and applied primarily to the Middle Ages; it works particularly badly for Protestant countries that thought better of chaste marriage than of celibate virginity. Virgin and whore persisted, but there's also the good wife, the scold, the blushing bride, the virtuous but sometimes married lady of Petrarchist tradition, the rich widow, the old witch. Nor were *all* ranks of society obsessed by clothes. The very poor were lucky to have rags.

I knew a distinguished writer once, who told his students 'Remember, the adjective is not your friend.'

At the risk of irritating [the author] I append some specific comments that include suggestions on writing. I hope he will forgive me – I'm a compulsive editor of the manuscripts I deal with and can hardly help myself. It is prudent to remember that, although some of the following details seem pedantic, readers are often impressed by such little elegancies as avoiding split infinitives, saving 'incredibly' to mean 'not worthy of belief,' thinking twice about using the largely empty word 'meaningful,' avoiding words such as 'message' that can seem critically naive ('When I want to send messages, said one famous Hollywood director, 'I use Western Union').

The essay's point that Spenser prefers a patriarchy is not surprising, although [the author] might want to use the word more precisely – patriarchy is government by fathers, and what they govern includes sons and stray males, so that not all males are patriarchal and indeed can bitterly resent the patriarch and even the patriarchy. Sexism isn't misogyny isn't patriarchy isn't fear of an engulfing mother isn't a belief that hierarchy governs all human relationships. One might distinguish these just a bit more.

The word 'demonized' is much overused in current critical discourse (I've seen it used to mean 'denigrated' or 'scolded'), but in this case it might be important to get things precise. Is Duessa a demon? If so, she isn't 'demonized' – I mean you can't 'demonize' a demon, right? If Spenser makes her a demon, then within the fiction she *is* a demon. But does he 'demonize' her? Is the Whore of Babylon demonic?

The pathos of friendship's difficulty for monarchs is also worth comment. Elizabeth had two problems: Cicero would doubt that she was capable of true friendship for two reasons: she's a woman and she cannot find an equal. That did not stop Henry III, say, from having friends, but his reward was to be (justly) accused of favouring his 'mignons.'

On the people and the dragon [in Book I]: there's a nice illustration in the 1575 Bishops Bible (Ezekiel, I think, or maybe Daniel) showing a very dead dragon with its legs in the air and lots of local folk clustered near it. The picture could illustrate Spenser. Maybe he saw it. If [the author] likes, I can send him a photocopy – it's a sweet picture.

Notes

1 'Versifying Connections: Daniel Rogers and the Sidneys', *Sidney Journal* 18.2 (2000): 1–36; 'The Wrath of Priapus: Rémy Belleau's "Jean qui ne peult" and Its Traditions', *Comparative Literature Studies* 37.1 (2000): 1–17; 'After the First Death, There Is No Other: Spenser, Milton and (Our) Death', in *Imagining Death*

in Spenser and Milton, ed. E. J. Bellamy, P. Cheney, and M. Schoenfeldt (Palgrave Macmillan, 2003); and 'Imperfect Pearls from France: Ronsard's Conceits Meet Donne's', Chapter 12 in this volume.

2 The MS, formerly the property of the Marquess of Hertford, is now Huntington MS 33188.

3 J. A. van Dorsten, *Poets, Patrons and Professors: Daniel Rogers and the Leiden Humanists* (Leiden and Oxford: Leiden and Oxford University Presses, 1962).

4 It is embedded in the *Mémoires* of Pierre de l'Estoile for the reign of Henri III and there dated September 1577; it exists in three MSS in the BnF: Bn. MS. fr. 6678, fols. 96 ff.; the one I found: MS Dupuy 843, fols. 89 ff.; and Bn MSS 500 Colbert 488, fols. 550ff.

Bibliography of works by Anne Lake Prescott

Books

Prescott, Anne Lake. *French Poets and the English Renaissance: Studies in Fame and Transformation*. New Haven: Yale University Press, 1978.

Prescott, Anne Lake. *Imagining Rabelais in Renaissance England*. New Haven: Yale University Press, 1998.

Prescott, Anne Lake. *Elizabeth and Mary Tudor*. The Early Modern Englishwoman: A Facsimile Library of Essential Works and Printed Writings, 1500–1640: Series I, Part Two, Volume Five. New York: Routledge, 2001.

Co-edited volumes

Black, Joseph, Anne Lake Prescott, et al., eds. *The Broadview Anthology of British Literature Volume 2: The Renaissance and the Early Seventeenth Century*. Broadview Press: Peterborough, 2006.

Cheney, Patrick and Anne Lake Prescott, eds. *Approaches to Teaching Shorter Elizabethan Poetry*. New York: Modern Language Association, 2000.

Dutcher, James M. and Anne Lake Prescott, eds. *Renaissance Historicisms: Essays in Honor of Arthur F. Kinney*. Newark: University of Delaware Press, 2008.

Maclean, Hugh and Anne Lake Prescott, eds. *Edmund Spenser's Poetry: Authoritative Texts, Criticism*. 3rd ed. New York: W. W. Norton, 1993.

Martin, Randall, Betty Travitsky, and Anne Lake Prescott, eds. *Women and Murder in Early Modern News Pamphlets and Broadside Ballads, 1573–1697*. Aldershot, England: Ashgate, 2005.

Prescott, Anne Lake, and Thomas Roche, William Oram, Andrew Escobedo, and Susannah Monta. *Spenser Studies: A Renaissance Poetry Annual* 13–30. New York: AMS Press, 1999–2015. Volumes 31–32. Chicago: Chicago University Press, 2018.

Spenser, Edmund. *Edmund Spenser's Poetry*. Edited by Andrew D. Hadfield and Anne Lake Prescott. A Norton Critical Edition, Fourth Edition. New York: W. W. Norton & Company 2014.

Thomas More, *Utopia*. Edited by Joseph Black, Anne Lake Prescott, et al. The Broadview Anthology of British Literature. Broadview Press: Peterborough, 2010.

Travitsky, Betty S. and Anne Lake Prescott, eds. *Female and Male Voices in Early Modern England: An Anthology of Renaissance Texts*. New York: Columbia University Press, 2000.

Journal articles

Prescott, Anne Lake. 'An Unknown Translation of Du Bartas'. *Renaissance News* 19 (1966): 12–13.

Prescott, Anne Lake. 'The Reception of Du Bartas in England'. *Studies in the Renaissance* 15 (1968): 144–73.

Prescott, Anne Lake. 'The Reputation of Clément Marot in Renaissance England'. *Studies in the Renaissance* 18 (1971): 173–202.

Prescott, Anne Lake. 'English Writers and Beza's Latin Epigrams: The Uses and Abuses of Poetry'. *Studies in the Renaissance* 21 (1974): 83–117.

Prescott, Anne Lake. 'Further Comments on More's Vision'. *Moreana* 54 (1977): 5–9.

Prescott, Anne Lake. 'Licia's Temple: Giles Fletcher the Elder and Number Symbolism'. *Renaissance and Reformation* 2 (1978): 170–81.

Prescott, Anne Lake. 'Thomas Nash (1588–1648) and Thomas More'. *Moreana* 59–60 (1978): 35–41.

Prescott, Anne Lake. 'The Washington Conference on St. Thomas More'. *Moreana* 62 (1979): 83–90.

Prescott, Anne Lake. 'Thomas More: The Man and His Age'. *Moreana* 70 (1981): 5–24.

Prescott, Anne Lake. 'A Sharper Look at Ridley's Book'. *Moreana* 82 (1984): 95–98.

Prescott, Anne Lake. 'The Stuart Masque and Pantagruel's Dreams'. *English Literary History* 51 (1984): 407–30.

Prescott, Anne Lake. 'The Thirsty Deer and the Lord of Life: Some Contexts for Amoretti 67–70'. *Spenser Studies* 6 (1985): 33–76.

Prescott, Anne Lake. 'A Response to Deborah Carmell, Volume VI'. *Spenser Studies* 7 (1986): 289–94.

Prescott, Anne Lake. 'The Succession: A Novel of Elizabeth and James'. *Sidney Newsletter* 6, no. 2 (1986): 26–28.

Prescott, Anne Lake. 'Humanism in the Tudor Jestbook'. *Moreana* 24 (1987): 5–16.

Prescott, Anne Lake. 'King David as a "Right Poet": Sidney and the Psalmist'. *English Literary Renaissance* 19 (1989): 131–51.

Prescott, Anne Lake. '*Translatio Lupae:* Du Bellay's Roman Whore Goes North'. *Renaissance Quarterly* 42 (1989): 397–419.

Prescott, Anne Lake. 'Spenser's Chivalric Restoration: From Bateman's "Travayled Pylgrime" to the Redcrosse Knight'. *Studies in Philology* 86, no. 2 (1989): 166–97.

Prescott, Anne Lake. 'Drayton's Muse and Selden's "Story": The Interfacing of Poetry and History in Poly-Olbion'. *Studies in Philology* 87 (1990): 128–35.

Prescott, Anne Lake. 'Triumphing over Death and Sin'. *Spenser Studies* 11 (1990): 231–32.

Prescott, Anne Lake. 'Evil Tongues at the Court of Saul: David as a Slandered Courtier'. *Journal of Medieval and Renaissance Studies* 21 (1991): 163–86.

Prescott, Anne Lake. 'Marginal Discourse: Drayton's Muse and Selden's "Story"'. *Studies in Philology* 88 (1991): 307–28.
Prescott, Anne Lake. 'Elizabeth's Garden of Virtue: Jacques Bellot's Sonnet Sequence for the Queen'. *ANQ: A Quarterly Journal of Short Articles, Notes and Reviews* 5, no. 2–3 (1992): 122–24.
Prescott, Anne Lake. 'Intertextual Topology: English Writers and Pantagruel's Hell'. *English Literary Renaissance* 23, no. 2 (1993): 244–66.
Prescott, Anne Lake. 'Recent Studies in the English Renaissance'. *Studies in English Literature, 1500–1900* 34, no. 1 (1994): 205–46.
Prescott, Anne Lake. 'Du Bellay in Renaissance England: Recent Work on Translation and Response'. *Oeuvres et Critiques* 20, no. 1 (1995): 121–28.
Prescott, Anne Lake. 'Divided State'. *English Literary Renaissance* 25, no. 3 (1995): 445–57.
Prescott, Anne Lake. 'James A. Riddell and Stanley Stewart, Jonson's Spenser: Evidence and Historical Criticism'. Pittsburgh: Duquesne. *Ben Jonson Journal* 4, no. 1 (1997): 187–95.
Prescott, Anne Lake. 'Mary Wroth, Louise Labé, and Cupid'. *Sidney Newsletter & Journal* 15, no. 2 (1997): 37–41.
Prescott, Anne Lake. 'Donne and Rabelais'. *John Donne Journal* 16 (1998): 37–58.
Prescott, Anne Lake. 'Foreign Policy in Fairyland: Henri IV and Spenser's Burbon'. *Spenser Studies* 14, no.1 (1999): 189–214.
Prescott, Anne Lake. 'Complicating the Allegory: Spenser and Religion in Recent Scholarship'. *Renaissance and Reformation / Renaissance et Réforme* 25, no. 4 (2001): 9–23.
Prescott, Anne Lake. 'Why Arguments over Communion Matter to Allegory: Or, Why Are Catholics Like Orgoglio'? *Reformation* 6, no. 1 (2002): 163–77.
Prescott, Anne Lake. 'The Ambivalent Heart: Thomas More's Merry Tales'. *Criticism* 45, no. 4 (2003): 417–33.
Prescott, Anne Lake. 'Postmodern More'. *Moreana* 40, no. 153–54 (2003): 219–39.
Prescott, Anne Lake. 'Du Bartas and Renaissance Britain: An Update'. *Oeuvres et Critiques* 29 (2004): 27–38.
Prescott, Anne Lake. 'Getting a Record: Stubbs, Singleton, and a 1579 Almanac'. *Sidney Journal* 22, no. 1–2 (2004): 131–37.
Prescott, Anne Lake. 'The Countess of Pembroke's Ruins of Rome'. *Sidney Journal* 23, no. 1–2 (2005): 1–17.
Prescott, Anne Lake. '"Formes of Joy and Art": Donne, David, and the Power of Music'. *John Donne Journal*, 25 (2006): 3–36.
Prescott, Anne Lake. 'Refusing Translation: The Gregorian Calendar and Early Modern English Writers'. *The Yearbook of English Studies* 36, no. 1 (2006): 1–11.
Prescott, Anne Lake. 'Mary Sidney's "Antonius" and the Ambiguities of French History'. *The Yearbook of English Studies* 38, no. 1/2 (2008): 216–33.
Prescott, Anne Lake. 'Teaching Donne on the Sidney Psalms'. *John Donne Journal* 27, no.1 (2008): 153–60.
Prescott, Anne Lake. 'Copies of the 1596 Faerie Queene: Annotations and an Unpublished Poem on Spenser'. *Spenser Studies* 23 (2008): 261–73.

Prescott, Anne Lake. 'Hills of Contemplation and Signifying Circles: Spenser and Guy Le Fèvre de la Boderie'. *Spenser Studies* 24 (2009): 155–83.
Prescott, Anne Lake. 'The 2011 Josephine Waters Bennett Lecture: From the Sheephook to the Scepter: The Ambiguities of David's Rise to the Throne'. *Renaissance Quarterly* 65, no. 1 (2012): 1–30.
Prescott, Anne Lake. 'Twice Beheaded: R. A. Lafferty's Thomas More'. *Moreana* 50, no. 191/92 (2013): 273–83.
Prescott, Anne Lake. 'Minor if Entertaining Post-Utopian Nowheres'. *Renaissance and Reformation / Renaissance et Réforme* 41, no. 3 (2018): 117–35.
Prescott, Anne Lake. 'The World of Renaissance Scholarship'. *English Literary Renaissance* 50, no. 1 (2020): 131–36.
Prescott, Anne Lake. 'Reading Marguerite de Navarre: An Aged Professor's Meditation'. *Criticism* 63, no. 12 (2021): 87–93.

Co-authored articles

Beilin, Elaine, Akiko Kusunoki, Mary Ellen Lamb, Katie Larson, Naomi Miller, Anne Lake Prescott, Martine van Elk, Susanne Woods, and Georgianna Ziegler. 'A Touchstone for Scholarship and Creativity: A Tribute to Margaret Hannay (1944–2016)'. *Early Modern Women* 11, no. 2 (2017): xi–xii.
Heninger, S. K., Susan C. Staub, John T. Shawcross, and Anne Lake Prescott. 'The Interface between Poetry and History: Gascoigne, Spenser, Drayton'. *Studies in Philology* 87, no. 1 (1990): 109–35.
Hieatt, A. K. and Anne Lake Prescott. 'Contemporizing Antiquity: The Hypnerotomachia and Its Afterlife in France'. *Word and Image* 8 (1992): 291–321.
Hieatt, A. Kent, Charles W. Hieatt, and Anne Lake Prescott. 'When Did Shakespeare Write "Sonnets 1609"'? *Studies in Philology* 88, no. 1 (1991): 69–109.
Kinney, Arthur and Anne Lake Prescott, et al. 'New Directions in Sidney Studies: From Here to Where'? *Sidney Newsletter* 9, no. 2 (1988): 19–54.
Kuin, Roger and Anne Lake Prescott. 'Versifying Connections: Daniel Rogers and the Sidneys'. *Sidney Journal* 18, no. 2 (2000): 1–35.
Kuin, Roger and Anne Lake Prescott. 'The Wrath of Priapus: Rémy Belleau's "Jean Qui Ne Peult" and Its Traditions'. *Comparative Literature Studies* 37, no. 1 (2000): 1–17.
May, Steven W. and Anne Lake Prescott. 'The French Verses of Elizabeth I'. *English Literary Renaissance* 24 (1994): 9–43.
Monta, Susannah B. and Anne Lake Prescott. 'Introduction'. *Spenser Studies* 34 (2020): 145–46.
Prescott, Anne Lake and A. Kent Hieatt. 'Shakespeare and Spenser'. *PMLA* 100, no. 5 (1985): 820–22.
Stillman, Robert E., Anne Lake Prescott, and Mary Ellen Lamb. 'Tribute to Roger Kuin'. *Sidney Journal* 40, no. 1 (2022): 1–2.
Sutch, Susie S. and Anne Lake Prescott. 'Translation as Transformation: Oliver de La Marcher's "Le Chevalier délibéré" and its Hapsburg and Elizabethan Permutations'. *Comparative Literature Studies* 25 (1988): 281–317.

Woods, Susanne, Barbara K. Lewalski, Georgianna Ziegler, Elaine Beilin, Anne Lake Prescott, and Susan M. Felch. 'Walking with Margaret'. *Spenser Review* 47 (2017). www.english.cam.ac.uk/spenseronline/review/item/47.1.1/ (accessed 30 November 2023).

Essays in books and collections

Prescott, Anne Lake. Introduction to *The Enchanted Doll*, by Mark Lemon. New York: Garland Press, 1976.

Prescott, Anne Lake. 'Anglo–French Relations'. In *A Critical Bibliography of French Literature: The Sixteenth Century*. Vol 2. Edited by Raymond La Charité, 672–77. Syracuse, NY: Syracuse University Press, 1984.

Prescott, Anne Lake. 'The Pearl of the Valois and Elizabeth I: Marguerite de Navarre's Miroir and Tudor England'. In *Silent But for the Word: Tudor Women as Patrons, Translators, and Writers of Religious Works*. Edited by Margaret P. Hannay, 61–77. Kent, OH: Kent State University Press, 1985.

Prescott, Anne Lake. 'Naming and Caring: The Theme of Stewardship in Paradise Lost'. In *Approaches to Teaching Milton's Paradise Lost*. Edited by Galbraith Crump, 157–64. New York: Modern Language Association, 1986.

Prescott, Anne Lake. 'Crime and Carnival at Chelsea: The Widow Edith and Thomas More's Household'. In *Miscellanea Moreana: Essays for Germain Marc'Hadour*. Edited by Clare Murphy, Henri Gibaud, and Mario di Cesare, 247–64. Binghamton, NY: Medieval & Renaissance Texts & Studies, 1989.

Prescott, Anne Lake. 'Reshaping Gargantua'. In *L'Europe de la Renaissance: Mélanges offerts à Marie-Thérèse Jones-Davies*. Edited by Jean-Claude Margolin and Marie-Madeleine Martinet, 477–91. Paris: Jean Touzot, 1989.

Prescott, Anne Lake. 'Musical Strains: Clément Marot's Roles as Psalmist and Courtier'. In *Contending Kingdoms: Historical, Psychological, and Feminist Approaches to the Literature of Sixteenth-century England and France*. Edited by Marie-Rose Logan and Peter Rudnytsky, 42–68. Detroit, MI: Wayne State University Press, 1991.

Prescott, Anne Lake. 'Is There a Reader in This Response? The Case of Robert Burton', in *Rabelais in Context: Proceedings of the 1991 Vanderbilt Conference*. Edited by Barbara Bowen. Birmingham, AL: Summa Publication, 1993.

Prescott, Anne Lake. Introduction to *Sir Thomas More in the English Renaissance: An Annotated Catalogue*, by Jackson C. Boswell, xi–xxxiv. Binghamton, NY: Medieval & Renaissance Texts & Studies, 1994.

Prescott, Anne Lake. 'Marginally Funny: Martha Moulsworth's Puns'. In *'The Muses Females Are': Martha Moulsworth and Other Women Writers of the English Renaissance*. Edited by Robert C. Evans and Anne C. Little, 85–90. West Cornwall, CT: Locust Hill Press, 1995.

Prescott, Anne Lake. 'From The Travayled Pilgrime to The Redcrosse Knight: Spenser's Chivalric Restorations'. In *Critical Essays on Edmund Spenser. Critical Essays on British Literature*. Edited by Suzuki, Mihoko. New York; London: G. K. Hall; Prentice Hall International, 1996.

Prescott, Anne Lake. 'The Odd Couple: Gargantua and Tom Thumb'. In *Monster Theory: Reading Culture*. Edited by Jeffrey Jerome Cohen, 75–95. Minneapolis: University of Minnesota Press, 1996.

Prescott, Anne Lake. 'Spenser (Re)Reading Du Bellay: Chronology and Literary Response'. In *Spenser's Life and the Subject of Biography*. Edited by Judith Anderson, Donald Cheney, and David Richardson, 131–45. Amherst: University of Massachusetts Press, 1996.

Prescott, Anne Lake. 'Housing Chessmen and Bagging Bishops: Space and Desire in Colonna, "Rabelais", and Middleton's Game at Chess'. In *Soundings of Things Done: Essays in Early Modern Literature in Honor of S. K. Heninger Jr.* Edited by Peter E. Medine and Joseph Wittreich, 215–33. Newark: University of Delaware Press, 1997.

Prescott, Anne Lake. 'Jonson's Rabelais'. In *New Perspectives on Ben Jonson*. Edited by James E. Hirsh, 35–54. Vancouver, BC: Fairleigh Dickinson University Press, 1997.

Prescott, Anne Lake. 'Rabelaisian Apocrypha and Satire in Early Canada: The Case of Robert Hayman'. In *Editer et traduire Rabelais à travers les âges*. Edited by Paul J. Smith, 101–16. Amsterdam: Rodopi, 1997.

Prescott, Anne Lake. 'Humor and Satire in the Renaissance'. In *The Cambridge History of Literary Criticism III: The Renaissance*. Edited by Glyn P. Norton. Cambridge: Cambridge University Press, 1999.

Prescott, Anne Lake. 'Rabelaisian (Non)Wonders and Renaissance Polemics'. In *Wonders, Marvels, and Monsters in Early Modern Culture*. Edited by Peter Platt, 133–44. Newark: University of Delaware Press, 1999.

Prescott, Anne Lake. 'The Evolution of Tudor Satire'. In *The Cambridge Companion to English Literature 1500–1600*. Edited by Arthur F. Kinney, 220–40. Cambridge: Cambridge University Press, 1999.

Prescott, Anne Lake. 'The Laurel and the Myrtle: Spenser and Ronsard'. In *Worldmaking Spenser: Explorations in the Early Modern Age*. Edited by Patrick Cheney and Lauren Silberman, 63–78. Lexington: University of Kentucky Press, 2000.

Prescott, Anne Lake. 'Pierre de La Primaudaye's French Academy: Growing Encyclopedic'. In *The Renaissance Computer: Knowledge Technology in the First Age of Print*. Edited by Jonathan Sawday and Neil Rhodes. New York: Routledge, 2000.

Prescott, Anne Lake. 'Barnfield's Spenser: "Great Collin" and the Art of Denial'. In *The Affectionate Shepherd: Celebrating Richard Barnfield*. Edited by Kenneth Borris and George Klawitter. Selinsgrove, PA: Susquehanna University Press, 2001.

Prescott, Anne Lake. 'Relocating Terra Firma: William Vaughan's Newfoundland'. In *Decentring the Renaissance: Canada and Europe in Multidisciplinary Perspective 1500–1700*. Edited by Carolyn Podruchny and Germain Warkentin, 125–40. Toronto, ON: University of Toronto Press, 2001.

Prescott, Anne Lake. 'Spenser's Shorter Poems'. In *The Cambridge Companion to Spenser*. Edited by Andrew Hadfield, 143–61. Cambridge: Cambridge University Press, 2001.

Prescott, Anne Lake. 'Divine Poetry as a Career Move: The Complexities and Consolations of Following David'. In *European Literary Careers: The Author* from *Antiquity to the Renaissance*. Edited by Patrick Cheney and Frederick A. de Armas, 206–30. Toronto, ON: Toronto University Press, 2002.

Prescott, Anne Lake. 'Family Grief: Mourning and Gender in Marguerite de Navarre's Les Prisons'. In *Grief and Gender 700–1700*. Edited by Jennifer Vaught and Lynne Dickson Bruckner, 105–19. Houndmills: Palgrave Macmillan, 2003.

Prescott, Anne Lake. 'Male Lesbian Voices: Ronsard, Tyard, and Donne Play Sappho'. In *Reading the Renaissance: Ideas and Idioms from Shakespeare to Milton*. Edited by Marc Berley, 109–29. Pittsburgh, PA: Duquesne University Press, 2003.

Prescott, Anne Lake. 'The (Robert) Green(e)ing of Louise Labé'. In *Opening the Borders: Inclusivity in Early Modern Studies Essays in Honor of James V. Mirollo*. Edited by Peter C. Herman, 133–49. Newark: University of Delaware Press, 2003.

Prescott, Anne Lake. '"And Then She Fell on a Great Laughter": Tudor Diplomats Read Marguerite de Navarre'. In *Culture and Change: Attending to Early Modern Women*. Edited by Margaret Mikesell and Adele Seeff, 41–65. Newark: Delaware University Press, 2003.

Prescott, Anne Lake. 'Sources'. In *A Critical Companion to Spenser Studies*. Edited by Bart van Es, 98–115. London: Palgrave Macmillan, 2006.

Prescott, Anne Lake. 'Tracing Astrophil's "Coltish Gyres": Sidney and the Horses of Desire'. In *Renaissance Papers 2005*. Edited by Christopher Cobb and M. Thomas Hester, 25–42. Martlesham, Suffolk: Boydell & Brewer, 2006.

Prescott, Anne Lake. 'Two Annes, Two Davids: The Sonnets of Anne Lok and Anne de Marquets'. In *Tradition, Heterodoxy and Religious Culture: Judaism and Christianity in the Early Modern Period*. Edited by Chanita Goodblatt and Theodore Howard Kreisel. Beer-Sheva: Ben-Gurion University of the Negev Press, 2006.

Prescott, Anne Lake. 'The Equinoctial Boar: Venus and Adonis in Spenser's Garden, Shakespeare's Epyllion and Richard III's England'. In *Shakespeare and Spenser: Attractive Opposites*. Edited by J. B. Lethbridge, 168–86. Manchester: Manchester University Press, 2008.

Prescott, Anne Lake. 'Making the *Heptaméron* English'. In *Renaissance Historicisms: Essays in Honor of Arthur F. Kinney*. Edited by James Dutcher and Anne Lake Prescott, 69–84. Newark: Delaware University Press, 2008.

Prescott, Anne Lake. 'Mary Sidney's French Sophocles: The Countess of Pembroke Reads Robert Garnier'. In *Representing France and the French in Early Modern English Drama*. Edited by Jean-Christophe Mayer, 68–89. Newark: University of Delaware Press, 2008.

Prescott, Anne Lake. 'More's Utopia: Medievalism and Radicalism'. In *A Companion to Tudor Literature*. Edited by Kent Cartwright, 277–94. Chichester: Wiley-Blackwell, 2010.

Prescott, Anne Lake. 'Spenser and French Literature'. In *The Oxford Handbook of Edmund Spenser*. Edited by Richard McCabe, 620–34. Oxford: Oxford University Press, 2010.

Prescott, Anne Lake. 'Afterlives'. In *The Cambridge Companion to Thomas More*. Edited by George M. Logan, 265–87. Cambridge: Cambridge University Press, 2011.

Prescott, Anne Lake. 'Menippean Donne'. In *The Oxford Handbook of John Donne*. Edited by Dennis Flynn, M. Thomas Hester, and Jeanne Shami, 158–79. Oxford: Oxford University Press, 2011.

Prescott, Anne Lake. 'Sibling Harps: The Sidneys and the Chérons Translate the Psalms'. In *Psalms in the Early Modern World*. Edited by Linda Phyllis Auster, Kari Boyd McBride, and David L. Orvis, 235–56. Farnham: Ashgate Publishing, 2011.

Prescott, Anne Lake. 'Du Bellay and Shakespeare's Sonnets'. In *The Oxford Handbook of Shakespeare's Poetry*. Edited by Jonathan Post, 134–50. Oxford: Oxford Academic, 2013.

Prescott, Anne Lake. 'Exploiting King Saul in Early Modern England'. In *Religious Diversity and Early Modern English Texts: Catholic, Judaic, Feminist and Secular Dimensions*. Edited by Arthur F. Marotti and Chanita Goodblatt, 178–94. Detroit, MI: Wayne State University Press, 2013.

Prescott, Anne Lake. 'Ronsard in England, 1635–1699'. In *French Connections in the English Renaissance*. Edited by Catherine Gimelli Martin and Hassan Melehy, 179–192. Farnham: Ashgate Publishing, 2013.

Prescott, Anne Lake. 'Perverse Delights: Cross Channel Trash Talk and Identity Politics'. In *Forms of Association: Making Publics in Early Modern Europe*. Edited by Paul Yachnin and Marlene Eberhart, 77–92. Amherst: University of Massachusetts Press, 2015.

Prescott, Anne Lake. 'Sir Philip Sidney's Psalms'. In *The Ashgate Research Companion to the Sidneys, 1500–1700*. Edited by Margaret P. Hannay and Mary Ellen Lamb, 283–94. London: Routledge, 2015.

Prescott, Anne Lake. 'Urquhart's Inflationary Universe'. In *The Culture of Translation in Early Modern England and France, 1500–1660*. Edited by Tania Demetriou and Rowan Tomlinson, 175–90. London: Palgrave Macmillan, 2015.

Prescott, Anne Lake. 'A Year in the Life of King Saul: 1643'. In *The Oxford Handbook of the Bible in Early Modern England, c. 1530–1700*. Edited by Kevin Killeen, Helen Smith, and Rachel Willie, 412–26. Oxford: Oxford University Press, 2015.

Prescott, Anne Lake. 'Spenser's French Connection'. In *Edmund Spenser in Context*. Edited by Andrew Escobedo, 264–72. Cambridge: Cambridge University Press, 2016.

Prescott, Anne Lake. 'Satire and Polemic'. In *The Oxford Handbook of Early Modern English Literature and Religion*. Edited by Andrew Hiscock and Helen Wilcox, 223–42. Oxford: Oxford University Press, 2017.

Prescott, Anne Lake. 'Menippos in the Classroom'. In *Teaching Modern British and American Satire*. Edited by Evan R. Davis and Nicholas D. Nace, 121–31. New York: Modern Language Association, 2019.

Prescott, Anne Lake. 'Spenser and Donne Look to the Continent'. In *Spenser and Donne: Thinking Poets*. Edited by Yulia Ryzhik. 108–17. Manchester: Manchester University Press, 2019.

Co-authored essays

Cheney, Patrick, and Anne Lake Prescott. 'Teaching Spenser's Marriage Poetry: Amoretti, Epithalamion, Prothalamion'. In *Approaches to Teaching Shorter*

Elizabethan Poetry. Edited by Patrick Cheney and Anne Lake Prescott, 226–38. New York: Modern Language Association, 2000.

Kuin, Roger, and Anne Lake Prescott. '"After the First Death there is No Other": Spenser, Milton, and (Our) Death'. In *Imagining Death in Spenser and Milton*. Edited by Elizabeth Bellamy, Patrick Cheney, and Michael Schoenfeldt, 78–94. Houndmills: Palgrave Macmillan, 2003.

Munro, Ian, and Anne Lake Prescott. 'Jest Books'. In *The Oxford Handbook of English Prose 1500–1640*. Edited by Andrew Hadfield, 343–59. Oxford: Oxford University Press, 2013.

Prescott, Anne Lake, and Lydia Kirsopp Lake. 'From "Amours" to Amores: Francis Thorius Makes Ronsard a Neolatin Lover'. In *French Connections in the English Renaissance*. Edited by Catherine Gimelli Martin and Hassan Melehy, 161–178. Farnham: Ashgate Publishing, 2013.

Travitsky, Betty S. and Anne Lake Prescott. 'Juxtaposing Genders: Jane Lead and John Milton with Betty', in Margaret Hannay and Suzanne Woods, eds, *Teaching Tudor and Stuart Women Writers*. Edited by Susanne Woods and Margaret P. Hannay. New York: Modern Language Association, 2001.

Travitsky, Betty S. and Anne Lake Prescott. 'Studying and Editing Early Modern English Women: Then and Now'. In *Women Editing/Editing Women: Early Modern Women Writers and the New Textualism*. Edited by Ann Hollinshead Hurley and Chanita Goodblatt, 1–16. Newcastle upon Tyne: Cambridge Scholars, 2009.

Translations and short essays

Translations of Ronsard's 'lesbian' poems in *Same-Sex Desire in the English Renaissance: A Sourcebook of Texts, 1470–1650*. Edited by Kenneth Borris. New York: Routledge, 2004.

Articles on French Literature, Rabelais, Burgundy, Giants, Titans, Belge, Burbon, Tantalus and Pilate, Mammon, Sclaunder. In *The Spenser Encyclopedia*. Edited by Donald Cheney, A. C. Hamilton, and David Richardson. Toronto, ON: Toronto University Press, 1990.

Short essays on Nicholas Grimald and French literature. In *Tudor England: An Encyclopedia*. Edited by Arthur F. Kinney and David W. Swain. New York: Garland, 2001.

Two short entries for *The Rabelais Encyclopedia*. Edited by Elizabeth C. Zegura. London: Bloomsbury, 2004.

Entries on Jane Anger, Thomas Nashe the Younger, and Michael Drayton for the *Oxford Dictionary of National Biography*.

Index

Literary works can be found under the authors' names. Italicized numbers indicate an illustration, and n after a number indicates a footnote on that page.

Absalom 114, 154
Acteon 71–72, 102n11, 232n5
Acuña, Hernando 18
Adams, Thomas 248–49
Aggas, Edgar 53
Ainsworth, Henry 85, 126
allegory 2–3, 5, 17–20, 22, 25, 27,
  30–32, 37–38, 41, 45n8, 50,
  62n4, 63n5, 68n47, 72, 103,
  137, 218, 230–31, 243, 252,
  277n17
 apocalyptical 61
 chess and 265–68, 272
 Christian 80, 82–83, 85, 101n4,
  101n5, 232n5
 David and 157n28, 161
 deer as 80, 82–83, 85, 101n4,
  101n5, 232n5
 in *The Faerie Queen* (Edmund
  Spenser) 17, 43n10, 46–68,
  62n4, 68n47, 68n48
 Francesco Colonna and 267
 in François Rabelais 267
 Game at Chess (Thomas Middleton)
  and 267–68, 276n19
 history and 46–68
 La Marche, Olivier de and 43n12
 in Marguerite de Navarre *Les
  Prisons* 219–20, 223
 personification 42n6
 pilgrimage 19
 prison as 219–20, 223
 Protestant 38
 quest 18
 in Stephen Bateman, *The Travayled
  Pylgrime* 18, 28, 38, 43n12
Alva, Duke 49
Anderson, Judith 61
Andrew of St. Victor 114
Andrewes, Lancelot 191–92
Apocrypha's Ecclesiasticus 80, 121
Aretino, Pietro 3, 239–40, 245–56
Ariosto, Ludovico 19, 207, 241, 243,
  252
Athanasius 10, 161–64, 169
 psalms of David and 163, 165–68,
  172
Augustine 81, 83, 85, 88, 126, 165–66

Babylon 184, 189
Bale, John 246
Barnes, Catherine 202n1
Baron, Hans 3
Baroque poetics 12
Barroway, Israel 170
Barthes, Roland 318
Bateman, Stephen 4–5, 10, 11, 17–45,
  44n13, 44n15
 The Travayled Pylgrime 17–45,
  42n5
  engraving, 'By the aged or olde
   man' *39*
  engraving, 'Here Understanding
   sheweth' *23*
  engraving, 'The armed Knight
   Signifieth' *20*

engraving, 'The Author an Memorie walking on foote' 33
engraving, 'The author and Memorie passeth the field' 29
engraving, 'The author and memorie riding forwarde' 31
engraving, 'The Author beholdeth the discourse' 35
engraving, 'The author being carried by his horse' 26
Bathsheba 114
Baxter, J. 247
Bellarmine, Cardinal 10, 168–69
Beza, Theodore 113, 118, 123, 128, 151
    Latin psalter and 125–26
    psalms and 9, 117, 120, 168
Biblia Sacra 126, 165
Bishops' Bible 119–20, 165, 175n7, 187
The Book of Common Prayer 10, 69, 87, 89–90, 108n44, 109
Book of Psalms 125, 167
Book of Samuel 114
Bourbon, Catherine de 6, 59, 66n37
Bourbon, Henri de, king of Navarre *see* Henri IV
Bourbons 54
Boyle, Elizabeth 69, 92
Boys, John 126
Breton, Nicholas 182
Browning, Robert 211
Bucer, Martin 9, 113, 116–17, 119–20, 126, 132n12, 137, 154, 167–68
Buchanan, George 245
Byfield, Nicholas 190–91

Calvin, Jean (John) 84–86, 113, 126, 266
    psalms and 9, 118, 120–21, 123–24, 139–40, 150, 168, 180
Campensis, Johannes 119
Capet, Hugh 53–54
Carleton, Dudley 48
Carolingians 54
Cartier, Jacques 152
Cary, Lucius 153
Catholicism 47, 51, 59, 260, 268
Cecil 58
Chamberlain, John 48
Charlemagne 53, 71

Charles, Prince 268
Charles I 126
Charles V 137
chess 276n8, 276n9, 276n13 *see also* allegory
    gender and 263
    literary theme 260–62, 262, 263–74, 276n15, 276n16, 278n25, 278n31
Christianity 9
Chronicles 1, 113
Chrysostom, John 85, 140, 166, 169
Church of England 59, 268
Clément, Jacques 51
Colonna, Francesco 2, 260–75, 275n2, 276–79
    Hypnerotomachia polifili 260–61, 262, 263, 266–67, 276n15
conceits 301–02, 317n6, 317n9
    in *Amours* (Pierre de Ronsard) 303
    English 293–94
    image and 293
    John Donne and 296–98, 303–04
    medieval 318
    Metaphysical 7, 8, 105n5, 281, 294, 288–89, 303–04, 313n1, 314n6, 314n9, 318
    Outrageous Exaggeration 299, 304
    personified Amour or Cupid 303
    Perverted Connotation 291, 298, 304
    Perverted Reference 298
    Pierre de Ronsard and 296–98
    Scientific Surprise 299, 304
Cope, Sir Anthony 120, 169
Cottrell, George 228–29
Countess of Pembroke *see* Sidney Mary
courtesan, literary tradition of 247, 256n2
Coverdale's Latin and English psalter 119
Cowper, William 138
Cranmer, Thomas 10, 86
Cromwell, Oliver 129
cross-gendering (male lesbian voices) 199–217
    in John Donne 199–205, 209
    in Pierre de Ronsard 201–06, 209–12
    in Pontus de Tyard 201, 206–12

Index 333

cross-gendering (male narrator)
  in *Les Prisons* (by Marguerite de Navarre) 223–30, 234n19, 234n23
  Marguerite de Navarre and 218, 221–31
Crowley, Robert 85
Cullen, Patrick 22

d'Alençon, Charles 220, 227
Dallington, Robert 261
Damiano, Odemira da 267
Daneau, Lambert 189
Daniel, in the lion's den 187, *188*
Daniel, Samuel 182, 187, 247, 249, 253
Dante Alighieri 219, 248
David 84, 86, 133n24, 133n29, 191–92
  Absalom and 114
  as anti-court poet 128
  aristocratic poets and 129
  biblical references to 114
  Christians and 118
  as a courtier 127, 131n8, 137
  English poets and 113
  English Protestants and 125
  as foreshadowing Christ 126, 135, 140, 149, 162, 178n20
  Goliath and 114, 138
  Jewish tradition and 118
  king Saul and 166
  life of 113–14, 116, 126–27
  lyrics of 114
  music and 166
  Nathan and *170–1*, 172
  politics and 127
  Renaissance readings of 160–79
  in Sidney's *Apology* 161–62, 170, 174n2
  slander and 113–34, 122–23, 125, 131n10
David, psalms of 114, 117–20, 123, 125–26, 137, 157n28, 190
  Renaissance readings of 113–34
  translations of 113, 116
de Bourbon, Catherine 6, 58–59, 66n37, 66n39
de Bourdeille, Pierre (Sieur de Brantôme) *see* de Brantôme, Pierre

de Brantôme, Pierre 1, 204–05
de la Heutterie, Charles 147
de Lorraine, Marguerite de 220
de Medici, Catherine 55, 150, 202, 210, 287
de Mornay, Philippe 168
de Navarre, Marguerite 8, 79–80, 84
  Clément Marot and 137–40, 148–51, 153
  deaths of family members 220–21, 232n11, 233n17
  Evangelical theology 218, 220–22, 226–27, 232n8, 232n15
  family of 223, 232n17, 232n20
  hunting theme and 80
  see also cross-gendering (male narrator)
de Navarre, Marguerite, works by
  Chansons spirituelles 73–77, 95, 97–99, 102n14, 103n17
  Heptaméron 218, 222, 224, 234n18
  Les Prisons 8–9, 218–38, 232n22
  Miroir de l'âme pécheresse 229
de Savoie, Louise 8, 221, 224, 226–27
deer 83, 106n28
  in *Amoretti 67-70* (Edmund Spenser) 72, 76, 80, 84
  David's psalm 42, 82
  as figure for David 86
  imagery 82
  as literary theme 69–112, 101n3, 101n4, 102n7, 102n11, 106n28, 107n33
  The Loving hind of Proverbs 5.19 (title page of Thomas Churchyard's *Discourse*) 94
  in Psalm 42, 69–112, *81*
  in religious texts 69–112
Defaux, Gerard 141
Dekker, Thomas 247
Derrida, Jacques 318
Desroches, Catherine 295
Desroches, Madeleine 295–96
d'Estampes, Mme. Anne Pisselou d'Heilly 75
d'Etaples, Lefèvre 140
Dionysis 51
Divels legend 53
Doeg 116, 118–19, 124–26, 128

Donne, John 7, 12, 182, 294, 304
  conceits in 288, 296–98, 303–04
  lesbian relations and 213n4, 214n8
  lesbian voices and 199–205, 209
  Sappho and 199–217, 213n4, 214n8, 215n9
Donne, John, works by
  'The Flea' 295–97
  'A Nocturnall upon St. Lucies Day' 299, 302–03, 312–13
  'Sappho to Philaenis' 1, 199–206, 209–11, 214n8
Dorat, Jean 201
Drayton, Michael 182, 187–88, 241, 247
Du Bartas, Guillaume de Salluste 127–28, 174n3
  Triumph of Faith 56
  Yvry 56-7, 60
Du Bellay, Joachim 4, 75, 91, 160, 188, 251–52, 284–85
  image of ruin in 253
  roman poetry of 246
  Rome and 188–89, 239–44, 246, 249–55
  satire and 257n5, 257n7, 257n8
Du Bellay, Joachim, works by
  Antiquitez de Rome 2, 180–1, 194n14, 241–42, 245–48, 250, 253, 255
  'La vielle courtisanne' 239–55
  L'Olive 105n23, 109n47
  'Songe' 245–46
duc de Mercueur 53
Duchess Renée of Ferrara 143
Duplessis-Mornay, Philippe 53–54
Durer, Albrecht, *Painter's Manuel* 261
Dutch Revolt 61

Edict of Nantes 62
Elizabeth I 6, 51–52, 66n37, 191–92
  brother Edward 226
  The Faerie Queen (Edmund Spenser) and 46–48, 60
  letters to Catherine de Bourbon 58–59
  letter to Henri IV 57–58
Elizabeth Tudor *see* Elizabeth I
Elyot, John 160

Ephesians 1:14 79
Ephesians 4:8 78–79
Erondelle, Pierre 49
Estienne, Robert 118, 145
  psalter of 123, 126, 132n17, 213n2
Evangelical theology 72, 118, 128, 132n17, 150, 226, 232n8, 232n18
Ezekiel 79, 122

Farnese, Alessandro 48
Felch, Susan 1–16
Feminism 3
Ferguson, Gary 222
Ferguson, Margaret 170–71
Fletcher, Giles 91
The Flower de Luce 50, 53, 64n12, 64n21
Francis I (François I) 137, 142–43, 148, 149, 150, 161, 168, 227
  ballade written to Marguerite 225
  David and 138–39
  death of 218, 222–23
  female subjectivity and 225
  king Saul and 135, 145
  poems of 8, 224–25
François-Hercule, duc d'Alençon 52
Francus 53

Gallagher, Lowell 61
Garnier, Robert 182
Gascoigne, George 72, 83
gender 199–217
  chess and 263–64
  homosexuality 199–217
  John Donne and 199–205, 209
  in *Les Prisons* (by Marguerite de Navarre) 218–38
  Pierre de Ronsard and 201–12
  Pontus Tyard and 201, 206–12
  Renaissance 199–217
  spirit and soul 229
  Valois dynasty and 225
  voicing poetry and 226
  see also cross-gendering (male lesbian voices); cross-gendering (male narrator); homosexuality

Geneva Bible 79, 119–21, 125, 129, 133n19, 137, 140, 182–87, 190
  David in 115, 123, 125–26
  Ezekiel 184–85, *185*
Geryon (Spenser's Geryoneo) 52
Gesner, Conrad 83
Gilby, Anthony 126
Gillebert, Pierre 241
Glasson, Simone 220
Goldberg, Jonathan 1, 12n2, 12n3
Golding, Arthur 120, 168, 180
Gosson, Stephen 172
Great Bible 119
Greenblatt, Stephen 3
grief 218–38, 227
  sonnets of mourning 303
Griffin, Robert 141–42, 150
Guise family 46, 51–52, 54
  Henry I, duc de Guise 48

Hannay, Margaret 192
Harington, John 172, 239
hart *see* deer
Harvey, Gabriel 48, 55–56, 60, 75
Hedrick, Donald 261
Helen of Troy 298
Heninger, S. K. 262
Henri de Navarre *see* Henri IV
Henri III 46–48, 51–53, 202
Henri IV 6, 55–56, 63n9, 65n30, 75, 119, 128
  allegory and 63n5
  conversion of 46, 57, 60, 62n3, 65n25, 65n27
  Hercules and 51–52, 61
  life of 50, 58
  myth of 63n6
  sister Catherine and 58, 66n37
  Spenser's Burbon (character) as allegory for 6, 46–50
  victory at Ivry 48, 56
Henry VII 45n23
Henry VIII 30–31, 119, 133n19, 151–52, 155n10, 159n41, 181, 193n3, 259n18, 275n2, 275n8
Herbert, George 129
Hercules 46, 51, 53, 56, 61

Hieatt, Kent 100, 105n21, 106n27, 110n49, 181, 193n49, 259n18, 275n2, 275n8
Holy League 46, 50–51, 59–60
homosexuality 199–217
  see also cross-gendering (lesbian voices); cross-gendering (male narrator); lesbian voices
Horace 70–72, 127, 169, 172, 247
Howell, Thomas 189
Hugh of St. Victor 83
Huguenots 51, 131n10, 132n14
Humston, Robert 189
hunting, as literary theme 69–112, 107n34
Hurault, Michel 48, 51–53

International Spenser Society 2
Isaiah 79–80, 87, 90, 247

Jerusalem 184–85, 188, 189–92, 246, 255
Jesuits 270
Jesus Christ 116, 122, 170
Johnson, William 87–88
Jonathan, son of Saul 122
Jud, Leon 118
Jung, Carl 230
Junius-Tremellius Bible 170

Kimhi, David 119
King James 133n19, 138, 268
Kipling, Gordon 18
Klawitter, George 200
Koller, Kathrine 17
Kristeller, Paul Oskar 3
Kristeva, Julia 9, 227–28
Kuin, Roger 5, 66n33, 280–316, 317–18

La Marche, Olivier de 21, 24, 36–37, 40, 43n12
Lacan, Jacques 228
Laumonier, Paul 202
Leicester, Robert Dudley, Earl of 61
lesbian voices 216n15
  John Donne 199–205, 209, 213n4, 214n8
  Pierre de Ronsard 201–06, 209–12
  Pontus de Tyard 201, 206–12

Limon, Jerzy 273
Lloyd, Lodowick 189
Lock, Anne 190
Lodge, Thomas 72, 241, 247
Louis XII 143
Luther, Martin 83, 85, 266
  psalms of David and 167

Malingre, Matthieu 152
mannerism, painting and 304
Marcellinus 163
Markham, Gervase 2, 4, 239, 251–52, 256n1, 257n5, 257n8
  The Famous Whore 239–40, 248, 250, 253, 255
    prostitution 248
    Rome 249
    translation of du Bellay's 'vielle courtesanne' 240–41, 248
Marlowe, Christopher 182, 244
Marot, Clément 75, 103n20, 117, 127, 134n31, 155n15, 156n18, 157n25, 159n41
  attacks on 146
  as courtier 135–59, 158n40
  David and 135–36, 141, 143–45
  death of 151
  flees France 135, 143, 150
  Francis I and 143
  Lutheranism and 137, 152
  Marguerite de Navarre and 143
  Ovid and 150
  pamphlet war 146
  as psalmist and courtier 135–59
  psalms and 154n6
  religion and 154n3, 155n16
  reputation of 151
  Saul and 135–36, 141
  scriptural poetry of 136
  translation of psalms by David 132n14, 137–40, 148, 152, 168
Marot, Clément, works by
  'Aux Dames de France' 153
  'Eglogue de Marot au Roy, soubz les noms de Pan & Robin' 148
  'Eglogue sur la Naissance du filz de Monseigneur le Daulphin' 150

Epigram 246 141–42
Epître 36 143, 319
Marotines, (songs by Marot) 151
Marot, Jean 147
Mary Stuart 51, 192
Masque of the League and the Spanyard discovered 48, 52–55
Masters, G. Mallary 230
Mayenne, Charles de Lorraine, duc de 48, 52, 54
Medea 224, 253, 291, 298
Merovingians 53, 54
metaphor
  Babylon and 184, 189
  biblical 184, 189
  chess and 270
  cities and 184–85, 189–92, 247, 258n12, 258n18
  David's psalms and 172
  deer as 107n35
  Jerusalem and 184–85, 189–92
  mirror 172
  Rome and 184–85, 187–89, 242, 244, 247–48, 253
  ruins and 180, 182–83, 189–90
Metaphysical style 281, 294, 298–99, 303–04
Meyer, Barbara 225
Middleton, Thomas 241, 268
  Game at Chess 2, 267–74
    Catholic vs Protestant 273–74
    Middleton's chessmen play the great game, title page *269*
    performance of 268, 272
    space and desire in 260–79
Milton, John 28, 34, 113, 317
Mirror for Magistrates 241, 247
Monta, Susannah 1–16
More, Thomas 231
Mueller, Janel 66n37, 201, 206
Munday, Anthony 248
mutability theme 181, 187
myth 51–52, 55, 230

Nathan 114, 164, 170–72
  David and *170–71*, 172
New Historicism 3, 5–6

Old Historicism 3, 5
Oram, Bill 319
Osiris 51
Ovid 136, 184, 190, 211, 245, 255, 257n8
  Clément Marot and 143–44, 150
  Heroides 200–01, 224
  Metamorphoses 219
Owen, Wilfred 302

Parker, Matthew 19, 164, 172, 187
  deer and 85
  psalms and 120, 175n6, 175n7
  translation of psalms by David 162–63, 166
Parr, Catherine 120
Paul, Saint 122
Peace of the Ladies 223–24
Petrarch, Francesco 95, 188–89, 206, 219, 241, 243, 258n10, 300
  hunting as literary theme in 69–70
  'I'vo pensando' 300
  Rome and 188
Petrarchismo 303–04
Pharamond, legendary king of France 53
Philaenis 1, 200–01, 209–11
Philip II of Spain 52
Platonic Androgyne 230
'The Pléiade' 210, 258n17, 304, 318
Pliny 83
Pocock, J.G.A. 3
Pollock, Sheldon 5
Ponsonby, William 77
Porete, Marguerite 220
Prescott, Anne Lake 1–16, 298
  allegory and 6
  career of 3
  comparative literary study and 4–5
  as editor 319
  and religious exegesis in the sixteenth century 9
  gender and 3, 7–9
  historicism and 5–7
  interpretive elegance 11–12
  literary history and 7
  literary terms and 7
  philology and 4

religion and 9–11
scholarly societies and 2–3
translation and 4–5
prostitution, theme of 246, 248–49
  in *The Famous Whore* (Gervase Markham) 239
  Jacobean stage 256
  Renaissance treatment of 245
  wolf as Italian slang 241
Protestantism 18, 75, 120, 151, 174n3, 177n13, 274
Protestants 46, 260
psalmists, Renaissance 127
psalms of David 9–10, 131n8, 169
  imagery and 177n13
  Marot's translation of 132n14, 137–40, 148, 152, 168
  Mary Sidney's translations of 5, 181–87, 191–92, 192n1
  Philip Sidney translations of 182, 187
  political significance and 120, 131n10
  translations of 123–24, 127, 131n10, 136, 149, 152
psalter, Huguenot 117
psalter, Latin 125–26
psalter, Sidney 182, 187
psalters, medieval 116
psalters, Tudor 119
psychoanalysis 3
Puttenham, George 76

Quarles, Francis 127
Quint, David 265

Rabelais, François 264–67, 272–73, 274
Rabelais, François, works by
  Cinquième livre 2, 75, 263, 272–73, 276n8, 276n17
  Gargantua et Pantagruel 263, 275n3
Ramachandran, Ayesha 1–16
Reformation 135–36, 192
Renaissance
  Catholics and 136
  gender and 199–217
  perspective 261–62

Renaissance Society of America 2–3
Renaissance studies 3
Robinson, R. 86
Rogers, Daniel 317
Rogers, Nehemiah 126–27
Roland 71
Ronsard, Pierre de 5, 12, 75, 201–07,
    209–12, 217n30, 244, 286,
    290, 298, 304
  conceit and 12, 288–90, 298
  Donne and 280–316
  Helen of Troy sonnet 299
  Marguerite de Navarre and 75
  Sappho and 199–217
Ronsard, Pierre de, works by
  Amours 284–96, 303
  'Cusin' 294–97
  'Elegie pour la mort de Marie'
    299–300, 303, 305–12
  Franciade 244
  Odes 304
  'Terre ouvre moy ton sein' 299,
    301–02
ruins
  aesthetic of 180
  discourse of 182–83, 187, 189–90

Sagon, Francis 146–48, 319
St. Basil 162, 165–67, 169
St. Catherine 139
Salmon, Don Pierre 116
Samuel 1 and 2 113, 122
Sandys, George 153
Sappho 1, 200–21, 207, 209, 211,
    215n12
Sarum liturgy 10
The Sarum Missal 87–88
Sarum Primer *171*
Sarum rite 69, 78, 84, 109n45
  sonnets and 87
Sasso 72
Saul 113–34, 166, 191
  court of 117, 123, 126
  slander in court of 113–34
  translators and 124
Saul, Arthur, *Famous game of chesse-
    play* 263–64, 267–68
Saul and Barbier, chess guide 267
Saulnier, V.-L. 243
Sedgwick, Eve 1

Servetus, Michael 114
Shakespeare, William 187–88, 205,
    211, 247
  Edmund Spenser and 181–82
  Geneva Bible and 125
  Sonnets and 253
Sidney, Mary 117, 129, 163, 187, 192,
    226
  Jerusalem in 182–83
  mutability and 183
  psalm translations 181–87, 191–92,
    192n1
  Rome in 182–83
  ruins in 181–83
  Sidney Psalter and 192
Sidney, Philip 9–11, 60, 117, 174n1,
    179n23, 226, 294, 301
  poetry and 160–62, 176n8, 178n16,
    178n17
  Protestantism and 174n3
  psalms and 175n7
  David and 160–62
  'right poet' and 166, 169–70,
    176n9
Sidney, Philip, works by
  Defence of Poesy (also *Apology for
    Poetry*) 126, 163, 169–72,
    177n12, 179n24, 303
  psalm translations 113, 117–18,
    129, 132n17, 160–74, 174n2,
    187, 195n21
Sidney, Robert 59
Skelton, John 114, 118
Society for the Study of Early Modern
    Women and Gender 2
Solomon 83, 122
Song of Songs 76, 80–81, 83–85, 90,
    109n44
Spanish Armada 52, 188–91, 249
Spenser, Edmund 5, 44n15, 45n22,
    104n23, 106n27
  chivalric restoration and 17–45
  historical events and 60–61
  Ireland and 46
  lineage and succession as themes 53
  myth and 61
  names of characters and 46
  prayer book and 93
  religion and 10, 11
  ruins aesthetic of 8

sonnets of 77, 88, 90, 92–93
Tasso and 70
Spenser, Edmund, works by *see also*
    The Faerie Queen (Edmund
    Spenser)
  Amoretti
    Amoretti 22 (Lenten poem) 78,
      88
    Amoretti 67-70 (Edmund
      Spenser) 5, 104n25, 106n31,
      107n33, 107n38
    Amoretti 67 95
    Amoretti 68 78, 96
    Amoretti 69 96
    Amoretti 70 96–97
    contexts for 69–112
    deer as literary theme 69–112
    religious calendar and 86–88,
      90–91, 93–94, 104n21
  Complaints 180, 182
  'The dying Pellican' 77
  Epithalamion 64n19, 75, 86, 92–93,
    109n45
  The Faerie Queen 6, 17, 24, 34, 36,
    41, 85, 115, 318
    Book I (Holiness) 17–41
    Book II (Temperance) 17, 71
    Book V (Justice) 46–62
    chivalry in 49
    European politics in 46–63,
      63n11, 64–68
    Flourdelis (character) 46
    history and 30–31, 61
    mythology and 46, 61
    Redcrosse knight (character) 17,
      25–29, 32, 37–38, 40, 43n13,
      44n17, 46, 63n9
    Sir Burbon (character
      representing Henri IV) 46–65,
      65n27, 68n46, 68n47, 69–75
    Stephen Bateman and 18–19, 21
    see also allegory
  Mother Hubberds Tale 125
  Ruines of Rome, (translation of Du
    Bellay's Antiquitez) 78,
    180–84, 186–88, 193n3, 242
  Visions of Bellay 186
The Spenser Encyclopedia 50
Sternhold-Hopkins 120, 126, 163,
  175n6, 194n6

Stringelius, Victorinus 86
Swan, John 189
Sylvester, Joshua 56–57

Taffin, Jean 190
Tallis, Thomas 162
Tasso, Torquato 69–72, 95
Tofte, Richard 188
Top, Alexander 126
translators, Geneva and 121
Traub, Valerie 1
Tremellius and Junius, *Biblia Sacra*
    126, 165
Tyard, Pontus de 199, 201, 206–12
    Oeuvres poétiques 206

Valerian, Ian-Pierre 81
Valerianus 83
Valois dynasty 46, 54, 225–26,
    231
van Dorsten, Jan 165, 317
Vatablus, Francis 9, 118–21, 123, 129,
    132n17
Vida, Marcus Hieronymus, *Scaccia
    ludus: Or, the Game of Chess*
    264, 267
Villiers, George, Duke of Buckingham
    268
Virgil, *Aeneid* 71
Vulgate Bible of 1535 116

Waddington, Raymond 225–26
Wallop, John 152
Warnke, Frank 290, 293–94, 304,
    315n19, 315n30
Watson, Christopher 138
Webbe, George 122
Whitney, Geoffrey 82, 180
Wilcox, Thomas 83
Williams, Sir Roger 49
Wills, Richard 169
Wind, Edgar 225
Wither, George 113, 128
Wodroephe, John 152
Wolfe, John 7, 51
Wyatt, Thomas 69, 113, 118, 127–28,
    131n10, 152, 209

Yachnin, Paul 267
Yandell, Catherine 204

EU authorised representative for GPSR:
Easy Access System Europe, Mustamäe tee 50,
10621 Tallinn, Estonia
gpsr.requests@easproject.com

www.ingramcontent.com/pod-product-compliance
Lightning Source LLC
Chambersburg PA
CBHW051557230426
43668CB00013B/1881